Security Technologies for the World Wide Web

Second Edition

For quite a long time, computer security was a rather narrow field of study that was populated mainly by theoretical computer scientists, electrical engineers, and applied mathematicians. With the proliferation of open systems in general, and of the Internet and the World Wide Web (WWW) in particular, this situation has changed fundamentally. Today, computer and network practitioners are equally interested in computer security, since they require technologies and solutions that can be used to secure applications related to electronic commerce. Against this background, the field of computer security has become very broad and includes many topics of interest. The aim of this series is to publish state-of-the-art, high standard technical books on topics related to computer security. Further information about the series can be found on the WWW at the following URL:

http://www.esecurity.ch/serieseditor.html

Also, if you'd like to contribute to the series by writing a book about a topic related to computer security, feel free to contact either the Commissioning Editor or the Series Editor at Artech House.

Recent Titles in the Artech House Computer Security Series

Rolf Oppliger, Series Editor

Computer Forensics and Privacy, Michael A. Caloyannides

Demystifying the IPsec Puzzle, Sheila Frankel

Developing Secure Distributed Systems with CORBA, Ulrich Lang and Rudolf Schreiner

Implementing Electronic Card Payment Systems, Cristian Radu

Implementing Security for ATM Networks, Thomas Tarman and Edward Witzke

Information Hiding Techniques for Steganography and Digital Watermarking,
    Stefan Katzenbeisser and Fabien A. P. Petitcolas, editors

Internet and Intranet Security, Second Edition, Rolf Oppliger

Non-repudiation in Electronic Commerce, Jianying Zhou

Secure Messaging with PGP and S/MIME, Rolf Oppliger

Security Fundamentals for E-Commerce, Vesna Hassler

Security Technologies for the World Wide Web, Second Edition, Rolf Oppliger

For a listing of recent titles in the *Artech House Computing Library*, turn to the back of this book.

Security Technologies for the World Wide Web

Second Edition

Rolf Oppliger

Artech House
Boston • London
www.artechhouse.com

Library of Congress Cataloging-in-Publication Data
Oppliger, Rolf.
    Security technologies for the World Wide Web / Rolf Oppliger.—2nd ed.
       p.   cm.—(Artech House computer security series)
    Includes bibliographical references and index.
    ISBN 1-58053-348-5 (alk. paper)
      1. Computer security.   2. World Wide Web (Information retrieval system)—Security measures.
      I. Title.   II. Series.
    QA76.9.A25 O67   2002
    005.8—dc21   2002032665

British Library Cataloguing in Publication Data
Oppliger, Rolf
    Security technologies for the World Wide Web.—2nd ed.—
    (Artech House computer security series)
    1. World Wide Web—Security measures
    I. Title
    005.8

ISBN 1-58053-348-5

Cover design by Christine Stone

© **2003 ARTECH HOUSE, INC.**
685 Canton Street
Norwood, MA 02062

International Standard Book Number: 1-58053-348-5
Library of Congress Catalog Card Number: 2002032665

10 9 8 7 6 5 4 3 2 1

To my daughter, Lara

Contents

Preface . . . .   *xv*

References. . . . .   *xx*

Acknowledgments. . . . .   *xxiii*

1   Introduction   1

    1.1   Internet.   1

    1.2   WWW.   5

    1.3   Vulnerabilities, threats, and countermeasures   8

    1.4   Generic security model.   10

        1.4.1   *Security policy*   12

        1.4.2   *Host security*.   13

        1.4.3   *Network security*.   13

        1.4.4   *Organizational security*   16

        1.4.5   *Legal security*.   17

    References.   17

2   HTTP Security.   21

    2.1   HTTP.   21

    2.2   User authentication, authorization,
and access control   26

2.3   Basic authentication.   29

2.4   Digest access authentication   34

2.5   Certificate-based authentication   41

2.6   Server configuration.   42

    2.6.1   Configuring HTTP basic authentication *42*

    2.6.2   Configuring HTTP digest access authentication *45*

2.7   Conclusions.   46

References.   48

3   **Proxy Servers and Firewalls** **49**

3.1   Introduction   49

3.2   Static packet filtering   54

3.3   Dynamic packet filtering or stateful inspection.   57

3.4   Circuit-level gateways   58

3.5   Application-level gateways   64

3.6   Firewall configurations.   68

    3.6.1   Dual-homed firewall *69*

    3.6.2   Screened host firewall *71*

    3.6.3   Screened subnet firewall. *72*

3.7   Network address translation   74

3.8   Configuring the browser.   76

3.9   Conclusions.   80

References.   83

4   **Cryptographic Techniques** **87**

4.1   Introduction   87

4.2   Cryptographic hash functions   90

4.3   Secret key cryptography.   92

    4.3.1   DES *93*

    4.3.2   Triple-DES. *93*

    4.3.3   IDEA *95*

    4.3.4   SAFER *95*

    4.3.5   Blowfish *95*

4.3.6 CAST-128 . . . . *95*

4.3.7 RC2, RC4, RC5, and RC6. . . . . *95*

4.3.8 AES *96*

4.4 Public key cryptography 96

4.4.1 RSA *100*

4.4.2 Diffie-Hellman *101*

4.4.3 ElGamal *102*

4.4.4 DSS *102*

4.4.5 ECC *102*

4.5 Digital envelopes 103

4.6 Protection of cryptographic keys 105

4.7 Generation of pseudorandom bit sequences 107

4.8 Legal issues 107

4.8.1 Patent claims *108*

4.8.2 Regulations *109*

4.8.3 Electronic and digital signature legislation *110*

4.9 Notation 111

References 113

5   Internet Security Protocols 117

5.1 Introduction 117

5.2 Network access layer security protocols 118

5.2.1 Layer 2 Forwarding Protocol *121*

5.2.2 Point-to-Point Tunneling Protocol *122*

5.2.3 Layer 2 Tunneling Protocol *124*

5.2.4 Virtual private networking. *124*

5.3 Internet layer security protocols 125

5.3.1 IP security architecture *128*

5.3.2 IPsec protocols *131*

5.3.3 IKE Protocol *136*

5.3.4 Implementations. *141*

5.4 Transport layer security protocols 143

5.5 Application layer security protocols 143

5.5.1 Security-enhanced application protocols *144*

5.5.2   *Authentication and key distribution systems* *144*

5.5.3   *Layering security protocols above the application layer* *145*

5.6   Conclusions   146

References   148

6   SSL and TLS Protocols   153

6.1   SSL Protocol   153

    6.1.1   *History* *153*

    6.1.2   *Architecture* *155*

    6.1.3   *SSL Record Protocol* *159*

    6.1.4   *SSL Handshake Protocol* *161*

    6.1.5   *Security analysis* *167*

    6.1.6   *Implementations* *169*

6.2   TLS Protocol   171

6.3   SSL and TLS certificates   175

6.4   Firewall traversal   178

    6.4.1   *SSL/TLS tunneling* *179*

    6.4.2   *SSL/TLS proxy servers* *181*

6.5   Conclusions   182

References   183

7   Certificate Management and Public Key Infrastructures.   185

7.1   Introduction   185

7.2   Public key certificates   187

    7.2.1   *PGP certificates* *188*

    7.2.2   *X.509 certificates* *190*

7.3   IETF PKIX WG   193

7.4   Certificate revocation   196

    7.4.1   *CRLs* *198*

    7.4.2   *OCSP* *199*

    7.4.3   *Alternative schemes* *200*

7.5   Certificates for the WWW.   201

     7.5.1   CA certificates. *201*

     7.5.2   Server or site certificates.   *203*

     7.5.3   Personal certificates. *204*

     7.5.4   Software publisher certificates. *205*

7.6   Conclusions.   207

References.   210

8   Authentication and Authorization Infrastructures   213

8.1   Introduction   213

8.2   Microsoft .NET Passport   216

     8.2.1   Overview. *217*

     8.2.2   .NET Passport user accounts. *219*

     8.2.3   .NET Passport SSI service *222*

     8.2.4   Complementary services. *228*

     8.2.5   Security analysis. *230*

8.3   Kerberos-based AAIs   231

     8.3.1   Kerberos *231*

     8.3.2   SESAME. *240*

     8.3.3   Windows 2000. . . . .   *240*

8.4   PKI-based AAIs   241

8.5   Conclusions.   245

References.   245

9   Electronic Payment Systems   249

9.1   Introduction   249

9.2   Electronic cash systems   255

9.3   Electronic checks   257

9.4   Electronic credit-card payments   259

9.5   Micropayment systems.   261

9.6   Conclusions.   262

References.   264

10   **Client-side Security** **267**

    10.1   Introduction   267

    10.2   Binary mail attachments.   271

    10.3   Helper applications and plug-ins   272

    10.4   Scripting languages   275

    10.5   Java applets.   278

           10.5.1   Security architecture *279*

           10.5.2   Security policy *281*

           10.5.3   Code signing *281*

    10.6   ActiveX controls.   283

    10.7   Security zones   288

    10.8   Implications for firewalls   291

    10.9   Conclusions.   293

    References.   294

11   **Server-side Security** **297**

    11.1   Introduction   297

    11.2   CGI   300

    11.3   Server APIs   309

    11.4   FastCGI   310

    11.5   Server-side includes   311

    11.6   ASP.   312

    11.7   JSP   313

    11.8   Conclusions.   314

    References.   314

12   **Privacy Protection and Anonymity Services** **317**

    12.1   Introduction   317

    12.2   Early work.   321

    12.3   Cookies   324

    12.4   Anonymous browsing.   328

           12.4.1   Anonymizing HTTP proxy servers *329*

           12.4.2   JAP *330*

	12.4.3	*Crowds*	330
	12.4.4	*Onion routing*	333
	12.4.5	*Freedom network*	336
12.5	Anonymous publishing.		336
	12.5.1	*JANUS and the rewebber service*	336
	12.5.2	*TAZ servers and the rewebber network*	338
	12.5.3	*Publius*	340
12.6	Voluntary privacy standards		341
	12.6.1	*Privacy seals*	341
	12.6.2	*P3P*	342
12.7	Conclusions		343
References			344

13 Intellectual Property Protection 347

13.1	Introduction		347
13.2	Usage control.		349
13.3	Digital copyright labeling		351
	13.3.1	*Introduction*	351
	13.3.2	*Categories of watermarking techniques*	352
	12.3.3	*Attacks*	355
13.4	Digital Millenium Copyright Act		356
13.5	Conclusions		357
References			358

14 Censorship on the WWW 359

14.1	Introduction		359
14.2	Content blocking		360
	14.2.1	*IP address blocking*	361
	14.2.2	*URL blocking*	363
14.3	Content rating and self-determination		365
14.4	Conclusions		371
References			373

15   **Risk Management** 375

    15.1   Introduction 375

    15.2   Formal risk analysis 378

    15.3   Alternative approaches and technologies 379

          15.3.1   Security Scanning *379*

          15.3.2   Intrusion Detection *381*

    15.4   Conclusions 382

    References 383

16   **Conclusions and Outlook** 385

      Abbreviations and Acronyms 389

      About the Author 403

      Index 405

Preface

During the past decade, I have been heavily involved in security issues related to TCP/IP-based networks.[1] The results of this work are summarized in *Authentication Systems for Secure Networks* [1], *Secure Messaging with PGP and S/MIME* [2], and—most importantly—the second edition of *Internet and Intranet Security* [3]. The three books overview and fully discuss the technologies that are available today and that can be used in TCP/IP-based networks to provide access control and communication security services. They are mainly written for computer scientists, electrical engineers, and network practitioners with some background in computer and communication security.

Some time ago, I was asked whether one of the books could be used to educate World Wide Web (WWW) professionals (e.g., Webmasters and Web server administrators) in security matters. Unfortunately, I realized that while the books cover most technologies used to secure applications for the WWW, they are written in a language that is inappropriate for Web professionals. Note that these folks are generally familiar with network operating system issues and communication protocols, but they are neither security experts nor cryptographic specialists. They may not even be interested in architectural details and design considerations for cryptographic technologies and protocols that are widely deployed.

Having in mind the Web professional who must be educated in security matters within a relatively short period of time, I decided to write a book that may serve as a security primer. While writing the book, I realized that

---

1. TCP/IP-based networks are networks that are based on the communications protocol suite. This protocol suite, in turn, is centered around the Transport Control Protocol (TCP) and the Internet Protocol (IP).

the result could also be used by Web users and application software developers. The resulting book, *Security Technologies for the World Wide Web*, was published in 2000. It overviewed and briefly discussed all major topics that are relevant for Web security. Unfortunately, and due to the dynamic nature of the field, it has become necessary to update the book and come up with a second edition after only a relatively short period of time. There are many new terms and buzzwords that need to be explained and put into perspective. Consequently, *Security Technologies for the World Wide Web, Second Edition* elaborates on some well-known security technologies that have already been covered in the first edition, as well as some more recent developments in the field.

First of all, it is important to note that the term *WWW security* means different things to different people:

▸ For Webmasters, it means confidence that their sites won't be hacked and vandalized or used as a gateway to break into their local area networks (LANs);

▸ For Web users, it means the ability to browse securely through the Web, knowing that no one is looking into their communications;

▸ Finally, for proponents of electronic commerce applications, it means the ability to conduct commercial and financial transactions in a safe and secure way.

According to [4], Web security refers to "a set of procedures, practices, and technologies for protecting Web servers, Web users, and their surrounding organizations." In this book, we mainly focus on the technologies that can be used to provide security services for the WWW. Some of these technologies are covered in detail, whereas others are only briefly introduced and left for further study. For example, most security problems and corresponding exploits that make press headlines are due to bugs and flawed configurations of specific Web servers, such as Microsoft's Internet Information Server (IIS). Due to their transient nature, however, bugs and configuration flaws are not addressed in this book. There are many books mainly on computer security and hacking that address these issues. All of these books suffer the problem that they generally obsolesce faster than new editions can be produced. Also, an increasingly large number of CERT[2] advisories, incident notes, and vulnerability notes can be used to provide this type of information.

---

2.   The acronym *CERT* stands for Computer Emergency Response Team.

The reader of *Security Technologies for the World Wide Web, Second Edition* gets an overview of all major topics that are relevant for the WWW and its security properties. As such, the book is intended for anyone who is concerned about security on the Web, is in charge of security for a network, or manages an organization that uses the WWW as a platform for providing information. It can be used for lectures, courses, and tutorials. It can also be used for self-study or serve as a handy reference for Web professionals. Further information can also be found in other books on WWW security. Among these books, I particularly recommend [4–6].[3] There are also some books that focus entirely on one specific cryptographic security protocol (i.e., the Secure Sockets Layer or Transport Layer Security protocol) that is widely deployed on the WWW [7, 8]. These books are recommended reading but are more narrow in scope than *Security Technologies for the World Wide Web*. Finally, there is also a frequently asked questions (FAQ) document available on the Web.[4]

While it is not intended that this book be read linearly from front to back, the material has been arranged so that doing so has some merit. In particular, *Security Technologies for the World Wide Web, Second Edition* has been organized in 15 chapters, summarized as follows:

▶ In Chapter 1, we introduce the topic and elaborate on the Internet, the WWW, vulnerabilities, threats, and countermeasures, as well as a model that can be used to discuss various aspects of security.

▶ In Chapter 2, we elaborate on the security features of the Hypertext Transfer Protocol (HTTP). Most importantly, we address the user authentication and authorization schemes provided by HTTP and some implementations thereof.

▶ In Chapter 3, we explain and address the implications of proxy servers and firewalls for Web-based applications.

▶ In Chapter 4, we introduce cryptographic techniques that are employed by many security technologies for the WWW. These techniques will be used in subsequent chapters.

▶ In Chapter 5, we overview and briefly discuss the cryptographic security protocols that have been proposed and partly implemented for the Internet (and that can also be used for the WWW).

---

3. Among these books only [6] has been updated in a second edition so far.

4. http://www.w3.org/Security/Faq

- In Chapter 6, we focus on two transport layer security protocols, namely the Secure Sockets Layer (SSL) and Transport Layer Security (TLS) protocols. These protocols are particularly important to secure Web-based applications.

- In Chapter 7, we address the problem of how to manage certificates and discuss the issues that surround public key infrastructures (PKIs).

- In Chapter 8, we broaden the topic addressed in Chapter 7 and discuss authentication and authorization infrastructures (AAIs).

- In Chapter 9, we overview and briefly discuss some electronic payment systems that can be used in e-commerce applications for the Internet or WWW.

- In Chapter 10, we focus on client-side security and the security implications of executable (or active) content (e.g., Java applets and ActiveX controls).

- In Chapter 11, we address server-side security and the security implications of some widely deployed server programming technologies (e.g., CGI and API scripts).

- In Chapter 12, we address the increasingly important field of privacy protection and anonymity services for the WWW.

- In Chapter 13, we overview and discuss some technologies that can be used for intellectual property protection.

- In Chapter 14, we address the politically relevant issues that surround censorship on the Internet or WWW.

- In Chapter 15, we elaborate on risk management.

- In Chapter 16, we draw conclusions and predict some future developments in the field.

Unlike the first edition, *Security Technologies for the World Wide Web, Second Edition* does not include a glossary. This is because in May 2000, an *Internet Security Glossary* was published as informational RFC 2828 (or FYI 36, respectively) [9]. This document can be used as a reference for anyone working in the field.[5] However, *Security Technologies for the World Wide Web,*

---

5. There are many other glossaries available on the Internet. Examples include a glossay compiled by Networks Associates, Inc. at http://www.pgp.com/glossary/default.asp and another glossary compiled by Rob Slade at http://victoria.tc.ca/int-grps/books/techrev/secgloss.htm.

Second Edition still includes a list of abbreviations and acronyms. References are included at the end of each chapter. This is also true for the various RFC documents that are relevant for WWW security.[6] At the end of the book, an About the Author section is included to tell you a little bit about me. Finally, there is an Index to help you find particular terms.

Some authors make a clear distinction between client-side security, server-side security, and document security, and structure their books accordingly (e.g., [4]). This book does not follow this approach but uses a functional organization instead. More precisely, the various chapters outlined above address zero, one, or even more than one of the above-mentioned classes of security issues.

There has been a long tradition in the computer and network security literature of providing various kinds of checklists. Again, *Security Technologies for the World Wide Web, Second Edition* breaks with this tradition, mainly because security is more than checking off items on checklists. The single most important thing in security is to understand the underlying concepts and technological approaches. If you understand them, it is a simple exercise to formulate and implement your own checklist(s).

While time brings new technologies and outdates current technologies, I have attempted to focus primarily on the conceptual approaches to providing security services for the WWW. The Web is changing so rapidly that any book is out of date by the time it hits the shelves in the bookstores (that's why this book had to go into a second edition after a relatively short period of time). By the time you read this book, several of my comments will probably have moved from the future to the present, and from the present to the past, resulting in inevitable anachronisms.

Due to the nature of this book, it is necessary to mention company, product, and service names. It is, however, important to note that the presence or absence of a specific name implies neither any criticism or endorsement, nor does it imply that the corresponding company, product, or service is necessarily the best available. For a more comprehensive products overview, I particularly recommend the Computer Security Products Buyer's Guide that's compiled and published annually by the Computer Security Institute (CSI) based in San Francisco, California.[7]

Whenever possible, I add some uniform resource locators (URLs) as footnotes to the text. The URLs point to corresponding information pages

---

6.   There are many RFC archives available. For example, RFC documents can be downloaded from `http://www.ietf.org/rfc`.

7.   `http://www.gocsi.com`

provided on the Web. While care has been taken to ensure that the URLs are valid, due to the dynamic nature of the Web, these URLs as well as their contents may not remain valid forever. Similarly, I use screen shots to illustrate some aspects related to the graphical user interfaces (GUIs). Unlike in the first edition, I use Microsoft Internet Explorer version 5.5 and Opera version 6.0 (instead of Netscape Navigator). Keep in mind, however, that software vendors, including Microsoft and Opera Software, tend to update and modify their GUIs periodically. Therefore, chances are that the GUI you currently use looks (slightly or completely) different than the one replicated in this book.

Finally, I would like to take the opportunity to invite you as a reader of this book to let me know your opinion and thoughts. If you have something to correct or add, please let me know. If I haven't expressed myself clearly please also let me know. I appreciate and sincerely welcome any comment or suggestion, in order to update the book periodically. The best way to reach me is to send an e-mail to `rolf.oppliger@esecurity.ch`. You can also visit the home page[8] of my company eSECURITY Technologies Rolf Oppliger and drop a message there. In addition, I have also established a home page for this book. The page is located at URL `http://WWW.esecurity.ch/Books/WWWsec2e.html`.

References

[1]   Oppliger, R., *Authentication Systems for Secure Networks*, Norwood, MA: Artech House, 1996.

[2]   Oppliger, R., *Secure Messaging with PGP and S/MIME*, Norwood, MA: Artech House, 2001.

[3]   Oppliger, R., *Internet and Intranet Security, Second Edition*, Norwood, MA: Artech House, 2002.

[4]   Stein, L. D., *Web Security: A Step-by-Step Reference*, Reading, MA: Addison-Wesley, 1998.

[5]   Rubin, A. D., D. Geer, and M. J. Ranum, *Web Security Sourcebook*, New York: John Wiley & Sons, 1997.

[6]   Garfinkel, S., with E. H. Spafford, *Web Security, Privacy & Commerce, Second Edition*, Sebastopol, CA: O'Reilly & Associates, 2001.

[7]   Thomas, S. A., *SSL & TLS Essentials: Securing the Web*, New York: John Wiley & Sons, 2000.

---

8.   http://www.esecurity.ch

[8]   Rescorla, E., *SSL and TLS: Designing and Building Secure Systems*, Reading, MA: Addison-Wesley, 2000.

[9]   Shirey, R., ''Internet Security Glossary,'' Request for Comments 2828, May 2000.

Acknowledgments

First, I want to express my thanks to all people who contributed to and were involved in the writing, publishing, and selling of the first edition of this book. Among these people, I am particularly grateful for the interest and support of Kurt Bauknecht, Dieter Hogrefe, Hansjürg Mey, and Günther Pernul. Also, I want to thank all buyers of the first edition; they have made it possible for me to update the book and to develop a second edition. Since publication of the first edition, many security professionals, colleagues, customers, and students have provided valuable comments, suggestions, pointers, and further material to me. I hope that this input was taken into proper consideration. Ruedi Rytz and my brother, Hans Oppliger, have been particularly helpful in finding mistakes and making the book more comprehensive and understandable. The same is true for John Yesberg, who has thoroughly reviewed the entire manuscript and provided many useful comments and hints. As with the first edition the staff at Artech House was enormously helpful in producing the second edition of this book. Among these people, I'd like to thank Tim Pitts, Ruth Harris, Judi Stone, and Jen Kelland. Above all, I want to thank my family—my wife Isabelle and our beloved children, Marc and Lara—for their encouragement, support, and patience during the writing of the book. Once again, they have tolerated the long writing hours into the night, the scattered papers and manuscripts, the numerous business trips, and many other inconveniences while I completed this edition of the book. Soon before the book went into production, our daughter, Lara, was born. Consequently, it is dedicated to her.

Introduction

Contents

1.1 Internet

1.2 WWW

1.3 Vulnerabilities, threats and countermeasures

1.4 Generic security model

References

As mentioned in the Preface, this book assumes that the reader is familiar with the fundamentals of computer networks and distributed systems in general, and TCP/IP networking in particular. You may refer to [1–4] for a comprehensive introduction, or Chapter 2 of [5] for a corresponding summary. Against this background, we overview the scope of the book in this chapter. In particular, we introduce the Internet and the World Wide Web (WWW) in Sections 1.1 and 1.2, distinguish between vulnerabilities, threats, and countermeasures in Section 1.3, and introduce a generic security model in Section 1.4.

1.1 Internet

The emerging use of TCP/IP networking has led to a global system of interconnected hosts and networks that is commonly referred to as *the Internet*.[1] The Internet was created initially to help foster communications among government-sponsored researchers and grew steadily to include educational institutions, government agencies, and commercial organizations. In fact, the Internet has experienced a triumphant advance during the past decade. Today, it is the world's largest

---

1. Note the definite article and the capital letter ''I'' in the term ''the Internet.'' More generally, the term *internet* is used to refer to any TCP/IP-based internetwork, whereas the term *intranet* is used to refer to a TCP/IP-based corporate or enterprise network.

1

computer network and has been doubling in size each year. With this phenomenal growth rate, the Internet's size is increasing faster than any other network ever created, including even the public-switched telephone network (PSTN).[2] Early in 1998, more than 2 million Web servers and more than 30 million computer systems were connected to the Internet [6] and these numbers have steadily increased meanwhile. Consequently, the Internet is may be seen as the basis and first incarnation of an information superhighway, or national information infrastructure (NII) as, for example, promoted by the U.S. government.[3]

But in spite of its exacting role, the initial, research-oriented Internet and its TCP/IP communications protocol suite were designed for a more benign environment than now exists. It could, perhaps, best be described as a collegial environment, where the users trusted each other and were interested in a free and open exchange of information. In this environment, the people on the Internet were the people who actually built the Internet. Later on, when the Internet became more useful and reliable, these people were joined by others with different ethical interests and behaviors. With fewer common goals and more people, the Internet steadily twisted away from its original intent.

Today, the Internet environment is much less collegial and trustworthy. It contains all the dangerous situations, nasty people, and risks that one can find in society as a whole. Along with the well-intentioned and honest users of the Internet, there are also people who intentionally try to break into computer systems connected to it. Consequently, the Internet is plagued with the kind of delinquents who enjoy the electronic equivalent of writing on other people's walls with spray paint, tearing off mailboxes, or hanging around in the streets annoying the neighborhood. In this environment, the openness of the Internet has turned out to be a double-edged sword. Since its very beginning, but especially since its opening in the 1990s and its ongoing commercialization, the Internet has become a popular target to attack. The number of security breaches has in fact escalated faster than the growth of the Internet as a whole.[4]

Security problems on the Internet receive public attention, and the media carry stories of high-profile malicious attacks via the Internet against

---

2. Only mobile networks experience similar growth rates.
3. http://nii.nist.gov
4. There are several statistics that illustrate this point. For example, refer to the publications of the Computer Security Institute (CSI) at http://www.gocsi.com or the reports and articles published by the CERT Coordination Center (CERT/CC) at http://www.cert.org.

government, business, and academic sites. Perhaps the first and still most significant incident was the Internet Worm, launched by Robert T. Morris, Jr. on November 2, 1988 [7, 8]. The Internet Worm flooded thousands of hosts connected to the Internet and woke up the Internet community accordingly. It gained a lot of publicity and led to increased awareness of security issues on the Internet. In fact, the computer emergency response team (CERT[5]) that is operated by the Software Engineering Institute at Carnegie Mellon University was created in the aftermath of the Internet Worm, and other CERTs have been founded in various countries around the world.[6] Today, the CERT at Carnegie Mellon University serves as the CERT Coordination Center (CERT/CC) for the Internet community.

Since the Internet Worm incident, reports of network-based attacks, such as password sniffing, IP spoofing, sequence number guessing, session hijacking, flooding, and other denial-of-service (DOS) attacks, as well as exploitations of well-known bugs and design limitations, have grown dramatically [9–11]. In addition, the use and wide deployment of executable content, such as provided by Java applets and ActiveX controls, has provided new possibilities to attack hosts or entire sites.[7]

Many Internet breaches are publicized and attract the attention of the Internet community, while numerous incidents go unnoticed. For example, early in 1994, thousands of passwords were captured by sniffer programs that had been remotely installed on compromised hosts on various university networks connected to the Internet. At the end of the same year, sequence number guessing attacks were successfully launched by Kevin Mitnick against several computing centers, including Tsutomu Shimomura's San Diego Center for Supercomputing [12]. This story actually shocked the world when it became *The New York Times* headline news on January 23, 1995. In 1996, several forms of DOS attacks were launched, such as e-mail bombing and TCP SYN flooding [13]. Also late in 1996, Dan Farmer conducted a security survey of approximately 2,200 computing systems on the Internet.[8] What he found was indeed surprising: Almost two-thirds of the more interesting Internet or Web sites had serious security problems that could have been exploited by determined attackers.

---

5. http://www.cert.org

6. Many of these CERTs are member organizations of the Forum of Incident Response and Security Teams (FIRST).

7. Refer to the WWW home page of DigiCrime at URL http://www.digicrime.com to convince yourself that executable content is in fact dangerous.

8. http://www.trouble.org/survey

Several Web sites of large companies and federal offices have been vandalized, and Webjacking has become a popular activity for casual Internet hackers.[9] More recently, macro viruses and distributed denial of service (DDoS) attacks have troubled the Internet community considerably. The trend to more and highly automated attacks is likely to continue in the future.

In spite of the fact that unscrupulous people make press headlines with various types of attacks, the vulnerabilities they exploit are usually well known. For example, security experts warned against passwords transmitted in cleartext at the very beginning of (inter)networking, and Robert T. Morris, Jr., described sequence number guessing attacks for BSD UNIX version 4.2 when he was with AT&T Bell Laboratories in 1985 [14, 15]. Some of the problems related to Internet security are a result of inherent vulnerabilities in the TCP/IP protocols and services, while others are a result of host configuration and access controls that are poorly implemented or too complex to administer. Additionally, the role and importance of system administration is often shortchanged in job descriptions, resulting in many administrators' being, at best, part-time and poorly prepared. This is further aggravated by the tremendous growth and speed of the Internet as a whole.

Today, individuals, commercial organizations, and government agencies depend on the Internet for communication and research, and thus have much more to lose if their sites are compromised. In fact, virtually everyone on the Internet is vulnerable, and the Internet's security problems are the center of attention, generating much fear throughout the computer and communications industries. Concerns about security problems have already begun to chill the overheated expectations about the Internet's readiness for full commercial activity, possibly delaying or preventing it from becoming a mass medium for the NII or the global information infrastructure (GII). Several studies have independently shown that many individuals and companies are abstaining from joining the Internet simply because of security concerns. At the same time, analysts are warning companies about the dangers of not being connected to the Internet. In this conflicting situation, almost everyone agrees that the Internet needs more and better security. In a workshop held by the Internet Architecture Board (IAB) in 1994, scaling and security were nominated as the two most important problem areas for the Internet architecture as a whole [16]. This has not

---

9. Note, however, that the real losses caused by Webjacking activities are comparably small, since the Web pages that are vandalized are often located outside the firewall in a so-called demilitarized zone (for easy access by the casual Web user).

changed so far and is not likely to change in the future [17]. It is particularly true for the WWW and Web-based applications.

1.2 WWW

The WWW is a virtual network that is overlaid on the Internet. It comprises all client[10] and server systems that communicate with one another using the *Hypertext Transfer Protocol* (HTTP). HTTP, in turn, is a simple client/server application protocol that is layered on top of a reliable transport service, such as provided by the Transport Control Protocol (TCP). The protocol defines how WWW resources[11] may be requested and transmitted across the Internet. In this book, we do not delve into the technical details of the HTTP specifications. Instead, we refer to the many books that address HTTP and its features. Among these books, I particularly recommend [18].

HTTP and the WWW were originally invented in the late 1980s by Tim Berners-Lee and his colleagues at the European Laboratory for Particle Physics (CERN[12]) located in Geneva, Switzerland. It was envisioned as a way of publishing physics papers on the Internet without requiring that physicists go through the laborious process of downloading a file and printing it out. As such, HTTP and the WWW have been in use since 1989. Note, however, that the first version of HTTP, referred to as HTTP/0.9 (i.e., HTTP version 0.9), was only a simple protocol for raw data transfer across the Internet.

HTTP was (and still is) a simple request/response protocol. This basically means that a client sends an HTTP request message to a server, and that the server sends back a corresponding HTTP response message. There are no multiple-step handshakes in the beginning as with other TCP/IP application protocols, such as Telnet or FTP. In the case of HTTP/0.9, the browser simply established a TCP connection to the appropriate port of the origin server and sent a request message like GET /index.html to the origin server. The origin server, in turn, responded with the contents of the requested resource (the file /index.html in the example above). In HTTP/0.9, there were no request headers, no request methods other than GET, and the response had to be a file written in a special language, namely the *hypertext markup*

---

10. In WWW parlance, HTTP clients are often called browsers. In this book, we are going to use the terms *HTTP client*, *client*, *browser*, and *Web browser* synonymously. Note, however, that most browsers provide client support for other application protocols in addition to HTTP, such as Telnet, FTP, and Gopher.

11. Examples of WWW resources include text and HTML files, GIF, and JPEG image files, or any other file that stores digitally encoded data in some specific format.

12. The acronym is derived from the French name of the research laboratory.

language (HTML). All current servers are capable of understanding and handling HTTP/0.9 requests, but the protocol is so simple that it is not very useful anymore.

After the first implementations of HTTP/0.9, the protocol was enhanced with some new features, such as request headers and additional request methods, as well as a message format that conforms to the multipurpose Internet mail extensions (MIME) specification originally proposed for Internet-based electronic messaging. The resulting HTTP/1.0 (version 1.0) specification was officially released in 1996 in RFC 1945 [19].

Compared to HTTP/0.9, HTTP/1.0 was a major step ahead. Nevertheless, HTTP/1.0 still did not sufficiently take into consideration the effects of hierarchical proxies, caching, the need for persistent connections, and virtual hosting. In addition, the proliferation of incompletely implemented applications calling themselves "compliant to HTTP/1.0" required a protocol version change in order for two communicating applications to determine each other's capabilities. Consequently, an updated version of the HTTP specification was drafted in 1997. After a 2 year trial period, the specification of HTTP/1.1 (version 1.1) was officially released in RFC 2616 [20] and submitted to the Internet standards track. The basic operation of HTTP/1.1 has remained the same as for HTTP/1.0 (and HTTP/0.9), and the protocol ensures that browsers and servers of different versions can correctly interoperate. More precisely, if the browser understands version 1.1, it uses HTTP/1.1 on the request line instead of HTTP/1.0. When the server sees this version number, it can make use of HTTP/1.1 features. If, however, an HTTP/1.1 server sees a lower version number, it adjusts its responses to use that protocol version instead. In addition to RFC 2616, there is an experimental RFC 2774 that describes an HTTP extension framework [21]. This framework is not addressed in this book.

Originally developed on NeXT computers, the WWW didn't really take off until a team of researchers at the National Center for Supercomputer Application (NCSA) of the University of Illinois wrote Mosaic, a browser for the X Window system. In the early 1990s, this browser soon became the standard against which all other browsers were compared. Marc Andreessen, who was the head of the original Mosaic development team, went on to cofound a start-up company called Mosaic Communications. The company first created a new browser called *Mozilla*.[13] Afterwards, the company was renamed Netscape Communications and the corresponding browser was renamed Netscape Navigator. After Microsoft released its own browser,

---

13. Note that sometimes browsers are still called *Mozilla*.

called the Internet Explorer, Netscape Communications and Microsoft started a tough competition for market share. The competition ended in 1998 when America Online (AOL) bought Netscape Communications. Netscape Navigator is still available and in use today, but it has lost a lot of market share. Instead of Netscape Navigator, a new browser called Opera[14] is used and widely deployed on the Internet today. Opera has been developed in Norway to meet the requirements of clients with limited computing power. As such, it is the browser of choice for many users of personal digital assistants (PDAs) and handheld computer devices. As of this writing, it is difficult to tell whether Microsoft Internet Explorer will increase its market share or loose it to a competitor, such as Opera.

HTTP and Web technologies are omnipresent on the Internet and an increasingly large number of Internet services have been redesigned and implemented so they can also be accessed from a standard off-the-shelf browser (instead of only a dedicated client software package). For example, most browsers implement the File Transfer Protocol (FTP)—in addition to HTTP—and can be used to electronically download files accordingly. Consequently, these browsers may serve as replacement tools for formerly used FTP clients. Also, many e-mail users regularly access their message stores using Web browsers and HTTP instead of e-mail user agents and message store access protocols, such as POP3 or IMAP4. In fact, Web-based messaging has become very popular in the recent past (especially among roaming users) and many companies have installed and are operating corresponding Web frontends to their messaging infrastructures. In the case of Microsoft Exchange, for example, Outlook Web Access may provide this kind of functionality.

Against this background, the term *Web services* has been created to become a new buzzword in the industry, and many software vendors have launched initiatives to promote Web services based on the *extensible markup language* (XML). Examples include Microsoft's .NET initiative and the Sun Open Net Environment (Sun ONE).[15] In either case, the *Web services markup language* (WSDL) is used to formally describe Web services in some structured and standardized way. Implementing a Web service means structuring data and operations inside of an XML document that complies with the *Simple Object Access Protocol* (SOAP) specification. The SOAP, in turn, is a simple and lightweight XML-based client/server protocol that

---

14. http://www.opera.com

15. In its latest material, Sun Microsystems uses the term *services on demand* to go one step further and to collectively refer to local applications, client/server applications, Web applications, and Web services.

defines a messaging framework for exchanging structured data and type information across the Web. It can be used in combination with any transport protocol or mechanism that is able to transport SOAP messages (also known as *SOAP envelopes*). Many programming or scripting languages can be used to implement a Web service and to construct, transmit, read, and process corresponding SOAP messages (e.g., Java and C#). Once a Web service has been implemented, it must be published somewehere that allows interested parties to find it. Information about how a client would connect to a Web service and interact with it must also be exposed somewhere accessible to them. This connection and interaction information is commonly referred to as binding information. *Universal description discovery and integration* (UDDI) registries are the primary means to publish, discover, and bind Web services. These registries contain the data structures and taxonomies used to describe Web services and Web service providers. A UDDI registry can be hosted either by private organizations or by third parties. More recently, IBM and Microsoft have announced the *Web services inspection language* (WSIL) specification to allow applications to browse Web servers for XML Web services. As such, WSIL promises to complement UDDI by making it easier to discover available services on Web sites not listed in the UDDI registries. By the time this book hits the shelves of bookstores, many new terms and acronyms will have been created and put in place. All of these technologies are not at the core of this book. Consequently, they are mentioned and put into perspective only where useful and appropriate. You may refer to many other books to learn about XML or Web services in general, and WSDL, SOAP, and UDDI in particular [22, 23]. You may also refer to the home page of the World Wide Web Consortium[16] (W3C) to get some further information about the latest acronyms and buzzwords.

1.3 Vulnerabilities, threats, and countermeasures

In general, a *vulnerability* refers to a weakness that can be exploited by somebody (e.g., an intruder) to violate a system or the information it contains. In a computer network or distributed system, passwords transmitted in cleartext often represent a major vulnerability. The passwords are exposed to eavesdropping and corresponding sniffing attacks. Similarly, the ability of a network host to boot with a network address that has originally been assigned to another host refers to another vulnerability

---

16. http://www.w3.org

that can be used to spoof that particular host and to masquerade accordingly. Unfortunately, the power of Web technology in general and HTTP in particular also makes the WWW vulnerable to a number of serious attacks.

A *threat* refers to a circumstance, condition, or event with the potential to either violate the security of a system or to cause harm to system resources. Computer networks and distributed systems are susceptible to a wide variety of threats that may be mounted either by intruders[17] or legitimate users. As a matter of fact, legitimate users are more powerful adversaries, since they possess internal information that is not usually available to intruders.

Finally, a *countermeasure* is a feature or function that either reduces or eliminates one (or several) system vulnerability(ies) or counters one (or several) threats. For example, the use of strong authentication techniques reduces the vulnerability of passwords transmitted in the clear and counters the threat of password sniffing and replay attacks. Similarly, the use of cryptographic authentication at the network layer effectively eliminates attacks based on machines spoofing other machines' IP addresses and counters IP spoofing attacks.

In essence, this book is about countermeasures that can be used and deployed to secure the WWW and applications that make use of it. Note, however, that security in general and WWW security in particular are vague terms that may mean various things to different people. The nature of security is such that it cannot be proven.[18] The very best we can show is resistance against a certain set of attacks we know and with which we are familiar. There is nothing in the world that can protect us against new types of attack. For example, timing attacks, differential fault analysis (DFA), and differential power analysis (DPA) are some of the latest tools in the never-ending competition between cryptographers and cryptanalysts.

In this book, we are not going to define the term *security* formally Instead, we focus on techniques and mechanisms that are available today and that can be used to provide security services (i.e., access control and communication security services) on the Web. The assumption is that if a WWW application is able to provide these security services, there are at least

---

17. The term *hacker* is often used to describe computer vandals who break into computer systems. These vandals call themselves hackers, and that is how they got the name, but in my opinion, they don't deserve it. In this book, we use the terms intruder and attacker instead.

18. In certain environments, specific security properties can be proven formally. This is, however, seldom completely proven.

some obstacles to overcome in order to successfully attack the application. If the security services are well designed and properly implemented, the resulting obstacles are far too big to be overcome by occasional intruders. Before we delve into the technical details, we want to briefly introduce a generic security model that explains and puts into perspective the various aspects of security.

1.4 Generic security model

Discussing security in computer networks and distributed systems is difficult, mainly because the term *security* is hard to define and even harder to quantify. Security is a subjective feeling that is perceived differently by different people. What somebody considers to be secure may be considered by somebody else to be completely insecure. An example to illustrate this point is an airplane flight: While many people consider flying to be secure, there are also people who refuse to fly mainly for security and safety reasons.

To convince a customer about the security and safety properties of a particular product or service is a difficult (marketing) task. How do you, for example, persuade a potential buyer about the security and safety properties of a specific car? A somehow unsatisfactory solution for a car dealer is to invite a potential buyer for a ride and to steer the car straight into the next tree. If the buyer remains uninjured, chances are that he or she is convinced about the security and safety properties of the car. Unfortunately, the car itself will be damaged and the dealer will have to give the buyer another one. The question that arises immediately is whether the security and safety properties of this car are equal to the ones from the other car.

Marketing professionals have come up with better solutions, such as tests conducted by independent consumer societies. The good marketing approach is aimed at increasing the reputation of a product or service in terms of security and safety. For example, in the car industry, Volvo has managed to steadily achieve this kind of reputation. Many people buy a Volvo car simply because they want to increase their security and safety when driving on the road. Unfortunately, a similar appreciation of security and safety properties is very immature in the information technology (IT) industry (if it exists at all).

In general, there are many aspects involved in securing a networked or distributed system, such as, for example, the WWW. First and foremost, there must be a security policy that formalizes the proper and improper use of the (networked or distributed) system, the possible threats against it, as well as countermeasures that must be employed to protect assets from these threats. Most importantly, the security policy is to specify the goals that should be achieved. For example, a possible goal for a corporate intranet would be that any access from external sites requires strong authentication of the requesting user at a security gateway. This goal can be achieved, for example, by using a one-time password or challenge-response system at the firewall. If another goal were the transparent encryption of the data traffic between internal and external sites, the use of Internet or transport layer security protocols would be another possibility to implement the security policy. After having specified a security policy, there are several aspects related to host, network, organizational, and legal security that all need to be addressed. The situation is comparable with politics and the military: politics may declare war, but the military must conduct it. Similarly, the security policy must specify the goals, but host and network security techniques and mechanisms must meet these goals. For example, the hosts must run a secure (network) operating system to protect internal resources against outside attacks. Similarly, the hosts must communicate over links that are considerably secure. Either the links are physically secure or they are secured through other means, such as cryptographic algorithms and protocols. Additionally, organizational security controls must be defined and put in place to enforce the technical (host and network) security techniques and mechanisms. If organizational security controls do not exist, everybody will try to do everything, effectively circumventing any security policy. Finally, legal security controls must ensure that if somebody misbehaves or maliciously attacks a system within the computer network or distributed system, he or she can be prosecuted and punished accordingly.

Following this line of argumentation, our generic security model for computer networks and distributed systems takes into account the following five aspects:

1. Security policy;

2. Host security;

3. Network security;

4. Organizational security;

5. Legal security.

These aspects are illustrated in Figure 1.1 and further addressed in the remaining part of this chapter. Whereas the rest of this book focuses exclusively on network security, the other aspects of security are equally

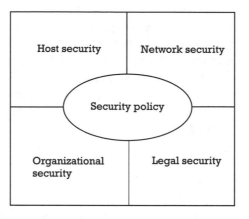

Figure 1.1 A generic security model for computer networks and distributed systems.

important and should also be considered with care. It is simply not possible to achieve security on the Web if these aspects are not adequately addressed. In fact, we have already mentioned in the Preface that most security breaches are due to software bugs that are exploited or configuration failures.

1.4.1 Security policy

As mentioned before, a security policy must specify the goals that should be achieved with regard to the security of a networked or distributed system. In fact, if a security policy is not specified, it is useless to talk about security in the first place. Put in other words: If one does not know what to protect and against what types of attacks this protection should hold, every security technology is fine and makes sense. Security often comes at some expense, often at the expense of some functionality that people want, and some monetary expense. A security policy should be a tool that guides a practitioner in working out which tradeoffs are acceptable, and which ones aren't. Many people new to the security field jump straight into technology and it is usually hard to convince them of the importance of policy.

The security policy should be specified by management, without taking into account the technical implementation and enforcement.[19] In fact, the security policy should be driven by requirements rather than technical considerations. Typical statements found in a security policy include phrases

---

19. While the policy should be written by management, it will often be the case that management doesn't understand what is required. A security practitioner will be required to present options to management, asking them to choose or endorse a policy.

such as "any access from the Internet to intranet resources must be strongly authenticated and properly authorized at the security gateway," or "any classified data must be properly encrypted for transmission."

1.4.2 Host security

Host security has traditionally addressed such questions as

▶ How to securely authenticate users;

▶ How to effectively control access to system resources;

▶ How to securely store and process data within the system;

▶ How to do the audit trail.

These and similar questions have been studied within the computer security community for quite a long time. A special field of study in this area is the evaluation and certification of IT systems and products. For example, the National Computer Security Center (NCSC) of the U.S. National Security Agency (NSA) developed the *Trusted Computer Security Evaluation Criteria* (TCSEC), also known as the "Orange Book," in the late 1980s [24]. In Europe, similar developments in Germany, France, the United Kingdom, and the Netherlands led to the *Information Technology Security Evaluation Criteria* (ITSEC) [25]. Europe, the United States, and Canada worked together and came up with *common criteria*.[20] The efforts were later joined by many other countries. In December 1999, ISO/IEC approved and published the Common Criteria version 2.1 as International Standard (IS) 15408. Note, however, that except for some government-sponsored programs, the idea of evaluating and certifying IT systems and products has not yet really taken off in the commercial world. This is particularly true for networked and distributed systems. The TCSEC has been interpreted [26] and people have drafted Common Criteria protection profiles for such systems, but there still remain many unsolved problems.

1.4.3 Network security

Network security addresses questions such as how to efficiently control access to computer networks and distributed systems, and how to securely transmit data between them.

---

20. http://csrc.nist.gov/cc

In network security parlance, one clearly distinguishes between a security service and a security mechanism:

▶ A *security service* is the performance of a set of useful or helpful functions and actions that can provide a particular quality or benefit to the requesting entity (e.g., user or client) as may be required by a security policy;

▶ A *security mechanism* can be used to provide one (or several) security service(s).

For example, user authentication is a security service that can be implemented with passwords or biometrics. Similarly, there are many encryption algorithms that can be used to provide data confidentiality services. In either case, one has to distinguish between specification and implementation. In short, a specification identifies what is needed, whereas an implementation provides it. This basically means that a security service (security mechanism) can be specified or implemented.

For example, the security architecture for the open systems inter-connection (OSI) reference model enumerates the following five classes of *security services* [27, 28]:

1. Authentication services;

2. Data confidentiality services;

3. Data integrity services;

4. Access control services;

5. Non-repudiation services.

Network users and applications must be able to selectively make use of services that conform to their security requirements. These requirements are individual by nature, and may vary from user to user or application to application. There are also some security services that are not enumerated in the OSI security architecture, such as anonymity services as further addressed in Chapter 12 of this book.

In addition to the security services mentioned above, the OSI security architecture also enumerates a couple of security mechanisms that can be used to implement the security services. In particular, the following eight *specific security mechanisms* are enumerated in the OSI security architecture:

1. Encipherment;

2. Digital signature mechanisms;

3. Access control mechanisms;

4. Data integrity mechanisms;

5. Authentication exchange mechanism;

6. Traffic padding mechanism;

7. Routing control mechanism;

8. Notarization mechanism.

Complementary to these specific security mechanisms, the OSI security architecture also enumerates the following five *pervasive security mechanisms:*

1. Trusted functionality;

2. Security labels;

3. Event detection;

4. Security audit trail;

5. Security recovery.

The OSI security architecture is extensively covered in the literature. In particular, Chapter 4 of [5] is dedicated entirely to the OSI security architecture. From a more practical point of view, it is appropriate to distinguish between access control and communication security services:

▸ *Access control services* are used to logically separate (inter)networks and to essentially control access to corporate networks which are also called intranets in the case of TCP/IP-based networks;

▸ *Communication security services* are used to protect communications within and between these networks. According to the OSI security architecture, communication security services include authentication, data confidentiality and integrity, as well as nonrepudiation services.

The predominant technology to provide access control services for corporate networks and intranets is the firewall technology as further addressed in Part II of [5] and Chapter 3 of this book. With regard to communication security services, many cryptographic protocols have been proposed for the various network layers of both the OSI reference model and the Internet model. These protocols are addressed in Part III of [5] and Chapters 5 and 6 of this book.

1.4.4 Organizational security

Any technical solution for host and network security must be backed up with organizational security controls. In fact, organizational security is required where technical host and network security mechanisms alone do not or only insufficiently work. A quotation from Richard H. Baker elaborates on the problem regarding technical versus organizational security [29]:

> Security continues to be and probably will always be a people problem. If you overlook that, you're in trouble.

According to this quotation, it is dangerous to depend on technical (host and network) security mechanisms alone. If people are not convinced about the need for the security mechanisms that are put in place, they will always try to circumvent them. In one of his later books, Baker has even been more succinct in this point [30]:

> The real challenges are human, not technical. Oldtimers will recognize a once-popular saying that the most important part of an automobile is the nut that holds the steering wheel. That's still true, even though a modern steering wheel may also contain an air bag and any number of controls and antitheft devices.

Our personal experience is in line with this quotation. In fact, human behavior is still the most important factor with regard to security and safety. Human behavior can be influenced by education and organizational security controls. Education is very important. If people understand the security controls they must rely on, they will make use of them instead of always trying to circumvent them. Additionally, organizational security controls must be put in place to make illegitimate procedures more difficult. Organizational security controls include directions and instructions that are released to define legitimate human behavior.

An analogy that may help better understand security in computer networks and distributed systems is the existing highway system, and the way we try to achieve safety and security on it.[21] In particular, we use and

---

21. Similar things could also be said for the airway system.

deploy several technical and organizational measures to achieve safe and secure traffic:

> On the technical side, we try to build highways in a way that minimizes the risks of careless drivers' being able to cause serious accidents. We also require drivers to have a license and cars to have passed a vehicle inspection test.

> On the organizational side, we have educational programs, traffic laws, and police to enforce these laws.

Using this analogy, it is obvious that we can learn several things from the way we handle security and safety in the real world.

1.4.5 Legal security

Finally, it is possible that host or network security techniques or mechanisms will fail and not provide sufficient protection against more sophisticated attacks. Similarly, it is possible that organizational security controls won't be able to back up technical deficiencies. In this case, it is important to have the possibility to legally prosecute the attacker(s). Consequently, legal security is a major topic with regard to computer networks and distributed systems.

Again, there is an analogy to better illustrate this point: We are all familiar with the postal delivery service. We send letters in envelopes in order to protect the confidentiality of the contents. In addition, we trust the employees of the postal delivery service not to open the envelopes and to respect the privacy of the mail accordingly. However, if we recognized that a letter was opened during its delivery, we would have cause to suspect the employee(s) of the postal delivery service of not respecting the privacy of the mail, and a case could even be brought to court. One can reasonably expect that similar legal security controls will be put in place in computer networks and distributed systems, such as the Web, and that the need for nonrepudiation services will be the major driving force for this development to happen.

References

[1]   Tanenbaum, A. S., *Computer Networks*, 3d ed., Englewood Cliffs, NJ: Prentice Hall, 1998.

[2]   Comer, D. E., and R. E. Droms, *Computer Networks and Internets*, 2nd ed., Englewood Cliffs, NJ: Prentice Hall, 1998.

[3]   Wilder, F., *A Guide to the TCP/IP Protocol Suite, Second Edition*, Norwood, MA: Artech House, 1998.

[4]   Comer, D., *Internetworking with TCP/IP: Vol. I: Principles, Protocols, and Architecture*, 4th ed., Englewood Cliffs, NJ: Prentice Hall, 2000.

[5]   Oppliger, R., *Internet and Intranet Security, Second Edition*, Norwood, MA: Artech House, 2002.

[6]   Zakon, R. H., "Hobbes' Internet Timeline," Request for Comments 2235, (FYI 32), November 1997.

[7]   Spafford, E. H., The Internet Worm: Crisis and Aftermath," *Communications of the ACM*, Vol. 32, 1989, pp. 678–688.

[8]   Rochlis, J. A., and M. W. Eichin, "With Microscope and Tweezers: The Worm from MIT's Perspective," *Communications of the ACM*, Vol. 32, 1989, pp. 689–703.

[9]   Denning, P. J., *Computers Under Attack: Intruders, Worms, and Viruses*, New York: ACM Press/Addison-Wesley, 1990.

[10]   Neumann, P. G., *Computer-Related Risks*, New York: ACM Press/Addison-Wesley, 1995.

[11]   Howard, J. D., "An Analysis of Security Incidents on the Internet 1989–1995," Ph.D. Thesis, Carnegie Mellon University, April 1997.

[12]   Shimomura, T., with J. Markoff, *Takedown*, New York: Hyperion, 1996.

[13]   Schuba, C. L., et al., "Analysis of a Denial of Service Attack on TCP," *Proceedings of IEEE Symposium on Security and Privacy*, 1997, pp. 208–223.

[14]   Morris, R. T., "A Weakness in the 4.2BSD UNIX TCP/IP Software," *Computer Science Technical Report* No. 117, Murray Hill, NJ: AT&T Bell Laboratories, 1985.

[15]   Bellovin, S. M., "Security Problems in the TCP/IP Protocol Suite," *ACM Computer Communication Review*, Vol. 19, No. 2, 1989, pp. 32–48.

[16]   Braden, R., et al., "Report of the IAB Workshop on Security in the Internet Architecture (February 8–10, 1994)," Request for Comments 1636, June 1994.

[17]   Bellovin, S., "Report of the IAB Security Architecture Workshop," Request for Comments 2316, April 1998.

[18]   Thomas, S., *HTTP Essentials: Protocols for Secure, Scaleable Web Sites*, New York: John Wiley & Sons, 2001.

[19]   Berners-Lee, T., R. Fielding, and H. Frystyk, "Hypertext Transfer Protocol—HTTP/1.0," Request for Comments 1945, May 1996.

[20]   Fielding, R., et al., "Hypertext Transfer Protocol—HTTP/1.1," Request for Comments 2616, June 1999.

[21]   Nielsen, H., P. Leach, and S. Lawrence, "An HTTP Extension Framework," Request for Comments 2774, February 2000.

[22]   Oellermann, W. L., Jr., *Architecting Web Services*, Berkeley, CA: Apress, 2001.

[23]   Graham, S., et al., *Building Web Services with Java: Making Sense of XML, SOAP, WSDL and UDDI*, Indianapolis, IN: Sams, 2001.

[24]   U.S. Department of Defense, *Trusted Computer System Evaluation Criteria*, Standard DoD 5200.28-STD, Fort George G. Meade, MD, 1985.

[25]   Commission of the European Communities, *Information Technology Security Evaluation Criteria*, Version 1.2, Directorate General XIII, 1991.

[26]   U.S. Department of Defense, *Trusted Network Interpretation of the Trusted Computer System Evaluation Criteria*, Fort George G. Meade, MD, 1987.

[27]   ISO/IEC 7498-2, Information Processing Systems—Open Systems Interconnection Reference Model—Part 2: Security Architecture, 1989.

[28]   ITU X.800, Security Architecture for Open Systems Interconnection for CCITT Applications, 1991.

[29]   Baker, R. H., *Computer Security Handbook*, New York: McGraw-Hill, 1991.

[30]   Baker, R. H., *Network Security: How To Plan for It and Achieve It*, New York: McGraw-Hill, 1995.

CHAPTER

2

Contents

2.1 HTTP

2.2 User authentication, authorization, and access control

2.3 Basic authentication

2.4 Digest access authentication

2.5 Certificate-based authentication

2.6 Server configuration

2.7 Conclusions

References

HTTP Security

HTTP is the main application protocol used on the WWW. In this chapter, we overview and briefly discuss HTTP and its basic security features. More specifically, we introduce HTTP and its mode of operation in Section 2.1, overview HTTP user authentication, authorization, and access control in Section 2.2, address HTTP basic authentication, HTTP digest access authentication, and certificate-based authentication in Sections 2.3 to 2.5, discuss the proper configuration of a Web server (i.e., Apache Web server) in Section 2.6, and draw some conclusions in Section 2.7.

2.1 HTTP

As mentioned in Chapter 1, HTTP is a simple request/response protocol that is used between a client (i.e., browser) and a Web server [1].[1] This basically means that the client requests information and the server provides the requested information using the HTTP. The information, in turn, may be represented by Web pages that are static or dynamically created. In many cases, the pages may be written in a specific format or language, such as HTML or XML. In the future, XML will be the preferred

---

1. In practice, the term *Web server* is used interchangeably to refer to the computer on which Web pages reside, and the program on the computer that receives HTTP request messages and sends back resources in corresponding response messages.

21

language for the information provided on the WWW (and elsewhere). This is particularly true for the use of XML in conjunction with complementary technologies, such as WSDL, SOAP, and UDDI registries (we have briefly reviewed these technologies in Chapter 1).

If the server provides static Web pages, the situation is comparably simple and the pages can be directly retrieved from the server's document tree. If, however, the server must provide dynamically created Web pages, the pages must be created by a specific program in response to an incoming HTTP request message. Historically, the first solution was to have these programs invoked using the Common Gateway Interface (CGI). Although CGI makes it simple to have a Web server perform a specific operation, such as a database lookup, it is not efficient because it requires that a separate program is started and a corresponding process is initialized for each incoming HTTP request message. There are some alternative technologies that can be used instead of CGI. For example, FastCGI is an open Web server interface that solves the performance problems inherent in CGI.[2] Also, many vendors provide proprietary application programming interfaces (APIs) for their Web servers. Examples include the Netscape Server API (NSAPI) from Netscape and the Internet Server API (ISAPI) from Microsoft. Last but not least, there are server-side technologies, such as ASP and JSP. The security implications of these technologies are further addressed in Chapter 11.

If a client wants to retrieve a resource (e.g., a static or dynamically created Web page) from a Web server, it must establish a TCP connection to the corresponding port (e.g., port 80 by default) of the server and send a corresponding HTTP request message to the server. In essence, the HTTP request message includes the following components:

- ▶ A request method that indicates the purpose of the HTTP request. The most important request method is GET. There are, however, other methods defined in the HTTP/1.1 specification (i.e., OPTIONS, HEAD, POST, PUT, DELETE, TRACE, and CONNECT). You may refer to RFC 2616 [1] for a complete and comprehensive description of these methods.

- ▶ A reference that indicates the resource to which the method should be applied (e.g., `http://www.esecurity.ch/index.html`). In theory, such a reference may be given in one of the following forms:

---

2.   Further information about FastCGI is available at `http://www.fastcgi.com`.

> ‣ A uniform resource locator (URL) [2, 3];

> ‣ A uniform resource name (URN) [4];

> ‣ A uniform resource identifier (URI) [5].

In practice, however, URLs are most widely used. Sometimes they are called URLs and sometimes they are called URIs (e.g., in many IETF protocol specifications).

> ‣ A string indicating the HTTP protocol version (e.g., HTTP/1.0 for version 1.0 of the HTTP);

> ‣ A MIME-like message containing request modifiers, client information, and possibly some body content.

Again, the exact format and syntax of HTTP messages (i.e., HTTP request and response messages) is specified in [1]. This RFC document is recommended reading for anybody working in the field.

As a working example, consider the situation in which a user wants to retrieve the home page of eSECURITY Technologies Rolf Oppliger. Therefore, the user simply enters www.esecurity.ch in the browser's address or URL field. The browser, in turn, does the following things on the user's behalf:

1. It uses the Internet Domain Name System (DNS) to retrieve the IP address of the Web server that hosts www.esecurity.ch.

2. It uses the client system's IP stack to establish a TCP connection to the Web server.[3] Since the user has not specified a port number at first place, the browser assumes that the Web server runs at port 80. Any other port is possible but must be specified in the URL (separated with a colon from the rest of the resource reference).

3. It composes an HTTP request message and uses the TCP connection to send the message to the server (it assumes the use of HTTP by default).

It is now up to the Web server to process the HTTP request message and to send back a corresponding HTTP response message.

---

3. HTTP communication usually takes place over TCP connections. The default port is TCP 80, but other ports can be used. This does not preclude HTTP from being implemented on top of any other protocol on the Internet, or on other networks. HTTP only presumes a reliable transport; any protocol that provides such guarantees can be used.

In the example given above, the browser would compose an HTTP request message that may look as follows:

```
GET http://www.esecurity.ch HTTP/1.0
Host: www.esecurity.ch
Proxy-Connection: Keep-Alive
User-Agent: Mozilla/4.0 (compatible; MSIE 5.5; Windows NT 4.0)
Accept: image/gif, image/jpeg, ...
Accept-Language: en
...
```

Note that this HTTP request message only includes a header part (i.e., the body part is empty). The header part, in turn, includes a number of HTTP headers. Each HTTP header provides specific information. For example, the Host header specifies that the requested Web site is www.esecurity.ch and the Proxy-Connection header specifies that the TCP connection that is going to be established between the browser and the proxy server must be kept alive and used to serve subsequent HTTP requests. Furthermore, the User-Agent header specifies what browser on what platform the user employs (i.e., Microsoft's Internet Explorer version 5.5 on a Windows NT version 4.0 system),[4] and the Accept and Accept-Language headers specify the MIME types and languages accepted by the browser. In addition, there is an increasingly large number of complementary HTTP headers that may be used in HTTP request and response messages.

In response to the HTTP request message, the Web server could send back an HTTP response message that consists of a status line, including the message's protocol version and a success or error code, followed by a MIME-like message containing some server information, entity meta information, and possibly some body content (separated with an empty line from the header). For example, a typical HTTP response message may look as follows:

```
HTTP/1.0 200 OK
Date: Mon, 03 Dec 2001 12:10:13 GMT
Server: Apache/1.3.20 (Unix) PHP/4.0.6 FrontPage/4.0.4.3
Last-Modified: Wed, 03 May 2000 08:01:16 GMT
ETag:"81dfc1-14e-390fdccc"
Accept-Ranges: bytes
Content-Length: 334
```

---

4. The term *Mozilla* is still in use today. Remember that from Chapter 1 that this is what Mosaic Communications called its first browser.

```
Content-Type: text/html
Proxy-Connection: Keep-Alive
<HTML>
  <HEAD>
    <TITLE>eSECURITY Technologies Rolf Oppliger</TITLE>
  </HEAD>
  <FRAMESET COLS="23%,*">
    <FRAME SRC="http://www.esecurity.ch/toc.html">
    <FRAME SRC="http://www.esecurity.ch/esecurity.html''
        NAME="view_frame">
  </FRAMESET>
  <NOFRAME>
  Your browser does not support frames.
  </NOFRAME>
</HTML>
```

The first line of the HTTP response message includes a status code. In this case, the status code 200 means that the HTTP request message is fine (i.e., OK) and that it is served. The HTTP response headers that follow give information either about the server (e.g., the `Server` header) or the returned resource (e.g., the `Date` and `Last-Modied` headers). In either case, a `Content-Type` header is required to inform the browser about the type of the provided resource. In the example given above, the content type `text/html` indicates a text document written in HTML. Finally, the HTTP response message may also include the requested resource (separated with an empty line from the header part). In this example, it is the `index.html` file that is found at the root of the requested server's document tree.

Most HTTP communication is initiated by the browser and consists of a request to be applied to a resource on some Web server. In the simplest case, this may be accomplished via a single TCP connection between the client and the server. A more complicated situation occurs when one or more intermediaries are present in the request/response chain. According to [1], there are three common forms of intermediary:

> ▶ A *proxy server* (or *proxy*) is a forwarding agent, receiving requests for a URL in its absolute form, rewriting all or part of the message, and forwarding the reformatted request toward the server identified by the URL.

> ▶ A *gateway* is a receiving agent, acting as a layer above some other server(s) and, if necessary, translating the requests to the underlying server's protocol.

▶ A *tunnel* acts as a relay point between two connections without changing the messages. Tunnels are used when the communication needs to pass through an intermediary (such as a firewall) even when the intermediary cannot understand the content of the messages.

This distinction is important because certain HTTP communication options may apply only to the connection with the nearest, nontunnel neighbor, only to the end-points of the request/response chain, or to all connections along the chain. Also, any party to the communication that is not acting as a tunnel may employ an internal cache for serving requests. The effect of a cache is that the request/response chain is shortened if one of the participants along the chain has a cached response applicable to that request. Not all responses are usefully cacheable, and some requests may contain modifiers that place special requirements on cache behavior (as explained later). In fact, there are a huge variety of architectures and configurations of caches and proxies currently being experimented with or deployed across the WWW. There are many things that need to be said about proxy servers, gateways, and tunnels. These things will be said in Chapter 3.

2.2 User authentication, authorization, and access control

In general, organizations run Web servers to make resources publicly available and accessible to as many users as possible. In this situation, the Web servers are typically configured to accept requests from anonymous users, and there is no need for user authentication, authorization, and access control. Sometimes, however, organizations run Web servers whose resources must not be available and accessible to anyone. For example, access to a Web server may be restricted to the employees of an organization, or certain resources may be accessible only to customers who have paid a subscription fee or have signed a nondisclosure agreement. In these cases, proper user authentication, authorization, and access control may be required.

Roughly speaking, the following techniques may be used to control access to resources located on a Web server:

▶ Restricting access by using hidden URLs (i.e., URLs that are kept secret);

▶ Restricting access to a particular group of computers based on those computers' address information (i.e., the computers' IP addresses or DNS hostnames);

▶ Restricting access to a particular group of users based on their identity information and corresponding credentials.

Obviously, the easiest way to restrict access is by storing the resources in hidden locations on the Web server's document tree. This refers to the technique of restricting access by using URLs that are kept secret and hidden. Hidden URLs (in the digital world) are about as secure as a key underneath a door mat (in the physical world). Nobody can access the resources unless they know which URLs to use. But anybody who knows a hidden URL has full access to the resource it refers to. Furthermore, the information is transitive. You might tell a friend of yours about a specific URL, and he might tell a friend of his or hers, and so on, until finally the URL gets posted to a mailing list or newsgroup, or it may even end up in a link in another HTML document. At this point, the URL may get registered by an automated program that sweeps through all the pages on a Web server, adding keywords from each page to a central database. If such a program follows the HTML link, it will add the formerly hidden URL, along with identifying index entries, to its database and make it accessible to a search engine accordingly. Thereafter, someone searching for the resource might be able to find it through the index service. In general, hidden URLs should only be used if its compromise and the loss of the resource's confidentiality does not pose any problem. Aviel D. Rubin, Daniel Geer, and Marcus J. Ranum have put this in other words [6]:

As everyone in the data security business is fond of saying, 'Obscurity is not security.' If you want to protect data, you will have to do better than naming it /tmp/nobody_would_guess_this_URL.html; you will need to provide a security mechanism.

Most Web servers allow their administrators to restrict access to a particular group of computers based on those computers' address information (e.g., the allow and deny directives in the case of the Apache Web server). The address information can be specified by the computers' IP addresses or DNS hostnames. In fact, restricting access to specific IP addresses or a range of IP addresses is relatively simple and works well for an organization that wishes to restrict access to people on its intranet. For example, you might consider restricting access to an intranet Web server to the range of IP addresses that has been assigned to your organization. Instead of specifying computers by IP addresses, most Web servers allow their administrators to restrict access on the basis of DNS hostnames. This has the advantage that IP addresses can be changed without having to change the Web server's configuration files, as well (as long as the DNS hostnames remain the same). The disadvantage of restricting access based on DNS hostnames is that the DNS itself can be attacked and misused. Either way, it is important to note that host-based addressing is not foolproof (e.g., IP spoofing can be used to transmit IP packets that appear to come from a different computer than the one actually used). In fact, the security of restricting access based on address information is comparable to the security of packet filtering as discussed in the next chapter.

Finally, restricting access to a particular group of users based on their identity information and corresponding credentials is the most effective way of controlling access to resources. For example, if the users of a Web server are widely dispersed (eventually using dynamically assigned IP addresses), or the administrator needs to be able to control access on an individual basis, it is necessary to implement a user-centric authentication and authorization scheme. In short, the process of verifying the identity of a requesting user is called *user authentication*, whereas the process of granting the privileges to access particular resources is called *user authorization*. In the simplest case, each user is given a username and a password. The username identifies the person who wishes to access the Web server, and the password authenticates the person. To increase security, more sophisticated user authentication schemes may be used.

Roughly speaking, setting up HTTP user authentication, authorization, and access control takes two steps:

1. A file containing the user authentication information must be created. Optionally, the set of users may be structured in some way (e.g., using groups).

2. The Web server must be told what resources to protect and which users to allow access (after proper authentication).

In the following sections, we address and briefly overview two HTTP user authentication schemes that are implemented and widely used today: basic authentication and digest access authentication. The authentication schemes specified in RFC 2617 [7] complement the HTTP/1.1 specification in RFC 2616 [1].[5]

---

5. Note that the HTTP digest access authentication scheme has been slightly modified and that RFC 2617 [7] supercedes RFC 2069.

2.3 Basic authentication

As mentioned above, the HTTP basic authentication scheme implements password-based authentication to protect and to control access to the resources of a server. The server, in turn, may be a Web server or an HTTP proxy server. The HTTP basic authentication scheme works similarly for both types of servers. As of this writing, the scheme is supported by all major browser and server software packages. On the client side, the scheme is supported by, for example, Netscape Navigator, Microsoft's Internet Explorer, and Opera. On the server side, the scheme is supported by almost all software packages, including, for example, Microsoft IIS and Apache.

If a browser requests a resource that is protected with the HTTP basic authentication scheme, the server challenges the browser to provide some valid authentication information (typically a username and a password). This is equally true for Web servers and HTTP proxy servers. The browser either remembers the authentication information from a previous HTTP session, or prompts the user to type in that information. In either case, the browser forwards the information to the server in the clear (this fact represents the most serious weakness and vulnerability of the HTTP basic authentication scheme).

For example, let us assume that a user wants his or her browser to retrieve the file index.html that is located in the protected directory /Demo/ HTTPBasicAuthentication/ at www.esecurity.ch. At first sight, the browser does not know that this file is protected with the HTTP basic authentication scheme. So it sends out a normal-looking HTTP request message. Remember from our previous discussions that such a message may start with the following request line:

    GET http://www.esecurity.ch/Demo/HTTPBasicAuthentication/HTTP/ 1.0

All other HTTP request headers basically remain the same. After having received the HTTP request message, the Web server recognizes that the requested file is located in a directory that is protected with the HTTP basic authentication scheme. As further explained below, the server recognizes that the file is protected because it is located in a directory that contains a specific file (i.e., the file .htaccess in the case of an Apache Web server). Instead of directly returning the requested file, the server generates an HTTP response message that includes the following two characteristic lines:

    HTTP/1.0 401 Unauthorized
    ...
    WWW-Authenticate: Basic realm="HTTP Basic Authentication Demo"

The first line informs the browser that the server has not been able to serve the request because the browser did not provide valid credentials. In our example, the status code 401 (i.e., "Unauthorized") reveals the fact that the server is a Web server (note that it could also be an HTTP proxy server). In the second line, the `WWW-Authenticate` header requests user credentials for the realm named "Basic Authentication Demo."

If the server were an HTTP proxy server, the HTTP response message would have the following two characteristic lines:

```
HTTP/1.0 407 Proxy Authentication Required
...
Proxy-Authenticate: Basic realm="HTTP Basic Authentication Demo"
```

Everything else would remain the same. In either case, the server may also return `Date`, `Server`, and possibly some other HTTP response headers. These headers are neither illustrated above nor discussed below (they are not very relevant from a security point of view).

The HTTP response message is received by the browser and the user is prompted to enter his or her password accordingly. For the server being a Web server, Figures 2.1 and 2.2 illustrate the prompts used by Microsoft's Internet Explorer and Opera. If the user obeys and properly enters his or her username and password (i.e., `rolf` and `test` in this example), the browser resends the HTTP request message that now carries an additional

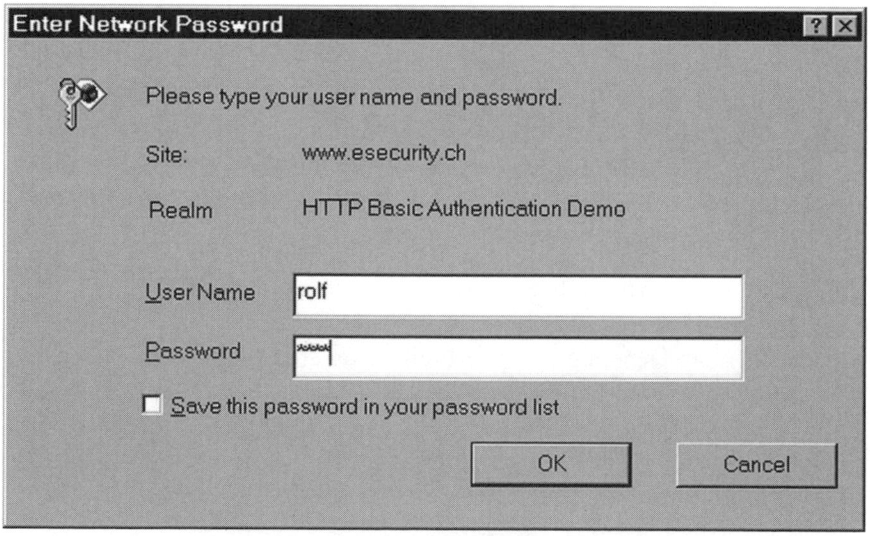

Figure 2.1 The Internet Explorer 5.5 Enter Network Password prompt using the HTTP basic authentication scheme. (© 2002 Microsoft Corporation.)

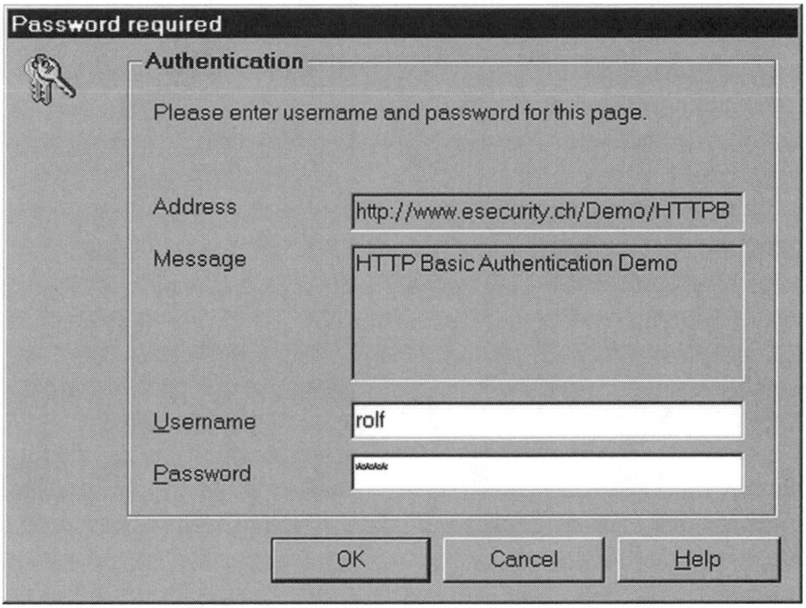

Figure 2.2 The Opera 6.0 Password required prompt using the HTTP basic authentication scheme. (© 2002 Opera Software.)

`Authorization` header (if the server were an HTTP proxy server, the browser would resend an HTTP request message with a `Proxy-Authoriza-tion` header). In our example, the `Authorization` header may look as follows:

`Authorization: Basic cm9sZjp0ZXN0`

The value `cm9sZjp0ZXN0` refers to the user's authentication information (i.e., the username and password separated with a colon) encoded using the Base-64 encoding scheme.[6] This basically works as follows:

1. Each character of the complete authentication information (i.e., `rolf:test`) is converted to its ASCII value (according to Table 2.1). The resulting string of hexademical values is `726F6C663A74657374` (each pair of hexademical values represents one ASCII character). Alternatively, the string of hexademical values may also be written as a bit string:

---

6.   The Base-64 encoding scheme is explained, for example, in Chapter 2 of [8].

Table 2.1 ASCII Characters with Hexadecimal Values

	0x00	0x10	0x20	0x30	0x40	0x50	0x60	0x70
+0	NUL	DLE		0	@	P	ʻ	p
+1	SOH	DC1	!	1	A	Q	a	q
+2	STX	DC2	"	2	B	R	b	r
+3	ETX	DC3	#	3	C	S	c	s
+4	EOT	DC4		4	D	T	d	t
+5	ENQ	NAK	%	5	E	U	e	u
+6	ACK	SYN	&	6	F	V	f	v
+7	BEL	ETB	ʼ	7	G	W	g	w
+8	BS	CAN	(	8	H	X	h	x
+9	HT	EM	)	9	I	Y	i	y
+A	LF	SUB	*	:	J	Z	j	z
+B	VT	ESC	+	;	K	[	k	{
+C	FF	FS	,	<	L	\	l		
+D	CR	GS	-	=	M	]	m	}
+E	SO	RS	.	>	N	^	n	
+F	SI	US	/	?	O	_	o	DEL

```
    7    2    6    F    6    C    6    6    3
  0111 0010 0110 1111 0110 1100 0110 0110 0011

    A    7    4    6    5    7    3    7    4
  1010 0111 0100 0110 0101 0111 0011 0111 0100
```

2. The bit string is rearranged and split into groups of six bits each.

```
  011100 100110 111101 101100 011001 100011
  101001 110100 011001 010111 001101 110100
```

3. Each group of six bits is represented by a new character in the Base-64 encoding scheme (according to Table 2.2). For example, the first substring 011100 refers to the decimal value 28 or the hexadecimal value 1C. Referring to Table 2.2, this value is represented by the letter c in the Base-64 encoding scheme. Similarly, the second substring 100110 refers to the decimal value 38 or hexadecimal value 26, and this value is represented by the letter m in the Base-64 encoding scheme. The resulting string can be constructed as follows:

```
  011100 100110 111101 101100 011001 100011
     28     38     61     44     25     35
     1C     26     3D     2C     19     23
      c      m      9      s      Z      j
```

Table 2.2 Characters Used in the Base-64
Encoding Scheme

	0x00	0x10	0x20	0x30
+0	A	Q	g	w
+1	B	R	h	x
+2	C	S	i	y
+3	D	T	j	z
+4	E	U	k	0
+5	F	V	l	1
+6	G	W	m	2
+7	H	X	n	3
+8	I	Y	o	4
+9	J	Z	p	5
+A	K	a	q	6
+B	L	b	r	7
+C	M	c	s	8
+D	N	d	t	9
+E	O	e	u	+
+F	P	f	v	/

101001	110100	011001	010111	001101	110100
41	52	25	23	13	52
29	34	19	17	D	34
p	0	Z	X	N	0

The first line represents the groups of six bits. The second and third line represent the corresponding decimal and hexadecimal values, whereas the fourth line represents the corresponding charcaters in the Base-64 encoding scheme. Consequently, the resulting string is cm9sZjp0ZXN0 and this string may serve as authentication information in the HTTP basic authentication scheme. Another example is given in [7]. The interested reader is invited to follow the above-mentioned steps to encode an arbitrary username and password pair, and to verify the correctness of his or her encoding result using a Web browser and a network monitoring tool.

In spite of the fact that the authentication information (i.e., the username and password separated with a colon) is Base-64-encoded, there is nothing that protects it against passive eavesdropping. In fact, anyone who intercepts the HTTP request message that is sent from the browser to the server can obtain the authentication information, decode the username and password (according to the Base-64 decoding scheme), and (mis)use this information illegitimately. To make things worse, HTTP is stateless and the browser reauthenticates itself each time it contacts the server (not just the first time). In order to make that transparent to the user, browsers usually cache the usernames and passwords and retransmit them automatically each time they contact the server. This is convenient but also causes many password transmissions that are transparent and "invisible" to the user (unfortunately, these retransmissions are not "invisible" for a passive attacker). More worrisome, it is generally not possible to log out an authenticated "HTTP session." This would require the browser to forget about the relevant user credentials. This is currently not a supported feature in most browsers. Last but not least, the most recent versions of some browsers provide the feature to remember a password forever, so that a user never has to type in the password again. As illustrated in Figure 2.1, this ability can be activated in Microsoft's Internet Explorer by employing the checkbox entitled "Save this password in your password list." From a security point of view, this feature is highly debatable. It is, however, convenient for the user and simplifies the user experience considerably. That's why people use it.

In summary, the HTTP basic authentication scheme is not secure. Although the passwords are stored on the server in encrypted form, they are passed from the browsers to the server in the clear[7] (or in Base-64-encoded form) for every single request. As such, they are exposed to eavesdropping and replay attacks.

2.4 Digest access authentication

Due to the fact that the HTTP basic authentication scheme must be considered to be weak and vulnerable, the complementary and inherently more secure *HTTP digest access authentication* scheme has been specified in [7] and submitted to the Internet standards track. Note, however, that the HTTP digest access authentication scheme still suffers from many known limitations and weaknesses (as discussed at the end of this section), and that it is intended as a simple replacement for the HTTP basic authentication scheme. More secure HTTP authentication schemes can be designed using public key certificates or authentication and key distribution systems, such as Kerberos [9].

Unfortunately (and contrary to the HTTP basic authentication scheme), the HTTP digest access authentication scheme is not widely deployed and

---

7.   This is similar to many other TCP/IP application protocols that lack strong user authentication, such as Telnet and FTP.

supported by Web browsers and servers.[8] On the client side, for example, the scheme is supported by the latest releases of Microsoft's Internet Explorer and Opera (the scheme is not supported by Netscape Navigator). On the server side, the scheme is supported by Microsoft IIS and Apache.[9]

Like the HTTP basic authentication scheme, the HTTP digest access authentication scheme implements a simple challenge-response mechanism to verify that the user knows a secret he or she shares with the server (i.e., the password). Unlike the HTTP basic authentication scheme, however, the verification is done without actually sending the secret in the clear. Instead, the HTTP digest access authentication scheme employs a one-way hash function (typically MD5[10]) to compute (on the browser side) and verify (on the server side) a digest value that is used to proof knowledge of the secret.

More specifically, when a browser requests a resource that is protected using the HTTP digest access authentication scheme, the server challenges the browser using a nonce (i.e., a randomly chosen value). The browser, in turn, must respond with a valid digest value to authenticate itself to the server. The digest value is computed from the following input parameters:

▸ The username;

▸ The user password (or a hash value thereof);

▸ The nonce;

▸ The HTTP access method;

▸ The URL of the requested resource.

Roughly speaking, the digest value is computed as follows:

$$h(h(A1):nonce:h(A2))$$

---

8. The major reason for this astonishing fact is that those products typically implement the SSL and TLS protocols. If the browser and server are communicating with HTTP on top of SSL or TLS (using HTTPS), the problem of password sniffing automatically goes away. The encrypted channel is set up before any HTTP header passes across the network, so the username and password are part of the encrypted SSL data stream and cannot be sniffed accordingly.

9. Digest access authentication as specified in [7] is implemented by the module `mod_auth_digest`. There is an older module, `mod_digest`, which implemented the older digest authentication scheme specified in RFC 2069.

10. An optional header may allow the server to specify the algorithm that must be used to create the one-way hash value. By default the MD5 algorithm as specified in RFC 1321 [10] is used. As further explained in Chapter 4, an MD5 hash value is 128 bits long. As such, it can be represented in 32 ASCII printable characters that each represent a hexadecimal number.

In this formula, h represents the one-way hash function,[11] $A1$ the expression that consists of the username, the realm string, and the user password (each component separated with a colon), and $A2$ the expression that consists of the HTTP access method and the requested URL (again, separated with a colon). There are some options that complicate the formula, but in principle, this is the way the browser has to compute the digest value it must encode as a response. Note that the user password is not sent in the clear. Instead, it is used as a secret input to the one-way hash function. As with the HTTP basic authentication scheme, the usernames and passwords must be prearranged and distributed out-of-band.

Let us assume that a browser wants to retrieve the `index.html` file located in the protected directory /Demo/HTTPDigestAccessAuthentication/ at `www.esecurity.ch`. Again, the browser does not know that this file is protected using the HTTP digest access authentication scheme. So it sends sends out a normal-looking HTTP request message. Remember from our previous discussions that this message may start with the following request line:

```
GET http://www.esecurity.ch/Demo/HTTPDigestAccessAuthentication/
    HTTP/1.0
```

All other HTTP request headers remain the same as in the previous example(s). After having received the HTTP request message, the Web server recognizes that the requested file is located in a directory of the Web server's document tree that is protected using the HTTP digest access authentication scheme. So it returns an HTTP response message that includes the following two characteristic lines (among other lines and HTTP headers):

```
HTTP/1.0 401 Unauthorized
...
WWW-Authenticate: Digest
    realm="HTTP Digest Access Authentication Demo",
    nonce="1011598310"
```

Again, if the server were an HTTP proxy server, it would return an HTTP response message with a 407 status code and a `Proxy-Authenticate` header. This case is not discussed in this book.

Contrary to the HTTP basic authentication scheme, the `WWW-Authenti-cate` header includes the keyword `Digest` (referring to the HTTP digest

---

11. Refer to Section 4.2 for an introduction to one-way hash functions.

access authentication scheme instead of Basic referring to the HTTP basic authentication scheme) as well as a comma-separated list of parameters. In our example, there are only two parameters (i.e., realm and nonce) with corresponding values:

▶ The realm parameter carries a string that is displyed to the user so he or she knows which username and password to use. As illustrated in Figure 2.3 for Opera, most browsers display this string in the prompt in which they ask the users to type in their username and password.

▶ The nonce parameter carries the random value that is used by the server to challenge the user (or the browser, repectively). The value is uniquely generated each time a 401 response message is compiled. The contents of the nonces are implementation dependent. An exemplary procedure to generate nonces (using time stamps and a secret key that is known only to the server) is given in [7]. In our example, the nonce is 1011598310.

As further addressed in [7], there are many other parameters that can be used in the WWW-Authenticate header. Most of them are optional. To keep

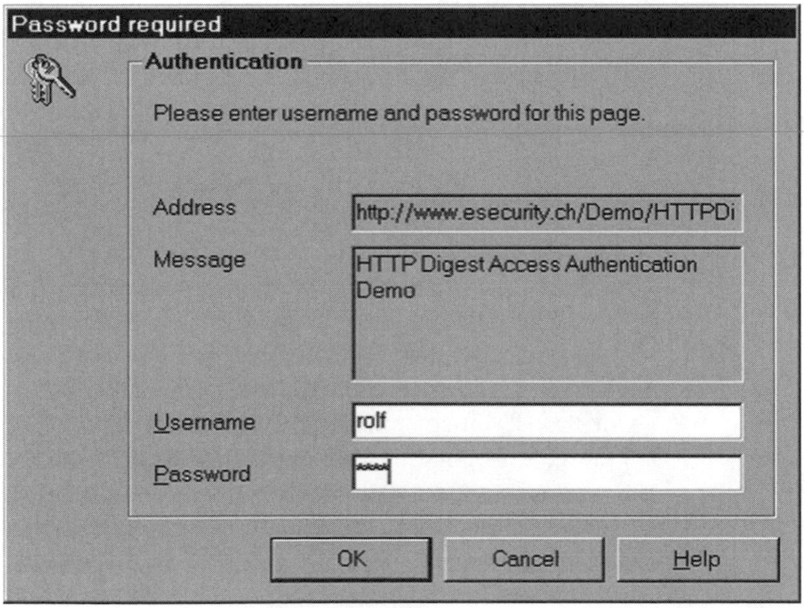

Figure 2.3 The Opera 6.0 Password required prompt using the HTTP digest access authentication scheme. (© 2002 Opera Software.)

the discussion sufficiently simple, we do not look into the synatx and semantics of these parameters.

In response to the HTTP response message, the browser prompts the user to enter his or her username and password. From a graphical user interface's point of view, this is very similar to the way the user is prompted in the HTTP basic authentication scheme. Figure 2.3 illustrates the prompt used by the Opera browser. If the user entered the requested information (i.e., the username and password), the browser would compute a response value and return it as part of an `Authorization` header in a second HTTP request message to the server. In our example, the `Authorization` header would look as follows:

```
Authorization: Digest
  username="rolf",
  realm="HTTP Digest Access Authentication Demo",
  uri="http://www.esecurity.ch/Demo/HTTPDigestAccessAuthen-
      tication/",
  algorithm=MD5,
  nonce="1011598310",
  response="2cbdf234349bbfbfa8460c2410acb445"
```

In this header, the `response` parameter carries the digest value that is needed to authenticate to the server. It is a 32-bit hexademical value that carries a one-way hash value (i.e., an MD5 hash value in this example) that is computed as described above. Due to the fact that the `WWW-Authenticate` header may include many optional parameters and that implementations should be compatible with a previous version of the HTTP digest access authentication scheme,[12] the actual format and procedures to compute and verify the hash values is quite complex. Consequently, we have used a simplified formula and you may refer to [7] to get a more comprehensive description and specification, as well as examples of HTTP request and response messages that conform to this specification.

Upon receiving an HTTP request message with a proper `WWW-Authenticate` header, the server must check the validity of the `response` value. In particular, it must look up the $A1$ hash value that corresponds to the submitted username, recompute the digest value, and compare the result to the response that was provided by the browser. If the values match, the user is assumed to be authentic. Note, however, that the server does not need to

---

12. As mentioned before, this version is called *HTTP Digest Authentication*, and it is specified in RFC document 2069.

know the user password in the clear. It is sufficient for the server to know the $A1$ hash value (i.e., the hash value of the username, the realm string, and the user password).

In the following chapter, we address the implications of proxy servers and firewalls for Web applications. As with the HTTP basic authentication, the use of proxy servers must be completely transparent in HTTP digest access authentication. That is, the proxy servers must forward the relevant headers (i.e., the WWW-Authenticate, Authorization, and some other headers) as they are. If a proxy server wanted to authenticate a client before a request is forwarded to a Web server, it would have to use appropriate Proxy-Authenticate and Proxy-Authorization headers as specified in [1]. Consequently, Web server authentication and HTTP proxy server authentication may coexist in the same challenge/response messages.

There is a potential difficulty in using an HTTP authentication scheme (i.e., HTTP basic authentication or HTTP digest access authentication) together with caching mechanisms implemented by HTTP proxy servers. Note that one goal of a proxy server is to cache resources that have been downloaded once to serve requests that are issued by multiple browsers. Consequently, if a resource has been downloaded by an authenticated browser, the resource may end up in a proxy cache, from where it may be redistributed to multiple (not authenticated) browsers. To protect against this redistribution, HTTP (since version 1.1) specifies that when a proxy server has received an HTTP request message containing an Authorization header, and a response message from relaying that request, it must not return that response message as a reply to any other request, unless one of the following two cache-control directives was sent in the corresponding original HTTP response message:

▶ If the original HTTP response message includes the must-revalidate cache-control directive, the proxy server can cache the resource and use it to serve further requests for the same resource. Each time the resource is requested, however, the proxy server must first reauthenticate the browser (using the HTTP request headers from the new request to allow the origin Web server to authenticate the browser).

▶ Alternatively, if the original HTTP response includes the public cache-control directive, the proxy server can cache the resource and use it to serve further requests for the same resource (without browser reauthentication).

In summary, the HTTP digest access authentication scheme solves the most severe security problem of the HTTP basic authentication scheme, namely, that passwords are transmitted in the clear (or in Base-64-encoded form that is equivalent to the unencrypted form). Instead of sending the username and password to the server, the browser uses the password to properly compute a response for the challenge provided by the server. As such, the password is never transmitted across the Internet. Provided that the user has picked a good (i.e., hard to guess) password, it is computationally infeasible for an attacker to derive the password from the response. For further protection, the user password may not be stored in the clear on the server side (where it could be stolen by someone with access to the server). Instead, only the hash value of the password may be stored. This is similar to the way that contemporary operating systems, such as UNIX or Windows NT, store passwords. As a final precaution, the requested URL is part of the response. Consequently, if the response is intercepted by an eavesdropper who attempts to play it back to gain illegitimate access to resources, he or she will be able to get access only to that single URL. More specifically, he or she will be unable to generate new responses to gain access to resources that are found in other branches of the document tree. Servers can further protect themselves against replay attacks by adding a timestamp to the nonces so that responses automatically expire after a relatively short period of time.

The HTTP digest access authentication scheme is intended as a simple replacement for the HTTP basic authentication scheme, and nothing more. In spite of all of its security features, the HTTP digest access authentication scheme still suffers from known limitations and weaknesses. For example, both the HTTP basic authentication scheme and the HTTP digest access authentication scheme are vulnerable to the man-in-the-middle attack (mainly because the server does not authenticate itself to the browser before it sends out the challenge).[13] Also, the HTTP digest access authentication scheme is (still) a password-based system and suffers from all the problems of such a system.

For example, digest authentication requires that the authenticating party (usually the server) store some data derived from the username and password in a user password file associated with a given realm. The security implications of this are that if this file is compromised, an attacker gains immediate access to documents on the server using this realm. On the other hand, a brute force attack would be necessary to obtain a user's password.

---

13. In a man-in-the-middle attack, an attacker spoofs a server and requests a browser to provide a user password.

This is why the realm is part of the hashed data stored in the file. It means that if one digest authentication password file is compromised, it does not automatically compromise others with the same username and password (though it does expose them to brute force attack). This is somewhat similar to the UNIX salt mechanism. There are two important security consequences of this:

1. The user password file must be protected as if it contained unencrypted passwords (that is why it is usually not stored in the document tree).

2. The realm name should be unique among all realms that any single user is likely to use. In particular, a realm name should include the name of the host doing the authentication (contrary to the example given previously in this chapter).

Furthermore, no provision is made in the specification of the HTTP digest access authentication scheme for the initial arrangement between the user and server to establish the user password. Consequently, the HTTP digest authentication scheme does not provide a complete answer to the need for security on the WWW. Also note that the HTTP digest access authentication scheme is only an authentication scheme that does not provide any data confidentiality or integrity services. This is where cryptographic security protocols, such as the Secure Sockets Layer (SSL) and Transport Layer Security (TLS) protocols, come into play.

2.5 Certificate-based authentication

The SSL and TLS protocols are the security technology of choice for the WWW and, indeed, most Web applications. As further addressed in Chapter 6, these protocols can be used to have a Web browser and a server authenticate each other,[14] establish a session key, and use this key to transparently encrypt, decrypt, and authenticate data segments that are exchanged between them. Consequently, this protocol can also be used to have a Web server (or HTTP proxy server) properly authenticate its users. This makes user authentication and authorization simple and straightforward. On the other side, however, it also requires that servers and browsers be equipped with public key certificates. Public key certificates and

---

14. Server-side authentication is mandatory in SSL and TLS, whereas client-side authentication is optional.

the establishment and use of corresponding infrastructures is further addressed in Chapters 7 and 8.

2.6   Server configuration

Based on the HTTP basic and digest access authentication schemes overviewed in the previous sections, Web server software packages usually provide support for user-based and group-based authorization and access control. For example, the Apache server allows an administrator to define authorized users, give them passwords, and place them in groups similar to the UNIX operating system. The syntax that is used to specify access control rules heavily depends on the Web server software in use. You may refer to the manual of your server software package for a description of the syntax that must be used. In the examples that follow, we refer to the Apache Web server software that is widely deployed today. Further information can be found at `http://httpd.apache.org/docs/howto/auth.html`.

2.6.1   Configuring HTTP basic authentication

To protect the contents of an Apache Web server with the HTTP basic authentication scheme, the following two configuration steps must be completed:

1. A password file must be created. The file must include the names and encrypted passwords of the legitimate and authorized users of the server. Because the file contains sensitive information, it should be stored outside of the document tree. To create and manage the password file, a utility called `htpasswd` may be used.[15] This utility creates entries that look as follows (for username `rolf` and password `test`):

    ```
    rolf:yIvSBWSuLs2N2
    ```

    Obviously, the first field includes the username (i.e., `rolf`) and the second field includes the encrypted password (i.e., `yIvSBWSuLs2N2`). The password is encrypted using the standard UNIX password encryption function [i.e., `crypt()`]. This basically means that the zero-string is encrypted using the password as a key, that a modified and slowed-down version of the DES serves as encryption

---

15. The `htpasswd` utility is typically located in the `bin` directory of the Apache installation.

algorithm, that an additional 12-bit value (i.e., a so-called salt) is used to seed the encryption, and that each encrypted password is Base-64-encoded as 13 printable characters (the first two characters representing the salt). Due to the salt mechanism, the password encryption function is nondeterministic, meaning that two users who have randomly chosen the same password may end up having encrypted passwords that look completely different. For example, `8DPEnfGmhy3f.`, `oC.DJuDdSwd4w`, and `N.Ecp9ZAWAPXE` are all valid and equivalent encodings of the username `rolf` and the encrypted password `test` (i.e., they all use different salt values). Optionally, a group file may be created to define that certain users belong together and may be treated as a group (mainly to simplify user management). Each group is defined by a group name and a list of members (i.e., users). For example:

```
family: isabelle marc lara rolf
```

In this case, a group named `family` is defined to include the members `isabelle`, `marc`, `lara`, and `rolf`. Note that for each of these members an entry in the password file must exist.

2.   The use of the password and group files must be configured on the server side. There are a number of server directives that can be used for this purpose:

  ▸ The `AuthType` directive is used to specify the authentication type being used (i.e., `Basic` or `Digest`).

  ▸ The `AuthName` directive is used to specify the authentication realm or name.

  ▸ The `AuthUserFile` directive is used to specify the location of the password file.

  ▸ The `AuthGroupFile` directive is used to specify the location of the group file, if any.

  ▸ The `Require` directive is used to specify the requirement(s) that must be satisfied in order to grant admission.

The directives can be placed in a `.htaccess` file in the particular directory being protected, or may go in a `<Directory>` section of the server's access configuration file (i.e., `access.conf`). To allow a directory to be restricted within an `.htaccess` file, however, the `access.conf` file must allow user authentication and authorization to be set up in .htaccess files. This is controlled by the AuthCong override. More specifically, the access.conf file must include AllowOverride AuthCong to allow user authentication and authorization in .htaccess files. In the explanations that follow, we assume the AuthCong override is included in the Web server's access configuration file.

Let's have a look at the server configuration that is used to protect the directory /Demo/HTTPBasicAuthentication at www.esecurity.ch. Protection is invoked by placing the following .htaccess file in the protected directory:

```
AuthType Basic
AuthName "HTTP Basic Authentication Demo"
AuthUserFile /home/esecurity.ch/conf/passwords
AuthGroupFile /home/esecurity.ch/conf/groups
require valid-user
```

Obviously, the first line indicates the use of the HTTP basic authentication scheme. The second line specifies the realm string that is used in the prompt to request the user to enter his or her password (this is illustrated in Figures 2.1 and 2.2). The third and fourth lines specify the location of the password and group files. Finally, the fifth line requires that any user provides his or her valid password to get access (in this case, the group file is not used at all). This part could be expanded to limit access to specific users or groups or specific access methods (e.g., GET). For example:

```
<LIMIT GET>
  require group family
</LIMIT>
```

limits user access to the members of the family group employing the HTTP GET method (in this case, the group file is used). In general, a <Limit> section is established between the <Limit> and </Limit> directives. It can be used to establish an access control policy for the directory. The format is <Limit X Y ...>, where each of the parameters is one of the HTTP access methods (e.g., GET, POST, PUT, or DELETE). Browsers that try to use one of the listed methods are restricted according to the rules listed within the section. If no method is listed, the restrictions apply to all methods. Multiple groups may be listed and multiple require directives may be used.

Using the htpasswd utility to create and manage a list of users in a password file, and maintaining a list of groups in a corresponding group file, is a relatively simple task. However, if the number of users becomes large, the server has a lot of processing to do in finding a user's authentication information. In fact, the server has to open the password file, look through it one line at a time until it finds the user that is trying to log in, and verify the password. In the worst case, if the username supplied is not there at all, every line in the file will need to be checked. On average, half of the file will need to be read before the user is found. To make things worse, this processing must be done for every request to access the protected realm (even though the user only enters his or her password once, the server has to reauthenticate on every request). This can be slow with a lot of users, and adds to the Web server load. Much faster access is possible using a database system. In the case of the Apache Web server, there are several database modules that may be used (e.g., `mod_auth_db` and `mod_auth_dbm`). The corresponding directives may change (e.g., `AuthDBUserFile` instead of `AuthUserFile` in the case of using Berkeley DB files and HTTP basic authentication) but the principle ideas remain the same. It is also possible to have an arbitrary external program check whether the given username and password are valid (this could be used to write an interface to check against any other database or authentication service). Modules are also available to check against the system password file or—more interestingly—to use a Kerberos authentication system.

2.6.2 Configuring HTTP digest access authentication

To protect the contents of an Apache Web server with the HTTP digest access authentication scheme, the following two configuration steps must be completed:

1. A password file must be created. For every legitimate and authorized user, the file must include the username, the realm string, and the user password in possibly encrypted form. Again, the file contains sensitive information and should be stored outside of the document tree. To create and manage the password file, a utility called `htdigest` can be used.[16] It creates entries like

    ```
    rolf:HTTP Digest Access Authentication Demo:672203b528e0-
    c29e08df53cba3f51b66
    ```

    for the username `rolf`, the realm string "HTTP Digest Access Authentication Demo," and the password `test`. Note that

---

16. Similar to the `htpasswd` utility, the `htdigest` utulity is typically located in the `bin` directory of the Apache installation.

the username and the realm string are not encrypted, and that the password is the only value that is encrypted. Contrary to the password encryption routine employed by the .htpasswd utility, however, the password encryption routine employed by the .htpasswd utility is deterministic, meaning that no salt is used, and that the same password is always encrypted and encoded to the same value (i.e., 672203b528e0c29e08df53cba3f51b66 in the example above). Optionally, a group file can be created to simplify user management. The syntax of the file is the same as the one employed by the HTTP basic authentication scheme.

2. The use of the password and group files must be configured on the server side. In addition to the directives that are available for the HTTP basic authentication scheme (i.e., AuthType, AuthName, and Require), the following two directives may be used to configure the use of the HTTP digest access authentication scheme:

  ‣ The AuthDigestFile directive is used to specify the location of the password file.

  ‣ The AuthDigestGroupFile directive is used to specify the location of the group file (if any).

  The placement of the directives is identical to the HTTP basic authentication scheme.

For example, the following .htaccess file may be used to protect the directory /Demo/HTTPBasicAuthentication at www.esecurity.ch:

```
AuthType Digest
AuthName "HTTP Digest Access Authentication Demo"
AuthDigestFile /home/esecurity.ch/conf/digests
AuthDigestGroupFile /home/esecurity.ch/conf/groups
require valid-user
```

The semantics of the directives should be clear. Again, access to the protected directory may be restricted to specific HTTP access methods (e.g., GET) using the <Limit> and </Limit> directives.

2.7 Conclusions

In the early days of the WWW, it was assumed that the resources made available by Web servers were inherently public and that there would be no need for such things as user authentication, authorization, and access control. Since then, however, the situation has changed fundamentally and the WWW is also used for the distribution of protected material. Consequently, there is urgent need for proper user authentication, authorization, and access control mechanisms.

The simplest mechanism to control access to Web resources is to use hidden URLs. Also, most Web servers can be configured to restrict access to a particular group of computers based on those computers' address information (IP addresses or DNS hostnames). Most importantly, some Web servers provide support for the HTTP user authentication and authorization schemes that are described in this chapter: HTTP basic authentication and HTTP digest access authentication. Unfortunately, the HTTP digest access authentication scheme is not widely deployed. This is because HTTP digest access authentication is always less secure than a full-fledged cryptographic security protocol, such as SSL or TLS. Consequently, some browsers implement SSL or TLS and leave beside HTTP digest access authentication. As mentioend in this chapter and further addressed in Chapter 6, SSL and TLS employ certificate-based authentication mechanisms.

In practice, many Web servers are configured to allow access to all users from computers located on the same network (i.e., intranet), whereas they allow access to other users only after proper authentication and authorization. For example, the .htaccess file of an Apache Web server could be extended as follows:

```
AuthType Basic
AuthName "HTTP Basic Authentication Demo"
AuthUserFile /home/esecurity.ch/conf/passwords
AuthGroupFile /home/esecurity.ch/conf/groups
Require valid-user
Allow from esecurity.ch
Satisfy any
```

The extension (i.e., the allow and satisfy directives) would make sure that either a valid user is requesting the resource (i.e., the require valid-user directive), or a request is originating from the esecurity.ch domain (i.e., the allow from esecurity.ch directive).[17] It is also possible to deny access for specific computers using the deny directive, and to define an order of preference (regarding the allow and deny directives). In general, it is

17. The satisfy any directive says that either of the two conditions must hold.

possible to express any access control condition using the allow, deny, order, and satisfy directives.

References

[1]   Fielding, R., et al., "Hypertext Transfer Protocol—HTTP/1.1," Request for Comments 2616, June 1999.

[2]   Berners-Lee, T., L. Masinter, and M. McCahill, "Uniform Resource Locators (URL)," Request for Comments 1738, December 1994.

[3]   Fielding, R., "Relative Uniform Resource Locators (URL)," Request for Comments 1808, June 1995.

[4]   Sollins, K., and L. Masinter, "Functional Requirements for Uniform Resource Names," Request for Comments 1737, December 1994.

[5]   Berners-Lee, T., R. Fielding, and L. Masinter, "Uniform Resource Identifiers (URI): Generic Syntax and Semantics," Request for Comments 2396, August 1998.

[6]   Rubin, A. D., D. Geer, and M. J. Ranum, *Web Security Sourcebook*, New York: John Wiley & Sons, Inc., 1997.

[7]   Franks, J., et al., "HTTP Authentication: Basic and Digest Access Authentication," Request for Comments 2617, June 1999.

[8]   Oppliger, R., *Secure Messaging with PGP and S/MIME*, Norwood, MA: Artech House, 2001.

[9]   Oppliger, R., *Authentication Systems for Secure Networks*, Norwood, MA: Artech House, 1996.

[10] Rivest, R. L., and S. Dusse, "The MD5 Message-Digest Algorithm," Request for Comments 1321, April 1992.

3

Proxy Servers and Firewalls

Contents

3.1 Introduction

3.2 Static packet filtering

3.3 Dynamic packet filtering or stateful inspection

3.4 Circuit-level gateways

3.5 Application-level gateways

3.6 Firewall configurations

3.7 Network address translation

3.8 Configuring the browser

3.9 Conclusions

References

In this chapter, we address proxy servers and firewalls as well as their implications for the WWW and Web-based applications. After a brief introduction in Section 3.1, we address the major firewall technologies (i.e., static packet filtering, dynamic packet filtering or "stateful" inspection, circuit-level gateways, and application-level gateways or proxy servers) in Sections 3.2 to 3.5. In Section 3.6, we overview and discuss firewall configurations that are used and widely deployed today. In Section 3.7, we address network address translation (NAT). In Section 3.8, we elaborate on the question of how to properly configure a browser to make use of proxy servers. In Section 3.9, we conclude with a discussion of the firewall technology as a whole. Note that the focus of this chapter is on how to get out of a corporate intranet (actually traversing a firewall). This is the usual situation one faces when dealing with firewalls. For mobile users and teleworkers, however, the situation is inverse and their primary focus is on how to get in a corporate intranet (e.g., to access an internal Web server). This leads to reverse proxies and the need for strong authentication mechanisms. These topics are further addressed in Chapter 6. Also, you may refer to part two of [1] for an overview and more comprehensive discussion of the firewall technology.

3.1 Introduction

While Internet connectivity offers enormous benefits in terms of increased availability and access to information, Internet

49

connectivity is not always a good thing, especially for sites with low levels of security. In fact, the Internet suffers from glaring security problems that, if ignored, could have disastrous impacts for unprepared sites. Inherent problems with the TCP/IP protocols and services, the complexity of host and site configuration, vulnerabilities introduced in the software development process, and a variety of other factors all contribute to making unprepared sites open for intruder activities.

Host security is generally hard to achieve and does not scale well in the sense that as the number of hosts increases, the ability to ensure that security is at a high level for each host usually decreases. Given the fact that secure management of just one single system can be a demanding task, managing many such systems could easily result in mistakes and omissions. A contributing factor is that the role of system administration is often undervalued and performed in a difficult situation. As a result of this situation, some systems will be less secure than others, and these systems will probably be the ones that ultimately break the security of either a site or an entire corporate intranet. This book does not address host and site security. There is an informational RFC document specifying a site security handbook [2]. You may refer to this document for a comprehensive overview about issues related to host and site security.

In days of old, brick walls were built between buildings in apartment complexes so that if a fire broke out, it would not spread from one building to another. Quite naturally, these walls were called *firewalls*.

Today, when a private network (i.e., an intranet) is connected to a public network (i.e., the Internet), its users are usually enabled to communicate with the outside world. At the same time, however, the outside world can also interact with the private network and its computer systems. In this situation, an intermediate system can be plugged between the private network and the public network to establish a controlled link, and to erect a security wall or perimeter. The aim of the intermediate system is to protect the private network from attacks that may originate from the outside world, and to provide a single choke point where security and audit can be imposed. Note that all traffic in and out of the private network can be enforced to pass through this single, narrow choke point. Also note that this point provides a good place to collect information about system and network use and misuse. As a single point of access, the intermediate system can record what occurs between the private network and the outside world. In analogy to physical firewalls, these intermediate systems are called *firewall systems*, or *firewalls* for short. In other literature, Internet firewalls are sometimes also referred to as *secure Internet gateways* or *security gateways*. In essence, a firewall system represents a blockade between a privately owned and protected network, which is assumed to be secure and trustworthy, and another network, typically a public network or the Internet, which is assumed to be insecure and untrustworthy. The purpose of the firewall is to prevent unwanted and unauthorized communications into or out of the protected network.

There are several possibilities to more formally define the term *firewall*. For example, according to [3], a *firewall* refers to ''an internetwork gateway that restricts data communication traffic to and from one of the connected networks (the one said to be 'inside' the firewall) and thus protects that network's system resources against threats from the other network (the one that is said to be 'outside' the firewall).'' This definition is fairly broad and not too precise.

In their pioneering book [4] and article [5] on firewalls and Internet security, William Cheswick and Steven Bellovin defined a firewall (system) as a collection of components placed between two networks that collectively have the following three properties:

1. All traffic from inside to outside, and vice versa, must pass through the firewall.

2. Only authorized traffic, as defined by the local security policy, will be allowed to pass.

3. The firewall itself is immune to penetration.

Note that these properties are design goals. A failure in one aspect does not necessarily mean that the collection is not a firewall, simply that it is not a good one. Consequently, there are different grades of security that a firewall can achieve. In either case, there must be a security policy for the firewall to enforce.

If one wants to exclude the fact that a simple packet filter can be called a firewall, one has to come up with an even more complex definition for the term *firewall*. In this case, a system can be called a firewall if it is able:

▸ To enforce strong authentication for users who wish to establish inbound or outbound[1] connections;

---

1. In this book, the terms *inbound* and *outbound* are used to refer to connections or IP packets from the point of view of the protected network, which is typically the intranet. Consequently, an outbound connection is a connection initiated from a client on an internal machine to a server on an external machine. Note that while the connection as a whole is outbound, it includes both outbound IP packets (those from the internal client to the external server) and inbound IP packets (those from the external server to the internal client). Similarly, an

> ‣ To associate data streams that are allowed to pass through the firewall with previously authenticated and authorized users.

Again, it is a policy decision if a data stream is allowed to pass through. Thus, this definition also leads to the necessity of an explicitly specified firewall policy, similar to the definition of Cheswick and Bellovin.

In this book, we make a clear distinction between packet filters (i.e., static or dynamic packet filters) and application gateways (i.e., circuit-level gateways or application-level gateways). It is interesting to note at this point that the last definition of a firewall requires the use of application gateways. Because application gateways operate at the higher layers of the OSI reference model, they typically have access to more information than packet-filtering devices and can therefore be programmed to operate more intelligently and to be more secure. Some vendors, perhaps for marketing reasons, blur the distinction between a packet filter and a firewall to the extent that they call any packet filtering device a firewall. This practice must be considered with care.

From a practical point of view, a firewall refers to a collection of hardware, software, and policy that is placed between a private network, typically a corporate intranet, and an external network, typically the Internet. As such, the firewall implements parts of a network security policy by enforcing that all data traffic is directed or routed to the firewall, where it can be examined and evaluated accordingly. A firewall seeks to prevent unwanted[2] and unauthorized communications into or out of a corporate intranet, and to allow an organization to enforce a policy on traffic flowing between the intranet and the Internet. Typically, a firewall also requires its users to authenticate themselves before any further action is deployed. The last definition given above has made this requirement mandatory. In this case, strong authentication mechanisms are used to replace password-based or address-based authentication schemes.

The general reasoning behind firewall usage is that without a firewall, a site is more exposed to inherently insecure host operating systems, TCP/IP protocols and services, and probes and attacks from the Internet. In a firewall-less environment, network security is a function of each host,

---

inbound connection is a connection initiated from a client on an external machine to a server on an internal machine. Following this terminology, the inbound interface for an IP packet refers to the physical network interface on a screening router on which the packet actually appeared, while the outbound interface refers to the physical network interface on which the packet will go out if it is not denied by the application of a specific packet-filtering rule.

2. The formalization of what "unwanted" communications refers to is generally a difficult task.

and all hosts must, in a sense, cooperate to achieve a uniformly high level of security. The larger the network, the less manageable it usually is to maintain all hosts at the same level of security. As mistakes and lapses in security become more common, break-ins can occur not only as a result of complex attacks, but also because of simple errors in configuration files and inadequately chosen passwords. Assuming that software is buggy, one can conclude that most host systems have security holes that can eventually be exploited by intruders. Firewalls are designed to run less software, and hence may potentially have fewer bugs, vulnerabilities, and security holes than conventional hosts. In addition, firewalls generally have advanced logging and monitoring facilities and can be professionally administered. With firewall usage, only a few hosts[3] are exposed to attacks from the Internet, which considerably simplifies the task of securing the intranet environment.

Later in this chapter, we will discuss the advantages and disadvantages of the firewall technology as a whole. Probably one of the main disadvantages is due to the fact that a firewall cannot protect sites and corporate intranets against insider attacks. For that matter, internal firewalls may be used to control access between different administration and security domains, or to protect sensitive parts of a corporate intranet. Internal firewalls are sometimes also called *intranet firewalls*. From a technical point of view, there is nothing that distinguishes an intranet firewall from an Internet firewall except for the policy it enforces.

More recently, the notion of *decentralized* or *personal firewalls* has become popular. A personal firewall protects a single system (e.g., a personal computer or laptop system) from network-based attacks. As such, personal firewalls are most often simple packet filters that can be configured by each user individually. Similar to intranet firewalls, personal firewalls work like "normal" firewalls and are not discussed separately in this book.

There are many books available that address firewall technologies (e.g., [1]). As a matter of fact, most books that have addressed Internet and intranet security in the past are actually books on firewalls [4, 6, 7], or put the main emphasis on firewalls [8]. There are also many research papers and reports that address specific topics related to firewalls. You may refer to the proceedings of any conference or workshop related to network security. As part of the Centre for Education and Research on Information Assurance and Security (CERIAS) at Purdue University, many resources related to Internet firewalls are available. In addition, there is the Firewalls Mailing List that is

---

3. Namely, the hosts that are part of the firewall.

archived at several sites.[4] Finally, a more or less comprehensive list of firewall products is available at `http://www.thegild.com/firewall`.

3.2   Static packet filtering

Generally speaking, a router is a dedicated internetworking device that runs a specialized operating system (e.g., Cisco IOS) to transfer packets between two or more physically separated network segments.[5] It operates at the network layer of the OSI reference model, or the Internet layer of the Internet model. As such, it routes IP packets by consulting tables that indicate the best path the IP packet should take to reach its destination. More accurately, a router receives an IP packet on one network interface and forwards it on another network interface, possibly in the direction of the destination IP address that is included in the IP header. If the router knows on which interface to forward the packet, it does so. Otherwise, it is not able to route the packet. In this case, the router usually returns the packet using an ICMP destination unreachable message to the source IP address.

Because every IP packet contains a source and a destination IP address, packets originating from or destined to a particular host or network segment can be selectively filtered by a packet-filtering device. Also, transport layer protocols such as TCP or UDP add a source and destination port number to each segment or datagram as part of their header information. These port numbers indicate which processes on each host finally will receive the data encapsulated within the IP packet. This information can also be used to selectively filter IP packets. In the late 1980s and early 1990s, several scientific papers and articles were published that described how to use packet filters to provide access control services for corporate intranets [9–13]. Some of these papers actually described the use of packet filtering in early firewall configurations at AT&T [10] and Digital Equipment Corporation (DEC) [11].[6]

Today, most commercial router products (e.g., Cisco routers) provide the capability to screen IP packets and filter them in accordance with a set of packet filter rules. Such routers are sometimes also called *screening routers*. In

---

4. E.g., `http://lists.gnac.net/firewalls`.
5. Despite the fact that most routers in use today are able to route multiple protocols, we mainly focus on IP routing in this book. This is because IP is by far the most dominant network layer protocol used in the Internet.
6. The DEC firewall was designed and implemented by Marcus J. Ranum. The same firewall was also used to secure the Web site of the White House at `http://www.whitehouse.gov`.

general, screening routers can provide an efficient mechanism to control the type of network traffic that can enter or leave a particular network segment. By controlling the type of network traffic that can enter or leave a network segment, they can also control the types of services that may exist. Services that eventually compromise the security of the network segment can be effectively and efficiently restricted.

As mentioned above, IP packets are usually filtered based on information that is found in packet headers:

▸ Protocol numbers;

▸ Source and destination IP addresses;

▸ Source and destination port numbers;

▸ TCP connection flags;

▸ Some other options.

Note that routers do not normally look at (TCP or UDP) port numbers when making routing decisions, but do for filtering purposes, knowing that the source and destination port number allow selective filtering based on the service being used. For example, a Telnet server usually listens at port 23, whereas an SMTP server usually listens at port 25. Selective filtering by port numbers also takes advantage of how ports are assigned. Although a Telnet server uses port 23 most of the time, a Telnet client port number is not fixed, but assigned dynamically. In a UNIX or Linux environment, for example, the client port is assigned a number greater than 1,023. Also note that screening routers can filter on any of the TCP connection flags, but that the SYN and ACK flags are the most frequently used flags for packet filtering (this is because these two flags collectively determine whether a TCP connection is established inbound or outbound). For example, all TCP segments except the first one (i.e., the TCP connection request message) carry an ACK flag.

Unfortunately, not all screening routers are able to filter IP packets based on all header fields mentioned earlier. For example, some screening routers are not able to consider the source port of an IP packet. This can make packet-filtering rules more complex and can even open up holes in the entire packet filtering scheme. There is, for example, such a problem if a site wishes to allow both inbound and outbound SMTP traffic for e-mail. Remember that in the case of a client establishing an SMTP connection to a server, the client's source port number would be randomly chosen at or above 1,024, and the destination port number would be 25, the port at which an SMTP server conventionally resides. Consequently, the SMTP server would return

IP packets with a source port number of 25 and a destination port number equal to the port number randomly chosen by the client. In this scenario, a packet filter must be configured to allow destination and source port numbers greater than 1,023 to pass through in either direction. If the router is able to filter on the source port, it can block incoming SMTP traffic with a destination port greater than 1,023 and a source port other than 25. Without this ability, however, the router cannot consider the source port and must therefore permit incoming SMTP traffic with a destination port greater than 1,023 and an arbitrary source port number. Consequently, legitimate but malicious users could conceivably make use of this situation and run servers at ports greater than 1,023 to circumvent the service access policy enforced by the packet filter. For example, a Telnet server that normally listens at port 23 could be told to listen at port 7,777 instead. Users on the Internet could then use a normal Telnet client to connect to this internal server even if the packet filter blocks destination port 23.

In addition to the header information itemized above, some packet-filtering devices also allow the administrator to specify packet-filtering rules based on which network interface an IP packet actually entered and on which interface the packet is destined to leave. Being able to specify filters on both inbound and outbound interfaces allows an administrator significant control over where the packet filter appears in the overall scheme and is very convenient for useful filtering on screening routers with more than two network interfaces. Unfortunately, for efficiency reasons, not all screening routers can filter on both inbound and outbound interfaces, and many routers implement packet filtering only on the outbound interface. Note that for outgoing IP packets, the filter rules can be applied when the router consults its routing tables to determine the interface to send the packet out on. At this point, however, the router no longer knows on which interface the packet entered; it has lost some important information.

Screening routers filter IP packets according to a set of packet filter rules. More accurately, when an IP packet arrives at a network interface of a filtering device, the packet headers are parsed. Each packet-filtering rule is applied to the packet in the order in which the packet-filtering rules are stored. If a rule blocks the transmission or reception of a packet, the packet is not allowed. If a rule allows the transmission or reception of a packet, the packet is allowed to proceed. If a packet does not satisfy any rule, it is either allowed or blocked depending on the firewall's "default" rule. In general, it is good practice to have a rule that will block IP packets that don't match any other rules.

Packet filters are stateless, meaning that each IP packet must be examined in isolation from what has happened in the past (and what will happen in the future), forcing the filter to make a decision to permit or deny each packet individually based upon the packet-filtering rules. Routers are generally optimized to shuffle IP packets quickly. The packet filters of a screening router take time and can defeat the overall optimization efforts. In fact, packet filtering is a slow operation that may considerably reduce routing throughput. Logging of IP packets also occurs without regard to past history, and enabling logging results in another hit on performance. More often than not, packet filtering and logging are not enabled in routers primarily to achieve better throughput and performance. If enabled and used, packet filtering and logging are typically installed at the interface between different administrative domains.

3.3 Dynamic packet filtering or stateful inspection

There is an increasingly large number of application protocols that make use of multiple connections and/or dynamically assigned port numbers. This makes it difficult to specify and set up appropriate packet-filtering rules. For example, FTP uses two TCP connections to transfer a file (i.e., an FTP control connection and an FTP data connection). Imagine a situation in which an intranet client wishes to establish an outbound FTP session to a server located on the Internet. According to the FTP specification, the client would first establish an outbound TCP connection from a randomly chosen port X to the FTP control port (i.e., port 21) of the server. Among other things, this connection would be used by the client to inform the server on which port Y it is going to listen for the incoming FTP data connection (using the PORT command of the FTP protocol). The server, in turn, would establish an inbound TCP connection from its FTP data port (i.e., port 20) to port Y on the client side. A file requested by the client would then be transferred on this TCP connection. Now imagine what happens if Internet connectivity is mediated through a screening router and the corresponding packet-filtering rules are configured in a restrictive way (meaning that inbound TCP connections are not allowed). In this situation, the second TCP connection (i.e., the FTP data connection) would be denied and the corresponding file transfer would not be able to take place. The underlying problem is that, due to the stateless nature of (static) packet filtering, it is not possible to recognize that the second TCP connection (i.e., the FTP data connection) logically belongs to the first TCP connection (i.e., the FTP control connection), and that the two connections collectively represent an FTP session. Consequently, the screening router simply sees an Internet server trying to establish an inbound TCP connection from server port 20 to client port Y. According to its policy and configuration, it is very likely that the screening router refuses this TCP connection. In the case of FTP, the problem can easily be solved using passive mode FTP.[7] There are, however, other application protocols that are more complex and for which a simple solution does not exist.

Remember that packet filters are stateless, meaning that each IP packet is examined in isolation from what has happened in the past, forcing the packet filter to make a decision to permit or deny each packet based upon the packet-filtering rules. Contrary to that, the notion and technology of *dynamic packet filtering* or *stateful inspection* was created by the developers of the FireWall-1 at CheckPoint Software Technologies, Ltd.[8] In short, stateful inspection refers to a technology in which a packet filter maintains state information about past IP packets to make more intelligent decisions about the legitimity of present and future IP packets. For example, a dynamic packet filter compares the first packet in a connection to the packet-filtering rules, and if the packet is permitted, state information is added to an internal database. One might think of this state information as representing an internal virtual circuit in the stateful inspection device on top of the transport layer association. This information permits subsequent packets in that association to pass quickly through the stateful inspection device. If the rules for a specific type of service require examining application data, then part of each packet must still be examined. As an example, FireWall-1 can react to seeing an FTP PORT command by creating a dynamic rule permitting a connection back from the FTP server to that particular port number on the client's side.

Dynamic packet filtering or stateful inspection provides much better possibilities to define packet-filtering rules and to filter IP packets (as compared to static packet filtering). In many situations, it makes sense to use stateful inspection to improve the capabilities (and security) of packet-filtering devices.

3.4   Circuit-level gateways

The idea of an application gateway is fundamentally different from a packet filter (i.e., a static or dynamic packet filter). This is equally true for

---

7. Using passive mode FTP, the FTP data connection is also established outbound.

8. The technology is covered by U.S. patent No. 5,606,668 that specifies a "system for securing inbound and outbound data packet flow in a computer network." The patent was granted to Checkpoint Software Technologies, Ltd., on February 25, 1997.

circuit-level gateways. In essence, a circuit-level gateway is a proxy server for TCP[9] (i.e., it is typically located and running on the firewall of a corporate intranet and it relays TCP connections).

More specifically, a circuit-level gateway does the following three things when a client wants to establish a TCP connection to a server:

1. It receives the TCP connection establishment request that is sent out by the client (because the client is configured to make use of the circuit-level gateway).

2. It authenticates and possibly authorizes the client (or the user behind the client).

3. It establishes a second TCP connection to the server on the client's behalf.

After having successfully established the second TCP connection, the circuit-level gateway simply relays application data forth and back.[10] As such, it does not interfere with the data stream. This differentiates a circuit-level gateway from an application-level gateway or proxy server that is able to understand the application protocol employed by the two endpoints of the connection. What this basically means is that the circuit-level gateway need not understand the application protocol in use. This simplifies the implementation and deployment of circuit-level gateways considerably.

The most important circuit-level gateway in use today is SOCKS.[11] It is a circuit-level gateway that follows a customized client approach, meaning that it requires customizations and modifications to the client software (i.e., no change is usually required to user procedures). More precisely, SOCKS requires modifications either to the client software or the TCP/IP stack to accommodate the interception at the firewall between the client and the server:

9. This statement is not completely true, as contemporary circuit-level gateways also are able to handle UDP-based application protocols. This will be explained later in this chapter.

10. Note that the only difference between a circuit-level gateway and a simple port forwarding mechanism is that with a circuit-level gateway, the client must be aware of the intermediate system, whereas in the case of a simple port-forwarding mechanism, the client need not be aware and may be completely oblivious of the existence of the intermediary. Also, a circuit-level gateway is generic, and any TCP connection can be handled by the same gateway (if enabled in its configuration). Contrary to that, a port-forwarding mechanism is usually specific to a given service, meaning that all qualifying TCP segments are forwarded to a specific port of a server.

11. http://www.socks.nec.com

▸ A client that has been modified to handle SOCKS interactions is commonly referred to as a "socksified" client. Following this terminology, most Web browsers (e.g., Microsoft's Internet Explorer) are socksified clients and issue SOCKS calls that are transparent to their users.

▸ Socksified TCP/IP stacks are also available, which may obviate the need for client software modifications.

In either case, the SOCKS server resides at the firewall and interacts with the socksified clients or TCP/IP stacks. There are no further changes required for the servers that may reside either on the Internet or intranet.

SOCKS and the original SOCKS protocol for communications between a socksified client and a SOCKS server was originally proposed in [14]. The original implementation consisted of two components: a SOCKS server or daemon (i.e., sockd) and a SOCKS library that can be used to replace regular Sockets calls in the client software. More specifically, the application developer has to recompile and link the client software with a few preprocessor directives to intercept and replace the regular TCP/IP networking Sockets calls with their SOCKS counterparts, as summarized in Table 3.1. This is sufficiently easy to be used on a large scale.

The design goal of SOCKS was to provide a general framework for TCP/IP applications to securely use (i.e., traverse) a firewall. Complying with these design goals, SOCKS is independent of any supported TCP/IP application protocol. When a socksified intranet client requires access to a server on the Internet, it must first open a TCP connection to the appropriate port on the SOCKS server residing on the firewall system (the SOCKS server conventionally listens at TCP port 1080). If this first TCP connection is established, the client uses the SOCKS protocol to have a second TCP connection to the server be established by the SOCKS server.

Table 3.1 Sockets Calls and SOCKS Counterparts

SOCKS Call	Socket Call
Rconnect	connect
Rbind	bind
Rlisten	listen
Rselect	select
Rgetsockname	getsockname
Raccept	accept

The SOCKS protocol used between the socksified client (i.e., the client using the SOCKS library routines) and the SOCKS server basically consists of the following two commands:

▸ The CONNECT command takes as arguments the IP address and port number of the server, as well as a username. It basically requests that the SOCKS server establishes a TCP connection to the given IP address and port number.

▸ The BIND command takes as arguments the client IP address and a username. It is used only in protocols that require the client to accept connections back from the server. As we saw previously, FTP is an example of such a protocol (since it requires the client to accept a data connection from the server).

In either case, the username is a string passed from the requesting client to the SOCKS server for the purposes of authentication, authorization, and accounting.

After having received a request (i.e., a CONNECT or BIND command), the SOCKS server evaluates the information provided by the client. The evaluation is performed against a sockd configuration file that may include a ruleset. Each rule in the set either permits or denies communications with one or several systems. In either case, the SOCKS server sends a reply back to the client. Among other things, the reply includes information indicating whether the request was successful. Once the requested second connection is established, the SOCKS server simply relays data back and forth between the client and the server (without looking into or interpreting the data stream).

The original SOCKS implementation was refined into a SOCKS package and a protocol that is widely deployed and commonly referred to as SOCKS Protocol version 4, or SOCKS V4. After the successful deployment of SOCKS V4, the IETF chartered an Authenticated Firewall Traversal (AFT) WG to "start with the SOCKS system described" in [14], and to "specify a protocol to address the issue of application-layer support for firewall traversal" in 1994.[12] The major result of the IETF AFT WG was the specification of the SOCKS protocol version 5 (SOCKS V5) in March 1996 [15].[13] As such,

---

12. http://www.ietf.org/html.charters/aft-charter.html
13. At the time of this writing, an updated version of the SOCKS Protocol version 5 specification is published as an Internet draft.

SOCKS V5 has been submitted to the Internet standards track as a proposed standard. It is possible and very likely that the protocol will become an Internet Standard.

As compared with SOCKS V4, SOCKS V5 provides some additional features. These features are related to user authentication, communication security, UDP support, and extended addressing schemes:

‣ In SOCKS V4, user authentication is relatively simple and straight-forward. It basically consists of a username that is sent from the socksified client to the SOCKS server as part of the CONNECT or BIND method. In addition to this simple authentication scheme, SOCKS V5 supports a handshake between the client and the SOCKS server for authentication method negotiation. The first message is sent by the client to the SOCKS server. It declares the authentication methods the client is currently able to support. The second message is sent from the SOCKS server back to the client. It selects a particular authentication method according to the SOCKS server's security policy. If none of the methods declared by the client meet the security requirements of the SOCKS server, communications are dropped. After the authentication method has been negotiated, the client and SOCKS server start the authentication process using the chosen method. Two authentication methods are specified in corresponding RFC documents: password-based authentication in [16] and Kerberos V5 GSS-API authentication in [17]. The approach for use of GSS-API in SOCKS V5 is to authenticate the client and server by successfully establishing a security context. This context can then be used to protect messages that are subsequently exchanged. Prior to use of GSS-API primitives, the client and server should be locally authenticated and have established default GSS-API credentials.

‣ Depending on the underlying authentication methods implemented via GSS-API, a client can negotiate with the SOCKS server about the security of subsequent messages. In the case of Kerberos V5, either integrity and/or confidentiality services are provided for the rest of messages, including the client's requests, the SOCKS server's replies, and all application data. Note that this feature is particularly well suited for use by reverse proxy servers, because it supports data encryption between clients (on the Internet) and the SOCKS server.

‣ SOCKS V4 is only able to handle TCP applications. Unfortunately, an increasingly large number of TCP/IP applications are making use of

UDP (e.g., applications that make use of real-time and/or multicast communications). Against this background, the SOCKS protocol has been extended to additionally provide support for UDP. More specifically, a new method, called UDP ASSOCIATE, has been added to the SOCKS V5 protocol specification [15]. The UDP ASSOCIATE request sent from the client to the SOCKS server is used to establish an association within the UDP relay process to handle UDP datagrams. According to this association, the SOCKS server relays UDP datagrams to the requesting client. Obviously, this approach is conceptually similar to stateful inspection or dynamic packet filtering as discussed above. The UDP association terminates when the TCP connection that the UDP ASSOCIATE request arrived on terminates. As a result, the SOCKS V5 library can now be used to socksify both TCP- and UDP-based applications.

‣ Finally, SOCKS V5 supports DNS names and IP version 6 addresses in addition to normal IP version 4 addresses.

Because of their fundamental differences, the SOCKS V5 protocol specification does not require any provision for supporting the SOCKS V4 protocol. However, it is a simple matter of implementation to enable SOCKS V5 servers to communicate with V5 and V4 clients. In fact, most SOCKS V5 servers that are available today provide backward compatibility.

In summary, a circuit-level gateway (e.g., a SOCKS server) provides an interesting technology and possibility to have applications and application protocols securely traverse a firewall. A clear advantage of circuit-level gateways is their generality, meaning that a circuit-level gateway can act as a proxy server for any application (not just one). Circuit-level gateways are particularly useful for applications for which application-level gateways (i.e., proxy servers) do not exist or are conceptually hard to design and implement. For example, an application protocol that is hard to deal with (using packet-filtering technologies and application-level gateways) is the Internet Inter-ORB Protocol (IIOP) that is used in environments and applications that conform to the Common Object Request Broker Architecture (CORBA). The difficulty stems from the fact that the IIOP makes use of UDP and dynamically assigned port numbers. Against this background, a group of vendors have jointly specified the use of SOCKS V5 to have IIOP communications securely traverse a firewall.[14] This is a technology that we

---

14. http://www.socks.nec.com/corba-firewall.pdf

will likely see deployed in the future. The generality of circuit-level gateways, however, also comes with some disadvantages. For example, a SOCKS server is not able to scan application data for specific commands or executable content (e.g., Java applets or ActiveX controls). Consequently, if a configuration must be optimized for maximum security, the use of application-level gateways is still the preferred option.

3.5 Application-level gateways

Contrary to a circuit-level gateway, an application-level gateway serves only one application protocol. To clarify this point, imagine the situation in which the packet filter of a firewall blocks all inbound Telnet and FTP sessions, unless the sessions are terminated by a bastion host (that is also part of the firewall configuration). The bastion host, in turn, hosts an application gateway that operates at the transport (circuit) or application layer. The situation is slightly different in either case:

▸ If the application gateway operates at the transport layer, a circuit-level gateway (e.g., a SOCKS server) must be running on the bastion host.

▸ If the application gateway operates at the application layer, there are basically two application-level gateways or proxy servers that must be running on the bastion host (i.e., one proxy server for Telnet and another proxy server for FTP).

In either case, a user who wishes to connect inbound to an intranet server must have his or her Telnet or FTP client connect to the application gateway running on the bastion host. The application gateway, in turn, would then authenticate and authorize the user. In the positive case, it would set up a secondary TCP connection to the intranet server and relay application data between the two TCP connections back and forth. If the application gateway were a circuit-level gateway, it would not look into the application data it relays. If, however, the application gateway were an application-level gateway, it would look into and fully control the application data stream. In an attempt to make it hard to retrieve internal files from systems located on the Internet, an application-level gateway could, for example, be configured in a way that permits the use of the FTP PUT command but denies the use of the FTP GET command. Similarly, an application-level gateway for HTTP could be configured to screen data traffic and filter out Java applets and ActiveX controls to protect internal hosts from mobile code and software-driven attacks (this kind of filtering is not possible in the case of circuit-level gateways).

From the client's point of view, interaction with an application gateway requires some additional steps. This is equally true for circuit-level gateways and application-level gateways. In the case of a SOCKS server the additional steps are hidden from the user and the corresponding client software must be modified to be aware of the SOCKS server (i.e., it must be "socksified").

In general, the use of an application gateway requires some customization and modification of either the user procedures or the client software:

▸ The customization and modification of the user procedures is a simple and straightforward approach to implementing application gateway support. Following this approach, the user first establishes a connection to the application gateway and then requests the establishment of a second connection to the server. An important benefit is that the customization of the user procedures, in general, requires no impact to client software. Given the extensive presence of client software, this approach is attractive for implementing Internet access (in fact, the first Internet firewalls worked that way). The main disadvantage of this approach is that the user has to be trained for an extra step to log on to the proxy server.

▸ The other approach to implementing application gateway support is to customize and modify the client software (similar to the process of "socksifying" a client). The main advantage of this approach is that it may provide transparency to users in accessing the Internet and traversing firewall systems. The main disadvantage, however, is that it obviously requires modifications to client software. This is not always possible and seldom easy to accomplish.

Note that both approaches have severe disadvantages, as they require customization and modification of either the user procedures or the client software. Which approach is simpler depends on the application, its availability in source code, and the organization that makes use of the application.[15]

Against this background, it would be nice to have a firewall that maintains all software modifications required for application gateway

---

15. For example, in large organizations, training users may be harder than modifying an application.

support in the firewall. In this case, neither the user procedures nor the client software would have to be customized or modified accordingly. This idea has led to the development of transparent firewalls.

In short, a *transparent firewall* is configured to listen on the network segment of the firewall for outgoing TCP connections and to autonomously relay these connections on the client's behalf. Note, however, that transparency is not necessarily provided in both directions. As a matter of fact, inbound transparency is seldom required or used, as users must usually authenticate themselves at a firewall system. Also note that a transparent firewall still requires that all messages to and from the Internet be transmitted through the firewall. However, the existence of the firewall system can be hidden entirely from both the user and the client software.

Let us have a look at an example in which a Telnet client tries to connect to a Telnet server making use of a proxy server. The procedure to establish a Telnet session can be summarized as follows:

1. The Telnet client acting on behalf of the user requests a TCP connection to the Telnet proxy server running on the firewall (at an arbitrary but fixed port number). If a screening router is put in front of the firewall, the connection must be authorized according to the corresponding packet-filtering rules.

2. The Telnet proxy server, in turn, may check the source IP address of the client machine. The connection request can be accepted or rejected according to some authorization and access control information.

3. In addition to the source IP address check of the client, the user may also need to authenticate himself or herself (e.g., using a username and password).

4. If the user is properly authenticated, the client must provide the address or name of the Telnet server (again, this step can be and will be made transparent to the user).

5. The Telnet proxy server then establishes a second TCP connection to the Telnet server. Again, this connection request may have to pass through a screening router. In this case, the packet-filtering rules of the screening router must be configured so that they let packets through that are originated by a firewall system.

6. After having established the second TCP connection to the Telnet server, the Telnet proxy server relays Telnet data between the two

connections. In addition, the Telnet proxy server also may scan the data traffic for specific Telnet commands and filter them out. Also, the Telnet proxy server may log all command executions to build an audit trail.

To properly authenticate the user, the Telnet proxy server must have access to some authentication and authorization information. This is generally true for any application-level gateway or proxy server that provides support for user-level authentication (not just Telnet proxy servers). In general, there are several user authentication and authorization schemes that an application-level gateway or proxy server could implement and use. In either case, the application-level gateway or proxy server must have access to some reference information it can use to verify whether the authentication information provided by a client (or user) is valid (e.g., a one-way hash value of a user password or the public key certificate of a user). The reference information can be stored either locally ·or remotely. If many firewall systems and network access servers (NAS) are put in place, the second approach is preferable since it makes it possible to aggregate security information at a single point. Typically, a standardized protocol is used to retrieve the reference information from a centralized security server. There are currently two competing protocol proposals:

• Livingston Enterprises, Inc., has developed and implemented a protocol called Remote Authentication Dial-In User Service (RADIUS) [18].[16] In short, the RADIUS protocol can be used to carry authentication, authorization, and configuration information between an NAS that desires to authenticate its users and a shared authentication or security server. Livingston Enterprises, Inc., also has made publicly and freely available corresponding RADIUS security server software. A companion protocol that can be used to carry accounting information between an NAS and a shared authentication or security server is specified in [19].

• The terminal access controller access control system (TACACS) was originally developed by BBN under ARPA funding in the early 1980s. It was used to authenticate users to terminal access computers on the ARPANET. Later, Cisco Systems developed, implemented, and deployed a family of protocols that are based on TACACS [20].

16. As of this writing, the IETF has made the RADIUS protocol a draft standard.

While the TACACS and extended TACACS (XTACACS) protocols are no longer in use, TACACS+ is a protocol in current use. Refer to the Cisco manuals for the corresponding TACACS, XTACACS, and TACACS+ commands.

Both protocols (RADIUS and the protocol family for the TACACS derivates) are widely supported by firewall systems and network access servers.

After having successfully authenticated and authorized the client (or user), a proxy server sets up a secondary TCP connection to the requested application server. From the user's point of view, a secondary authentication may now be required and actually take place, since the application server may want to authenticate and authorize the client (or user) as well. This secondary authentication step is beyond the scope of the firewall. If the user is successfully authenticated and authorized, the application server usually starts serving the request.

In summary, application-level gateways and proxy servers provide a sophisticated and advanced technology to secure TCP-based applications and application protocols for the WWW. Commercial firewalls typically come along with proxy server support for Telnet, FTP, SMTP, HTTP, and many other TCP-based applications and application protocols. There are advantages and disadvantages that should be kept in mind when discussing the suitability of application-level gateways and proxy servers. The advantages are related to user authentication and authorization, application protocol control, logging, and accounting. Contrary to that, the disadvantages are related to the fact that a proxy server must be built specifically for each application protocol, that application gateways (i.e., circuit-level and application-level gateways) are notoriously bad at handling UDP-based application protocols, and that it is necessary to know the application protocol in order to code and set up a proxy server.

3.6   Firewall configurations

A firewall configuration is an arrangement of packet filters and application gateways. In theory, there are many possibilities for combining these components. In practice, however, there are only three firewall configurations that are deployed: dual-homed firewall, screened host firewall, and screened subnet firewall. These configurations are overviewed and briefly discussed next.

3.6.1   Dual-homed firewall

In TCP/IP parlance, the term *multihomed host* refers to a host with multiple network interfaces. Usually, each network interface is connected to a separate network segment, and the multihomed host can typically forward or route IP packets between these network segments. If, however, IP forwarding and IP routing are disabled on the host, it provides isolation between the network segments and may be used in a firewall configuration accordingly. To disable IP routing is usually a relatively simple and straightforward task. It basically means to turn off any program that might be advertising the host as a router. To disable IP forwarding is considerably more difficult and may require modifying the operating system kernel. Fortunately, a number of operating system vendors provide a simple possibility to modify the kernel and to turn off IP forwarding accordingly.

A dual-homed host is a special case of a multihomed host, namely, one that has exactly two network interfaces. Again, IP routing and IP forwarding can be disabled to provide isolation between the two network segments the dual-homed host physically interconnects.

As illustrated in Figure 3.1, a simple *dual-homed firewall* configuration may consist of a dual-homed host that serves as a bastion host. IP routing and IP forwarding are disabled so that IP packets can no longer be routed or forwarded between the two network interfaces. Consequently, data can only be transferred from one network interface to the other if there is an application-level gateway (or proxy) process to do it. Note that Figure 3.1 is simplified in the sense that the routers are not shown (they are assumed to be part of the intranet and Internet environments). In contrast, Figure 3.2 shows a more detailed configuration of a dual-homed firewall. In this configuration, the bastion host's external network interface is

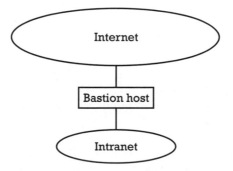

Figure 3.1   A simple dual-homed firewall configuration.

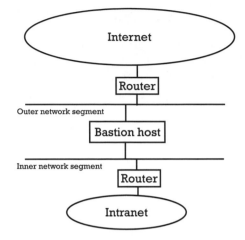

Figure 3.2 A more realistic configuration of a dual-homed firewall.

connected to an outer network segment and the bastion host's internal network interface is connected to an inner network segment:[17]

▸ The outer network segment is connected with a screening router to the Internet.[18] The aim of the screening router is to ensure that any outbound IP packet carries the IP address of the bastion host as its source IP address, and that any inbound IP packet carries the IP address of the bastion host as its destination IP address. The packet-filtering rules must be configured accordingly.

▸ Similarly, the inner network segment hosts a screening router that is interconnected to the intranet. The aim of this screening router is to make sure that any outbound IP packet carries the IP address of the bastion host as its destination IP address, and that any inbound IP packet carries the IP address of the bastion host as its source IP address. Again, the packet-filtering rules must be configured accordingly.

In the firewall configuration illustrated in Figure 3.2, the outer network segment can be used to host server systems that are intended to be publicly accessible, such as public Web servers, DNS servers with public information,

17. In some literature, the outer network segment is labeled *red* and the inner network segment is labeled *blue* to refer to their different sensitivity and security status.
18. Consequently, this router serves as an access router.

and access servers for other networks (e.g., modem pools for the PSTN or ISDN). This is common practice to make server systems and corresponding services publicly available and accessible from the Internet.

It is fairly obvious that the bastion host (and the application gateways running on it) can be replicated an arbitrary number of times in a dual-homed firewall configuration (e.g., to improve performance). The resulting configuration is sometimes also called a *parallel dual-homed firewall*. It may consist of several bastion hosts that are all connected to the same inner and outer network segments.

The dual-homed firewall is a simple and highly secure firewall configuration. The security originates from the fact that all data must pass an application gateway to get from one network interface of the bastion host to the other. There is no possibility of bypassing the bastion host or its application gateways. There are, however, also several disadvantages that are important in practice, and that should be considered with care accordingly:

▸ Performance is a problem because the bastion host may become a bottleneck (note that all data must pass the bastion host).

▸ The bastion host represents a single point of failure. If it crashes, Internet connectivity is also lost.

▸ There are some practical problems related to TCP/IP application protocols with no proxy support (e.g., proprietary protocols). In this case, the dual-homed firewall configuration turns out to be rather inflexible, and this inflexibility could turn out to be disadvantageous.

In summary, the dual-homed firewall configuration is secure but rather inflexible. Contrary to this, the screened host and screened subnet firewall configurations discussed next are more flexible but less secure. Consequently, where throughput and flexibility are important or required, these configurations may be the preferable choices.

3.6.2 Screened host firewall

As illustrated in Figure 3.3, a *screened host firewall* configuration basically consists of a screening router that interconnects the intranet to the Internet, and a bastion host that is logically situated on the intranet. Contrary to the bastion host of a dual-homed firewall, the bastion host of a screened host firewall is single-homed, meaning that it has only one network interface

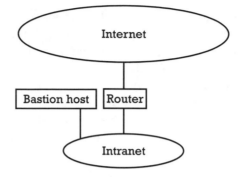

Figure 3.3 A simple configuration of a screened host firewall.

that interconnects it with an internal network segment (i.e., a network segment that is part of the intranet).

In a screened host firewall configuration, the screening router has to make sure that IP packets destined for intranet systems are first sent to an appropriate application gateway on the bastion host. If a specific TCP/IP application protocol is assumed to be secure, the screening router also can be configured to bypass the bastion host and to send the corresponding IP packets directly to the destination system. For very obvious reasons, this possibly increases flexibility but also decreases security.

Similar to the dual-homed firewall configuration, the bastion host and its application gateways can also be replicated an arbitrary number of times in the screened host firewall configuration. In fact, this is likely to be the preferred configuration, as different application gateways are typically running on different hosts (all of them representing bastion hosts for the applications they serve as a gateway).

In summary, the screened host firewall configuration is very simple and straightforward. As compared with the dual-homed firewall configuration, it is more flexible but also potentially less secure. This is because the bastion host can be bypassed (i.e., by configuring the screening router that interconnects the intranet and the Internet accordingly). Due to the dual-homed nature of the bastion host, this is not possible in the dual-homed firewall configuration.

3.6.3 Screened subnet firewall

As illustrated in Figure 3.4, a *screened subnet firewall* configuration basically consists of a subnet that is screened by a single-homed bastion host. The outer screening router has to make sure that all (or at least most) data pass

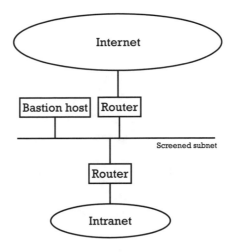

Figure 3.4 A screened subnet firewall configuration.

an application gateway running on a bastion host. Consequently, the bastion host screens the subnet located between the outer and the inner screening router, and this screened subnet is sometimes also referred to as a *demilitarized zone* (DMZ).[19] Similar to the other configurations discussed thus far, the bastion host can be replicated an arbitrary number of times in a screened subnet firewall configuration. Each bastion host may provide a specific service. In fact, the resulting separation of servers and services is an interesting feature from a security point of view. A screened subnet firewall configuration with multiple bastion hosts is illustrated in Figure 3.5.

Note that the two screening routers provide redundancy in that an attacker would have to subvert both routers in order to access intranet systems. Also note that the bastion host and the additional servers on the DMZ could be set up to be the only systems seen from the Internet; no other system name would be known or used in a DNS database that is made accessible to the outside world.

A screened subnet firewall configuration can be made more flexible by permitting certain services to pass around the bastion host and the corresponding application gateways. As an alternative to passing services directly between the intranet and Internet, one may also place the systems that need these services directly on the screened subnet. In fact, this would be the preferred configuration but is not always possible (e.g., if the placement of the systems on the screened subnet represents an unacceptable

19. The DMZ is named after the strip of no-man's-land between North and South Korea.

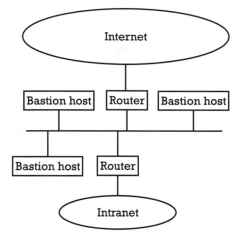

Figure 3.5 A screened subnet firewall configuration with multiple bastion hosts.

tradeoff between security and functionality). Again, we refer to the importance of policy.

In summary, the screened subnet firewall configuration is flexible and provides a reasonable level of security. As such, it has been the firewall configuration of choice for many network security professionals in the past.

3.7 Network address translation

Many contemporary firewall systems provide support for what is known as *network address translation* (NAT). NAT basically means that an organization can use private IP addresses on its own network (i.e., the intranet) to increase its address space.[20] If IP packets are sent to the Internet, the private IP addresses are dynamically converted to IP addresses that have been officially assigned to the organization and that are routable on the Internet. Similarly, if IP packets are received from the Internet, the officially assigned IP addresses are converted back to the appropriate private IP addresses.

---

20. In IP version 4, IP addresses are 32 bits long. The resulting address space is 2^{32}. Due to the popularity and wide deployment of Internet technologies, this address space is almost used (i.e., almost all IP addresses have been officially assigned to organizations. Against this background, the use of private IP addresses (i.e., IP addresses that are not routable on the Internet) provides a viable solution to overcome the lack of officially assigned IP addresses. IP version 6 will use IP addresses that are 128 bits long. The resulting address space is 2^{128}. Consequently, there should be enough IP addresses for all future purposes.

Based on the private IP addresses, the IP packets are then routed on the intranet to their appropriate destination.

In RFC 1918 and BCP 5 [21], three blocks of the IP address space are reserved for private use. The blocks are summarized in Table 3.2.

A firewall that supports NAT works similarly to a transparent firewall. IP packets with external destination IP addresses are routed to the network segment that hosts the firewall configuration. The firewall, in turn, grabs the IP packets that request a TCP connection establishment and establishes the connection on behalf of the client. In addition, a firewall that supports NAT also substitutes the private IP addresses (used on the intranet) with officially assigned IP addresses (used on the Internet). Obviously, this substitution is reversed in the opposite direction.

For example, let's look at a company that is officially assigned an IP class C address. For its internal use, the company uses IP addresses from the 20-bit block itemized in Table 3.2 (i.e., 172.16.0.0 to 172.31.255.255). As illustrated in Figure 3.6, an FTP client (on the left) with a private IP address C wants to retrieve a file from a destination FTP server with IP address S located somewhere on the Internet (on the right). Therefore, the client makes use of a transparent firewall with IP address F (in the middle). The transparent firewall, in turn, actively supports NAT.

In this situation, the following steps are performed to establish a connection between the FTP client and the FTP server:

1. The FTP client sends out a TCP connection establishment request message to port 21 of the destination FTP server (the notation c@C > 21@S indicates that a message is sent out from source IP address C and port number c to destination IP address S and port number 21).

Table 3.2 Private IP Address Blocks [21]

10.0.0.0–10.255.255.255	24-bit block
172.16.0.0–172.31.255.255	20-bit block
192.168.0.0–192.168.255.255	16-bit block

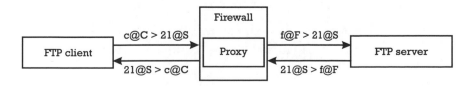

Figure 3.6 A firewall supporting NAT.

Because the FTP server is not directly reachable by the client, the message is forwarded to the network segment that hosts the firewall and its proxy servers.

2. The FTP proxy server of the firewall grabs the initial TCP connection establishment request message, authenticates and authorizes the user, and eventually forwards the message to the destination FTP server. In this case, however, the message source is initialized with an IP address F and a randomly chosen and dynamically assigned port number (the port number is specific for this particular FTP session).

3. The destination FTP server receives the TCP connection establishment request message and eventually establishes a TCP connection to the FTP proxy server. Any FTP command that is sent out by the FTP client is then automatically forwarded by the FTP proxy server to the destination FTP server.

In the opposite direction, FTP application data are sent from the destination FTP server to the proxy server of the firewall, and from the proxy server to the FTP client. Note that in this direction, the source IP address is usually not substituted by the proxy server, and that officially assigned IP addresses may appear on the intranet accordingly (in the source IP address fields).

Transparent application gateways provide the most recent and most sophisticated firewall technology available today. Whenever possible, this technology should be the preferred one to use, as it does not require user procedures or client software to be modified. Unfortunately, most firewalls that implement this technology must also use NAT. The IETF has debated NAT for some time and there is considerable feeling that it is an unfortunate technical approach that is justified only when an organization is unable to acquire adequate IP address space. Because of its increased address space, the use and wide deployment of IP version 6 (IPv6) will make NAT obsolete in the future.[21]

3.8 Configuring the browser

First of all, it is important to note that most parts of a firewall configuration are transparent and "invisible" to the Web user and his or her browser. For

---

21. One may also argue in the opposite direction, namely, that NAT will make IPv6 obsolete.

example, packet filters and screening routers operate on the IP packets originated or received by particular hosts without having the corresponding users be able to influence the packet filtering behavior. Similarly, the use of a transparent firewall doesn't have to be configured on the browser side (this is the idea of transparency). Also, a user doesn't have to care whether a firewall is configured as dual-homed or screened subnet. (i.e., the browser configuration is the same in either case).

If, however, a firewall is not transparent and uses application gateways (i.e., a circuit-level gateway or application-level gateways), a Web user locating behind that firewall must configure his or her browser to properly interact with the application gateways that are running on the bastion host(s). This is true for any traffic destined to external IP addresses. The browser must know how to reach these addresses. For internal IP addresses, there is usually no need to use application gateways and configure browsers accordingly.

Using Microsoft's Internet Explorer, for example, the user can configure the browser using the local-area network (LAN) Settings panel as illustrated in Figure 3.7.[22] According to the screenshot of this figure, there are basically three possibilities to configure the browser:

1. Have the browser automatically detect the settings.

2. Use an automatic configuration script.

3. Manually configure the use of one (or several) proxy server(s).

In practice, the second and third possibilities are most often used. In fact, it is always possible to manually configure the use of one (or several) proxy server(s). If only one proxy server is used (e.g., an HTTP proxy server), its use can be directly configured in the lower section of the "Local Area Network (LAN) Settings" panel.

If, however, a proxy server must be specified for more than one application protocol, the Advanced button may be pressed to open the Proxy Settings panel, as illustrated in Figure 3.8. In this panel, the use of proxy servers can be configured for HTTP, HTTPS (named "Secure" in Microsoft's Internet Explorer), FTP, Gopher, and SOCKS. Obviously, it is possible to specify only one proxy server and to activate the checkbox entitled "Use the same proxy server for all protocols." It is also possible to

---

22. The Local Area Network (LAN) Settings panel can be found in the Connections tab of the Tools > Internet Options ... menu.

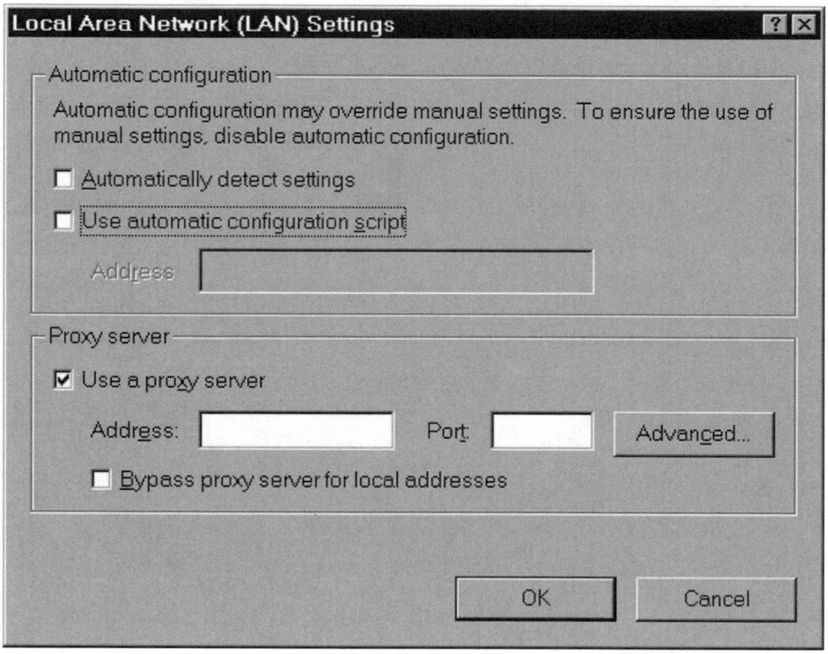

Figure 3.7 Configuring Microsoft's Internet Explorer using the Local Area Network (LAN) Settings panel. (© 2002 Microsoft Corporation.)

specify Internet addresses that may be contacted directly (i.e., without having to go through a proxy server). These addresses are named ''Exception'' in Microsoft's Internet Explorer.

The manual configuration of proxy servers does not scale in intranet environments. In this situation, it is usually more convenient to use an automatic configuration script. Automatic configuration scripts were originally introduced by Netscape Communications under the term proxy auto-config (PAC) files. Consequently, a PAC file is typically named proxy.pac. In short, a PAC file is written in a scripting language (e.g., JavaScript) and provides the following function:

```
function FindProxyForURL(url, host)
{
}
```

There are two arguments for a FindProxyForURL function call: url specifies the full URL being accessed, and host specifies the hostname extracted from the URL (this is only for convenience, since it is the same string as between :// and the first : or / after that). The FindProxyForURL function returns a string describing the configuration. If the return string is

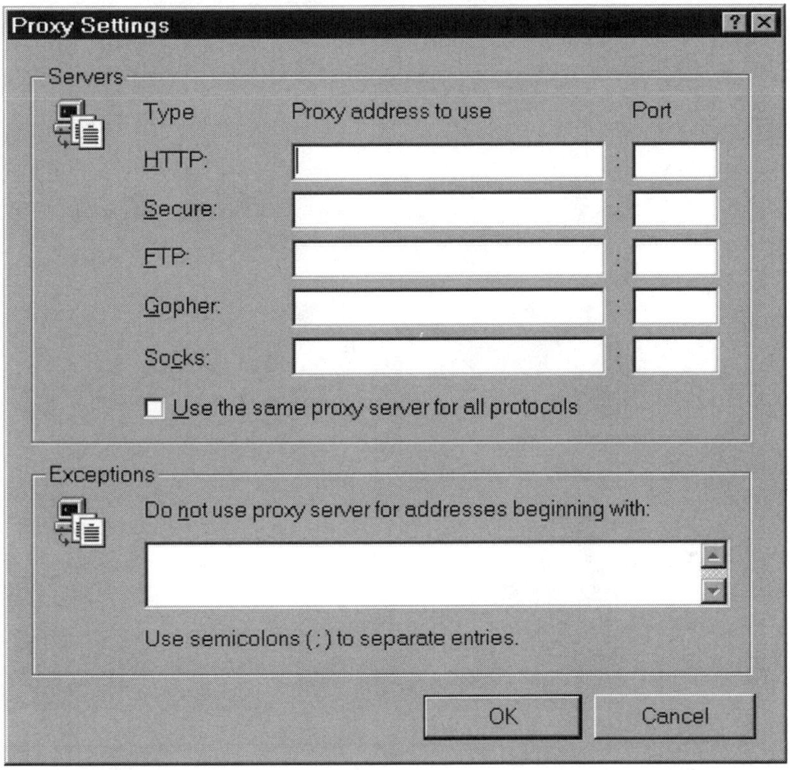

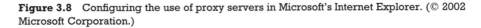

Figure 3.8 Configuring the use of proxy servers in Microsoft's Internet Explorer. (© 2002 Microsoft Corporation.)

null, no proxies should be used. The string can contain any number of the following building blocks, separated by a semicolon:

‣ DIRECT—In this case, connections should be made directly, without using any proxies;

‣ PROXY host:port—In this case, the specified proxy server should be used;

‣ SOCKS host:port—In this case, the specified SOCKS server should be used.

The use of a PAC file is very convenient to have all browsers in an intranet environment use the same proxy settings.

As illustrated in Figure 3.9, the Opera browser can also be configured to make use of proxy servers or PAC files using the Proxy servers panel. Similar

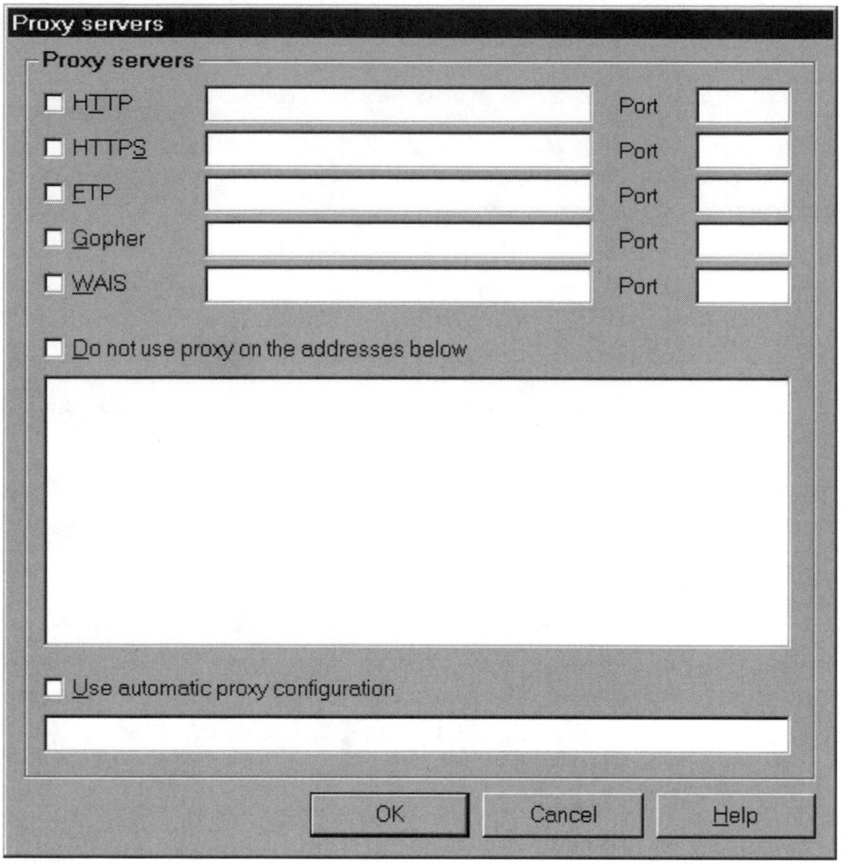

Figures 3.9 Configuring the use of proxy servers in the Proxy servers panel of Opera. (© 2002 Opera Software.)

to Microsoft's Internet Explorer, proxy servers can be specified for HTTP, HTTPS, FTP, and Gopher. Unlike Microsoft's Internet Explorer, however, Opera supports WAIS but does not support SOCKS. This may change in the future, because WAIS is seldom used.

3.9 Conclusions

Today, many companies and organizations want to have interconnectivity between their internal computer systems and the global Internet. As such, they interconnect their intranets to the Internet and try to control access using firewalls. Depending on the basic components and configuration, there are several grades of firewall protection that can be obtained. For example, there is no security by allowing unrestricted access between a corporate intranet and the Internet. Next, packet filters can be added to obtain a certain level of data traffic interception, and stateful inspection technologies may help to make more intelligent decisions whether to forward particular IP packets. Also, the firewall can include both packet filters and application gateways. A variety of circuit-level and application-level gateways can be added along with different strengths of the corresponding authentication mechanisms. Similarly, the firewall can also reside on a secure operating system,[23] thereby improving the underlying security for the firewall code and files. Finally, the firewall can provide support for Internet layer security protocols to build secure tunnels between firewall-protected sites and to build virtual private networks (VPNs) accordingly. Similarly, intrusion detection systems may be used to detect illegitimate attempts to access the intranet environment. Last but not least, a company can also deny any access to and from the Internet, thereby ensuring isolation and complete security from the outside world. Although this is seemingly a theoretical option in these euphoric times for Internet access, it is still the only prudent approach to follow for certain highly secure environments.

Firewall systems are a fact of life on the Internet today. If properly implemented and deployed, they provide efficient and effective access control services for corporate intranets. Consequently, more and more network managers are setting up firewalls as their first line of defense against outside attacks. Nevertheless, the firewall technology has remained an emotional topic within the Internet community. Let's briefly summarize the main concerns:

▶ Firewall advocates consider firewalls as important additional safe-guards, because they aggregate security functions in a single point, simplifying installation, configuration, and management.

▶ Firewall detractors are usually concerned about the difficulty of using firewalls, requiring multiple logins and other out-of-band mechanisms, as well as their interference with the usability and vitality of the Internet as a whole. They claim that firewalls foster a false sense of security, leading to lax security within the firewall perimeter.

---

23. In this context, a secure operating system refers to an operating system that is hardened and minimized, meaning that anything not urgently required for the firewall's functionality is stripped off.

At minimum, firewall advocates and detractors both agree that firewalls are a powerful tool for network security, but that they aren't by any means a panacea or a magic bullet for all network and Internet-related security problems. For example, any firewall can be circumvented by tunneling unauthorized application protocols in authorized ones. For example, if a firewall is configured to deny POP traffic between an intranet client and an Internet server, it is always possible to tunnel POP traffic inside HTTP. In fact, there are many tools that support this kind of tunneling and make it transparent to the user. Consequently, firewalls should not be regarded as a substitute for careful security management within a corporate intranet. Also, a firewall is useful only if it handles all traffic to and from the Internet. This is not always the case, since many sites permit dial-in access to modems that are located at various points throughout the site. This is a potential back door and could negate all the protection provided by the firewall. A much better method for handling modems is to concentrate them into a modem pool. In essence, a modem pool consists of several modems connected to a terminal server. A dial-in user connects to the terminal server and then connects from there to other internal hosts. Some terminal servers provide security features that can restrict connections to specific hosts, or require users to authenticate themselves. Obviously, RADIUS, TACACS, and TACACS+ can again be used to secure communications between the terminal server and a centralized security server. Sometimes, authorized users also wish to have a dial-out capability. These users, however, need to recognize the vulnerabilities they may be creating if they are careless with modem access. A dial-out capability may easily become a dial-in capability if proper precautions are not taken. In general, dial-in and dial-out capabilities should be considered in the design of a firewall and incorporated into it. Forcing outside users to go through the strong authentication of the firewall should be reflected in the firewall policy.

In summary, firewall systems provide basic access control services for corporate intranets. A pair of historical analogies can help us better understand the role of firewall technology for the current Internet [22]:

▸ Our Stone-Age predecessors lived in caves, each inhabited by a family whose members knew each other quite well. They could use this knowledge to identify and authenticate one another. Someone wanting to enter the cave would have to be introduced by a family member trusted by the others. History of human society has shown that this security model is too simple to work on a large scale. As families grew in size and started to interact with one another, it was no longer possible for all family members to know all other members of the community, or even to reliably remember all persons who had ever been introduced to them.

▸ In the Middle Ages, our predecessors lived in castles and villages surrounded by town walls. The inhabitants were acquainted with each other, but they did not trust each other. Instead, identification and authentication, as well as authorization and access control, were centralized at a front gate. Anyone who wanted to enter the castle or village had to pass the front gate and was thoroughly checked there. Those who managed to pass the gate were implicitly trusted by all inhabitants. But human history has shown that this security model doesn't work either. For one thing, town walls don't protect against malicious insider attacks; for another, town walls and front gates don't scale easily (since they are so massive). Many remnants of medieval town walls bear witness to this lack of scalability.

Using the above analogies, the Internet has just entered the Middle Ages. The simple security model of the Stone Age still works for single hosts and local area networks. But it no longer works for wide area networks in general and the Internet in particular. As a first—and let's hope intermediate—step, firewalls have been erected at the Internet gateways. Because they are capable of selectively dropping IP packets, firewalls also restrict the connectivity of the Internet as a whole. The Internet's firewalls are thus comparable to the town walls and front gates of the Middle Ages. Screening routers correspond to general-purpose gates, while application gateways correspond to more specialized gates. Today, we don't see town walls anymore. Instead, countries issue passports to their citizens to use worldwide for identification and authentication. It is possible and very likely that the Internet will experience a similar development and that trusted parties will issue locally or globally accepted certificates for Internet principals. These certificates could then be used to provide complementary security services, such as authentication, data confidentiality and integrity, and nonrepudiation services. The tool to achieve this goal is cryptography. The following chapters elaborate on cryptography and its use providing security services on the WWW.

References

[1]   Oppliger, R., *Internet and Intranet Security, Second Edition*, Norwood, MA: Artech House, 2002.

[2]   Fraser, B., "Site Security Handbook," Request for Comments 2196, September 1997.

[3]   Shirey, R., "Internet Security Glossary," Request for Comments 2828, May 2000.

[4]   Cheswick, W. R., and S. M. Bellovin, *Firewalls and Internet Security: Repelling the Wily Hacker*, Reading, MA: Addison-Wesley, 1994.

[5]   Cheswick, W. R., and S. M. Bellovin, "Network Firewalls," *IEEE Communications Magazine*, September 1994, pp. 50–57.

[6]   Siyan, K., and C. Hare, *Internet Firewalls and Network Security*, Indianapolis, IN: New Riders Publishing, 1995.

[7]   Zwicky, E. D., et al., *Building Internet Firewalls*, 2nd Edition, Sebastopol, CA: O'Reilly & Associates, 2000.

[8]   Garfinkel, S., and G. Spafford, *Practical UNIX and Internet Security*, 2nd ed., Sebastopol, CA: O'Reilly & Associates, 1996.

[9]   Mogul, J. C., "Simple and Flexible Datagram Access Controls for UNIX-Based Gateways," *Proceedings of the USENIX Summer Conference*, 1989, pp. 203–221.

[10]   Cheswick, B., "The Design of a Secure Internet Gateway," *Proceedings of the USENIX Summer Conference*, 1990, pp. 233–237.

[11]   Ranum, M. J., "A Network Firewall," *Proceedings of World Conference on System Administration Security*, July 1992, pp. 153–163.

[12]   Chapman, D. B., "Network (In)Security Through IP Packet Filtering," *Proceedings of USENIX UNIX Security Symposium III*, September 1992, pp. 63–76.

[13]   Avolio, F., and M. J. Ranum, "A Network Perimeter with Secure Internet Access," *Proceedings of the Internet Society Symposium on Network and Distributed System Security*, February 1994, pp. 109–119.

[14]   Koblas, D., and M. R. Koblas, "SOCKS," *Proceedings of USENIX UNIX Security III Symposium*, September 1992, pp. 77–82.

[15]   Leech, M., et al., "SOCKS Protocol Version 5," Request for Comments 1928, March 1996.

[16]   Leech, M., "Username/Password Authentication for SOCKS V5," Request for Comments 1929, March 1996.

[17]   McMahon, P., "GSS-API Authentication Method for SOCKS Version 5," Request for Comments 1961, June 1996.

[18]   Rigney, C., et al., "Remote Authentication Dial-In User Service (RADIUS)," Request for Comments 2138, April 1997.

[19]   Rigney, C., "RADIUS Accounting," Request for Comments 2139, April 1997.

[20] Finseth, C., "An Access Control Protocol, Sometimes Called TACACS," Request for Comments 1492, July 1993.

[21] Rekhter, Y., et al., "Address Allocation for Private Internets," Request for Comments 1918 (BCP 5), February 1996.

[22] Oppliger, R., "Internet Kiosk: Internet Security Enters the Middle Ages," *IEEE Computer*, Vol. 28, October 1995, pp. 100–101.

Contents

4.1 Introduction

4.2 Cryptographic hash functions

4.3 Secret key cryptography

4.4 Public key cryptography

4.5 Digital envelopes

4.6 Protection of cryptographic keys

4.7 Generation of pseudorandom bit sequences

4.8 Legal Issues

4.9 Notation

References

Cryptographic Techniques

In this chapter, we introduce and briefly overview some cryptographic techniques that are used in the rest of the book. More specifically, we introduce the topic in Section 4.1; address cryptographic hash functions, secret key cryptography, and public key cryptography in Sections 4.2, 4.3, and 4.4, respectively; address digital envelopes in Section 4.5; and elaborate on some techniques to protect private keys and generate pseudorandom bit sequences in Sections 4.6 and 4.7. Finally, we discuss some legal issues that surround the use of cryptography in Section 4.8, and introduce a notation that can be used to describe cryptographic protocols and applications in Section 4.9.

Note that this chapter is far too short to provide a comprehensive overview about all cryptographic techniques that are relevant for WWW security. For this purpose, you must read one (or several) of the many books on cryptography that are available today. Among these books, I particularly recommend [1–7].

4.1 Introduction

According to [4], the term *cryptography* refers to the study of mathematical techniques related to various aspects of information security such as confidentiality, data integrity, entity authentication, and data origin authentication. It is commonly agreed that cryptography is a major enabling technology for network security, and that cryptographic algorithms and protocols are essential building blocks:

‣ A *cryptographic* algorithm is an algorithm defined by a sequence of steps precisely specifying the actions required to calculate a specific function of the input data. Most of the time, cryptographic algorithms are used to achieve specific security objectives.

‣ A *cryptographic* protocol is a distributed algorithm defined by a sequence of steps precisely specifying the actions required of two or more entities.

Cryptographic algorithms and protocols are being studied in both theory and practice. The aim is to design and come up with algorithms and protocols that are both secure and practical. Note, however, that there are at least two basic approaches to discussing the security of cryptographic algorithms and protocols:

‣ *Computational security* measures the computational effort required to break a specific cryptographic algorithm or protocol. An algorithm or protocol is said to be computationally secure if the best method for breaking it requires at least n operations, where n is some specified, usually very large, number. The problem is that no known practical algorithm or protocol can be proven to be secure under this definition. In practice, an algorithm or protocol is called *computationally secure* if the best known method of breaking it requires an unreasonably large amount of computational resources (e.g., time or memory). Another approach is to provide evidence of computational security by reducing the security of an algorithm or protocol to some well-studied problem that is thought to be difficult. For example, it may be possible to prove that an algorithm or protocol is secure if a given integer cannot be factored or a discrete logarithm cannot be computed. Algorithms and protocols of this type are sometimes called provably secure, but it must be understood that this approach only provides a proof of security relative to the difficulty of solving another problem, not an absolute proof of security.

‣ *Unconditional security* measures the security of a cryptographic algorithm or protocol when there is no upper bound placed on the amount of computational resources an adversary has at hand. Consequently, an algorithm or protocol is called unconditionally secure if it cannot be broken, even with infinite time and memory.

The computational security of a cryptographic algorithm or protocol can be studied from the point of view of computational complexity, whereas the unconditional security cannot be studied from this point of view because computational resources are allowed to be infinite. The appropriate framework in which unconditional security must be studied is probability theory, and the application thereof in communication or information theory [8, 9].

Unconditional security is preferable from a security point of view, because it protects against an infinitely powerful adversary. Unfortunately, unconditional security is generally hard and expensive to achieve in many cases, and sometimes impossible. For example, theory shows that unconditionally secure encryption systems use very long keys, making them unsuitable for most practical applications. Similarly, there is no such thing as an unconditionally secure public key cryptosystem. The best we can achieve is provable security, in the sense that the problem of breaking the public key cryptosystem is arguably at least as difficult as solving a complex mathematical problem. Consequently, one is satisfied with computational security, given some reasonable assumptions about the computational power of a potential adversary. But keep in mind that the security that a computationally secure cryptographic algorithm or protocol may provide is, for the most part, based on the perceived difficulty of a mathematical problem, such as the factorization problem or the discrete logarithm problem in the case of public key cryptography. Confidence in the security of such systems may be high because the problems are public and many minds have attempted to attack them. However, the vulnerability remains that a new insight or computing technology may defeat this type of cryptography. There are at least two recent developments that provide some evidence for this intrinsic vulnerability:

▸ In 1994, Peter W. Shor proposed randomized polynomial-time algorithms for computing discrete logarithms and factoring integers on a quantum computer, a computational device based on quantum mechanical principles [10, 11]. Note that it is not known how to build a quantum computer of a useful size; it is not even known to be possible at all.

▸ Also in 1994, Len M. Adleman[1] demonstrated the feasibility of using tools from molecular biology to solve an instance of the directed Hamiltonian path problem, which is known to be hard[2] [12]. The problem instance was encoded in molecules of deoxyribonucleic acid (DNA), and the steps of the computation were performed with

---

1. Len M. Adleman is a coinventor of the Rivest, Shamir, and Adleman (RSA) cryptosystem.
2. According to theoretical computer science, the directed Hamiltonian path problem is NP-complete.

standard protocols and enzymes. Adleman notes that while the currently available fastest supercomputers can execute approximately 10^{12} operations per second, it is plausible for DNA computers to execute 10^{20} or even more operations per second. Moreover, a DNA computer would be far more energy efficient than existing supercomputers. Similar to the quantum computer, it is not clear at present whether it is feasible to actually build a DNA computer with such performance characteristics. Further information on DNA computing can be found in the relevant literature (e.g., [13]).

Should either quantum computers or DNA computers ever become practical, they would have a tremendous impact on modern cryptography. In fact, many cryptographic algorithms and protocols that are computationally secure would be rendered worthless. This is particularly true for algorithms and protocols that make use of public key cryptography.

Cryptographic algorithms and protocols are used to establish secured channels (both in terms of authenticity and integrity, as well as confidentiality). Note the subtle difference between a *secure* channel and a *secured* channel. Certain channels are assumed to be secure, including trusted couriers and personal contacts between communicating parties, whereas other channels may be secured by physical or cryptographic techniques. Physical security may be established through physical means, such as dedicated communication links with corresponding access controls put in place, or the use of *quantum cryptography*. Contrary to conventional cryptography, the security of quantum cryptography does not rely upon any complexity-theoretic or probability-theoretic assumptions, but is based on the Heisenberg uncertainty principle of quantum physics [14]. As such, quantum cryptography is immune to advances in computing power and human cleverness. In the future, quantum cryptography may provide a physical alternative to unconditionally secure cryptographic algorithms and protocols. In the meantime, however, conventional and computationally secure cryptographic algorithms and protocols are much easier to use and deploy. Consequently, we are not going to delve into the details of quantum cryptography in this book. You may refer to any book mentioned above to get information about quantum cryptography.

4.2 Cryptographic hash functions

According to [4], a *hash function* is a function h that has, as a minimum, the following two properties:

1. h maps an input x of arbitrary finite bit-length, to an output $h(x)$ of fixed bit-length (compression);

2. Given h and x, $h(x)$ is easy to compute (ease of computation).

In addition, hash functions that are relevant for cryptographic applications (i.e., cryptographic hash functions) may fulfill one or several of the following requirements:

▸ A hash function is *preimage resistant* (or *one-way*) if for essentially all prespecified outputs, it is computationally infeasible to find any input that hashes to that output, that is, to find any preimage x' such that $h(x') = y$ when given any y for which a corresponding input is not known.

▸ A hash function is *second-preimage resistant* (or *weak collision resistant*) if it is computationally infeasible to find any second input that has the same output as any specified input, that is, given x, to find a second preimage $x' \neq x$ such that $h(x) = h(x')$.

▸ A hash function is *collision resistant* (or *strong collision resistant*) if it is computationally infeasible to find any distinct inputs x, x' that have the same output, that is, such that $h(x) = h(x')$.

In the literature, the term *one-way hash function* (OWHF) or *weak one-way hash function* is often used to refer to a hash function that is both preimage resistant and second-preimage resistant, whereas the term *collision resistant hash function* (CRHF) or *strong one-way hash function* is often used to refer to a hash function that is collision resistant. Furthermore, the term *cryptographic hash function* is used to refer to either of them (i.e., OWHF or CRHF).

Mainly because of their efficiency, *cryptographic hash functions* are of central importance for cryptographic algorithms and protocols. For example, cryptographic hash functions can be used to compute and verify digests for arbitrary messages. In this context, these functions may also be called *message digest algorithms*, and in this book we use both terms synonymously and interchangeably. Also, keyed cryptographic hash functions can be used to compute and verify *message authentication codes* (MACs). Almost all cryptographic security protocols make use of MACs in one way or another.

All definitions given above are not precise in a mathematically strong sense, because they do not resolve what the terms *easy* and *computationally infeasible* actually mean. Nevertheless, we want to use these definitions in this book. It is important to note that the existence of OWHF (or even

CRHF) is still an unproven assumption and that, until today, no function has been shown to be preimage resistant (i.e., one-way) in a mathematically pure sense. Obviously, a sufficiently large domain prohibiting an exhaustive search is a necessary but not sufficient condition for a function to be preimage resistant.

Most cryptographic hash functions in use today work on similar principles. They have a basic compression function that is iteratively applied on subsequent blocks of data (until the result of the last compression step is taken as output value). Examples of cryptographic hash functions include MD2 [15], MD4 [16], MD5 [17], and the Secure Hash Algorithm 1 (SHA-1) [18]. MD2, MD4, and MD5 produce 128-bit hash values, whereas SHA-1 produces 160-bit hash values. RIPEMD is another example of an iterative cryptographic hash function. It was developed as part of a European research project and is basically a variation of MD4. RIPEMD-160 is a strengthened version of RIPEMD producing another 160-bit hash value [19]. As of this writing, MD5 and SHA-1 are by far the most widely used and deployed cryptographic hash functions. Due to some recent results in the cryptanalysis of MD5, SHA-1 is the preferred choice.

4.3 Secret key cryptography

Secret key cryptography refers to traditional cryptography. In this kind of cryptography, a secret key is established and shared between communicating peers, and the key is used to encrypt and decrypt messages on either side. Because of its symmetry, secret key cryptography is often referred to as *symmetric cryptography*.

The use of a secret key cryptosystem is overviewed in Figure 4.1. We assume that A on the left side wants to send a confidential message to B on the right side. A therefore shares a secret key K with B. This key may be preconfigured manually or distributed by a key distribution center (KDC). Note that during its initial distribution, K must be secured in terms of confidentiality, integrity, and authenticity. This is usually done by having the KDC encrypt K with secret keys that it shares with A and B, respectively. With regard to the use of cryptographic algorithms and protocols, persons are usually represented by cryptographic implementations (e.g., crypto boxes that implement an encryption algorithm). In Figure 4.1, the cryptographic implementations are represented with black rectangles that are located in front of A or B, respectively. A (or the crypto box representing A) encrypts a plaintext message P by applying an encryption function E and the key K, and sends the resulting ciphertext $C = E_K(P)$ to B. On the other side, B

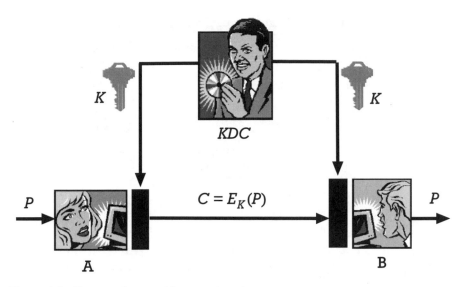

Figure 4.1 The use of a secret key cryptosystem.

(or the crypto box representing B) decrypts C by applying the decryption function D and the key K. B therefore computes $D_K(C) = D_K(E_K(P)) = P$, and recovers the plaintext P accordingly.

Secret key cryptography has been in use for many years in a variety of forms. Two basic categories of secret key cryptosystems are *block ciphers* and *stream ciphers*. As their names suggest, block ciphers operate on blocks of data (e.g., 64 bits), whereas stream ciphers operate on data one bit or byte at a time.

Examples of secret key cryptosystems that are in widespread use are itemized in Table 4.1 and overviewed next.[3] Again, you may refer to [4] for a comprehensive description of the cryptosystems and the corresponding encryption and decryption algorithms.

4.3.1 DES

The Data Encryption Standard (DES) is still the most well-known and widely deployed secret key cryptosystem in use today. It was originally designed by a group of researchers at IBM and published as Federal Information Processing Standard (FIPS) 46 in 1977 [20]. As such, it has been used for the encryption of unclassified information by the U.S. National Institute of Standards and Technology (NIST) for almost a quarter of a century.

---

3. Note that the cryptosystems are randomly chosen and that there are many others one may discuss.

Table 4.1 Secret Key Cryptosystems

Algorithm Name	Main Mode	Effective Key Length
DES	Block cipher	56 bits
Triple-DES (3DES)	Block cipher	112 or 168 bits
IDEA	Block cipher	128 bits
SAFER	Block cipher	64 or 128 bits
Blowfish	Block cipher	Variable from 1 up to 448 bits
CAST-128	Block cipher	128 bits
RC2, RC5, and RC6	Block cipher	Variable from 1 up to 2,048 bits
RC4	Stream cipher	Variable from 1 up to 2,048 bits

DES operates as a block cipher with 64-bit blocks, 16 rounds, and a variable key length up to 56 bits. In electronic code book (ECB) mode, DES encrypts data in discrete blocks of 64 bits. To improve its cryptographical strength, DES is often used in cipher block chaining (CBC) mode. In this mode, the encryption of each block depends on the contents of the previous one, preventing an interloper from tampering with the message by rearranging the encrypted blocks. Furthermore, there are two modes that can be used to turn DES into a stream cipher: cipher feedback (CFB) mode and output feedback (OFB) mode.

DES's 56-bit effective key length was sufficiently secure during its first two decades of operation, but it is far too short today. In fact, it has become feasible to perform an exhaustive key search in a reasonable amount of time.[4]

4.3.2 Triple-DES

One way to improve the cryptographical strength of a secret key cryptosystem with limited key length (e.g., DES) is to apply the algorithm multiple times. Applying the algorithm twice does not improve the situation, because of the existence of a specific cryptanalytical attack.[5] Consequently, at least three applications are necessary for a security improvement, and the threefold application of DES is called Triple-DES (3DES). It can be used with two or three different keys, and the resulting secret key cryptosystems are

---

4. http://www.eff.org/descracker
5. The attack is called *meet-in-the-middle* attack. It requires that a known plaintext is encrypted with all possible keys, and that a corresponding ciphertext is decrypted with all possible keys. If an encryption result matches a decryption result in the middle, a key candidate is found (that's why the attack is called meet-in-the-middle attack). The key candidate must be verified using another plaintext-ciphertext pair.

usually called two-key 3DES or three-key 3DES, respectively. Many contemporary applications use 3DES as a replacement for DES. Note, however, that the use of 3DES is not very efficient (in fact, it is approximately three times slower than DES), and that there are many real-time applications that require faster encryption algorithms.

4.3.3 IDEA

The International Data Encryption Algorithm (IDEA) was developed by Xuejia Lai and James Massey in the early 1990s at the ETH Zurich, Switzerland [21]. IDEA is a 64-bit block cipher that uses a 128-bit key. The algorithm is patented and must be licensed for commercial use.

4.3.4 SAFER

After having developed IDEA, James Massey proposed SAFER K-64 and SAFER K-128. As their names suggest, SAFER K-64 uses a 64-bit key [22], whereas SAFER K-128 uses a proprietary key schedule algorithm that is able to accommodate 128-bit keys. Furthermore, SAFER K-64 uses 6 rounds, whereas SAFER K-128 recommends 10 rounds (12 maximum).

4.3.5 Blowfish

The Blowfish algorithm was developed by Bruce Schneier [23]. It is a DES-like encryption algorithm that can be used as a block cipher with 64-bit blocks, 16 rounds, and variable key lengths up to 448 bits.

4.3.6 CAST-128

The term *CAST* refers to a design procedure for a family of DES-like encryption algorithms with variable key size and numbers of rounds. In RFC 2144, a 128-bit CAST encryption algorithm is specified [24]. This algorithm is called CAST-128 and is used and widely deployed for Internet applications.

4.3.7 RC2, RC4, RC5, and RC6

RC2, RC4, RC5, and RC6 are secret key cryptosystems with variable key lengths that were designed by Ronald L. Rivest for RSA Security, Inc.:

- RC2 is a block cipher (block size is 64 bits), designed as a replacement for DES.

- RC4 is a stream cipher.

- RC5 is a block cipher that is configurable with regard to word length and number of rounds (in addition to the ley length).

- RC6 is a recent proposal to improve RC5.

The RC2 and RC4 algorithms were originally protected by trade secrets, but were disassembled, reverse-engineered, and anonymously posted to a Usenet newsgroup in 1996 and 1994, respectively.

4.3.8 AES

In November 2001, the U.S. NIST officially released FIPS 197 that specifies an Advanced Encryption Standard (AES) to replace DES [25]. The AES emerged from a proposal called Rijndael that originated from Belgium. You may refer to `http://www.esat.kuleuven.ac.be/~rijmen/rijndael` for more information about the Rijndael algorithm. In addition, there is an official AES home page[6] hosted by the U.S. NIST.

4.4 Public key cryptography

The idea of using one-way functions, which can only be inverted if a certain secret (a so-called trapdoor) is known, has led to the invention of *public key cryptography* or *asymmetric cryptography* [26].[7] Today, public key cryptography is a battlefield for mathematicians and theoretical computer scientists. We are not going to delve into the mathematical details. Instead, we address public key cryptography from a practical point of view. From this point of view, a public key cryptosystem is simply a cryptosystem in which a user has a pair of mathematically related keys:

- A *public key* that can be published without doing any harm to the system's overall security;

---

6. `http://csrc.nist.gov/encryption/aes`
7. In spite of the fact that [26] is commonly used to refer to the invention of public key cryptography, similar ideas were pursued by Ralph C. Merkle.

▶ A *private key* that is assumed to never leave the possession of its owner.

For both the public and private keys, it must be computationally infeasible for an outsider to derive one from the other.

The use of a public key cryptosystem is overviewed in Figure 4.2. Again, A and B represent users, and the dark rectangles located in front of them represent the implementations of the cryptographic algorithms and protocols in use. A and B each has a key pair (k_A, k_A^{-1}) and (k_B, k_B^{-1}). The private keys k_A^{-1} and k_B^{-1} must not be revealed to anyone, whereas the public keys k_A and k_B must be publicly available in certified form. This basically means that they are digitally signed by a *certification authority* as further addressed below.

If A wants to securely transfer a plaintext message P to B, she does the following things:

1. She gets the public key of B (i.e., k_B) from an authentic source.

2. She encrypts P with k_B.

3. She sends the resulting ciphertext $C = E_{k_B}(P)$ to B. (The term $E_{k_B}(P)$ is abbreviated with $E_B(P)$ in Figure 4.2).

On the other side, B uses his private key k_B^{-1} to successfully decrypt $P = D_{k_B^{-1}}(C) = D_{k_B^{-1}}(E_{k_B}(P))$.

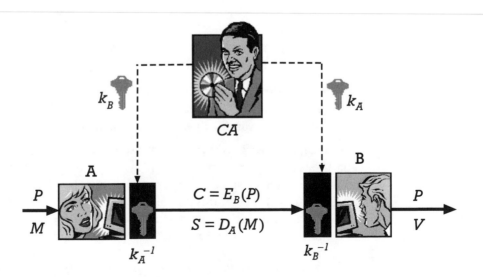

Figure 4.2 The use of a public key cryptosystem.

A public key cryptosystem can be used not only to protect the confidentiality of a message, but also to protect its authenticity and integrity. If A wants to protect the authenticity and integrity of a message M, she creates a digital signature $S = D_{k_A}(M)$ (the term $D_{k_A}(M)$ is abbreviated with $D_A(P)$ in Figure 4.2) for M and send it together with the message to B. Using the public key of A (i.e., k_A), B can now verify the digital signature. Consequently, the value V in Figure 4.2 represents a boolean value (i.e., either the digital signature is correctly verified or it is not).

Digital signatures provide an electronic analog of handwritten signatures for electronic documents, and—similar to handwritten signatures—digital signatures must not be forgeable, recipients must be able to verify them, and the signers must not be able to repudiate them later. However, a major difference between a handwritten signature and a digital signature is that the digital signature cannot be constant, but must be a function of the document on which it appears. If this were not the case, a digital signature, because of its electronic nature, could be copied and attached to arbitrary documents.

Arbitrated digital signature schemes are based on secret key cryptography. In such a scheme, a trusted third party (TTP) validates the signature and forwards it on the signer's behalf. Obviously, this does not scale and requires a TTP that may become a bottleneck. Consequently, digital signature schemes should come along without TTPs taking an active role. They usually require the use of public key cryptography: Signed messages are sent directly from signers to recipients. In essence, a *digital signature scheme* consists of the following:

▸ A key-generation algorithm that randomly selects a public key pair;

▸ A signature algorithm that takes as input a message and a private key, and that generates as output a digital signature for the message;

▸ A signature verification algorithm that takes as input a digital signature and a public key, and that generates as output a message and an information bit according to whether the signature is valid for the message.

A comprehensive overview and discussion of public-key-based digital signature schemes are given in [27]. According to the OSI security architecture, a digital signature refers to data appended to, or a cryptographic transformation of, a data unit that allows a recipient of the data unit to prove the source and integrity of the data unit and protect against forgery (e.g., by the recipient). Consequently, there are two classes of digital signatures:

1. A *digital signature giving message recovery* refers to the situation in which a cryptographic transformation is applied to a data unit.

In this case, the data is automatically recovered if the recipient verifies the signature.

2. A *digital signature with appendix* refers to the situation in which some cryptographically protected data is appended to the data unit. In fact, the data represents a digital signature and can be decoupled from the data unit that it signs.

The structure of a digital signature giving message recovery (a) and a digital signature with appendix (b) are illustrated in Figure 4.3. A dark rectangle represents an encrypted message part, whereas a white rectangle represents a message part that is not encrypted.

In the case of digital signatures with appendix, the bandwidth limitation of public key cryptography is unimportant because of the use of one-way hash functions as auxiliaries. A can use her private key k_A^{-1} to compute a digital signature $S = D_A(M)$ or $S = D_A(h(M))$ for message M. In the second case, h refers to a cryptographic hash function that is applied to M before generating the digital signature. In summary, A does the following things when she computes and sends to B a digital signature with appendix for message M:

1. She uses a cryptographic hash function h to compute $h(M)$.

2. She encrypts $h(M)$ with her private key k_A^{-1}. The result represents the digital signature that is appended to the message.

3. She transmits M and the digital signature to B.

On the other side, B does the following things to verify the signature:

1. He hashes the message M with the same cryptographic hash function h.

2. He decrypts the digital signature with A's public key (i.e., k_A).

3. He verifies whether the two values match or not (the signature is verified only if the values match).

(a)

(b)

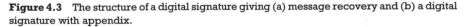

Figure 4.3 The structure of a digital signature giving (a) message recovery and (b) a digital signature with appendix.

The use of public key cryptography considerably simplifies the problem of key distribution. Note that in Figure 4.2, instead of providing A and B with a unique session key that is protected in terms of confidentiality, integrity, and authenticity, the trusted third party, which is now called a *certification authority* (CA), has only to provide A and B with the public key of the communicating peer. This key is public in nature and need not be protected in terms of confidentiality. Nevertheless, the use of public key cryptography requires an authentication framework that binds public keys to user identities. As further addressed in Chapter 7, a *public key certificate* is a certified proof of such binding vouched for by a TTP acting as a CA. According to *Webster's Dictionary*, the term *certificate* refers to a document stating the truth. In the digital world we live in today, the term is mostly used to refer to a collection of information to which a digital signature has been affixed by some authority who is recognized and trusted by some community of certificate users. According to this definition, there exist various types of certificates that potentially may serve many purposes. In either case, a certificate is a form of credentials. Examples of credentials used in daily life are the driver's license, Social Security card, and birth certificate. Each of these credentials has some information on it identifying its owner and some authorization stating that someone else has confirmed the information.

A public key (or digital) certificate consists of three main elements:

1. A public key;

2. Certificate information that refers to the certificate owner's identity, such as his or her name;

3. One or more digital signatures.

The aim of the digital signature(s) on the certificate is to state that the other certificate information has been attested to by some other person or entity.

A digital certificate can be one of a number of different formats, including, for example, PGP and ITU-T X.509. Again, this point is further addressed in Chapter 7. In the following sections, we overview some public key cryptosystems that are in widespread use today.

4.4.1 RSA

The most widely used public key cryptosystem is RSA, invented by Ronald L. Rivest, Adi Shamir, and Len M. Adleman at MIT in 1977 [28]. The RSA cryptosystem gets its security from the difficulty and intractability of the integer factorization problem. What this means is that it is fairly simple to multiply two large prime numbers, but difficult to compute the prime factors of a large number. One of the nice properties of RSA is that the same operation (i.e., exponentiation modulo a large number) can be used for both message encryption and decryption, as well as digital signature generation and verification. This is not the case for most other public key cryptosystems.

Mathematically spoken, the RSA public key cryptosystem requires two distinct large primes (p and q). Denote $n = pq$ and $\phi(n) = (p-1)(q-1)$, where ϕ refers to *Euler's totient function*. Each user chooses a large number $d > 1$ such that $gcd(d, \phi(n)) = 1$ and computes the number e ($1 < e < \phi(n)$) that satisfies the congruence $ed \equiv 1 \pmod{\phi(n)}$. The numbers n and e constitute the public key, whereas the remaining items p, q, $\phi(n)$, and d form the private information. More commonly, d is referred to as the private key.

Against this background, message encryption and decryption work as follows:

▸ To encrypt, one raises the plaintext block P to the power of e and reduces modulo n: $C = P^e \pmod{n}$;

▸ To decrypt, one raises the ciphertext block C to the power of d and reduces modulo n: $P = C^d \pmod{n}$.

Digital signature generation and verification uses the same algorithms with different keys (the private key is used to digitally sign a message, whereas the public key is used to verify the signature).

The RSA public key cryptosystem was protected by U.S. Patent No. 4,405,829 "Cryptographic Communications System and Method," issued and granted to MIT on September 20, 1983. The patent expired on September 20, 2000. Outside the United States, the RSA public key cryptosystem has never been protected by a patent.

4.4.2 Diffie-Hellman

In 1977, Whitfield Diffie and Martin Hellman proposed a key agreement protocol that allows participants to agree on a key over an insecure public channel [26]. The protocol gets its security from the difficulty and intractability of the discrete logarithm problem in a finite group, such as the multiplicative group of a finite field. What this basically means is that, in general, the inverse operation of the exponentiation function is the logarithm function. There are efficient algorithms for computing logarithms in many groups; however, one does not know a polynomial-time algorithm for computing discrete logarithms in cyclic groups. For example, for a very large prime number p and two smaller numbers y and a, it is computationally intractable to find an x that satisfies the equation $y = a^x \bmod p$.

Mathematically speaking, the Diffie-Hellman key agreement protocol requires a finite cyclic group G of order $|G|$ and generator a. To agree on a session key, A and B secretly choose elements x_A and x_B in G. These elements represent A and B's private keys. A and B then compute their public keys $y_A = a^{x_A}$ and $y_B = a^{x_B}$, and exchange these public keys over an unsecured public channel. Finally, A and B compute $K_{AB} = y_B^{x_A} = a^{x_B x_A}$ and $K_{BA} = y_A^{x_B} = a^{x_A x_B}$. Note that $K_{AB} = K_{BA}$, so this value can actually be used as a shared secret or session key to secure communications between A and B. Also note that an eavesdropper seeing either or both of the public keys cannot derive either private key nor the shared secret, because of the difficulty of the discrete logarithm problem.

The Diffie-Hellman key agreement protocol was protected by U.S. Patent No. 4,200,770, "Cryptographic Apparatus and Method," issued and granted to Stanford University on April 29, 1980. The patent expired in 1997. Similar to the RSA public key cryptosystem, the Diffie-Hellman key agreement protocol has never been protected by a patent outside the United States.

4.4.3 ElGamal

In the early 1980s, Taher ElGamal adapted the Diffie-Hellman key agreement protocol and came up with a public key cryptosystem that can be used for data encryption and digital signatures [29, 30]. Contrary to RSA, however, the ElGamal algorithms for data encryption and decryption are different from the the ElGamal algorithms for digital signature generation and verification. This is no serious drawback but is also not advantageous from an implementor's point of view.

Unlike many other public key cryptosystems, the ElGamal public key cryptosystem has not been patented in the U.S.

4.4.4 DSS

In the early 1990s, the U.S. NIST published the Digital Signature Standard (DSS) as a viable alternative to RSA signature schemes. The DSS refers to an optimized modification of the ElGamal cryptosystem that can be used only for digital signature generation and verification [31].

4.4.5 ECC

More recently, the use of elliptic curve cryptography (ECC) has attracted a lot of interest. ECC-based public key cryptosystems obtain their security from the difficulty and intractability of the elliptic curve discrete logarithm problem (that uses groups of points on elliptic curves). As illustrated in Table 4.2, a number of different types of cryptography have been defined over elliptic curves. The resulting ECC-based public key cryptosystems seem to be advantageous with regard to their security properties (meaning that smaller keys are required for a similar level of security). As such, they are particularly useful in situations where small keys are required (e.g., mobile and wireless applications).

Unlike RSA, the general category of ECC is not patented. Individual companies, however, have filed patents for specific efficiency or security algorithms that are related to ECC. Most importantly, the Certicom Corporation[8] holds several patents in this field.

4.5 Digital envelopes

There are advantages and disadvantages related to both secret and public key cryptography. For example, the use of secret key cryptography is efficient but does not scale well beyond a certain number of participants. Furthermore, secret key cryptography does not provide the possibility to digitally sign data. Conversely, public key cryptography solves the scalability and digital signature problems but is highly inefficient in terms of computational resources.

In an attempt to combine the advantages of secret and public key cryptography, a hybrid scheme may be used. In short, a hybrid scheme combines secret and public key cryptography to produce a scheme that is as efficient and effective as possible. For example, the *digital envelope* is a hybrid scheme that is heavily used in many applications. The aim of a digital envelope is similar to a letter envelope: It must protect the confidentiality of a message. As such, the digital envelope provides a digital analog for

Table 4.2 ECC-Based Public Key Cryptosystems

Acronym	Text
ECDH	Elliptic curve Diffie-Hellman key agreement
ECDSA	Elliptic curve digital signature algorithm
ECES	Elliptic curve encryption scheme
ECMQV	Elliptic curve MQV key agreement
ECNRA	Elliptic curve Nyberg-Rueppel signature scheme with appendix

---

8. http://www.certicom.com

the letter envelope in the physical world (hopefully with better security properties).

When A wants to send a confidential message M to B, she can generate a digital envelope for M and send the envelope to B. On the sender's side the procedure is as follows:[9]

1. A retrieves B's public key k_B from a directory service or from a local repository.

2. A randomly generates a transaction key K from a secret key cryptosystem.

3. A encrypts M with K (the result is $\{M\}K$).

4. A encrypts K with k_B (the result is $\{K\}k_B$).

5. A concatenates $\{M\}K$ with $\{K\}k_B$, and sends the result to B.

Upon receipt of $\{M\}K$ and $\{K\}k_B$, B uses his private key k_B^{-1} to decrypt the message. The two-step procedure is as follows:

1. B decrypts $\{K\}k_B$ with k_B^{-1} (the result is K).

2. B decrypts $\{M\}K$ with K (the result is M).

Obviously, an alternative procedure would be to directly encrypt the message M with B's public key k_B, and to send the result, $\{M\}k_B$, to B. However, the use of a digital envelope has at least two advantages compared with this simple scheme:

▸ First, the use of a digital envelope is more efficient. Remember from our previous discussions that public key cryptography is computationally expensive compared with secret key cryptography. Consequently, encrypting a message with a public key requires more computational resources than encrypting a message with a secret key. The longer the message, the more efficient and advantageous the use of secret key cryptography.

▸ Second, the use of a digital envelope is more appropriate for messages sent to multiple recipients. If A wanted to send a message M to

---

9.   The notation used is introduced in Section 4.9.

recipients $B_1, B_2, \ldots, B_n$ $(n > 1)$, she would have to build $\{M\}k_{B_i}$ for each recipient B_i $(i = 1, \ldots, n)$ individually. The resulting message would grow in proportion to the number of recipients. For example, if A wanted to send a 1-MB file to $n = 4$ recipients $(B_1, \ldots, B_4)$, the resulting messages would fill 4 MB of data. Contrary to that, the use of digital envelopes considerably reduces this amount of data. If the public keys of the $n = 4$ recipients are 1,024 bits long each, the digitally enveloped message would sum up to 1 MB $+ 4 \times 1$ KB $=$ 1.004 MB of data.

Consequently, the use of digital envelopes is almost always advantageous, as compared with public key cryptography used for bulk data encryption.

4.6 Protection of cryptographic keys

Any system that uses cryptographic techniques has to deal with keys that must be protected against passive and active attacks. This is equally true for session keys that originate from a secret key cryptosystem and private keys that originate from a public key cryptosystem. If such a key is locally stored on a computer system, it is vulnerable to access and misuse by unauthorized users. In fact, file permissions alone are often not adequate for protecting cryptographic keys on most computer systems, though they are part of an overall solution. Cryptographic keys protected only by file permissions are generally vulnerable to intruders and the accidental missetting of permissions.

Encryption is an accepted solution for protecting cryptographic keys stored on removable media, such as floppy disks. The use of encryption, however, also requires access to some other key that must be protected from disclosure. Consequently, the use of encryption to protect cryptographic keys leads to a recursion, and this recursion can only be stopped by making some key derivable from otherwise available information. The recommended advice is to make this information a passphrase selected by the user. A passphrase is different from a password in that no restrictions are usually placed on its length or value. This accomplishes two useful features:

1. The domain from which the passphrase is chosen is limited only by the input device of the user.

2. The user can select an easily remembered value, such as a favorite quotation or other concatenation of easily remembered words.

The key that is used to actually encrypt and protect another key (e.g., the user's private key) is derived from the user's passphrase. A possibility to compute a random-looking hash value from a user's passphrase is to use an OWHF. Whenever the private key is needed (e.g., to decrypt an encryption key or to digitally sign a message), the user enters his or her passphrase, the cryptographic key is derived, the private key is decrypted, and then the private key is available for use. Typically, the file that is used to store the encrypted private key also includes a one-way hash value of the private key. Checking the hash value after decrypting the file contents provides a fast mechanism for determining if the correct passphrase was entered by the user. Without the hash value check, the only mechanism by which the private key's value can be checked would be to use it and see if it works. This may be computationally expensive.

If a user's private key is stored in encrypted form, the user must enter his or her passphrase to decrypt and locally use the key. From a security point of view, this is the optimal behavior. However, users quickly become irritated if they must send or receive more than a few messages during a session (because they have to reenter their passphrase multiple times). Consequently, many products include a feature that allows the passphrases to be kept in memory and users to choose usability over security. This badly hurts the overall security of the products (because the passphrases are vulnerable in memory and can be attacked accordingly).

In summary, the combination of file permissions and passphrase-derived encryption provides some nondisclosure protection for cryptographic keys (if the users choose appropriate passphrases). In addition, there are some cryptographic techniques (e.g., cryptographic camouflage as further addressed in [32]) that can be used to provide better protection for locally stored private keys. Even better protection is provided if the file containing the encrypted cryptographic key is stored on a removable media, such as a floppy disk. Best possible protection is available if the key is stored in some tamper-resistant hardware device, such as a smart card, a PCMCI card, or a USB token. Recent research and development activities also focus on the use of alternative hardware devices, such as cellular phones, personal digital assistants (e.g., Palm Pilots), or any other device that implements the Wireless Application Protocol (WAP). There is arguably no single best hardware token to store cryptographic keys. Any device the user usually carries around with him or her is a potentially good hardware token and may serve this purpose (perhaps after some modification).

4.7 Generation of pseudorandom bit sequences

Many cryptographic systems use sequences of random (or pseudorandomly generated) bits. For example, if an e-mail message is digitally enveloped, an encryption key—sometimes also called *session key*—must be randomly selected by the sender of the message. This key is used to encrypt and digitally envelope the message. Also, random or pseudorandom numbers are required to initially generate public key pairs.

Randomness is a statistical property of a sequence of values. In the case of bit values, the requirement is for an adversary to be unable to predict the next bit in a sequence even when all previously generated bits are known. The problem is that if it is possible to predict some of the sequence of bits used, it may be possible to reduce the size of the domain from which the key being generated is selected. If the domain is significantly reduced, an exhaustive key search may become feasible.

Locating a source of unpredictable bits presents a unique challenge on most computer systems (because a hardware source of unpredictable bits is usually not available). Consequently, a whole branch of cryptographic research is dedicated to the problem of how to generate pseudorandom bit sequences using only software. In fact, there are various approaches to address this problem. For example, one software-based approach is to use a cryptographically strong OWHF to hash a large amount of information with limited unpredictability available. Such information can, for example, be derived from the current status of the computer system (using corresponding system commands) or the mouse movements and position of keyboard strokes. Because a OWHF generates a fixed size quantity, the process is iterated as many times as are necessary to get the required number of bits.

In 1994, an informational RFC was published that addresses the problem of how to randomly or pseudorandomly generate bit sequences [33]. It recommends the use of hardware and shows that the existing hardware on many systems can be used for this purpose. Also, it provides suggestions for ameliorating the problem when a hardware solution is not available.

4.8 Legal issues

There are some legal issues to keep in mind when using cryptographic techniques. In particular, there are patent claims; regulations for the import, export, and use of cryptography; and legislation for electronic and digital signatures. Some legal issues are briefly mentioned next. You may refer to [34, 35] for more information about the legal implications of using cryptography.

4.8.1 Patent claims

Patents applied to computer programs are usually called *software patents*. In the U.S. computer industry, software patents are a subject of ongoing controversy. Some of the earliest and most important software patents granted by the U.S. Patent and Trademark Office were in the field of cryptography. These software patents go back to the late 1960s and early 1970s. Although computer algorithms were widely thought to be unpatentable at that time, cryptography patents were granted because they were written as patents on encryption devices built in hardware. Indeed, most early encryption devices were built in hardware because general-purpose computers simply could not execute the encryption algorithms fast enough in software. For example, IBM obtained several patents in the early 1970s on its Lucifer algorithm, which went on to become the DES. Today, many secret key cryptosystems also are covered by patent claims. For example, DES is patented but royalty-free, whereas IDEA is patented and royalty-free for noncommercial use, but requires a license for commercial use. Later in the 1970s, many pioneers in the field of public key cryptography filed and obtained patents for their work. Consequently, the field of public key cryptography is largely governed by a couple of software patents. Some of them have already expired (e.g., the Diffie-Hellman and RSA patents) or are about to expire soon.

Outside the United States, the patent situation is quite different. For example, patent law in Europe and Japan differs from U.S. patent law in one very important aspect. In the United States, an inventor has a grace period of one year between the first public disclosure of an invention and the last day on which a patent application can be filed. In Europe and Japan, there is no grace period. Any public disclosure instantly forfeits all patent rights. Because the inventions contained in the original patents related to public key cryptography were publicly disclosed before patent applications were filed, these algorithms were never patentable in Europe and Japan.[10]

Under U.S. patent law, patent infringement is not a criminal offense, and the penalties and damages are the jurisdiction of the civil courts. It is the responsibility of the user of a particular cryptographic algorithm or technique to make sure that correct licenses have been obtained from the corresponding patent holders. If these licenses do not exist, the patent holders can sue the user in court. Therefore, most products that make use of cryptographic algorithms or techniques include the licenses required to use them.

---

10. As a consequence of the lack of patent claims, public key cryptography has been more widely adapted in European countries and in Japan.

Finally, it is important to note that the IETF has a special requirement with regard to the use of patented technology in Internet standards track protocols. In fact, before approving a protocol specification for the Internet standards track, a written statement from a patent holder is required stating that a license will be made available to applicants under reasonable terms and conditions.

4.8.2 Regulations

There are different regulations for the use and export of cryptographic techniques.[11] For example, France had some regulations for the use of cryptographic techniques and some countries from the Far East still have them as well. On the other side, there are some countries that require that specific data be encrypted to certain standards. This is particularly true for medical data.

With regard to the export of cryptographic techniques, the situation is even more complicated. For example, the United States regulates the export of cryptographic systems and technical data regarding them. More specifically, U.S. export controls on commercial encryption products are administered by the Bureau of Export Administration (BXA) in the Department of Commerce (DoC). Regulations governing exports of encryption are found in the Export Administration Regulations (EAR). Consequently, if a U.S. company wants to sell cryptographic systems and technical data overseas, it must have export approval by the BXA according to the EAR.

On January 14, 2000, the BXA published a regulation implementing the White House's announcement of a new framework for U.S. export controls on encryption items (the announcement was made on September 16, 1999). The policy is in response to the changing global market, advances in technology, and the need to give U.S. industry better access to these markets, while continuing to provide essential protections for national security.[12] The regulation enlarges the use of license exceptions, implements the changes agreed to at the Wassenaar Arrangement[13] on export controls for conventional arms and dual-use goods and technologies in December 1998,

---

11. There are typically no regulations for the import of cryptographic techniques.

12. http://www.bxa.doc.gov/Encryption

13. The Wassenaar Arrangement is a treaty originally negotiated in July 1996 and signed by 31 countries to restrict the export of dual-use goods and technologies to specific countries considered to be dangerous. The countries that have signed the Wassenaar Arrangement include the former Coordinating Committee for Multilateral Export Controls (COCOM) member and cooperating countries, as well as some new countries such as Russia. The COCOM was an international munitions control organization that also restricted the export of cryptography as a dual-use technology. It was formally dissolved in March 1994. More recently, the Wassenaar

and eliminates the deemed export rule for encryption technology. In addition, new license exception provisions are created for certain types of encryption, such as source code and toolkits. There are some countries exempted from the regulation (i.e., Cuba, Iran, Iraq, Libya, North Korea, Sudan, and Syria). In these countries, some or all technologies and products mentioned in this book will not be available. In all other countries, most technologies and products mentioned in this book will be available.

4.8.3 Electronic and digital signature legislation

In the recent past, many countries have enacted electronic or digital signature laws in an effort to facilitate electronic commerce (e-commerce) and e-commerce applications:

▸ In the European Union (EU), the European Parliament and the Council of the European Union adopted Directive 1999/93/EC on a community framework for electronic signatures[14] on December 13, 1999. The purpose of the directive was (and still is) to facilitate the use of electronic signatures and to contribute to their legal recognition in Europe. According to the directive, EU "member states shall bring into force the laws, regulations and administrative provisions necessary to comply with this Directive before 19 July 2001." As of this writing, several EU member states already have an electronic signature law or are about to draft and enact one.

▸ In the United States, former president Bill Clinton signed the Electronic Signatures in Global and National Commerce Act (E-SIGN) on June 30, 2000. The E-SIGN Act implements a national uniform standard for all electronic transactions that encourages the use of electronic signatures, electronic contracts, and electronic records by providing legal certainty for these instruments when signatories comply with its standards. The E-SIGN Act became effective on October 1, 2000.

Arrangement was updated. The participating countries of the Wassenaar Arrangement are Argentina, Australia, Austria, Belgium, Bulgaria, Canada, Czech Republic, Denmark, Finland, France, Germany, Greece, Hungary, Ireland, Italy, Japan, Luxembourg, the Netherlands, New Zealand, Norway, Poland, Portugal, The Republic of Korea, Romania, Russian Federation, Slovak Republic, Spain, Sweden, Switzerland, Turkey, Ukraine, United Kingdom, and the United States. Further information on the Wassenaar Arrangement can be found on the Web by following the URL http://www.wassenaar.org.

14. http://europa.eu.int/comm/internal_market/en/media/sign

In addition, many countries outside the EU and the United States have enacted electronic or digital signature laws or are about to work out the legal details thereof (e.g., some countries in Asia).

Unfortunately, the formal specification of requirements for both certification service providers and cryptographic devices that can be used to securely store private keys and generate digital signatures (e.g., smart cards or USB tokens) is very difficult and challenging. For example, how do you measure and quantify the security and trustworthiness of a commercial certification service provider? What criteria are relevant? How do you take into account organizational criteria? Similarly, how do you measure and quantify the security of a cryptographic device that is used to store private keys and/or digitally sign documents? Does the device, for example, really sign what the user sees on the screen (i.e., what you sign is what you see) or can it be spoofed with wrong input data? Keep in mind that the cryptographic device runs in a potentially hostile environment and that any kind of spoofing attack is possible there.

The requirements for certification service providers and cryptographic devices tend to be either too strong or too weak:

▸ If the requirements are too strong, their implementation may become too expensive and prohibitive in practice. This is basically what happened in Germany when the first version of a signature law was put in place a couple of years ago.

▸ If the requirements are too weak, their implementation—or the security thereof—may be challenged in court. Consequently, the legal value of the resulting electronic or digital signatures may not be very high. Against this background, it will be very interesting to see the E-SIGN Act be applied in practice.

Against this background, it will be interesting to see the requirements of future electronic and digital signature legislations. In either case, there is still a long way to go until we use electronic or digital signatures the same way we use handwritten signatures in daily life. In the meantime, however, digital signatures may serve as evidence gathering tools.

4.9 Notation

As mentioned before, a cryptographic protocol is a distributed algorithm defined by a sequence of steps precisely specifying the actions required of two or more entities to achieve a specific security objective. The following notation is used in this book to describe cryptographic protocols:

- Capital letters, such as A, B, C, ..., are used to refer to principals. Note that many publications on cryptography and cryptographic protocols use names, such as Alice and Bob, to refer to principals. This is a convenient way of making things unambiguous with relatively few words, because the pronoun "she" can be used for Alice, and "he" can be used for Bob. However, the advantages and disadvantages of this naming scheme are controversial, and we are not going to use it in this book.

- K is used to refer to a secret key. A secret key is basically a key of a secret key cryptosystem.

- The pair (k, k^{-1}) is used to refer to a public key pair, whereas k is used to refer to the public key and k^{-1} is used to refer to the corresponding private key.

In either case, key subscripts are used to indicate principals. In general, capital letter subscripts are used for long-term keys, and small letter subscripts are used for short-term keys. For example, K_A is used to refer to A's long-term secret key, whereas k_b is used to refer to B's short-term public key.

- The term $\{M\}K$ is used to refer to a message M that is encrypted with the secret key K. Since the same key K is used for decryption, $\{\{M\}K\}K$ equals M. If K is used to compute and verify a message authentication code (MAC) for message M, then the term $\langle M \rangle K$ is used to refer to the MAC.

- Similarly, the term $\{M\}k$ is used to refer to a message M that is encrypted with the public key k. The message can only be decrypted with the corresponding private key k^{-1}. If a public key cryptosystem is used to digitally sign messages, the private key is used for signing, and the corresponding public key is used for verifying signatures. Referring to the terminology of the OSI security architecture, the term $\{M\}k^{-1}$ is used to refer to a digital signature giving message recovery, and $\langle M \rangle k^{-1}$ is used to refer to a digital signature with appendix. Note that in the second case, $\langle M \rangle k^{-1}$ in fact abbreviates $M, \{h(M)\}k^{-1}$, with h being an OWHF or CRHF.

Finally, the term $X \ll Y \gg$ is used to refer to a public key certificate that has been issued by X for Y's public key. It implies that X has verified Y's identity and certified the binding of Y's long-term public key k_Y with its identity.

References

[1] Koblitz, N.I., *A Course in Number Theory and Cryptography*, 2nd ed., New York: Springer-Verlag, 1994.

[2] Stinson, D., *Cryptography Theory and Practice*, Boca Raton, FL: CRC Press, 1995.

[3] Schneier, B., *Applied Cryptography: Protocols, Algorithms, and Source Code in C*, 2nd ed., New York: John Wiley & Sons, 1996.

[4] Menezes, A., P. van Oorschot, and S. Vanstone, *Handbook of Applied Cryptography*, Boca Raton, FL: CRC Press, 1996.

[5] Mollin, R.A., *An Introduction to Cryptography*, Boca Raton, FL: CRC Press, 2000.

[6] Buchmann, J., *Introduction to Cryptography*, New York: Springer, 2000.

[7] Goldreich, O., *Foundations of Cryptography: Basic Tools*, Cambridge, UK: Cambridge University Press, 2001.

[8] Shannon, C. E., "A Mathematical Theory of Communication," *Bell System Technical Journal*, Vol. 27, No. 3/4, July/October 1948, pp. 379–423, 623–656.

[9] Shannon, C. E., "Communication Theory of Secrecy Systems," *Bell System Technical Journal*, Vol. 28, No. 4, October 1949, pp. 656–715.

[10] Shor, P. W., "Algorithms for Quantum Computation: Discrete Logarithms and Factoring," *Proc. IEEE 35th Annual Symposium Foundations Computer Science*, 1994, pp. 124–134.

[11] Shor, P. W., "Polynomial-Time Algorithms for Prime Factorization and Discrete Logarithms on a Quantum Computer," *SIAM Journal of Computing*, October 1997, pp. 1484–1509.

[12] Adleman, L. M., "Molecular Computation of Solutions to Combinatorial Problems," *Science*, November 1994, pp. 1021–1024.

[13] Paun, G., G. Rozenberg, and A. Salomaa, *DNA Computing: New Computing Paradigms*, New York: Springer-Verlag, 1998.

[14] Bennett, C. H., G. Brassard, and A. K. Ekert, "Quantum Cryptography," *Scientific American*, October 1992, pp. 50–57.

[15] Kaliski, B., "The MD2 Message-Digest Algorithm," Request for Comments 1319, April 1992.

[16]   Rivest, R. L., "The MD4 Message-Digest Algorithm," Request for Comments 1320, April 1992.

[17]   Rivest, R. L., and S. Dusse, "The MD5 Message-Digest Algorithm," Request for Comments 1321, April 1992.

[18]   U.S. National Institute of Standards and Technology (NIST), "Secure Hash Standard (SHS)," FIPS PUB 180-1, April 1995.

[19]   Dobbertin, H., A. Bosselaers, and B. Preneel, "RIPEMD-160: A Strengthened Version of RIPEMD," *Proceedings of Fast Software Encryption Workshop*, 1996, pp. 71–82.

[20]   U.S. National Institute of Standards and Technology (NIST), "Data Encryption Standard," FIPS PUB 46, January 1977.

[21]   Lai, X., *On the Design and Security of Block Ciphers*, Ph.D. thesis, ETH No. 9752, ETH Zürich, Switzerland, 1992.

[22]   Massey, J. L., "SAFER K-64: A Byte-Oriented Block Ciphering Algorithm," *Proceedings of Fast Software Encryption Workshop*, 1994, pp. 1–17.

[23]   Schneier, B., "Description of a New Variable-Length Key, 64-Bit Block Cipher (Blowfish)," *Proceedings of Fast Software Encryption Workshop*, 1994, pp. 191–204.

[24]   Adams, C., "The CAST-128 Encryption Algorithm," Request for Comments 2144, May 1997.

[25]   U.S. National Institute of Standards and Technology (NIST), "Advanced Encryption Standard (AES)," FIPS PUB 197, November 2001.

[26]   Diffie, W., and M. E. Hellman, "New Directions in Cryptography," *IEEE Transactions on Information Theory*, IT-22(6), 1976, pp. 644–654.

[27]   Pfitzmann, B., *Digital Signature Schemes*, Berlin, Germany: Springer-Verlag, 1996.

[28]   Rivest, R. L., A. Shamir, and L. Adleman, "A Method for Obtaining Digital Signatures and Public-Key Cryptosystems," *Communications of the ACM*, 21(2), February 1978, pp. 120–126.

[29]   ElGamal, T., "Cryptography and Logarithms over Finite Fields," Ph.D. thesis, Stanford University, 1984.

[30]   ElGamal, T., "A Public Key Cryptosystem and a Signature Scheme Based on Discrete Logarithm," *IEEE Transactions on Information Theory*, IT-31(4), 1985, pp. 469–472.

[31]   U.S. National Institute of Standards and Technology (NIST), *Digital Signature Standard (DSS)*, FIPS PUB 186, May 1994.

[32]   Hoover, D. N., and B. N. Kausik, "Software Smart Cards via Cryptographic Camouflage," *Proceedings of IEEE Symposium on Security and Privacy*, 1999.

[33] Eastlake, D., S. Crocker, and J. Schiller, ''Randomness Recommendations for Security,'' Request for Comments 1750, December 1994.

[34] Baker, S. A., and P. R. Hurst, *The Limits of Trust: Cryptography, Governments, and Electronic Commerce*, Cambridge, MA: Kluwer Law International, 1998.

[35] Diffie, W., and S. Landau, *Privacy on the Line: The Politics of Wiretapping and Encryption*, Cambridge, MA: MIT Press, 1998.

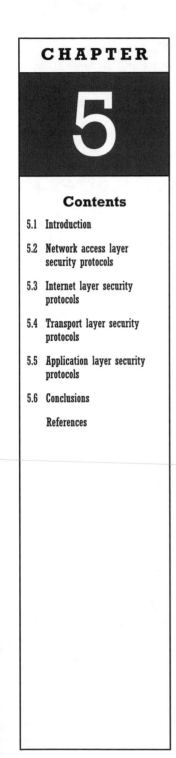

CHAPTER

5

Contents

5.1 Introduction

5.2 Network access layer
security protocols

5.3 Internet layer security
protocols

5.4 Transport layer security
protocols

5.5 Application layer security
protocols

5.6 Conclusions

References

Internet Security Protocols

In this chapter, we overview and briefly discuss some cryptographic security protocols that have been proposed, specified, and partly implemented for the Internet and that can also be used on the WWW. In particular, we introduce the topic in Section 5.1, address security protocols for the network access, Internet, transport, and application layers in Sections 5.2 to 5.5, and draw some conclusions in Section 5.6.

5.1 Introduction

There is a strong consensus that providing security services in computer networks and distributed systems requires the use of cryptographic techniques, and that these techniques must be integrated into security protocols accordingly. This is also true for the Internet and the WWW. Consequently, many cryptographic security protocols have been proposed, specified, implemented, and deployed on the Internet and the WWW in the past. Some of these protocols have been successful, whereas others have not found their market shares and have disappeared accordingly.

In the case of TCP/IP-based networks, cryptographic security protocols can operate at any layer of the corresponding communications protocol suite. Consequently, there are proposals for providing security services at the network access, Internet, transport, and application layers. There are even some proposals to provide security services above the application layer. All of these possibilities are overviewed and briefly

117

discussed in the sequel. Keep in mind, however, that the treatment in this book is rather short, and that a more detailed overview and discussion can be found in Part III of [1]. Also, the chapter provides a long list of references for further study.

5.2 Network access layer security protocols

In the Internet model and protocol stack, the network access layer handles issues related to local area networking and dial-up connectivity. Protocols that operate at this layer include Ethernet (IEEE 802.3), token bus (IEEE 802.4), token ring (IEEE 802.5), FDDI, and protocols for serial line dial-up networking, such as the Serial Line IP Protocol (SLIP) and—most importantly—the Point-to-Point Protocol (PPP) [2]. SLIP and PPP both define encapsulation mechanisms for transporting multiprotocol data across layer two point-to-point links (e.g., serial lines). In short, an encapsulation mechanism specifies how protocol data units (PDUs) from one protocol are encapsulated in PDUs of another protocol, and how these PDUs are then transported through the network. For all practical purposes, Ethernet is the most widely used and deployed technology for local area networking, and PPP is the most widely deployed protocol for dial-up networking.

In the late 1980s, the IEEE started to address issues related to LAN and metropolitan-area network (MAN) security. In particular, the IEEE 802.10 working group (WG) was formed in May 1988 to address LAN and MAN security. Meanwhile, the IEEE 802.10 WG specified several *standards for interoperable LAN/MAN security* (SILS) that are compatible with existing IEEE 802 and OSI specifications [3, 4]. Unfortunately, SILS has not been commercially successful, and there are hardly any products that implement the standards. Consequently, we do not address the work of the IEEE 802.10 WG. Instead, we elaborate on recent work that has been done to secure dial-up connections using PPP with security enhancements.

First of all, we consider the problem that a European conference attendee traveling in the United States faces if he or she wants to connect his or her laptop computer to his or her corporate intranet in Europe (e.g., to read e-mail messages or download a presentation). There are at least two solutions for this problem:

1. A very obvious solution for the problem is to use the public-switched telephone network (PSTN) or the integrated services digital network (ISDN) to connect to a remote access server (RAS)

located on the corporate intranet (e.g., a modem pool), to set up a PPP connection, and to use this connection to log in to the destination server located on the corporate intranet. The major advantages of this solution are availability and simplicity, whereas the major disadvantages are related to security and costs:

> The problem related to security is that the data traffic between the laptop computer and the intranet server goes unencrypted and unprotected.

> The problem related to costs is that the user is charged a long-distance call (or the company is charged the fees in the case of a modem pool with free charging or dial-back facilities).

2. A more sophisticated solution for the problem is to use a virtual private network (VPN) channel or tunnel. As we discuss later, there are many technologies that refer to and make use of the term VPN. Some of these technologies use cryptography to encapsulate data traffic and to establish and maintain cryptographically protected tunnels between the communicating peers. There are basically two approaches to create such a tunnel:

> One possibility is to encapsulate a given network layer protocol, such as IP, IPX, or AppleTalk, inside PPP, to cryptographically protect the PPP frames and to encapsulate the data inside a tunneling protocol, which is typically IP (but could also be ATM or Frame Relay). This approach is commonly referred to as *layer 2 tunneling* because the passenger of the tunneling scheme is actually a layer 2 protocol (i.e., PPP).

> Another possibility is to encapsulate a given network layer protocol, such as IP, IPX, or AppleTalk, directly into a tunneling protocol, such as 3Com's Virtual Tunneling Protocol (VTP), and to encapsulate the data inside another network layer protocol (e.g., IP) that is used to tunnel the data through the Internet. This approach is commonly referred to as *layer 3 tunneling* because the passenger of the tunneling scheme is actually a layer 3 protocol (i.e., VTP).

Figure 5.1 illustrates and puts into perspective the layer 2 tunneling and layer 3 tunneling encapsulation schemes (for IPX encapsulated inside IP). In either case, the protected part of the data is IPX. The major advantages of VPN tunnels are related to the fact that data traffic is encapsulated in IP

Layer 2 tunneling

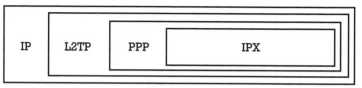

Layer 3 tunneling

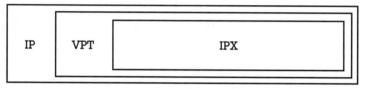

Figure 5.1 The layer 2 and layer 3 tunneling encapsulation schemes.

packets that can be routed over the Internet and that cryptographic techniques can then be used to protect the IP packets.

The first solution is simple and straightforward; it does not deserve further explanation. In the following sections we elaborate on the second solution. In particular, we briefly overview and partly discuss the layer 2 forwarding/tunneling protocols that have been proposed and deployed in the past (layer 3 tunneling protocols are addressed in the following section).

Today, there is a strong consensus that the Layer 2 Tunneling Protocol (L2TP) is the preferred choice for applications that want to use layer 2 tunneling. Following the terminolgy introduced by the L2TP specifications, the following terms and acronyms are used (instead of POP and RAS[1]):

  ▸ A *remote system* or *dial-up client* is a computer system or router that is typically the initiator of a layer 2 tunnel.

  ▸ An *L2TP access concentrator* (LAC) is a node that acts as one side of a layer 2 tunnel endpoint and is a peer to the layer 2 tunneling protocol server (e.g., the L2TP network server discussed next). As such, the LAC sits between the remote system or dial-up client and the server and forwards packets to and from each. The connection from the LAC to the remote system is either local or a PPP link.

---

1. Because the term *RAS* is heavily used in the PPTP implementation of Microsoft, we use it when we discuss MS-PPTP later in this chapter.

 ‣ Finally, an *L2TP network server* (LNS) is a node that acts as one side of a layer 2 tunnel endpoint (typically the recipient) and is a peer to the LAC. As such, the LNS is the logical termination point of a PPP session that is being tunneled from the remote system by the LAC.

Note that the LAC and the LNS require a common understanding of the encapsulation protocol so that layer 2 frames (e.g., PPP frames) can be successfully transmitted and received across the Internet. Also note that in this terminology, a network access server (NAS) is a device that provides access to users across a remote access network, such as the PSTN or ISDN. As such, the NAS may serve as either a LAC, LNS, or both.

5.2.1   Layer 2 Forwarding Protocol

Historically, the first layer 2 forwarding/tunneling protocol was the *Layer 2 Forwarding* (L2F) Protocol originally developed and proposed by Cisco Systems. It addressed two areas of standardization:

 ‣ The encapsulation of layer 2 frames (i.e., PPP frames) within the L2F protocol. Each L2F frame, including an L2F header and a payload, is then encapsulated and sent within an IP packet or a UDP datagram, respectively. Contrary to more recent layer 2 forwarding/tunneling protocol proposals, the L2F protocol does not take into account the use of cryptography to protect the confidentiality of the encapsulated layer 2 frames.

 ‣ The connection management for the layer 2 tunnel (i.e., how the tunnel is initiated and terminated).

Both areas are specified in RFC 2341 [5]. According to this specification, the L2F protocol uses the well-known UDP port 1701 (for both source and destination ports).

Because the L2F protocol is only of historical value,[2] we do not delve into the technical details of the L2F protocol specification. You may refer to the referenced RFC document if you are interested in history (or if you are an administrator in charge of installing and configuring an implementation of the L2F protocol).

---

2.   Note that the category of the referenced RFC document is historic.

5.2.2 Point-to-Point Tunneling Protocol

Similar to the L2F protocol, the *Point-to-Point Tunneling Protocol* (PPTP) was
originally developed and designed to solve the problem of creating and
maintaining VPN tunnels over public TCP/IP-based networks using the PPP
[6, 7].[3] The PPTP is the result of joint efforts of Microsoft and a set of product
vendors, including, for example, Ascend Communications, 3Com/Primary
Access, ECI Telematics, and U.S. Robotics. These companies originally
constituted the PPTP Forum, whose resulting PPTP specification was made
publicly available and submitted to the IETF Point-to-Point Protocol
Extensions (PPPEXT[4]) WG for possible consideration as an Internet
Standard in 1996.[5]

A typical deployment of the PPTP starts with a remote system or dial-up
client, such as a laptop computer, that must be interconnected to an LNS
located on a corporate intranet using an LAC. As such, the PPTP can be used
to encapsulate PPP frames in IP packets for transmission over the Internet or
any other publicly accessible TCP/IP-based network. More specifically, the
remote system can connect to the LNS in two ways:

1. If the remote system supports PPTP, it can directly use it to connect
    to the LNS.

2. If, however, the remote system does not support PPTP, it can use
    PPP to connect to an Internet service provider's LAC, and this LAC
    can then use PPTP to connect to the LNS.

In the first case, the situation is comparably simple. The remote system
first establishes a PPP connection to the Internet service provider's LAC and
then uses PPTP to send encapsulated PPP frames to the LNS. The IP packets
that encapsulate the PPP frames are simply forwarded by the LAC.

In the second case, however, the LAC must use the PPTP to encapsulate
the PPP frames in IP packets on behalf of the remote system. Consequently,
the LAC must play the role of an intermediate or proxy server in one way or
another. In fact, there are two connections. The first connection uses the PPP
to interconnect the remote system and the LAC, whereas the second
connection uses the PPTP to interconnect the LAC and the LNS. PPP frames
received by the LAC are encapsulated in IP packets using the PPTP.

---

3. http://www.microsoft.com/technet/winnt/winntas/technote/pptpudst.asp
4. http://www.ietf.org/html.charters/pppext-charter.html
5. Note that the IETF PPPEXT WG is situated in the IETF's Internet area (not in the security area).

In either case, the PPTP uses a sophisticated encapsulation scheme to tunnel PPP frames through the Internet (or any other TCP/IP-based network that interconnects the LAC and the LNS). In fact, network or Internet layer protocol data units (e.g., IP packets, IPX packets, or NetBEUI messages) are first framed using PPP. The resulting PPP frames are then encapsulated using a generic routing encapsulation (GRE) header [8] as well as an IP header that is used to route the frame through the Internet. Finally, the resulting IP packets are framed with still another media-specific header before they can be forwarded to the interface connected to the Internet.

In addition to the data channel that uses IP encapsulation to transmit data, the PPTP uses a TCP connection for signaling. The corresponding messages that are sent or received over this connection are used to query status and to convey signaling information between the LAC (i.e., the PPTP client) and the LNS (i.e., the PPTP server). The control channel is always initiated by the PPTP client to the PPTP server using TCP port number 1723. In most cases, it is a bidirectional channel where the client can send messages to the server and vice versa. Note that the notion of an outband signaling channel is something very specific for PPTP. Most other security protocols (e.g., the IPsec protocols) use inband signaling, meaning that signaling information is transported together with the protected data units.

The PPTP specification does not mandate the use of specific algorithms for authentication and encryption. Instead, it provides a framework for the negotiation of particular algorithms. This negotiation is not specific to PPTP, and relies on existing PPP option negotiations contained within the PPP compression protocol (CCP) [9], the challenge handshake authentication protocol (CHAP) [10], and some other PPP extensions and enhancements. Also outside the world of the PPTP, PPP sessions have been able to negotiate compression algorithms as well as authentication and encryption algorithms [11, 12].

In spite of the fact that the PPTP specification was submitted to the IETF PPPEXT WG for consideration as an Internet Standard, its standardization effort has been abandoned. Microsoft's implementation of the PPTP (i.e., MS-PPTP) is heavily used in Windows NT environments. Outside these environments, however, neither MS-PPTP nor another implementation of PPTP is widely deployed.

Using MS-PPTP, the client and the server typically authenticate each other using MS-CHAP [13], which is Microsoft's version of the CHAP, and encrypt data using the *Microsoft Point-to-Point Encryption* (MPPE) protocol [14].

As outlined in [15], MS-PPTP has severe flaws in both its design and implementation. This is particularly true for MS-PPTP version 1, but it is also true for MS-PPTP version 2 (e.g., [16, 17]). Consequently, the use of MS-PPTP cannot be recommended from a security point of view.

5.2.3 Layer 2 Tunneling Protocol

In June 1996, Microsoft and Cisco Systems proposed and submitted a combination of MS-PPTP and the L2F protocol to the IETF PPPEXT WG. The proposal was named *Layer 2 Tunneling Protocol* (L2TP) [18]. This collaborative protocol specification was particularly good news, as it meant that there would be just one industrywide IETF specification for a layer 2 tunneling and VPN dial-up protocol.

Similar to the L2F protocol and PPTP, the L2TP facilitates the tunneling of encapsulated PPP frames across an intervening network in a way that is as transparent as possible to both end users and applications. Contrary to the other protocols, however, L2TP uses and even requires the use of IPsec security associations (SAs) to cryptographically protect data that are transmitted between LACs and LNSs.

After this initial release, the L2TP specification was further refined. In August 1999, a preliminary release was published in RFC 2661 [19] and submitted to the Internet standards track. As such, the L2TP is likely to replace both the L2F protocol and PPTP in the future (in both Microsoft and Cisco products).

5.2.4 Virtual private networking

In summary, the L2F protocol, PPTP, and L2TP provide means for virtual private networking. Consequently, a final word is due on the use of these protocols for virtual private networking. According to RFC 2828, a *virtual private network* (VPN) is "a restricted-use, logical computer network that is constructed from the system resources of a relatively public, physical network (such as the Internet), often by using encryption, and often by tunneling links of the virtual network across the real network" [20]. According to this definition, the use of encryption is not mandatory for VPNs. Consequently, there are some alternative technologies and notions of virtual private networking in use today. These technologies use controlled route leaking (i.e., route filtering) or label switching instead of cryptography to provide VPN facilities.

For example, *multiprotocol label switching* (MPLS) is a technology that can be used to implement something similar to closed user groups (CUGs) in a TCP/IP-based network [21, 22]. In short, MPLS makes sure that IP packets cannot reach hosts that are not legitimate members of a specific host group.

Note, however, that there is no cryptographic protection in use, and that an MPLS subscriber has to trust the network provider not to eavesdrop on its communications and not to manipulate the IP traffic accordingly. Sometimes this level of trust may be justified. Sometimes, however, this level of trust may not be justified and the subscriber is then well advised to look into and consider the use of VPN technologies that employ cryptography in one way or another.

5.3 Internet layer security protocols

In most network architectures and corresponding communications protocol stacks, network layer protocol data units are transmitted in the clear, meaning that they are not cryptographically protected during their transmission. Consequently, it is relatively simple to do malicious things, such as inspecting the contents of the data units, forging the source or destination addresses, modifying the contents, or even replaying old data units. There is no guarantee that data units received are in fact from the claimed originators (i.e., the claimed source addresses), that they are delivered to the proper recipients, that they contain the original contents, and that the contents have not been inspected by an eavesdropper while the data units were transmitted from the originators to the recipients. The lack of built-in security is particularly true for IP packets.

Against this background, the idea of having a standardized network or Internet layer security protocol (to protect network or Internet layer protocol data units) is not new, and several protocols had been proposed before the IETF IPSEC WG started to meet:

▸ The *Security Protocol 3* (SP3) was a network layer security protocol jointly developed and proposed by the U.S. National Security Agency (NSA) and the National Institute of Science and Technology (NIST) as part of the secure data network system (SDNS) suite of security protocols [23]. Outside the U.S. military, the SDNS and its security protocols have not seen widespread use. This is particularly true for SP3.

▸ The *Network Layer Security Protocol* (NLSP) was developed by the ISO to secure the Connectionless Network Protocol (CLNP) [24]. Similar to IP in the Internet model, CLNP provides a connectionless and un-reliable network layer service to the higher layers in the OSI reference model. As such, the aim of the NLSP is to secure the network layer service and to provide some basic security services to the higher layers. The NLSP is an incompatible descendent of SP3.

▶ The *Integrated NLSP* (I-NLSP) was originally developed and proposed by the U.S. NIST to provide security services for both IP (i.e., IPv4) and CLNP.[6] Again, the security function of I-NLSP is roughly similar to that of SP3, although some details differ. For example, I-NLSP provides some additional functionality, such as security label processing.

▶ A protocol named *swIPe* was yet another experimental Internet layer security protocol that was developed and prototyped by John Ioannidis and Matt Blaze [25]. The prototype implementation is publicly and freely available on the Internet.[7]

The network and Internet layer security protocols listed are more alike than they are different. In fact, they all use secure encapsulation as their basic enabling technique. What this basically means is that authenticated or encrypted network layer protocol data units are contained within other data units. In the case of secure IP encapsulation, for example, outgoing plaintext IP packets are authenticated or encrypted and encapsulated in new IP packets by adding new IP headers that are used to route the packets through the internetwork. At the peer systems, the incoming IP packets are decapsulated, meaning that the outer IP headers are stripped off and the inner IP packets are authenticated or decrypted and then forwarded to the intended recipients.

An encapsulated IP packet is illustrated in Figure 5.2. Note that the original IP header and IP payload (together with some additional data) are

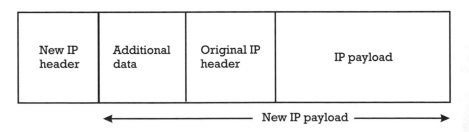

Figure 5.2 Encapsulated IP packet.

---

6. I-NLSP was specified in an Internet-Draft that expired long ago.

7. ftp://ftp.csua.berkeley.edu/pub/cypherpunks/swIPe/swipe.tar.Z

treated as the payload for the new IP packet, that this payload is the one that is protected, and that a new IP header must be prepended to the new payload. Consequently, the new IP header must not be encrypted, since it must be used to route (or tunnel) the new IP packet through the (inter)network. Such an encapsulation or tunneling scheme is convenient, since it means that no changes are required to the existing Internet routing infrastructure: authenticated or encrypted IP packets have an unencrypted, normal-looking outer IP header, and this IP header can be used to route and process the packet as usual. This transparency is convenient for the large-scale deployment of encapsulation and tunneling schemes in general, and IP encapsulation or tunneling in particular. In fact, similar IP encapsulation or tunneling schemes can be used to transfer multicast or IPv6 traffic through unicast or IPv4 networks.

When the IETF started to develop the next version of IP (i.e., IPv6), it was commonly agreed that this version had to incorporate strong security features (at least for users who desire security). The security features had to be algorithm-independent so that the cryptographic algorithms could be altered without affecting the other parts of an implementation. Further-more, the security features should be useful in enforcing a wide variety of security policies, and yet they should be designed in a way that avoids adverse impacts on Internet users who do not need security services for the protection of their IP traffic at all.

Against this background, the IETF chartered an IPSEC WG in 1992. The aim was to define a security architecture (mainly for IPv6), and to standardize both an IP Security Protocol (IPSP) and a related Internet Key Management Protocol (IKMP). Soon it was realized that the same security architecture that was being developed for IPv6 could also be used for IPv4. Consequently, the charter of the IETF IPSEC WG was revised to target both IPv6 and IPv4, and the resulting security architecture had to be the same. The main difference is that the security mechanisms specified in the IP security architecture have to be retrofitted into IPv4 implementations, whereas they must be present in all IPv6 implementations at the beginning.

In August 1995, the IETF IPSEC WG published a series of RFC documents that collectively specified a first version of the IP security architecture and the IPSP [26–30]. This version was incomplete and rushed to publication, mainly to satisfy a perceived industry need. Nevertheless, the IESG approved the IPSP specification to enter the Internet standards track as a Proposed Standard, and the participants of the IETF IPSEC WG continued their work to refine the IP security architecture and the IPSP specifi-cation, as well as to standardize the IKMP [31, 32]. The discussion on the standardization of the IKMP was very controversial. In the end, two protocol proposals, namely, the Internet Security Association and Key Management Protocol (ISAKMP) and the OAKLEY Key Determination Protocol, were merged to become the IKMP. Furthermore, the acronym IPSP was replaced with the term *IPsec protocols* (as it consists of two subprotocols), and the acronym IKMP was replaced with the term *Internet Key Exchange* (IKE). Consequently, the IP security architecture as we understand it today comprises both a set of IPsec protocols and the IKE protocol.

In November 1998, the IETF IPSEC WG published a series of RFC documents that collectively specify a revised version of the IP security architecture [33], including revised versions of the IPsec [34–39] and IKE [40–42] protocols.[8] In addition, an informational RFC was published that provides a road map for the various documents that are released under the auspices of the IETF IPSEC WG [43]. Further information about the current status of the various protocol specifications can be found on the home page of the IETF IPSEC WG.[9] In addition, there are several books that address IPsec and virtual private networking [44–46]. Among these books, I particularly recommend [46].

Soon after the release of the revised series of RFC documents, it was realized that two topics deserved further study:

1. The use of policies in IPsec environments;

2. The use of IPsec technologies to secure remote access services.

In early 2000, the IETF chartered an IP Security Policy (IPSP)[10] WG to address the first topic and an IP Security Remote Access (IPSRA)[11] WG to address the second topic. You may refer to the home pages of the two WGs to get an overview about the current status of their work.

5.3.1 IP security architecture

As mentioned above, the IP security architecture comprises an entire suite of security protocols. The suite includes the IPsec protocols and the IKE protocol. The IPsec protocols comprise the Authentication Header (AH) and Encapsulating Security Payload (ESP) subprotocols. Similarly, the IKE

---

8. As of this writing, the protocol specifications refer to proposed standards.
9. http://www.ietf.org/html.charters/ipsec-charter.html
10. http://www.ietf.org/html.charters/ipsp-charter.html
11. http://www.ietf.org/html.charters/ipsra-charter.html

protocol has evolved from two major key management protocol proposals (i.e., ISAKMP and OAKLEY).

A high-level overview of the IP security architecture is given in Figure 5.3. In short, an IPsec module is a (hardware or software) module that implements the IPsec architecture and its protocols. The primary goal of an IPsec module is to secure IP traffic that is sent to or received from another IPsec module. What this basically means in terms of security services and mechanisms is specified in a corresponding *security association* (SA). The aim of the IKE protocol is to establish SAs and the aim of the IPsec protocols is to make use of these SAs. On either side of an SA, the security parameters of that SA (e.g., encryption algorithm and session key) are stored in a *security association database* (SAD). Each SA and corresponding entry in the SAD is indexed with three values:

▶ A *security parameters index* (SPI);

▶ An IP destination address;

▶ A security protocol identifier (i.e., AH or ESP).

As will be explained later, each IPsec-protected packet carries an SPI value that can be used by the recipient to retrieve the correct SA parameters from its SAD. In addition to the SAD, there is a security policy database (SPD) in each IPsec module. The SPD provides detailed specifications of the security services accorded to each packet.

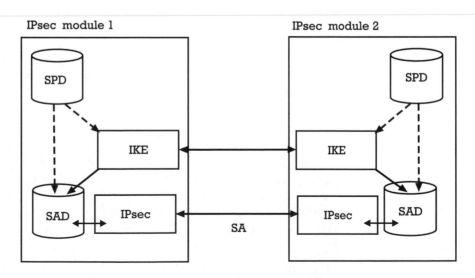

Figure 5.3   High-level overview of the IP security architecture.

In accordance with this high-level overview, the concept of an SA is at the core of the IP security architecture. An SA specifies the security services and mechanisms that must be implemented and used between two endpoints or IPsec modules. The endpoints, in turn, may be hosts or network security gateways, such as IPsec-enabled routers or application gateways. For example, an SA may require the provision of data confidentiality services through the use of the IPsec ESP protocol (this protocol will be explained later). Furthermore, the SA may specifiy the parameters for this protocol, such as the encryption algorithm (e.g., the DES algorithm), the mode of operation (e.g., the CBC mode), and its initialization vector (IV). The SA is a simplex (unidirectional) connection or relationship. Security services are afforded to an SA by the use of AH, or ESP, but not both. If both AH and ESP protection is applied to a data stream, then two SAs must be established and maintained. Similarly, to secure bidirectional communications between two hosts or security gateways, two SAs (one in each direction) are required. The term *SA bundle* refers to a set of SAs through which traffic must be processed to satisfy a specific security policy.

The IPsec architecture allows the user or system administrator to control the granularity at which security services are offered. In the first series of RFCs, three approaches toward how to feed SAs with security parameters and cryptographic keys were distinguished:

1. *Host-oriented keying* has all users on one host share the same session key for use on traffic destined for all users on another host.

2. *User-oriented keying* lets each user on one host have one or more unique session keys for the traffic destined for another host (such session keys are not shared with other users).

3. *Session-unique keying* has a single session key being assigned to a given IP address, upper-layer protocol, and port number triple (in this case, a user's FTP session may use a different key than the same user's Telnet session).

From a security point of view, user-oriented and session-unique keying are superior and therefore preferred. This is due to the fact that in many cases, a single computer system will have at least two suspicious users that do not mutually trust each other. When host-oriented keying is used and mutually suspicious users exist on a system, it is sometimes possible for a user to determine the host-oriented key by cryptanalytical attacks. Once this user has improperly obtained the key in use, he or she can either read another user's encrypted traffic or forge traffic from this particular user.

Some possible attacks that follow and take advantage of this line of argumentation can be found in [47, 48]. When user-oriented or session-unique keying is used, certain kinds of attack from one user onto another user's data traffic are simply not possible. Unfortunately, the distinction between the three keying approaches is no longer used in the current protocol specifications of the IETF IPSEC WG. In reality, all we see today is host-oriented keying.

The SPD of an IPsec implementation defines at a high level of abstraction the security requirements for the IP packets that are forwarded or routed. As such, the SPD is established and maintained by a user or system administrator (or by an application operating within constraints established by either of them). Each entry in the SPD defines the traffic to be protected, how to protect it, and with whom the protection is shared. For each IP packet entering or leaving the IPsec implementation, the SPD must be consulted for the possible application of the IPsec security services. More specifically, an SPD entry may define one of the three actions to take upon a traffic match:

1. *Discard:* A packet is not let in or out.

2. *Bypass:* A packet is let in and out without applying IPsec security services.

3. *Apply:* A packet is only let in or out after having applied IPsec security services.

As such, the SPD provides access control enforcement equivalent to a (static) packet filter.

In general, the IPsec protocols (i.e., AH and ESP) are largely independent of the associated SA and key management techniques and protocols, although the techniques and protocols involved do affect some of the security services offered by the protocols. The IPsec protocols and the complementary IKE protocol are overviewed next.

5.3.2 IPsec protocols

According to the terminology introduced in the OSI security architecture, the IPsec protocols provide the following security services:

- A data origin authentication service;

- A connectionless data integrity service (including protection against replay attacks);

> • A data confidentiality service;

> • An access control service;

> • A limited traffic flow confidentiality service.

The security services are provided at the Internet layer, offering protection for IP and upper-layer protocols. As mentioned previously, the security services are provided by two subprotocols, namely, the AH and the ESP. Each protocol can be used to protect either only the upper-layer payload of an IP packet or the entire IP packet. This distinction is handled by considering two different modes of operation:

1. *Transport mode* is used to protect the upper-layer payload of an IP packet.

2. *Tunnel mode* is used to protect an entire IP packet (in this case, IP encapsulation is used as an enabling technique).

Figure 5.4 illustrates the IPsec transport and tunnel modes. In transport mode, an IPsec header (i.e., an AH or ESP header) is inserted between the original IP header and payload (i.e., the TCP segment or UDP datagram). In tunnel mode, the original IP packet is encapsulated into another IP packet. What this means is that there are two IP headers:

1. An inner IP header that carries the original IP header (specifying the original source and destination IP addresses);

2. An outer IP header that carries the new IP header (specifying new source and destination IP addresses).

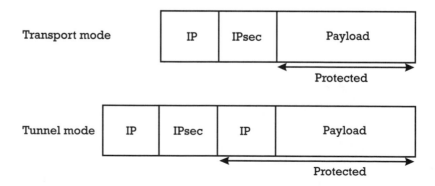

Figure 5.4 IPsec transport and tunnel modes.

The tunnel mode IPsec header appears between the outer IP header and the inner IP header.

Both IPsec protocols—AH and ESP—can operate in either transport or tunnel mode. Transport mode is typically used to secure IP traffic between two endpoints (i.e., computer systems), whereas tunnel mode is typically used to secure IP traffic between two points that are not necessarily the endpoints of the communications. For example, one of the points may be a security gateway for a corporate intranet. In this case, the IP traffic is encapsulated (i.e., using IPsec in tunnel mode) between the remote system and the security gateway (making sure that the systems located on the corporate intranet must not be able to handle IPsec). Note that whenever either endpoint is a security gateway (e.g., a router or firewall), IPsec must be used in tunnel mode (in the case where traffic is destined for a security gateway, e.g., SNMP commands, the security gateway is acting as a host, and transport mode is also allowed).

5.3.2.1 Authentication header

The IPsec AH protocol provides data origin authentication and connection-less data integrity for IP packets (collectively referred to as "authentication" in this section). The precision of the authentication is a function of the granularity of the SA with which AH is employed. Depending on which cryptographic algorithm is used and how keying is performed, the AH may also provide non-repudiation of origin services. Finally, the AH may offer an antireplay service at the discretion of the receiver, to help counter specific DOS attacks.

The IANA has assigned the protocol number 51 for the AH protocol, so the header immediately preceding the AH must include 51 in its protocol or next header field. As specified in RFC 2402 [34] and illustrated in Figure 5.5, the AH header consists of the following fields:

- An 8-bit Next Header field;
- An 8-bit Payload Length field;
- A 16-bit field that is reserved for future use;
- A 32-bit SPI field;
- A 32-bit Sequence Number field;
- A variable-length $n \times 32$–bit Authentication Data field.

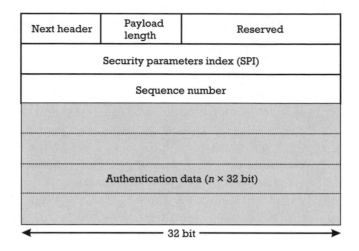

Figure 5.5 The authentication header (AH) format.

The authentication data is computed by using an authentication algorithm and a cryptographic key specified in the corresponding SA. The sender computes the data before sending the IP packet, and the receiver verifies it upon reception. Several algorithms for authentication data computation and verification have been proposed in the past. The HMAC construction is explained in [49]. In short, the HMAC construction takes as input the message M and the authentication key K, and produces as output the following expression:

$$HMAC_K(M) = h(K \oplus opad, h(K \oplus ipad, M))$$

To compute $HMAC_K(M)$, the key K and an inner pad value *ipad* (*ipad* refers to the byte 0x36 repeated several times) are first added modulo 2. The result is concatenated with the message M and hashed with the OWHF h (which can be either MD5 or SHA-1). Similarly, the result is concatenated with the sum of K and an outer pad value *opad* (*opad* refers to the byte 0x5C repeated several times) modulo 2. Finally, this result is hashed with the appropriate one-way hash function h (MD5 or SHA-1), and the resulting authentication data is truncated to 96 bits.[12] Depending on the OWHF in use, the resulting HMAC constructions are

---

12. The truncation was introduced because of a desire to achieve a specific packet alignment goal, to avoid devoting all 128 or 160 bits to the authentication function, and to have a uniform size MAC, whether MD5 or SHA-1 is employed.

called HMAC-MD5-96 (in the case of MD5) and HMAC-SHA-1-96 (in the case of SHA-1).

Because the AH protocol does not provide data confidentiality services, implementations thereof may be widely deployed, even in countries where controls on encryption would preclude deployment of technology that potentially offered data confidentiality services. Consequently, AH is an appropriate protocol to employ when confidentiality is not required.

5.3.2.2 Encapsulating security payload

As its name suggests, the IPsec ESP protocol uses IP encapsulation to provide data confidentiality and partial traffic flow confidentiality (in tunnel mode and with the invocation of padding data to hide the size of an IP packet). Similar to the AH, the ESP protocol also provides authentication (referring to data origin authentication and connectionless data integrity services). Note, however, that the scope of the authentication offered by the ESP is narrower than that for the AH (i.e., the IP headers below the ESP header are not protected). If only the upper-layer protocols need to be authenticated, then ESP authentication is an appropriate choice and is more space efficient than use of an AH encapsulating an ESP.

The IANA has assigned the protocol number 50 for the ESP protocol, so the header immediately preceding the ESP must include 50 in its protocol or next header field. The ESP format is specified in RFC 2406 [38] and illustrated in Figure 5.6. It consists of the following fields:

- A 32-bit SPI field (not encrypted);
- A 32-bit Sequence Number field (not encrypted);
- A variable-length Payload Data field;
- A variable-length Padding field;
- An 8-bit Pad Length field;
- An 8-bit Next Header field;
- In addition, the ESP may also include a variable-length $n*32$-bit Authentication Data field.

In RFC 2405, the DES in cipher block chaining (CBC) mode with an explicit initialization vector (IV) is introduced as the default algorithm to encrypt the ESP Payload Data field [37]. But this default algorithm may be replaced by any other algorithm at will. For example, RFC 1851 specifies

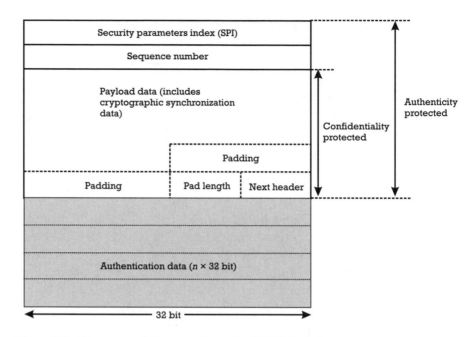

Figure 5.6 The encapsulating security payload (ESP) format.

the experimental use of 3DES. In the future, it is possible and very likely that we will see more AES implementations instead of DES or 3DES implementations. Unfortunately, export, import, and use of specific encryption algorithms may be regulated in some countries. The algorithms for computing the authentication data are the same as the ones suggested for the AH.

Note that both AH and ESP are also vehicles for access control, based on the distribution of cryptographic keys and the management of traffic flows relative to these security protocols. Also note that full protection from traffic analysis is not provided by any of the two IPsec subprotocols. At the most, tunnel mode ESP can provide a partial traffic flow confidentiality service. In fact, the ESP protocol can be used to create a secure tunnel between two security gateways. In this case, anyone eavesdropping on the communications between the security gateways is not able to see what hosts are actually sending and receiving IP packets from behind the security gateways. Nevertheless, it is fair to mention that only a few Internet users worry about traffic analysis at all.

5.3.3 IKE Protocol

The IP security architecture mandates support for both manual and automated SA and key management (using a key management protocol).

For several years, the IETF IPSEC WG had been struggling with competing proposals for an automated SA and key management protocol:

- IBM proposed a Modular Key Management Protocol (MKMP) for its IP Secure Tunnel Protocol (IPST) [50].

- Sun Microsystems proposed and is using its Simple Key-Management for Internet Protocols (SKIP) [51].

- Phil Karn originally proposed and prototyped a Photuris Key Management Protocol[13] [52, 53] that is conceptually similar to the Station-to-Station (STS) protocol originally proposed in [54]. The Photuris protocol combines an ephemeral Diffie-Hellman key exchange with a subsequent authentication step to protect against man-in-the-middle attacks. To protect the participanting peers against resource clogging attacks, the Photuris protocol introduced a cookie exchange.

- Hugo Krawczyk proposed a variation and generalization of the Photuris protocol, called Photuris Plus or SKEME [55].

- Because Bill Simpson (one of the coauthors of the latest Photuris Key Management Protocol specification) refused to make changes to protocol specification in accordance with suggestions provided by the IETF IPSEC WG chairs, the Photuris Key Management Protocol was dropped from consideration and Hilarie Orman drafted a version of the Photuris and SKEME protocols that was called OAKLEY Key Determination Protocol [56]. In this protocol, several parameters are negotiable, including, for example, the mathematical structure in which the Diffie-Hellman key exchange is supposed to take place and the authentication method that is being used.

- The NSA Office of INFOSEC Computer Science proposed a general Internet Security Association and Key Management Protocol (ISAKMP).

In the first half of the 1990s, the developers of the various key management protocols competed with one another within the IETF IPSEC WG. There were basically two groups: (a) SKIP and (b) the group of Photuris-like protocols, including, for example, the OAKLEY Key Determination

---

13. Phil Karn was later joined by Bill Simpson to write the experimental Photuris protocol specifications.

Protocol. Also, because of the fact that SKIP does not make use of SAs at all, the ISAKMP is useful only for the protocols of group (b). Consequently, the two major contenders were SKIP and ISAKMP/OAKLEY.

In September 1996, the IETF Security Area Director[14] posted a document to the Internet to end the controversy. In this document, the two contenders (i.e., SKIP and ISAKMP/OAKLEY) were reviewed, and it was concluded that ISAKMP/OAKLEY should become the mandatory standard (SKIP can still become an elective standard).

In short, ISAKMP defines how two peers communicate, how the messages they use to communicate are constructed, and through which state transitions they go to secure their communications. It provides the means to authenticate a peer, to exchange information for a key exchange, and to negotiate security services. It does not, however, define how a particular authenticated key exchange is done, nor does it define the attributes necessary for an SAs. These issues are left to a specific key exchange protocol, such as OAKLEY. As such, ISAKMP is a general-purpose security exchange protocol that may be used for policy negotiation and establishment of keying material for a variety of needs. The specification of what IKE is being used for is done in a *domain of interpretation* (DOI). The IP security DOI for ISAKMP is specified in RFC 2407 [40]. More specifically, RFC 2407 defines how ISAKMP can be used to negotiate IKE and IPsec SAs. If and when IKE is used by other protocols, they will each have to define their own DOI.[15] In other words, ISAKMP defines the language to establish authenticated session keys, whereas OAKLEY defines the steps two peers must actually take to establish the keys. Together they constitute the IKE protocol.

The IKE protocol is a request-response type of protocol with an initiator and a responder. The IKE initiator is the party that is instructed by its IPsec module to establish an SA or SA bundle as a result of an outbound packet matching an SPD entry. The SPD of IPsec is used to instruct IKE what to establish but does not instruct IKE how to do so. In fact, how IKE establishes the IPsec SAs is based on its own policy settings. IKE defines policy in terms of protection suites. Each protection suite must define at least an encryption algorithm, a hash algorithm, a Diffie-Hellman group, and a method for authentication. IKE's policy database then is the list of all protection suites weighted in order of preference.

The establishment of an IPsec SA (or an SA bundle) using IKE is a two-phase process:

---

14. The IETF Security Area Director was (and still is) Jeffrey Schiller from MIT.
15. At the time of this writing, no other DOI is available.

- In phase one, an IKE SA is established. The IKE SA defines the way in which the two peers communicate, for example, which algorithm to use to encrypt IKE traffic, how to authenticate the remote peer, and so on.

- In phase two, the IKE SA is used to establish any given number of IPsec SAs between the communicating peers. The IPsec SAs established by IKE may optionally have perfect forward secrecy (PFS[16]) of the keys and, if desired, also of the peer identity.

5.3.3.1 Phase one: establishing an IKE SA

The establishment of an IKE SA basically consists of three steps and corresponding exchanges:

1. A cookie exchange;

2. A value exchange;

3. An authentication exchange.

In short, the cookie exchange protects the responder from simple resource clogging attacks. Once initiator and responder cookies have been established, a value exchange and a subsequent authentication exchange are used to implement an authenticated Diffie-Hellman key exchange, and to provide the initiator and responder with an authenticated shared secret accordingly.

Cookie Exchange: To protect the responder from simple resource clogging attacks, the initiator must provide a valid cookie whenever he or she wants to enter a value exchange and initiate a computationally expensive Diffie-Hellman key exchange accordingly. A valid cookie, in turn, is a value that can be computed and verified only by the responder. For example, it can be a keyed one-way hash value of the initiator's and responder's IP addresses and port numbers. In this case, the key must be known only to the responder.

---

16. For a key agreement protocol based on public key cryptography, PFS ensures that a session key derived from a set of long-term public and private keys will not be compromised if one of the private keys is compromised in the future.

Value Exchange: A value exchange establishes a shared secret key between the communicating peers. In general, there is more than one way to establish a key, but IKE always uses a Diffie-Hellman key exchange. Consequently, the act of doing a Diffie-Hellman key exchange is not negotiable, but the parameters to use are. In fact, IKE borrows five groups from the OAKLEY specification; three are traditional exchanges doing exponentiation modulo a large prime, and two are elliptic curve groups. Upon completion of the value exchange, the two peers share a key and this key still needs to be authenticated.

Authentication Exchange: In a final step, the Diffie-Hellman key and, therefore, the IKE SA must be authenticated. There are five methods of authentication defined in IKE: preshared keys, digital signature using DSS, digital signature using RSA, and two methods that use an encrypted nonce exchange with RSA.

There are basically two modes and corresponding exchanges that can be used in phase one: a main mode exchange and an aggressive mode exchange.

1. In a *main mode exchange*, the request and response messages for each of the three exchanges are sent and received one after the other, totaling six messages.

2. Contrary to that, some of the messages are sent together in an *aggressive mode exchange*, totaling three messages. Most important, an aggressive mode exchange cannot use cookies to protect against resource clogging attacks.

In short, aggressive mode is faster but main mode is more flexible. Once Phase One is completed, Phase Two may commence and the required IPsec SAs may be created.

5.3.3.2 Phase two: establishing IPsec SAs

Contrary to Phase One, there is a single Phase Two exchange, and this exchange has been named *quick mode exchange*. This exchange negotiates IPsec SAs under the protection of the IKE SA, which was created in Phase One. The keys used for the IPsec SAs are, by default, derived from the IKE secret state. Pseudorandom nonces are exchanged in quick mode and hashed with the secret state to generate keys and guarantee that all SAs have unique keys. All such keys do not have the property of PFS as they are all derived from the same root key (i.e., the IKE shared secret). To provide PFS, Diffie-Hellman public values, and the group from which they are derived, are exchanged along the nonces and IPsec SA negotiation parameters. The resulting secret is used to generate the IPsec SA keys to guarantee PFS.

5.3.4 Implementations

As illustrated in Figure 5.7, there are three possibilities to implement the IPsec architecture (with or without key management) and to place the implementation in a host or security gateway:

- The most simple and straightforward possibility is to integrate the IPsec protocols into a native IP implementation (a). This is applicable to hosts and security gateways, but requires access to the corresponding source code.

- Another possibility is provided by so-called bump-in-the-stack (BITS) implementations (b). In these implementations, IPsec is implemented underneath an existing IP stack, between the native IP implementation and the local network drivers. Source code access for the IP stack is not required in this case, making it appropriate for use with legacy systems. This approach, when adopted, is usually employed with hosts.

- A somewhat related possibility is provided by so-called bump-in-the-wire (BITW) implementations (c). Similar to BITS implementations, source code access for the IP stack is not required for BITW implementations. But in addition to BITS implementations, additional hardware in the form of outboard cryptographic processors are

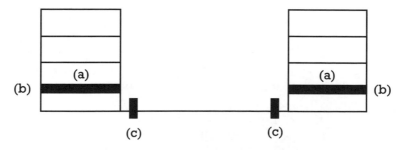

Figure 5.7 The three possibilities to implement the IPsec architecture.

typically used. This is a common design feature of network security systems used by the military, and of some commercial systems as well. BITW implementations may be designed to serve both hosts and security gateways.

As of this writing, most IPsec implementations are either BITS or BITW. For example, PGPnet is a BITS implementation, whereas most firewall products that support IPsec for virtual private networking are BITW implementations. The dominance of BITS or BITW implementations is expected to change in the future, because more vendors of networking software have integrated or are about to integrate the IPsec protocols into their products. For example, Windows 2000 comes along with IPsec support and the Cisco IOS also provides support for the IPsec protocols in the more recent releases.

From an implementation point of view, it is important that the key management protocol in use (e.g., IKE protocol) implements a standardized API. The IETF IPSEC WG has specified a corresponding PF_KEY key management API version 2 [57].

There are advantages and disadvantages related to security protocols that operate at the Internet layer in general, and the IPsec protocols in particular:

 ‣ The main advantage is that applications need not be changed to use the IPsec protocols. Another advantage is that providing security at the Internet layer works for both TCP- and UDP-based applications. This is advantageous because a steadily increasing number of applications are based on UDP that is hard to secure at the transport layer.

 ‣ The main disadvantage is that IP stacks must either be changed or extended. Because of the inherent complexity of the IKE protocol, the changes or extensions are not trivial. In the long term, high-speed networking may also provide a performance problem. As of this writing, it is not clear whether encryption rates and key agility properties of IPsec implementations will meet the performance requirements of future high-speed networks.

Because of the disadvantages of providing security at the Internet layer, some alternative approaches have appeared in the past (as discussed in the other sections of this chapter). The current trend in industry suggests that the IPsec protocols will primarily be used for virtual private networking and connecting mobile users to corporate intranets.

5.4 Transport layer security protocols

Again, the idea of having a standardized transport layer security protocol is not new, and several protocols had been proposed before the IETF TLS WG even started to meet:

▸ The security protocol 4 (SP4) is a transport layer security protocol that was developed by the NSA and NIST as part of the secure data network system (SDNS) suite of security protocols [58].

▸ The transport layer security protocol (TLSP) was developed and standardized by the International Organization for Standardization (ISO) [59].

▸ Matt Blaze and Steven Bellovin from AT&T Bell Laboratories developed an encrypted session manager (ESM) software package that operates at the transport layer [60].

In Internet application programming, it is common to use a generalized interprocess communications facility (IPC) to work with different transport layer protocols. Two popular IPC interfaces are BSD sockets and the transport layer interface (TLI), found on System V UNIX derivates. One idea that comes to mind first when trying to provide security services for TCP/IP applications is to enhance an IPC interface such as BSD sockets with the ability to authenticate peer entities, to exchange secret keys, and to use these keys to authenticate and encrypt data streams transmitted between the communicating peer entities. Netscape Communications Corporation followed this approach when it specified a *secure sockets layer* (SSL) and a corresponding SSL Protocol. The idea was later adopted by the IETF *transport layer security* (TLS) WG that is tasked to develop a security protocol for the transport layer. Due to their importance on the marketplace for network security solutions, we address the SSL and TLS protocols separately in the following chapter.

5.5 Application layer security protocols

In general, there are three approaches to provide security services at or above the application layer. First, the services can be integrated into each application protocol individually. Second, a generic security system can be built that provides the possibility to incorporate security services into arbitrary application programs. Third, it is possible to leave the application layer as it is and to provide security services above it.[17]

5.5.1 Security-enhanced application protocols

There are several application protocols that have been enhanced to provide integrated security services. For example, the Secure Shell (SSH) is a widely used and deployed protocol that serves as a secure replacement for terminal access and file transfer [61, 62]. DNS Security, or DNSSEC in short, refers to a set of security extensions and enhancements for DNS [63]. Furthermore, there are several cryptographic file systems that have been developed and proposed in the past. Examples include the Cryptographic File System (CFS) [64, 65] and the Andrew File System (AFS) [66].

With regard to Web security, the IETF chartered a Web Transaction Security (WTS) WG[18] in 1995. The goal of the WG was to "develop requirements and a specification for the provision of security services to Web transaction." The starting point was the specification of the Secure Hypertext Transfer Protocol (S-HTTP) that had been developed and was originally proposed by Eric Rescorla and Allan Schiffman on behalf of the CommerceNet consortium in the early 1990s.[19] S-HTTP version 1.0 was publicly released in June 1994 and distributed by the CommerceNet consortium. Since 1995, the S-HTTP specification has been further refined under the auspices of the IETF WTS WG. In August 1999, the S-HTTP was specified and released in an experimental RFC document [67] (complemented by other RFC documents). Due to the success and widespread deployment of SSL and TLS, S-HTTP and the IETF WTS WG silently disappeared.

5.5.2 Authentication and key distribution systems

In the 1990s, a considerable amount of work had been done to develop authentication and key distribution systems that can be used by arbitrary applications to incorporate security services. Examples include the following authentication and key distribution systems:

---

17. In [1], the third approach is discussed in a separate chapter with the title "Message Security Protocols."
18. http://www.ietf.org/html.charters/wts-charter.html
19. Launched in 1994 as a nonprofit organization, CommerceNet is dedicated to advancing electronic commerce on the Internet. Its almost 600 member companies and organizations seek solutions to technology issues, sponsor industry pilots, and foster market and business development. The CommerceNet consortium is available on-line at http://www.commerce.net.

- Kerberos, originally developed at MIT;

- Network Security Program (NetSP), developed by IBM;

- SPX, developed by DEC;

- The Exponential Security System (TESS), designed and developed at the University of Karlsruhe.

In addition, there are several extensions to the basic Kerberos authentication system, such as those provided by Yaksha, SESAME (secure European system for applications in a multivendor environment), and the Distributed Computing Environment (DCE) developed by the Open Group.[20] In this section we are not going to describe and discuss the authentication and key distribution systems mentioned above. Instead we refer to [68]. Kerberos will be overviewed and discussed in Section 8.3, when we talk about Kerberos-based authentication and authorization infrastructures (AAIs).

The important thing to keep in mind is that an authentication and key distribution system is to provide an API that makes it simple to secure any application protocol. The API of choice is the Generic Security Services API (GSS API) as specified by the IETF Common Authentication Technology (CAT) WG.[21]

5.5.3 Layering security protocols above the application layer

In addition to security-enhanced application protocols and authentication and key distribution systems, it is possible to layer security protocols above the application layer (i.e., leave the application protocols as they are). In this case, one may use any given (insecure) application protocol and secure the stream of bits and bytes before it is submitted to the application.

There are bascially two approaches that can be mentioned in this context: secure messaging (e.g., PGP or S/MIME as further addressed in [69]) and XML security as specified by the World Wide Web Consortium (W3C). In fact, the use of XML makes it possible to encrypt or digitally sign data segments (e.g., messages) in a standardized way before they are transmitted in computer networks or distributed systems. The corresponding

---

20. The Open Group was formed in early 1996 by the consolidation of two open-systems consortia, namely the Open Software Foundation (OSF) and the X/Open Company Ltd. The Open Group includes a large number of computer vendors, including IBM, DEC, and Microsoft.

21. http://www.ietf.org/html.charters/cat-charter.html

specifications are known as *XML Encryption* and *XML Digital Signatures*. Because XML security is a very new and still transient topic, it is not further addressed in this book. Note, however, that the IETF XMLDSIG WG[22] has been asked "to develop an XML compliant syntax used for representing the signature of Web resources and portions of protocol messages (anything referenceable by a URI) and procedures for computing and verifying such signatures." In March 2001, the WG came up with a specification that has been submitted to the Internet standards track [70].

In April 2002, Microsoft Corporation, IBM Corporation, and VeriSign, Inc. jointly proposed an architecture and a road map to properly address security within a Web service environment. The specifications that are currently being developed build upon foundational technologies, such as SSL/TLS, SOAP, WSDL, XML Digital Signatures, and XML Encryption. As of this writing, the only specification that is available is the WS-Security specification. In short, it describes how to attach digital signature and encryption headers to SOAP messages. In addition, it describes how to attach security tokens, including binary security tokens such as X.509 certificates and Kerberos tickets, to messages. In addition to the WS-Security specification, there are many specifications in the queue. Examples include the WS-Policy, WS-Trust, WS-Privacy, WS-SecureConversation, WS-Federation, and WS-Authorization specifications. You may refer to `http://www-106.ibm.com/developerworks/library/ws-secmap` for a corresponding overview.

5.6 Conclusions

In this chapter we overviewed and briefly discussed some cryptographic security protocols that can be used to provide communication security services for TCP/IP-based networks. While most of these protocols are similar in terms of security services they provide as well as cryptographic algorithms and techniques they employ, they vary fundamentally in the manner in which they provide the security services and their placement within the TCP/IP communications protocol suite. In particular, we have seen protocols for the network access, Internet, transport, and application layer.

Given this variety of cryptographic security protocols, we ask at least two questions:

---

22. `http://www.ietf.org/html.charters/xmldsig-charter.html`

1. Which security protocol is the best?

2. Which layer is best suited to provide communication security services?

With regard to the first question, the cryptographic security protocols have unique and partly incomparable advantages and disadvantages. For example, the IPsec and IKE protocols provide support for many parameters and options that are negotiable between the communicating peers, whereas the SSL and TLS protocols are rather strict in terms of parameters and options that must be implemented and supported. Given this situation and its diversity, it is very difficult or even impossible to have the protocols compete with each another and to actually decide which one is the best. Fortunately, most security protocols provide a reasonable level of security. In fact, most of them use the same or very similar cryptographic techniques and algorithms (e.g., the HMAC construction for message authentication, DES, 3DES, or AES for bulk data encryption, and RSA for entity authentication and key exchange). Only a few protocols have been shown to be weak and have serious security problems (e.g., MS-PPTP). Note, however, that this is only an example and that there are probably more weak than strong protocols in use today. This is particularly true for proprietary and unpublished security protocols that one sometimes finds in commercial products.

If deciding which security protocol is the best is difficult if not impossible, the next question is which layer is best suited to provide communication security services. This question is simpler to answer mainly because it addresses classes of security protocols (instead of individual security protocols). In order to further simplify the discussion (and to reduce the variety of layers that can provide communication security services), one usually distinguishes between lower layers (i.e., the network access and Internet layers) and higher layers (i.e., the transport and application layers, as well as the provision of security services above the application layer). In either case, there are arguments to provide security services at either the lower or higher layers in a given protocol stack:

▸ In short, the proponents of providing security services at the lower layers argue that lower-layer security can be implemented transparently to users and application programs, effectively killing many birds with a single stone.

▸ Contrary to that, the proponents of providing security services at the higher layers argue that lower-layer security attempts to do too many things, and that only protocols that work at higher layers can meet application-specific security needs and provide corresponding security services both effectively and efficiently.

Unfortunately, both arguments are true in some sense and there is no generally agreed-upon best layer to provide security services. The best layer actually depends on the security services that are required in a given environment and the application environment in which the services must be implemented and deployed. For example, nonrepudiation services are typically provided at the higher layers, whereas data confidentiality services can also be provided at the lower layers. Also, in an application environment where one can assume users to have smartcards and public key certificates the implementation and provision of non-repudiation services is usually simple and straightforward. In either case, the end-to-end argument originally proposed in [71] also applies for security and provides a strong argument for providing security services at the higher layers. In short, the end-to-end argument says that the function in question (e.g., a security function) can completely and correctly be implemented only with the knowledge of the application standing at the endpoints of the communications system. Therefore, providing that function as a feature of the communications system itself is not possible (sometimes an incomplete version of the function provided by the communications system may be useful as a performance enhancement).

References

[1]   Oppliger, R., *Internet and Intranet Security, Second Edition*, Norwood, MA: Artech House, 2002.

[2]   Simpson, W., "The Point-to-Point Protocol (PPP)," Request for Comments 1661, STD 51, July 1994.

[3]   IEEE 802.10, "IEEE Standards for Local and Metropolitan Area Networks: Interoperable LAN/MAN Security (SILS)," 1998.

[4]   IEEE 802.10c, "Supplements to IEEE Std 802.10, Interoperable LAN/MAN Security (SILS): Key Management (Clause 3)," 1992.

[5]   Valencia, A., M. Littlewood, and T. Kolar, "Cisco Layer Two Forwarding (Protocol) L2F," Request for Comments 2341, May 1998.

[6]   Scott, C., P. Wolfe, and M. Erwin, *Virtual Private Networks*, 2nd ed., Sebastopol, CA: O'Reilly & Associates, 1998.

[7]   Brown, S., *Implementing Virtual Private Networks*, New York: McGraw-Hill, 1999.

[8]   Hanks, S., et al., "Generic Routing Encapsulation (GRE)," Request for Comments 1701, October 1994.

[9]   Rand, D., "The PPP Compression Control Protocol (CCP)," Request for Comments 1962, June 1996.

[10]   Simpson, W., "PPP Challenge Handshake Authentication Protocol (CHAP)," Request for Comments 1994, August 1996.

[11]   Meyer, G., "The PPP Encryption Control Protocol (ECP)," Request for Comments 1968, June 1996.

[12]   Blunk, L., and J. Vollbrecht, "PPP Extensible Authentication Protocol (EAP)," Request for Comments 2284, March 1998.

[13]   Zorn, G., and S. Cobb, "Microsoft PPP CHAP Extensions," Request for Comments 2433, October 1998.

[14]   Pall, G. S., and G. Zorn, "Microsoft Point-to-Point Encryption (MPPE) Protocol," Request for Comments 2118, April 1998.

[15]   Schneier, B., and P. Mudge, "Cryptanalysis of Microsoft's Point-to-Point Tunneling Protocol," *Proceedings of ACM Conference on Communcations and Computer Security*, November 1998.

[16]   Zorn, G., "Microsoft PPP CHAP Extensions, Version 2," Request for Comments 2759, January 2000.

[17]   Schneier, B., and P. Mudge, "Cryptanalysis of Microsoft's PPTP Authentication Extensions (MS-CHAPv2)," June 1999.

[18]   Shea, R., *L2TP: Implementation and Operation*, Reading, MA: Addison-Wesley, 1999.

[19]   Townsley, W., et al., "Layer Two Tunneling Protocol 'L2TP'," Request for Comments 2661, August 1999.

[20]   Shirey, R., "Internet Security Glossary," Request for Comments 2828, May 2000.

[21]   Davie, B. S., and Y. Rekhter, *MPLS: Technology and Applications*, San Francisco, CA: Morgan Kaufmann Publishers, 2000.

[22]   Black, U., *MPLS and Label Switching Networks*, Englewood Cliffs, NJ: Prentice Hall, 2001.

[23]   Nelson, R., "SDNS Services and Architecture," *Proceedings of National Computer Security Conference*, 1987, pp. 153–157.

[24]   ISO/IEC 11577, Information Technology—Telecommunications and Information Exchange Between Systems—Network Layer Security Protocol, Geneva, Switzerland, 1993.

[25] Ioannidis, J., and M. Blaze, "The Architecture and Implementation of Network-Layer Security Under Unix," *Proceedings of the USENIX UNIX Security Symposium IV*, October 1993, pp. 29–39.

[26] Atkinson, R. J., "Security Architecture for the Internet Protocol," Request for Comments 1825, August 1995.

[27] Atkinson, R. J., "IP Authentication Header," Request for Comments 1826, August 1995.

[28] Atkinson, R. J., "IP Encapsulating Security Payload," Request for Comments 1827, August 1995.

[29] Metzger, P., and W. Simpson, "IP Authentication Using Keyed MD5," Request for Comments 1828, August 1995.

[30] Karn, P., P. Metzger, and W. Simpson, "The ESP DES-CBC Transform," Request for Comments 1829, August 1995.

[31] Atkinson, R. J., "Towards a More Secure Internet," *IEEE Computer*, Vol. 30, January 1997, pp. 57–61.

[32] Oppliger, R., "Security at the Internet Layer," *IEEE Computer*, Vol. 31, No. 9, September 1998, pp. 43–47.

[33] Kent, S., and R. Atkinson, "Security Architecture for the Internet Protocol," Request for Comments 2401, November 1998.

[34] Kent, S., and R. Atkinson, "IP Authentication Header," Request for Comments 2402, November 1998.

[35] Madson, C., and R. Glenn, "The Use of HMAC-MD5-96 Within ESP and AH," Request for Comments 2403, November 1998.

[36] Madson, C., and R. Glenn, "The Use of HMAC-SHA-1-96 Within ESP and AH," Request for Comments 2404, November 1998.

[37] Madson, C., and N. Doraswamy, "The ESP DES-CBC Cipher Algorithm with Explicit IV," Request for Comments 2405, November 1998.

[38] Kent, S., and R. Atkinson, "IP Encapsulating Security Payload (ESP)," Request for Comments 2406, November 1998.

[39] Glenn, R., and S. Kent, "The NULL Encryption Algorithm and Its Use with IPsec," Request for Comments 2410, November 1998.

[40] Piper, D., "The Internet IP Security Domain of Interpretation for ISAKMP," Request for Comments 2407, November 1998.

[41] Maughan, D., et al., "Internet Security Association and Key Management Protocol (ISAKMP)," Request for Comments 2408, November 1998.

[42] Harkins, D., and D. Carrel, "The Internet Key Exchange (IKE)," Request for Comments 2409, November 1998.

[43] Thayer, R., and N. Doraswamy, "IP Security Document Roadmap," Request for Comments 2411, November 1998.

[44] Doraswamy, N., and D. Harkins, *IPSec: The News Security Standard for the Internet, Intranets, and Virtual Private Networks*, Upper Saddle River, NJ: Prentice Hall, 1999.

[45] Kaufman, E., and A. Neuman, *Implementing IPSec: Making Security Work on VPNs, Intranets, and Extranets*, New York: John Wiley & Sons, 1999.

[46] Frankel, S., *Demystifying the IPsec Puzzle*, Norwood, MA: Artech House, 2001.

[47] Bellovin, S. M., "Problem Areas for the IP Security Protocols," *Proceedings of the 6th USENIX Security Symposium*, 1996, pp. 1–16.

[48] Bellovin, S. M., "Probable Plaintext Cryptanalysis of the IP Security Protocols," *Proceedings of the Symposium on Network and Distributed System Security*, 1997, pp. 155–160.

[49] Oehler, M., and R. Glenn, "HMAC-MD5 IP Authentication with Replay Prevention," Request for Comments 2085, February 1997.

[50] Cheng, P. C., et al., "A Security Architecture for the Internet Protocol," *IBM Systems Journal*, Vol. 37, No. 1, 1998, pp. 42–60.

[51] Caronni, G., et al., "SKIP—Securing the Internet," *Proceedings of WET ICE '96, Workshops on Enabling Technologies: Infrastructure for Collaborative Enterprises*, June 1996, pp. 62–67.

[52] Karn, P., and W. Simpson, "Photuris: Session-Key Management Protocol," Request for Comments 2522, March 1999.

[53] Karn, P., and W. Simpson, "Photuris: Extended Schemes and Attributes," Request for Comments 2523, March 1999.

[54] Diffie, W., P. C. van Oorshot, and M. J. Wiener, "Authentication and Authenticated Key Exchanges," *Designs, Codes and Cryptography*, Norwell, MA: Kluwer Academic Publishers, 1992, pp. 107–125.

[55] Krawczyk, H., "SKEME: A Versatile Secure Key Exchange Mechanism for Internet," *Proceedings of Internet Society Symposium on Network and Distributed System Security*, February 1996.

[56] Orman, H., "The OAKLEY Key Determination Protocol," Request for Comments 2412, November 1998.

[57] McDonald, D., C. Metz, and B. Phan, "PF_KEY Key Management API, Version 2," Request for Comments 2367, July 1998.

[58] Nelson, R., "SDNS Services and Architecture," *Proceedings of National Computer Security Conference*, 1987, pp. 153–157.

[59] ISO/IEC 10736, *Information Technology—Telecommunications and Information Exchange Between Systems—Transport Layer Security Protocol*, Geneva, Switzerland, 1993.

[60] Blaze, M., and S. M. Bellovin, "Session-Layer Encryption," *Proceedings of USENIX UNIX Security Symposium*, June 1995.

[61] Ylönen, T., "SSH—Secure Login Connections over the Internet," *Proceedings of USENIX UNIX Security Symposium*, July 1996.

[62] Barrett, D. J., and R. E. Silverman, *SSH, the Secure Shell: The Definitive Guide*, Sebastopol, CA: O'Reilly & Associates: 2001.

[63] Eastlake, D., "Domain Name System Security Extensions," Request for Comments 2535, March 1999.

[64] Blaze, M., "A Cryptographic File System for UNIX," *Proceedings of ACM Conference on Computer and Communications Security*, November 1993, pp. 9–16.

[65] Blaze, M., "Key Management in an Encrypting File System," *Proceedings of USENIX Summer Conference*, June 1994, pp. 27–35.

[66] Howard, J. H., "An Overview of the Andrew File System," *Proceedings of USENIX Conference*, 1988, pp. 23–26.

[67] Rescorla, E., and A. Schiffman, "The Secure HyperText Transfer Protocol," Request for Comments 2660, August 1999.

[68] Oppliger, R., *Authentication Systems for Secure Networks*, Norwood, MA: Artech House, 1996.

[69] Oppliger, R., *Secure Messaging with PGP and S/MIME*, Norwood, MA: Artech House, 2000.

[70] Eastlake, D., J. Reagle, and D. Solo, "XML-Signature Syntax and Processing," Request for Comments 3075, March 2001.

[71] Saltzer, J. H., D. P. Reed, and D. D. Clark, "End-to-End Arguments in System Design," *ACM Transactions on Computer Systems*, Vol. 2, No. 4, November 1984, pp. 277–288.

6

Contents

6.1 SSL Protocol

6.2 TLS Protocol

6.3 SSL and TLS certificates

6.4 Firewall traversal

6.5 Conclusions

References

SSL and TLS Protocols

As mentioned in the previous chapter, there are two transport layer security protocols that are of utmost importance for the security of Web-based applications: the SSL and TLS protocols. In this chapter, we elaborate on the two protocols. More specifically, we overview and briefly discuss the protocols in Sections 6.1 and 6.2, address SSL and TLS certificates in Section 6.3, and elaborate on firewall traversal in Section 6.4. Finally, we draw some conclusions in Section 6.5.

6.1 SSL Protocol

In this section, we elaborate on the history, architecture, two subprotocols (i.e., the SSL Record Protocol and SSL Handshake Protocol), security analysis, and implementations of the SSL protocol.

6.1.1 History

In general, there are several possibilities to cryptographically protect HTTP data traffic. For example, in the early 1990s the CommerceNet[1] consortium proposed S-HTTP that was basically a security-specific enhancement of HTTP. An implementation of S-HTTP was made publicly available in a modified version of

---

1. http://www.commerce.net

the NCSA Mosaic browser that users had to purchase (contrary to the "normal" NCSA Mosaic browser that was publicly and freely available on the Internet).

At the same time, however, Netscape Communications introduced SSL and a corresponding protocol with the first version of Netscape Navigator.[2] Contrary to the CommerceNet consortium, Netscape Communications did not charge its customers for the implementation of its security protocol. Consequently, SSL became the predominant protocol to provide security services for HTTP data traffic after 1994, and S-HTTP silently sank into oblivion.

So far, there have been three versions of SSL:

1. SSL version 1.0 was used internally only by Netscape Communications. It contained some serious flaws and was never released in public.

2. SSL version 2.0 was incorporated into Netscape Navigator versions 1.0 through 2.x. It had some weaknesses related to specific incarnations of the man-in-the-middle attack. In an attempt to leverage public uncertainty about SSL's security, Microsoft also introduced the competing *Private Communication Technology* (PCT) Protocol in its first release of Internet Explorer in 1996.

3. Netscape Communications responded to Microsoft's PCT challenge by introducing SSL version 3.0 that addressed the problems in SSL 2.0 and added some new features. At this point, Microsoft backed down and agreed to support SSL in all versions of its TCP/IP-based software (although its own software still supports PCT for backward compatibility).

The latest specification of SSL 3.0 was officially released in March 1996.[3] It is implemented in all major browsers, including, for example, Microsoft Internet Explorer 3.0 (and higher), Netscape Navigator 3.0 (and higher), and Opera. As discussed later in this chapter, SSL 3.0 has also been adapted by the IETF TLS WG. In fact, the TLS 1.0 protocol specification is a derivative of

---

2.   On August 12, 1997, Netscape Communications was granted U.S. patent 5,657,390 entitled "Secure Socket Layer Application Program Apparatus and Method" for the technology employed by the SSL protocol.

3.   The SSL 3.0 specification was drafted by Alan O. Freier and Philip Karlton of Netscape Communications, as well as Paul C. Kocher of Cryptography Research.

SSL 3.0. In the following two sections, we focus only on the SSL and TLS protocols; the PCT protocol is not further addressed in this book.

6.1.2 Architecture

The architecture of SSL and the corresponding SSL protocol are illustrated in Figure 6.1. According to this figure, SSL refers to an intermediate (security) layer between the transport layer and the application layer. SSL is layered on top of a connection-oriented and reliable transport service, such as provided by TCP. It is conceptually able to provide security services for arbitrary TCP-based application protocols, not just HTTP. As a matter of fact, one major advantage of transport layer security protocols in general, and the SSL protocol in particular, is that they are application-independent, in the sense that they can be used to transparently secure any application protocol layered on top of TCP. Figure 6.1 illustrates several exemplary application protocols, including NSIIOP, HTTP, FTP, Telnet, IMAP, IRC, and POP3. They can all be secured by layering them on top of SSL (the appended letter S in the corresponding protocol acronyms indicates the use of SSL). Note, however, that SSL has a strong client-server orientation and does not really meet the requirements of peer application protocols.

In short, the SSL protocol provides communication security that has three basic properties:

1. The communicating parties (i.e., the client and the server) can authenticate each other using public key cryptography.

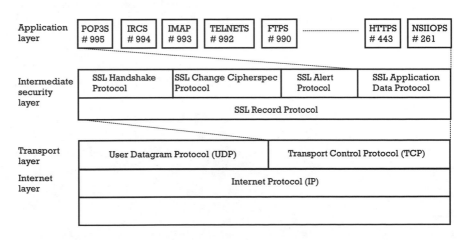

Figure 6.1 The architecture of SSL and the SSL protocol.

2. The confidentiality of the data traffic is protected, as the connection is transparently encrypted after an initial handshake and session key negotiation has taken place.

3. The authenticity and integrity of the data traffic is also protected, as messages are transparently authenticated and integrity-checked using MACs.

Nevertheless, it is important to note that SSL does not protect against traffic analysis attacks. For example, by examining the unencrypted source and destination IP addresses and TCP port numbers, or examining the volume of transmitted data, a traffic analyst can still determine what parties are interacting, what types of services are being used, and sometimes even recover information about business or personal relationships. We have already mentioned in this book that users generally consider the threat of traffic analysis to be relatively low, and so the developers of SSL have not attempted to address it, either. Furthermore, SSL does not protect against attacks directed against the TCP implementation, such as TCP SYN flooding[4] or session hijacking attacks.[5]

To use SSL protection, both the client and server must know that the other side is using SSL. In general, there are three possibilities to address this issue:

1. Use dedicated port numbers reserved by the Internet Assigned Numbers Authority (IANA). In this case, a separate port number must be assigned for every application protocol that uses SSL.

2. Use the normal port number for every application protocol, and to negotiate security options as part of the (now slightly modified) application protocol.

3. Use a TCP option to negotiate the use of a security protocol, such as SSL, during the normal TCP connection establishment phase.

The application-specific negotiation of security options (i.e., the second possibility) has the disadvantage of requiring each application protocol to be modified to understand the negotiation process. Also, defining a TCP option (i.e., the third possibility) would be a fine solution, but has not been

---

4. This attack requires the flooding of a TCP implementation with SYN messages.
5. This attack targets an endpoint of a TCP connection and tries to take over the connection.

seriously discussed so far. In practice, separate port numbers have been reserved and assigned by the IANA for every application protocol that may run on top of SSL or TLS (i.e., the first possibility).[6] Note, however, that the use of separate port numbers also has the disadvantage of requiring two TCP connections if the client does not know what the server supports. First the client must connect to the secure port, and then to the unsecure port, or vice versa. It is very possible that future protocols will abandon this approach and go for the second possibility. For example, the Simple Authentication and Security Layer (SALS) defines a method for adding authentication support to connection-based application protocols [1]. According to the SALS specification, the use of authentication mechanisms is negotiable between the client and server of a given application protocol. As of this writing, SALS is primarily used to secure communications between IMAP4 clients and servers. It is not clear at the moment whether SALS or similar mechanisms will also be used to secure other application protocols.

The port numbers assigned by the IANA for application protocols that run on top of SSL/TLS are summarized in Table 6.1 and partly illustrated in Figure 6.1. Note that some acronyms for application protocols that run on top of SSL/TLS have changed since publication of the first edition of this book. Today, the "S" indicating the use of SSL is consistently appended (postfixed) to the acronyms of the corresponding application protocols (in some earlier terminologies, the S was inconsistently used and prepended (prefixed) to some acronyms).

Table 6.1 Port Numbers Assigned for Application Protocols That Run on Top of SSL/TLS

Keyword	Port	Description
nsiiops	261	IIOP name service over TLS/SSL
https	443	HTTP over TLS/SSL
smtps	465	SMTP over TLS/SSL (former ssmtp)
nntps	563	NNTP over TLS/SSL (former snntp)
ldaps	636	LDAP over TLS/SSL (former sldap)
ftps-data	989	FTP (data) over TLS/SSL
ftps	990	FTP (control) over TLS/SSL
telnets	992	TELNET over TLS/SSL
imaps	993	IMAP4 over TLS/SSL
ircs	994	IRC over TLS/SSL
pop3s	995	POP3 over TLS/SSL (former spop3)

---

6. http://www.isi.edu/in-notes/iana/assignments/port-numbers

In general, an SSL session is stateful and the SSL protocol must initialize and maintain the state information on either side of the session. The corresponding session state information elements, including a session ID, a peer certificate, a compression method, a cipher spec, a master secret, and a flag that indicates whether the session is resumable, are summarized in Table 6.2. An SSL session can be used for several connections, and the corresponding connection state information elements are summarized in Table 6.3. They include cryptographic parameters, such as server and client random byte sequences, server and client write MAC secrets, server and client write keys, an initialization vector, and a sequence number. In either case, it is important to note that communicating parties may use multiple simultaneous SSL sessions and sessions with multiple simultaneous connections.

As illustrated in Figure 6.1, the SSL protocol consists of two main parts, the SSL Record Protocol and several SSL subprotocols layered on top of it:

Table 6.2   SSL Session State Information Elements

Element	Description
Session ID	Identifier chosen by the server to identify an active or resumable session state
Peer certificate	X.509 version 3 certificate of the peer entity
Compression method	Algorithm used to compress data prior to encryption
Cipher spec	Specification of the data encryption and MAC algorithms
Master secret	48-byte secret shared between the client and server
Is resumable	Flag that indicates whether the session can be used to initiate new connections

Table 6.3   SSL Connection State Information Elements

Element	Description
Server and client random	Byte sequences that are chosen by the server and client for each connection
Server write MAC secret	Secret used for MAC operations on data written by the server
Client write MAC secret	Secret used for MAC operations on data written by the client
Server write key	Key used for data encryption by the server and decryption by the client
Client write key	Key used for data encryption by the client and decryption by the server
Initialization vector	Initialization state for a block cipher in CBC mode. This field is first initialized by the SSL Handshake Protocol Thereafter, the final ciphertext block from each record is preserved for use with the following record
Sequence number	Each party maintains separate sequence numbers for transmitted and received messages for each connection

▸ The *SSL Record Protocol* is layered on top of a connection-oriented and reliable transport layer service, such as provided by TCP, and provides message origin authentication, data confidentiality, and data integrity services (including such things as replay protection).

▸ The SSL subprotocols are layered on top of the SSL Record Protocol to provide support for SSL session and connection establishment management.

The most important SSL subprotocol is the SSL Handshake Protocol. This protocol, in turn, is an authentication and key exchange protocol that can be used to negotiate, initialize, and synchronize security parameters and corresponding state information located at either endpoint of an SSL session or connection.

After the SSL Handshake Protocol has completed, application data can be sent and received using the SSL Record Protocol and the negotiated security parameters and state information elements. The SSL Record and Handshake Protocols are overviewed next.

6.1.3 SSL Record Protocol

The SSL Record Protocol receives data from higher layer SSL subprotocols and addresses data fragmentation, compression,[7] authentication, and encryption. More precisely, the protocol takes as input a data block of arbitrary size, and produces as output a series of SSL data fragments (further referred to as SSL records) of less than or equal to $2^{14} - 1 = 16,383$ bytes each.

The various steps of the SSL Record Protocol that lead from a raw data fragment to an SSLPlaintext (fragmentation step), SSLCompressed (compression step), and SSLCiphertext (encryption step) record are illustrated in Figure 6.2. Finally, each SSL record contains the following information fields:

▸ Content type;

▸ Protocol version number;

▸ Length;

---

7. Data compression as addressed by the SSL Record Protocol is not supported by the major SSL implementations in use today.

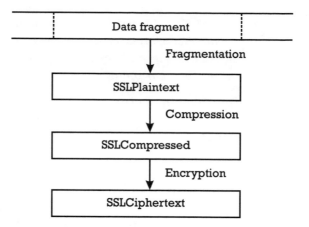

Figure 6.2 The SSL Record Protocol steps.

‣ Data payload (optionally compressed and encrypted);

‣ MAC.

The content type defines the higher layer protocol that must be used to subsequently process the SSL record data payload (after proper decompression and decryption). The protocol version number determines the SSL version in use (typically 3.0). Each SSL record data payload is compressed and encrypted according to the current compression method and cipher spec defined for the SSL session. At the start of each SSL session, the compression method and cipher spec are usually defined as null. They are both set during the initial execution of the SSL Handshake Protocol. Finally, a MAC is appended to each SSL record. It provides message origin authentication and data integrity services. Similar to the encryption algorithm, the algorithm that is used to compute and verify the MAC is defined in the cipher spec of the current session state. By default, the SSL Record Protocol uses a MAC construction that is similar but still different from the newer HMAC construction specified in RFC 2104 [2]. There are three major differences between the SSL MAC construction and the HMAC construction:

1. The SSL MAC construction includes a sequence number in the message before hashing to protect against specific forms of replay attacks.

2. The SSL MAC construction includes the record length.

3. The SSL MAC construction uses concatenation operators, whereas the HMAC construction uses the addition modulo 2.

All these differences exist mainly because the SSL MAC construction predates adoption of the HMAC construction in almost all Internet security protocol specifications. The HMAC construction was also adopted for the more recent TLS protocol specification.

As illustrated in Figure 6.1, several SSL subprotocols are layered on top of the SSL Record Protocol. Each subprotocol may refer to specific types of messages that are sent using the SSL Record Protocol. The SSL 3.0 specification defines the following three SSL protocols:

▸ Alert Protocol;

▸ Handshake Protocol;

▸ ChangeCipherSpec Protocol.

In short, the SSL Alert Protocol is used to transmit alerts (i.e., alert messages) via the SSL Record Protocol. Each alert message consists of two parts, an alert level and an alert description.

The SSL Handshake Protocol is the major SSL subprotocol. It is used to mutually authenticate the client and the server and to exchange a session key. As such, the SSL Handshake Protocol is overviewed and briefly discussed in the following section.

Finally, the SSL ChangeCipherSpec Protocol is used to change between one cipher spec and another. Although the cipher spec is normally changed at the end of an SSL handshake, it can also be changed at any later point in time.

In addition to these SSL subprotocols, an SSL Application Data Protocol is used to directly pass application data to the SSL Record Protocol.

6.1.4 SSL Handshake Protocol

The SSL Handshake Protocol is the main SSL subprotocol that is layered on top of the SSL Record Protocol. Consequently, SSL handshake messages are supplied to the SSL record layer, where they are encapsulated within one or more SSL records, which are processed and transmitted as specified by the compression method and cipher spec of the current SSL session, and the cryptographic keys of the corresponding SSL connection. The aim of the SSL Handshake Protocol is to have a client and server establish and maintain state information that is used to secure communications. More specifically, the protocol is to have the client and server agree on a common SSL protocol version, select the compression method and cipher spec, optionally authenticate each other, and create a master secret from which the various session keys for message authentication and encryption may be derived.

In short, an execution of the SSL Handshake Protocol between a client C and a server S can be summarized as follows (the messages that are put in square brackets are optional):

$$1 : C \longrightarrow S : \text{CLIENTHELLO}$$
$$2 : S \longrightarrow C : \text{SERVERHELLO}$$
$$[\text{CERTIFICATE}]$$
$$[\text{SERVERKEYEXCHANGE}]$$
$$[\text{CERTIFICATEREQUEST}]$$
$$\text{SERVERHELLODONE}$$
$$3 : C \longrightarrow S : [\text{CERTIFICATE}]$$
$$\text{CLIENTKEYEXCHANGE}$$
$$[\text{CERTIFICATEVERIFY}]$$
$$\text{CHANGECIPHERSPEC}$$
$$\text{FINISHED}$$
$$4 : S \longrightarrow C : \text{CHANGECIPHERSPEC}$$
$$\text{FINISHED}$$

When the client C wants to connect to the server S, it establishes a TCP connection to the HTTPS port (not included in the protocol description) and sends a CLIENTHELLO message to the server in step 1 of the SSL Handshake Protocol execution. The client can also send a CLIENTHELLO message in response to a HELLOREQUEST message or on its own initiative to renegotiate the security parameters of an existing connection. The CLIENTHELLO message includes the following fields:

‣ The number of the highest SSL version understood by the client (typically 3.0);

‣ A client-generated random structure that consists of a 32-bit timestamp in standard UNIX format, and a 28-byte value generated by a pseudorandom number generator;

‣ A session identity the client wishes to use for this connection;

‣ A list of cipher suites that the client supports;

‣ A list of compression methods that the client supports.

Note that the session identity field should be empty if no SSL session currently exists or if the client wishes to generate new security parameters.

In either case, a nonempty session identity field is to specify an existing SSL session between the client and the server (i.e., a session whose security parameters the client wishes to reuse). The session identity may be from an earlier connection, this connection, or another currently active connection. Also note that the list of supported cipher suites, passed from the client to the server in the CLIENTHELLO message, contains the combinations of cryptographic algorithms supported by the client in order of preference. Each cipher suite defines both a key exchange algorithm and a cipher spec. The server will select a cipher suite or, if no acceptable choices are presented, return an error message and close the connection accordingly. After having sent the CLIENTHELLO message, the client waits for a SERVERHELLO message. Any other message returned by the server except for a HELLOREQUEST message is treated as an error at this point in time.

In step 2, the server processes the CLIENTHELLO message and responds with either an error or SERVERHELLO message. Similar to the CLIENTHELLO message, the SERVERHELLO message includes the following fields:

▸ A server version number that contains the lower version of that suggested by the client in the CLIENTHELLO message and the highest supported by the server;

▸ A server-generated random structure that also consists of a 32-bit timestamp in standard UNIX format, and a 28-byte value generated by a pseudorandom number generator;

▸ A session identity corresponding to this connection;

▸ A cipher suite selected by the server from the list of cipher suites supported by the client;

▸ A compression method selected by the server from the list of compression algorithms supported by the client.

If the session identity in the CLIENTHELLO message was nonempty, the server looks in its session cache for a match. If a match is found and the server is willing to establish the new connection using the corresponding session state, the server responds with the same value as supplied by the client. This indicates a resumed session and dictates that both parties must proceed directly to the CHANGECIPHERSPEC and FINISHED messages as addressed further below. Otherwise, this field contains a different value identifying a new session. The server may also return an empty session identity field to indicate that the session will not be cached and therefore cannot be resumed later. Also note that in the SERVERHELLO message, the server selects a cipher suite and a compression method from the lists provided by the client in the CLIENTHELLO message. The key exchange, authentication, encryption, and message authentication algorithms are determined by the cipher suite selected by the server and revealed in the SERVERHELLO message. The cipher suites that have been defined for the SSL protocol are essentially the same as the ones that are specified for the TLS protocol (as summarized in Tables 6.4 to 6.7).

In addition to the SERVERHELLO message, the server may also send other messages to the client. For example, if the server is using certificate-based authentication (which is currently almost always the case), the server sends its site certificate to the client in a corresponding CERTIFICATE message. The certificate must be appropriate for the selected cipher suite's key exchange algorithm, and is generally an X.509v3 certificate. The same message type will be used later for the client's response to the server's CERTIFICATERequest message. In the case of X.509v3 certificates, a certificate may actually refer to an entire chain of certificates, ordered with the sender's certificate first followed by any CA certificates proceeding sequentially upward to a root CA (that will be accepted by the client).

Next, the server may send a SERVERKEYEXCHANGE message to the client if it has no certificate, a certificate that can be used only for verifying digital signatures, or uses the FORTEZZA token-based key exchange algorithm (KEA).[8] Obviously, this message is not required if the site certificate includes an RSA public key that can be used for encryption. Also, a nonanonymous server can optionally request a personal certificate to authenticate the client. It therefore sends a CERTIFICATERequest message to the client. The message includes a list of the types of certificates requested, sorted in order of the server's preference, as well as a list of distinguished names for acceptable CAs. At the end of step 2, the server sends a SERVERHELLODone message to the client to indicate the end of the SERVERHELLO and associated messages.

Upon receipt of the SERVERHELLO and associated messages, the client verifies that the server site certificate (if provided) is valid,[9] and checks that the security parameters provided in the SERVERHELLO message are indeed acceptable. If the server has requested client authentication, the client sends

---

8. Netscape Communications was paid a large amount of money by the NSA to include support for the FORTEZZA KEA in the SSL protocol specification.
9. A server site certificate is considered to be valid if its server's common name field entry matches the host part of the URL the client wants to access.

a CERTIFICATE message that includes a personal certificate for the user's public key to the server in step 3. Next, the client sends a CLIENT-KEYEXCHANGE message, whose format depends on the key exchange algorithm selected by the server:

▶ If RSA is used for server authentication and key exchange, the client generates a 48-byte premaster secret,[10] encrypts it with the public key found in the site certificate or the temporary RSA key from the SERVERKEYEXCHANGE message, and sends the result back to the server in the CLIENTKEYEXCHANGE message. The server, in turn, uses the corresponding private key to decrypt the premaster secret. We will return to this key exchange algorithm later in this section when we talk about a specific attack.

▶ If FORTEZZA tokens are used for key exchange, the client derives a token encryption key (TEK) using the KEA. The client's KEA calculation uses the public key from the server certificate along with some private parameters in the client's token. The client sends public parameters needed for the server to also generate the TEK, using its private parameters. It generates a premaster secret, wraps it using the TEK, and sends the result together with some initialization vectors to the server as part of the CLIENTKEYEXCHANGE message. The server, in turn, can decrypt the premaster secret accordingly. This key exchange algorithm is not widely used in practice.

▶ If a Diffie-Hellman key exchange is performed, the server and client exchange their public parameters as part of the SERVERKEYEXCHANGE and CLIENTKEYEXCHANGE messages. Obviously, this is only required if the Diffie-Hellman public parameters are not included in the site and personal certificates. The negotiated Diffie-Hellman key can then be used as premaster secret. Because a Diffie-Hellman key exchange involves both parties in a key exchange, the resulting key exchange is less vulnerable to weak pseudorandom number generators in client software packages. Consequently, it is possible and very likely that we will see more widespread use of the Diffie-Hellman key exchange in the future.

---

10. The premaster secret is 48 bytes long and consists of 2 bytes specifying the protocol version and 46 bytes of randomly generated data.

For the RSA, FORTEZZA, and Diffie-Hellman key exchanges, the same algorithms are used to convert the premaster secret into a 48-byte master secret (stored in the corresponding SSL session state), and to derive session keys for encryption and message authentication from this master secret. Nevertheless, some key exchange algorithms, such as the FORTEZZA token-based key exchange, may also use their own procedures for generating encryption keys. In this case, the master secret is only used to derive keys for message authentication. The procedures to derive master and session keys, as well as initialization vectors, are fully described in the SSL protocol specification and are not further addressed in this book.

If client authentication is required, the client also sends a CERTIFICATE-VERIFY message to the server. This message is used to provide explicit verification of the user's identity based on the personal certificate. It is only sent following a client certificate that has signing capability (all certificates except those containing fixed Diffie-Hellman parameters). Finally, the client finishes step 3 by sending a CHANGECIPHERSPEC message and a corresponding FINISHED message to the server. The FINISHED message is always sent immediately after the CHANGECIPHERSPEC message to verify that the key exchange and authentication processes were successful. As a matter of fact, the FINISHED message is the first message that is protected with the newly negotiated algorithms and session keys. It can only be generated and verified if these keys are properly installed on both sides. No acknowledgment of the FINISHED message is required; parties may begin sending encrypted data immediately after having sent the FINISHED message. The SSL Handshake Protocol execution finishes up by also having the server send a CHANGECIPHERSPEC message and a corresponding FINISHED message to the client in step 4.

After the SSL handshake is complete, a secure connection is established between the client and the server. This connection can now be used to send application data that is encapsulated by the SSL Record Protocol. More accurately, application data may be fragmented, compressed, encrypted, and authenticated according to the SSL Record Protocol, as well as the session and connection state information that is now established (according to the execution of the SSL Handshake Protocol).

The SSL Handshake Protocol can be shortened if the client and server decide to resume a previously established (and still cached) SSL session or duplicate an existing SSL session. In this case, only three message flows and a total of six messages are required. The corresponding message flows can be summarized as follows:

$$1 : C \longrightarrow S : \text{ClientHello}$$
$$2 : S \longrightarrow C : \text{ServerHello}$$
$$\text{ChangeCipherSpec}$$
$$\text{Finished}$$
$$3 : S \longrightarrow C : \text{ChangeCipherSpec}$$
$$\text{Finished}$$

In step 1, the client sends a ClientHello message to the server that includes a session identity to be resumed. The server, in turn, checks its session cache for a match. If a match is found, and the server is willing to resume the connection under the specified session state, it returns a ServerHello message with the same session identity in step 2. At this point, both the client and the server must send ChangeCipherSpec and Finished messages to each other in steps 2 and 3. Once the session reestablishment is complete, the client and server can begin exchanging application data.

In summary, the SSL protocol can be used to establish secure TCP connections between clients and servers. In particular, it can be used to authenticate the server, to optionally authenticate the client, to perform a key exchange, and to provide message authentication, as well as data confidentiality and integrity services for arbitrary application protocols layered on top of TCP. Although it may seem that not providing client authentication goes against the principles that should be espoused by a secure system, an argument can be made that the decision to optionally support it helped SSL gain widespread use in the first place. Support for client authentication requires public keys and personal certificates for each client, and because SSL support for HTTP must be embedded in the corresponding browser software, requiring client authentication would involve distributing public keys and personal certificates to every user on the Internet. In the short term, it was believed to be more crucial that consumers be aware of with whom they are conducting business than to give the merchants the same level of assurance. Furthermore, because the number of Internet servers is much smaller than the number of clients, it is easier and more practical to first outfit servers with the necessary public keys and site certificates. As of this writing, however, support for client-side public keys and personal certificates is growing as people generally push the use of PKI technologies.

6.1.5 Security analysis

A comprehensive security analysis of SSL 3.0 was performed by Bruce Schneier and David Wagner in 1996 [3]. Except for some minor flaws and worrisome features that could be easily corrected without overhauling the basic structure of the SSL protocol, they found no serious vulnerability or security problem in their analysis. Consequently, they concluded that the SSL protocol provides excellent security against eavesdropping and other passive attacks, and that people implementing the protocol should be aware of some sophisticated active attacks.

A few months later, however, Daniel Bleichenbacher from Bell Laboratories found an adaptive chosen ciphertext attack against protocols based on the public key cryptography standard (PKCS) #1 [4]. The attack was published in 1998 [5]. In short, an RSA private key operation (a decryption or digital signature operation) can be performed if the attacker has access to an oracle that, for any chosen ciphertext, returns only 1 bit telling whether the ciphertext corresponds to some unknown block of data encrypted using PKCS #1.

To understand the Bleichenbacher attack, it is necessary to have a look at PKCS #1. In fact, there are three block formats specified in PKCS #1: block types 0 and 1 are used for RSA digital signatures, and block type 2 is used for RSA encryption. Recall from our previous discussion that if the RSA algorithm is used for server authentication and key exchange, the client randomly generates a 46-byte premaster secret, prepends the two bytes 03 (the SSL protocol version number) and 00 to the premaster secret, encrypts the result using the public key of the server, and sends it in a CLIENTKEYEXCHANGE message to the server. As such, the CLIENTKEYEXCHANGE message carrying the encrypted premaster secret must conform to the format specified in PKCS #1 block type 2. The format is illustrated in Figure 6.3.

Now, assume there is an attacker who can send an arbitrary number of randomly looking messages to an SSL server, and the server responds for each of these messages with a bit indicating whether a particular message is correctly encrypted and encoded according to PKCS #1 (the server thus acts as an oracle). Under this assumption, Bleichenbacher developed an attack to illegitimately perform an RSA operation with the private key of the server (either a decryption or a digital signature operation). When applied to decrypt a premaster secret of a previously sent CLIENTKEYEXCHANGE message, the attacker can rebuild the premaster secret and the session keys that are

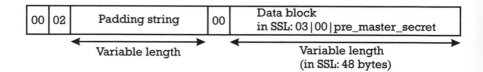

Figure 6.3   PKCS #1 block format for encryption.

derived from it accordingly. Consequently, the attacker can then decrypt the entire session (if he or she has monitored and stored the data stream of that session).

The attack is primarily of theoretical interest. Note that experimental results have shown that typically between 300,000 and 2 million chosen ciphertexts are required to actually perform the (decryption or digital signature) operation. To make things worse, the attack can only be launched against an SSL server that is available on-line (since it must act as an oracle). From the attacker's point of view, it may be difficult to send this huge number of chosen ciphertexts to the SSL server without causing the server administrator to become suspicious.

There are several possibilities to protect against the Bleichenbacher attack. First of all, it is not necessary for the server to respond with an error message after having received a CLIENTKEYEXCHANGE message that does not conform to PKCS #1. Another possibility is to change the PKCS #1 block format for encryption and to remove the leading 00 and 02 bytes, as well as the 00, 03, and 00 bytes in the middle of the message (as illustrated in Figure 6.3). Finally, another possibility is to use plaintext-aware encryption schemes, such as the one proposed by Mihir Bellare and Phillip Rogaway [6], or any other public key cryptosystem that is provably secure against adaptive chosen ciphertext attacks [7].[11] For example, in the aftermath of the publication of Bleichenbacher's results, IBM launched a marketing initiative to promote such a cryptosystem jointly developed by Ronald Cramer and Victor Shoup [8].

Before Bleichbacher published his attack, he had been collaborating with RSA Laboratories to update PKCS #1 and to specify a version 2 that is secure against adaptive chosen ciphertext attacks [9]. Meanwhile, all major vendors of SSL servers have incorporated and implemented PKCS #1 version 2 into their products. Unfortunately, PKCS #1 version 2 has also turned out be be vulnerable against specific types of chosen ciphertext attacks [10].

6.1.6 Implementations

As of this writing, the SSL protocol is by far the most pervasive security protocol for the Internet in general, and the WWW in particular. For example, most banks that offer their services over the Internet have their corresponding home banking client software based on SSL. This decision also

---

11. Note that plaintext awareness always implies security against chosen ciphertext attacks.

conforms to the strategic view of the European Committee for Banking Standards (ECBS).[12]

There are many implementations of SSL.[13] Examples include *SSLref*, a reference implementation of SSL from Netscape Communications; *SSLeay*, an internationally distributed implementation written by Eric Young in Australia; and *OpenSSL*, an open source implementation of SSL.[14] Last but not least, there is an interesting software called *Stunnel* that can be used to add SSL protection to existing TCP-based application servers in a UNIX environment without requiring changes to the corresponding code. The software can be invoked from the Internet daemon (i.e., `inetd`) as a wrapper for any number of services or run standalone, accepting network connections itself for a particular service. Refer to the Stunnel home page[15] for further information about the software package.

In addition to these SSL implementations, most browsers and Web servers have been modified to incorporate support for SSL. For example, the Apache Web server has been modified to make use of SSLeay [11]. Typically, Web servers that use SSL (or TLS) are called *secure* or *commerce* servers. Note, however, that these servers are not necessarily more secure than any other Web server; they just support SSL to secure the data traffic that is transmitted between the client and the server. Most SSL-enabled products support the RC4 algorithm for encryption and the MD2 and MD5 one-way functions for hashing.

For obvious reasons, the use of SSL slows the speed of a browser interacting with an HTTPS server. This performance degradation is in fact noticeable by the user. It is primarily due to the public key encryption and decryption operations that are required to initialize the SSL session and connection state information elements. In practice, users experience an additional pause of a few seconds between opening a connection to the HTTPS server and retrieving the first HTML page from it. Because SSL is designed to cache the master secret between subsequent sessions, this delay affects only the first SSL connection between the browser and the server. Compared with the session establishment, the additional overhead of

---

12. In May 1997, the ECBS published TR401 V1 entitled "Secure Banking over the Internet." The document is electronically available and can be downloaded from the home page of the ECBS at `http://www.ecbs.org`.

13. In the first edition of this book, the problem of using SSL- and TLS-enabled software products with limited cryptographic strength was also addressed. Due to the liberalized U.S. export controls, this problem has become obsolete in most parts of the world. Consequently, we are not going to repeat the discussion in this edition of the book.

14. `http://www.openssl.org`

15. `http://www.stunnel.org`

encrypting and decrypting the data traffic using one of the supported encryption algorithms, such as DES, RC2, or RC4, is practically insignificant (and not necessarily noticeable by the user). Consequently, for users that have a fast computer and a relatively slow network connection to an HTTPS server, the overhead of SSL is insignificant, especially if a large amount of data is sent afterward over the SSL session or over multiple SSL sessions that use a shared master secret. However, administrators of very busy SSL servers should consider getting either extremely fast computers or hardware assistance for the public key operations.

6.2   TLS Protocol

Early in 1996, the IETF chartered a TLS WG within the security and transport areas. The objective of the IETF TLS WG was to write Internet standards track RFCs for a TLS protocol using the currently available specifications of SSL (2.0 and 3.0), PCT (1.0), and SSH version 2 as a basis.[16]

Shortly before the IETF meeting in December 1996, a first TLS 1.0 document was released as an Internet-Draft. The document was essentially the same as the SSL 3.0 specification. In fact, it was the explicit strategy of the IETF TLS WG to have the TLS 1.0 specification be based on SSL 3.0, as opposed to SSL 2.0, PCT 1.0, SSH version 2, or any other transport layer security protocol proposal. At least three major modifications were suggested for SSL 3.0 to be incorporated into TLS 1.0:

1. The HMAC construction developed in the IETF IPsec WG should be adopted and consistently used in TLS 1.0.

2. The FORTEZZA token-based KEA should be removed from TLS 1.0, since it refers to a proprietary and unpublished technology. Instead, a DSS-based key exchange mechanism should be included in TLS 1.0.

3. The TLS Record Protocol and the TLS Handshake Protocol should be separated out and specified more clearly in related documents.

After having adopted these modifications, the resulting TLS protocol was specified in a series of Internet-Drafts. In January 1999, the TLS protocol

---

16. Note that at this point in time the SSH protocol had been investigated by the IETF TLS WG, and that the IETF later chartered a SECSH WG to update and standardize the SSH protocol independently of the TLS protocol. The SSH protocol is overviewed and discussed in Chapter 16.

version 1.0 was specified in RFC 2246 [12] and submitted to the Internet standards track (as a Proposed Standard). The differences between TLS 1.0 and SSL 3.0 are not huge, but they are significant enough that TLS 1.0 and SSL 3.0 do not easily interoperate. Nevertheless, TLS 1.0 does incorporate a mechanism by which a TLS implementation can back down to SSL 3.0.

Similar to the SSL protocol, the TLS protocol is a layered protocol that consists of a TLS Record Protocol and several TLS subprotocols layered on top of it:

- On the lower layer, the *TLS Record Protocol* takes messages to be transmitted, fragments them into manageable data blocks (so-called TLS records), optionally compresses them, computes and appends a MAC to each record, encrypts the result, and transmits it. Again, similar to SSL, the resulting records are called TLSPlaintext, TLSCompressed, and TLSCiphertext. A received TLSCiphertext record, in turn, is decrypted, verified, decompressed, and reassembled before it is delivered to the appropriate application protocol. A TLS connection state is the operating environment of the TLS Record Protocol. It specifies compression, encryption, and message authentication algorithms, and determines parameters for these algorithms, such as encryption and MAC keys and IVs for a connection in both the read and write directions. There are always four connection states in memory: the current read and write states and the pending read and write states. All records are processed under the current read and write states. The security parameters for the pending states are set by the TLS Handshake Protocol, and the handshake protocol selectively makes either of the pending states current, in which case the appropriate current state is disposed of and replaced with the pending state; the pending state is then reinitialized to an empty state.

- On the higher layer, there are several TLS subprotocols layered on top of the TLS Record Protocol. For example, the *TLS Handshake Protocol* is used to negotiate session and connection information elements that comprise a session identifier, a peer certificate, a compression method, a cipher spec, a master key, and a flag whether the session is resumable and can be used to initiate new connections. These items are used to create security parameters for use by the TLS Record Protocol when protecting application data. In addition, there are a *TLS Change Cipher Spec Protocol* and a *TLS Alert Protocol*. Both are similar to the corresponding SSL protocols (and are not further addressed in this book).

After a TLS handshake has been performed, the client and server can exchange application data messages. These messages are carried by the TLS Record Protocol and fragmented, compressed, authenticated, and encrypted accordingly. The messages are treated as transparent data to the TLS record layer.

The cipher suites that are specified for TLS 1.0 are summarized in Table 6.4.[17] The key exchange and encryption mechanisms, as well as the one-way hash function that are used in a particular cipher suite, are all encoded in its name. For example, the cipher suite TLS_RSA_WITH_RC4_128_MD5 uses RSA public key encryption for key exchange, RC4 with 128 bit session keys for encryption, and MD5 for computing one-way hash function results. Similarly, the cipher suite TLS_DH_DSS_WITH_3DES_EDE_CBC_SHA uses

Table 6.4 TLS 1.0 Cipher Suites As Specified in [12]

Cipher Suite
TLS_NULL_WITH_NULL_NULL
TLS_RSA_WITH_NULL_MD5
TLS_RSA_WITH_NULL_SHA
TLS_RSA_EXPORT_WITH_RC4_40_MD5
TLS_RSA_WITH_RC4_128_MD5
TLS_RSA_WITH_RC4_128_SHA
TLS_RSA_EXPORT_WITH_RC2_CBC_40_MD5
TLS_RSA_WITH_IDEA_CBC_SHA
TLS_RSA_EXPORT_WITH_DES40_CBC_SHA
TLS_RSA_WITH_DES_CBC_SHA
TLS_RSA_WITH_3DES_EDE_CBC_SHA
TLS_DH_DSS_EXPORT_WITH_DES40_CBC_SHA
TLS_DH_DSS_WITH_DES_CBC_SHA
TLS_DH_DSS_WITH_3DES_EDE_CBC_SHA
TLS_DH_RSA_EXPORT_WITH_DES40_CBC_SHA
TLS_DH_RSA_WITH_DES_CBC_SHA
TLS_DH_RSA_WITH_3DES_EDE_CBC_SHA
TLS_DHE_DSS_EXPORT_WITH_DES40_CBC_SHA
TLS_DHE_DSS_WITH_DES_CBC_SHA
TLS_DHE_DSS_WITH_3DES_EDE_CBC_SHA
TLS_DHE_RSA_EXPORT_WITH_DES40_CBC_SHA
TLS_DHE_RSA_WITH_DES_CBC_SHA
TLS_DHE_RSA_WITH_3DES_EDE_CBC_SHA
TLS_DH_anon_EXPORT_WITH_RC4_40_MD5
TLS_DH_anon_WITH_RC4_128_MD5
TLS_DH_anon_EXPORT_WITH_DES40_CBC_SHA
TLS_DH_anon_WITH_DES_CBC_SHA
TLS_DH_anon_WITH_3DES_EDE_CBC_SHA

17. More recently, the use of the AES has been specified in RFC 3268.

the Diffie-Hellman key exchange algorithm (DH) for key exchange, the digital signature standard (DSS) to compute and verify digital signatures, Triple-DES in CBC mode for encryption, and SHA-1 for computing one-way hash function results. Consequently, a TLS cipher suite is always named TLS_X_WITH_Y_Z, where X refers to the key exchange algorithm, Y to the encryption algorithm, and Z to the one-way hash function that is being used.

The key exchange and encryption algorithms, as well as the one-way hash functions that are specified in TLS 1.0, are itemized and further explained in Tables 6.5 to 6.7. In Table 6.6, the type of a cipher indicates whether it is a stream cipher or a block cipher running in CBC mode. Similarly, the key length indicates the number of bytes that are used for generating the encryption keys, whereas the expanded key length indicates the number of bytes actually fed into the encryption algorithm. Finally, the effective key bits measure how much entropy is in the key material being fed into the encryption routine, and the IV size measures how much data needs

Table 6.5 TLS 1.0 Key Exchange Algorithms As Specified in [12]

Key Exchange Algorithm	Description	Key Size Limit
DHE_DSS	Ephemeral DH with DSS signatures	None
DHE_DSS_EXPORT	Ephemeral DH with DSS signatures	DH = 512 bits
DHE_RSA	Ephemeral DH with RSA signatures	None
DHE_RSA_EXPORT	Ephemeral DH with RSA signatures	DH = 512 bits
DH_anon	Anonymous DH, no signatures	None
DH_anon_EXPORT	Anonymous DH, no signatures	DH = 512 bits
DH_DSS	DH with DSS-based certificates	None
DH_DSS_EXPORT	DH with DSS-based certificates	DH = 512 bits
DH_RSA	DH with RSA-based certificates	None
DH_RSA_EXPORT	DH with RSA-based certificates	DH = 512 bits
NULL	No key exchange	N/A
RSA	RSA key exchange	None
RSA_EXPORT	RSA key exchange	RSA = 512 bits

Table 6.6 TLS 1.0 Encryption Algorithms As Specified in [12]

Cipher	Type	Key Length	Expanded Key Length	Effective Key Size [bits]	IV Size	Block Size
NULL	Stream	0	0	0	0	N/A
IDEA_CBC	Block	16	16	128	8	8
RC2_CBC_40	Block	5	16	40	8	8
RC4_40	Stream	5	16	40	0	N/A
RC4_128	Stream	16	16	128	0	N/A
DES40_CBC	Block	5	8	40	8	8
DES_CBC	Block	8	8	56	8	8
3DES_EDE_CBC	Block	24	24	168	8	8

Table 6.7 TLS 1.0 One-Way Hash Functions As Specified in [13]

Hash Function	Hash Size	Padding Size
NULL	0	0
MD5	16	48
SHA	20	40

to be generated for the IV. All numbers except the effective key size are given in bytes (i.e., 8 bits).

TLS 1.0 as specified in RFC 2246 [12] was submitted to the IESG for consideration as a Proposed Standard for the Internet in January 1999. Meanwhile, two other standards track RFC documents and have been officially released by the IETF TLS WG:

▸ RFC 2712 specifies the addition of Kerberos Cipher Suites to TLS [14].

▸ RFC 2817 specifies how to upgrade to TLS Within HTTP/1.1 [15].

In addition, an informational RFC document specifies the use of HTTP over TLS (i.e., HTTPS) [16]. Finally, there are various Internet-Drafts specifying specific issues related to TLS or the use of TLS to secure TCP-based application protocols. Refer to the home page of the IETF TLS WG for an overview about the most recent developments and achievements.

6.3 SSL and TLS certificates

When Netscape Communications released its first version of Netscape Navigator with SSL support, it was faced with a practical problem: the SSL protocol required the existence of one or several CAs to make it work, but there were no CAs offering their services to the general public. Consequently, Netscape Communications turned to RSA Data Security, Inc., which had supplied the public key technology software on which Netscape Navigator was actually based. For several years RSA Data Security, Inc. had operated its own CA, called RSA Certification Services. The CA's primary reason for existence was to enable protocols that required certification services. In 1995, RSA Data Security, Inc. spun off its certification services division to a new company called VeriSign, Inc.[18]

---

18. http://www.verisign.com

Since then, each successive version of Netscape Navigator has added technology to allow for creation of a marketplace for commercial CAs and CA services. The first version contained a certificate for a single root CA. The second version still came with support for only a single root CA, but allowed other root CAs to be dynamically loaded with the user's permission. Netscape Navigator 3.0 came preloaded with certificates for 16 root CAs. In addition, the browser also contained a user interface for viewing the currently loaded certificates, deleting certificates, and adding more. The number of preconfigured and loaded certificates has steadily increased in all later releases of Netscape Navigator. This is equally true for all other browsers, including, for example, Microsoft's Internet Explorer and Opera. In fact, certificate management becomes an inportant issue for the usability of contemporary browsers.

For example, Figure 6.4 illustrates Microsoft Internet Explorer's Certificate Manager. There are basically four sets of certificates that can be managed using the Certificate Manager:

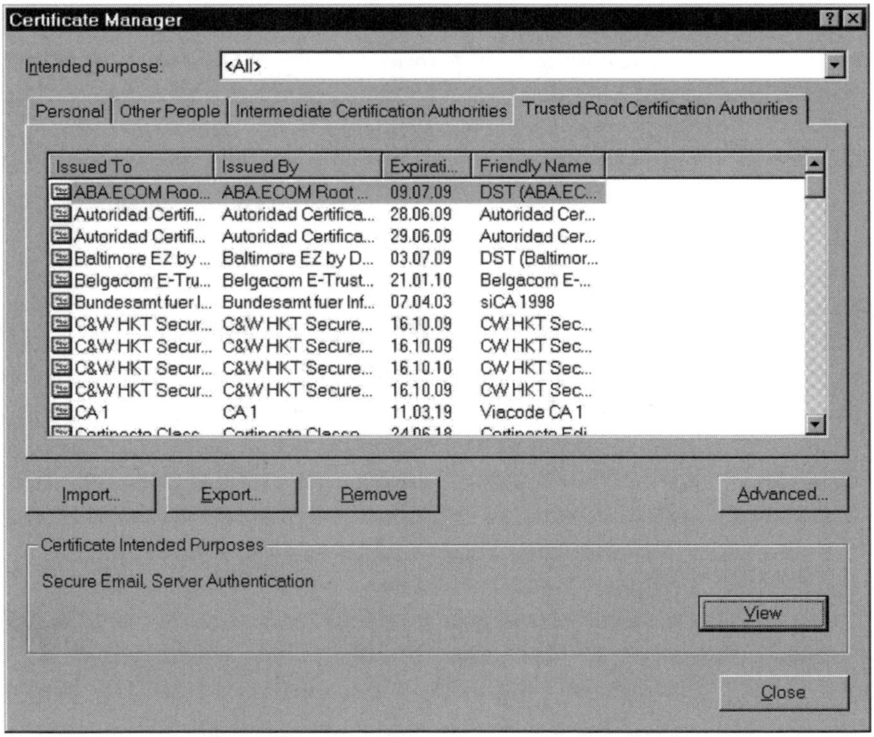

Figure 6.4 Microsoft Internet Explorer's Certificate Manager. (© 2002 Microsoft Corporation.)

- Personal certificates;
- Other peoples' certificates;
- Intermediate CAs' certificates;
- Trusted root CAs' certificates.

Personal certificates are certificates that belong to the current user of the browser, whereas other peoples' certificates belong to other people (as the name suggests). Other peoples' certificates are mainly used for secure messaging (i.e., S/MIME). In addition, trusted root CAs' and intermediate CAs' certificates are used to verify the certificates of both Web sites and other people. Trusted root CAs' certificates are implictly trusted by the user because they come preloaded with the browser's software distribution (i.e., the browser assumes that the user will trust these root CAs' certificates, without even asking him or her). This fact must be considered with care.

Other browsers use similar control panels and mechanisms to manage personal and CA certificates. For example, Figure 6.5 illustrates Opera's Preferences panel. If a user presses the Authorities... button, he or she comes to a screen where one can manage the certificates of trusted root CAs. This screen is illustrated in Figure 6.6. Again, there is a long list of CAs that

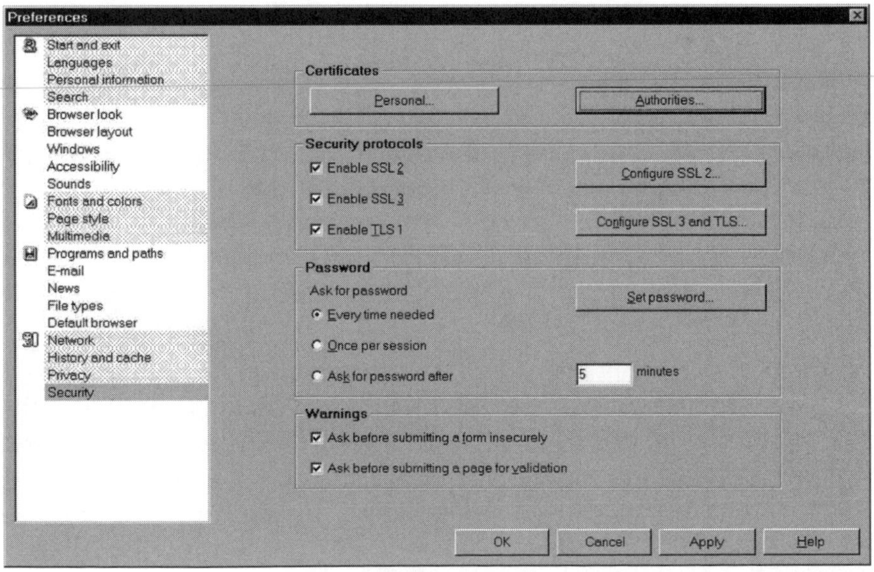

Figure 6.5 The Preferences panel in the Opera 6.0 browser. (© 2002 Opera Software.)

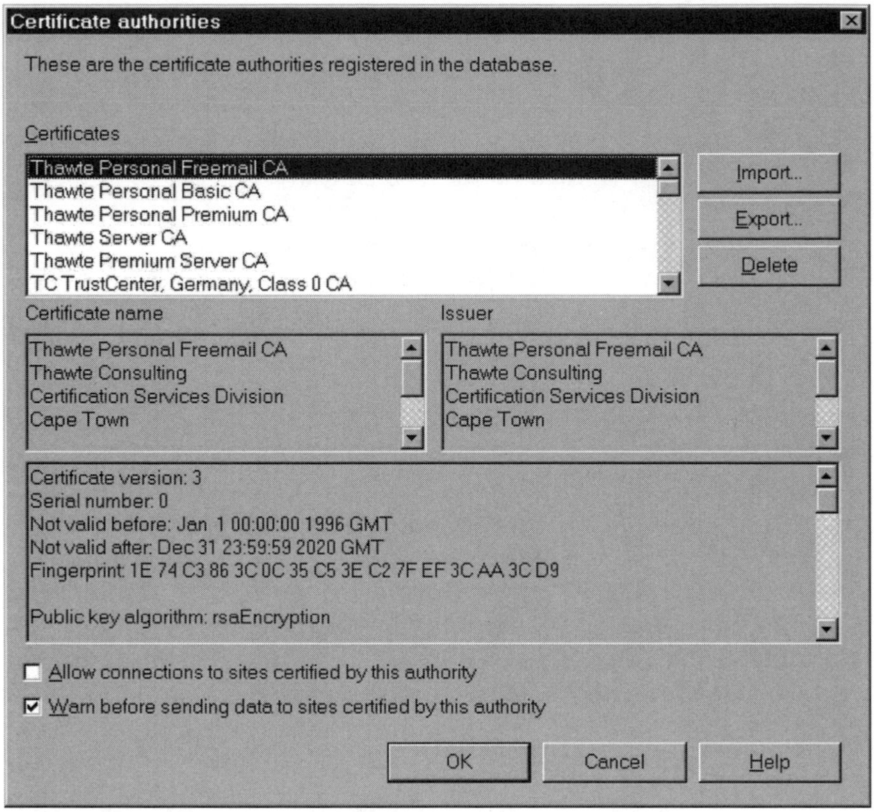

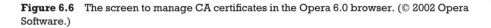

Figure 6.6 The screen to manage CA certificates in the Opera 6.0 browser. (© 2002 Opera Software.)

are configured to be trustworthy. The management of public key certificates is further addressed in the following chapter.

6.4 Firewall traversal

As of this writing, SSL and TLS in general, and HTTPS in particular, are widely used and deployed on the Internet and the WWW. Unfortunately, the protocols do not easily interoperate with application gateways (i.e., circuit-level gateways and application-level gateways). Note that an SSL or TLS connection is always established on an end-to-end basis, and that any application gateway or proxy server running at the firewall (between the client and the origin server) must be considered to be a man-in-the-middle. Also note that different protocols generally have different requirements for proxy servers. Consequently, firewall traversal represents an important problem area for SSL and TLS.

In general, an application protocol can either be proxied or tunneled through a proxy server:

▸ When we say that an application protocol is being proxied, we actually mean that the corresponding proxy server is aware of the specifics of the protocol and can understand what is happening on the protocol level. This allows such things as protocol-level filtering, access control, accounting, and logging. Examples of protocols that are usually proxied include Telnet, FTP, and HTTP.

▸ Contrary to that, we say that an application protocol is being tunneled when we actually mean that the corresponding proxy server (which is basically acting as a circuit-level gateway) is not aware of the specifics of the protocol and cannot understand what is happening on the protocol level accordingly. It is simply relaying, or tunneling, the data between the client and the server, and does not necessarily understand the protocol being used. Consequently, it cannot perform such things as protocol-level filtering, access control, and logging to the same extent as is possible for a full-fledged proxy server. Examples of protocols that are usually tunneled by proxy servers or circuit-level gateways include SSL-enhanced protocols, such as HTTPS, as well as the IIOP used in CORBA environments.

In an intranet environment, outbound SSL/TLS connections are often tunneled, whereas inbound SSL/TLS connections are proxied most of the times.

6.4.1 SSL/TLS tunneling

In an early attempt to address the problem of having SSL or HTTPS traffic going through a proxy-based firewall, Ari Luotonen from Netscape Communications proposed an SSL Tunneling Protocol that allows an HTTP proxy server to act as a tunnel for SSL-enhanced protocols. The protocol allows an SSL (or HTTPS) client to open a secure tunnel through an HTTP proxy server that resides on a firewall. When tunneling SSL, the proxy server must not have access to the data being transferred in either direction (for the sake of confidentiality). The proxy server must merely know the source and destination addresses (IP addresses and port numbers), and possibly, if the proxy server supports user authentication, the name of the requesting user. Consequently, there is a handshake between the browser and the proxy server to establish the connection between the browser and the remote server through the intermediate proxy server. To make the SSL tunneling extension be backward compatible, the handshake must be in the same format as normal HTTP/1.0 requests, so that proxy servers without support for this feature can still determine the request as impossible for them to service, and provide proper error notifications. As such, SSL tunneling is not really SSL specific. It is rather a general way to have a third party establish a connection between two endpoints, after which bytes are simply copied back and forth by this intermediary.

The SSL Tunneling Protocol is simple and straightforward. It uses a special HTTP method (i.e., CONNECT) and requires the browser to use this method to connect to the remote server.[19] More specifically, the browser connects to the proxy server and uses the CONNECT method to specify the hostname and the port number to connect to (the hostname and port number are separated by a colon). The host:port part is then followed by a space and a string specifying the HTTP version number (e.g., HTTP/1.0) and the line terminator. After that, there is a series of zero or more HTTP request header lines, followed by an empty line. Consequently, the first line of a CONNECT request message may look as follows:

CONNECT www.esecurity.ch:443 HTTP/1.0

After having received this message, the proxy server ties to establish a TCP connection to port 443 of www.esecurity.ch. If the server accepts the connection, the proxy server acts as a relay between the browser and the server. At this point in time, the browser and the server can start using SSL or TLS to establish a secure connection between them.

The SSL tunneling handshake is freely extensible using arbitrary HTTP/1.0 headers. For example, to enforce client authentication, the proxy may use the 407 status code and the Proxy-authenticate response header to ask the client to provide some authentication information to the proxy. Consequently, the SSL tunneling sequence looks as follows:

HTTP/1.0 407 Proxy authentication required
Proxy-authenticate: ...

In this case, the client would send the required authentication information in a message that looks as follows:

CONNECT www.esecurity.ch:443 HTTP/1.0
Proxy-authorization: ...

19. Meanwhile, the HTTP CONNECT method has become part of the HTTP specification.

Note that the CONNECT method provides a lower level function than the other HTTP methods. Think of it as some kind of an escape mechanism for saying that the proxy server should not interfere with the transaction, but merely serve as a circuit-level gateway and forward the data stream. In fact, the proxy server should not need to know the entire URL that is being requested—only the information that is actually needed to serve the request, such as the hostname and port number of the origin Web server. Consequently, the proxy server cannot verify that the protocol being spoken is really SSL, and the proxy server configuration should therefore explicitly limit allowed (tunneled) connections to well-known SSL ports, such as 443 for HTTPS or 563 for NNTPS (the port numbers are assigned by the IANA). As of this writing, SSL tunneling is supported by most HTTP proxy servers and browsers that are commercially available, including Microsoft Internet Explorer, Opera, and Netscape Navigator.

6.4.2 SSL/TLS proxy servers

As mentioned above, the primary use of SSL tunneling is to let internal users within a corporate intranet access external HTTPS servers on the Internet (in this case, it is seldom necessary to check the destination port number, because outbound HTTP connections are allowed in most security policies). Nevertheless, SSL tunneling can also be used in the opposite direction, namely, to make internal HTTPS servers visible and accessible to the outside world (to the users located on the Internet). In this case, however, the proxy server acts as an inbound proxy[20] for the SSL data traffic. What this basically means is that HTTPS connections originating from the outside world are simply relayed by the inbound proxy to the internal HTTPS servers, where the requesting users should be strongly authenticated. Therefore, the internal Web servers must implement the SSL or TLS protocol. Unfortunately, this is not always the case and most internal Web servers are still not SSL- or TLS-enabled (and do not represent HTTPS servers accordingly). In this case, the inbound proxy must authenticate the requesting clients and connect them to the appropriate internal Web servers. To make this possible (and to make these servers visible to the outside world), several SSL/TLS gateways or SSL/TLS proxy servers have

---

20. In the literature, inbound proxies are called *reverse proxies* most of the time. In this book, however, we use the term *inbound proxy*, as there is no reverse functionality involved. In fact, a reverse proxy is doing nothing differently than a normal proxy servers. The only difference is that it primarily serves inbound (instead of outbound) connections.

been developed and are being marketed today. For example, a group of researchers from the DEC Systems Research Center proposed the use of a combination of SSL client authentication (at the inbound proxy) and URL rewriting techniques in a technology called *secure Web tunneling* [16]. A similar technology to access internal Web servers has been developed and complemented with a one-time password system by a group of reseachrers at AT&T Laboratories [17].[21]

A final word is necessary due to the fact that use of the SSL and TLS protocols to secure (i.e., encrypt) HTTP data traffic also negatively influences the usefulness of proxy servers for caching. If a resource is encrypted end-to-end, it is encrypted in a way that is useful only for the server and one particular client (i.e., the client that has requested the resource and holds the corresponding session key). Consequently, there is no use in caching the encrypted resource for other clients.

6.5 Conclusions

In this chapter, we focused on a pair of security protocols that have been proposed for the transport layer. In particular, we overviewed and discussed the SSL and TLS protocols. Given the current situation on the Internet security market, it is possible and very likely that the TLS protocol will be one of the most important security protocols for the Internet. This is particularly true for the HTTP and the WWW. It is, however, also true for other applications (protocols) layered on top of TCP. For example, one can reasonably expect that future releases of software packages for Telnet, FTP, SMTP, POP3, and IMAP4 will implement and support the TLS protocol as well.

Both the SSL and the TLS protocols are layered on top of TCP. They neither address nor meet the security requirements of applications and application protocols that are layered on UDP. Unfortunately, there is an increasingly large number of applications and application protocols layered on UDP (e.g., protocols for real-time or multicast communications). For all these applications and application protocols, the SSL and the TLS protocols do not provide a viable solution. There are at least two conclusions one can draw from this situation:

---

21. http://www.research.att.com/projects/absent

- There is room for further research to address the question of how to secure UDP-based applications on the transport layer (e.g., a preliminary study is done in [18]).

- There is room for security protocols that operate either below or above the transport layer.

The second conclusion is particularly important, as it counters the argument that all other security protocols have become obsolete with the wide deployment of SSL/TLS. In the previous chapter, we overviewed and discussed other security protocols that operate below or above the transport layer.

References

[1] Myers, J., "Simple Authentication and Security Layer," Request for Comments 2222, October 1997.

[2] Krawczyk, H., M. Bellare, and R. Canetti, "HMAC: Keyed-Hashing for Message Authentication," Request for Comments 2104, February 1997.

[3] Wagner, D., and B. Schneier, "Analysis of the SSL 3.0 Protocol," *Proceedings of 2nd USENIX Workshop on Electronic Commerce*, November 1996, pp. 29–40.

[4] Bleichenbacher, D., "Chosen Ciphertext Attacks Against Protocols Based on the RSA Encryption Standard PKCS #1," *Proceedings of CRYPTO '98*, August 1998, pp. 1–12.

[5] RSA Data Security, Inc., *PKCS #1: RSA Encryption Standard*, Redwood City, CA, November 1993.

[6] Bellare, M., and P. Rogaway, "Optimal Asymmetric Encryption," *Proceedings of EUROCRYPT '94*, 1994, pp. 92–111.

[7] Bellare, M., et al., "Relations Among Notions of Security for Public-Key Encryption Schemes," *Proceedings of CRYPTO '98*, August 1998.

[8] Cramer, R., and V. Shoup, "A Practical Public Key Cryptosystem Provably Secure Against Adaptive Chosen Ciphertext Attack," *Proceedings of CRYPTO '98*, August 1998, pp. 13–25.

[9] Kaliski, B., and J. Staddon, "PKCS #1: RSA Cryptography Specifications Version 2.0," Request for Comments 2437, October 1998.

[10] Manger, J., "A Chosen Ciphertext Attack on RSA Optimal Asymmetric Encryption Padding (OAEP) as Standardized in PKCS#1 v2.0," *Proceedings of CRYPTO '01*, August 2001, pp. 230–238.

[11]   Laurie, B., and P. Lauried, *Apache: The Definitive Guide*, Sebastopol, CA: O'Reilly & Associates, 1997.

[12]   Dierks, T., and C. Allen, "The TLS Protocol Version 1.0," Request for Comments 2246, January 1999.

[13]   Abadi, M., et al., "Secure Web Tunneling," *Proceedings of 7th International World Wide Web Conference*, April 1998, pp. 531–539.

[14]   Medvinsky, A., and M. Hur, "Addition of Kerberos Cipher Suites to Transport Layer Security (TLS)," Request for Comments 2712, October 1999.

[15]   Khare, R., and S. Lawrence, "Upgrading to TLS Within HTTP/1.1," Request for Comments 2817, May 2000.

[16]   Rescorla, E., "HTTP over TLS," Request for Comments 2818, May 2000.

[17]   Gilmore, C., D. Kormann, and A. D. Rubin, "Secure Remote Access to an Internal Web Server," *Proceedings of ISOC Symposium on Network and Distributed System Security*, February 1999.

[18]   Mittra, S., and T. Y. C. Woo, "A Flow-Based Approach to Datagram Security," *Proceedings of ACM SIGCOMM*, September 1997.

CHAPTER

7

Contents

7.1 Introduction

7.2 Public key certificates

7.3 IETF PKIX WG

7.4 Certificate revocation

7.5 Certificates for the WWW

7.6 Conclusions

References

Certificate Management and Public Key Infrastructures

In Chapter 4, we introduced public key cryptography and the notion of public key certificates. In Chapters 5 and 6, we then used these certificates in cryptographic security protocols without addressing the question on how to manage them and how to establish and operate a public key infrastructure (PKI). These questions are addressed in this chapter. More specifically, we introduce the topic in Section 7.1, focus on public key certificates in Section 7.2, overview and discuss the work of the relevant IETF Working Group (i.e., IETF PKIX WG) in Section 7.3, address certificate revocation in Section 7.4, elaborate on certificates for the WWW in Section 7.5, and conclude with some final remarks in Section 7.6. Further information about the topic can be found in [1–3], Chapter 13 of [4], and Chapter 19 of [5]. Also, note that the topic is very dynamic and that you are invited to use the sources for further information mentioned throughout the chapter to update yourself periodically.

7.1 Introduction

According to RFC 2828 [6], the term *certificate* refers to "a document that attests to the truth of something or the ownership of something." Historically, the term was coined and first used by Loren M. Kohnfelder to refer to a digitally signed record holding a name and a public key [7]. As such, the certificate attests to the legitimate ownership of a public key and attributes a public key to a principal, such as a person, a hardware device, or any other entity. As discussed in Chapter 4, the resulting certificates are called *public key certificates*. They are used by many cryptographic security protocols, such as IPsec and IKE, SSL/TLS, and S/MIME. According to RFC 2828 [6], a public key certificate is a special type of digital certificate, namely, one "that binds a system entity's identity to a public key value, and possibly to additional data items." As such, it is a digitally signed data structure that attests to the ownership of a public key.

More generally and in accordance with RFC 2828, a certificate can be used not only to attest to the legitimate ownership of a public key (in the case of a public key certificate), but also to attest to the truth of any property attributable to a certificate owner. This more general class of certificates is commonly referred to as *attribute certificates* and will be discussed in the following chapter. In short, the major difference between a public key certificate and an attribute certificate is that the former includes a public key (i.e., the public key that is certified), whereas the latter includes a list of attributes (i.e., the attributes that are certified). In either case, the certificates are issued (and possibly revoked) by authorities that are recognized and trusted by some community of users. In the case of public key certificates, these authorities are called *certification authorities* (CAs).[1] In the case of attribute certificates, however, these authorities are called *attribute authorities* (AAs).

In short, a PKI consists of one (or several) CA(s). According to RFC 2828 [6], a PKI is "a system of CAs that perform some set of certificate management, archive management, key management, and token management functions for a community of users" that employ public key cryptography.[2] Another way to look at a PKI is as an infrastructure that can be used to issue, validate, and revoke public keys and public key certificates. As such, a PKI comprises a set of agreed-upon standards, CAs, structures among multiple CAs, methods to discover and validate certification paths, operational and management protocols, interoperable tools, and supporting legislation. In the past couple of years, PKIs have experienced a hype and many companies and organizations have announced their intentions to provide certification services to the general public. Unfortunately, only

1. In the past, CAs were often called trusted third parties (TTPs). This is particularly true for CAs that are operated by government bodies.
2. The last part of the sentence is particularly important, because in the past many people felt like having to enter the field of PKIs without having a legitimate reason to do so (if, for example, they are not using public key cryptography in the first place).

a few of these companies and organizations have succeeded and actually provide such services that can be taken seriously.

Many standardization bodies are working in the field of public key certificates and PKIs. Most importantly, the Telecommunication Standardization Sector of the International Telecommunication Union (ITU-T) has released and is periodically updating a recommendation that is commonly referred to as ITU-T X.509 [8], or X.509 in short. Meanwhile, the ITU-T recommendation X.509 has also been adopted by many other standardization bodies, including, for example, the ISO/IEC JTC1 [9]. Furthermore, many standardization bodies work in the field of profiling ITU-T X.509 for specific application environments.[3] For example, there is an IETF WG (i.e., the IETF PKIX WG) that is chartered to profile the use of ITU-T X.509 on the Internet. Due to the existence of this IETF WG, the W3C is not actively working in this field.

7.2 Public key certificates

There are several types and formats of public key certificates. All of them contain at least the following three pieces of information:

‣ A public key;

‣ Some naming information;

‣ One or more digital signatures.

The public key is the raison d'être for the public key certificate in the first place.

The naming information is used to identify the owner of the public key certificate, such as his or her name. In the past, there has been some confusion about the naming scheme that is appropriate for the global Internet. For example, the ITU-T recommendation X.500 introduced the notion of a distinguished name (DN) that can be used to uniquely identify an entity (i.e., a public key certificate owner) in a globally unique namespace. There are other examples of globally unique namespaces on the Internet, the most prominent being the DNS. The existence and usefulness of globally unique namespaces, however, has also been challenged

---

3. To *profile* ITU-T X.509—or any general standard or recommendation—basically means to fix the details with regard to a specific application environment. The result is a profile that elaborates on how to use and deploy ITU-T X.509 in the environment.

in the past (e.g., [10]). Most important, the Simple Distributed Security Infrastructure (SDSI) architecture and initiative [11] have evolved from the argument that a globally unique namespace is not appropriate for the global Internet, and that logically linked local namespaces provide a simpler and more realistic model [12]. As such, work on SDSI inspired establishment of a Simple Public Key Infrastructure (SPKI) WG within the IETF. The WG was tasked with producing a certificate infrastructure and operating procedure to meet the needs of the Internet community for trust management in as easy, simple, and extensible a way as possible. It published a pair of experimental RFC documents [13, 14] before its activities were abandoned in 2001.

Finally, the digital signature(s) is (are) used to attest to the fact that the other two items (i.e., the public key and the naming information) actually belong together. This part of a public key certificate turns the certificate into something useful.

As of this writing, there are two practically relevant formats for public key certificates[4]: Certificates used for Pretty Good Privacy (PGP) or OpenPGP (i.e., PGP certificates) and certificates that conform to the ITU-T recommendation X.509 (i.e., X.509 certificates) and are used for many contemporary security protocols and applications. They use different certificate formats and trust models.[5]

7.2.1   PGP certificates

PGP is used and deployed for secure messaging on the Internet. It refers to both a standard and a software package. As mentioned above, PGP uses a special certificate format and a cumulative trust model.

The distinguishing feature of the PGP certificate format is that it allows potentially multiple user identities (user IDs) and signatures per certificate. What this basically means is that a PGP certificate is issued for a public key and that multiple user IDs can be associated with this key. Furthermore, multiple signatures can certify the fact that a specific user ID is associated

---

4.   There are also other certificate formats, such as the format for certificates that conform to the Wireless Transport Layer Security (WTLS) specifications that is used to secure the Wireless Application Protocol (WAP). Due to the uncertain future of WAP and WTLS, we don't look at these certificates in this book.

5.   The term *trust model* refers to the set of rules a system or application uses to decide whether a certificate is valid. In the direct trust model, for example, a user trusts a public key certificate because he or she knows where it came from and considers this entity as trustworthy. In addition to the direct trust model, there is a cumulative trust model (employed, for example, by PGP certificates) and a hierarchical trust model (employed, for example, by ITU-T X.509 certificates).

with the public key. Consequently, there is a one-to-many relationship between the public key of a PGP certificate and the user IDs associated with it, and there is another one-to-many relationship for each of these user IDs and the signatures that are associated with it. Contrary to that, we will see below that the X.509 certificate format is much simpler. It allows only one user ID associated with a public key and one signature that certifies this association. The situation is illustrated in Figure 7.1. The left side illustrates the structure of a PGP certificate, whereas the right side illustrates the structure of an X.509 certificate.

Technically spoken, a PGP certificate is a data structure that includes the following fields:

- *Version number:* This field is used to identify which version of PGP was used to create the public key pair (of which the public key is associated with the certificate).

- *Public key:* This field is used to hold the public key and a corresponding algorithm identifier (i.e., RSA, Diffie-Hellman, or DSS).

- *Certificate owner information:* This field is used to hold identity information about the certificate owner and the holder of the corresponding private key. As discussed above, it may include several identities and signatures.

- *Self-signature:* This field is used to hold a self-signature for the certificate. As its name suggests, a self-signature is generated by the certificate owner using the private key that corresponds to the public key associated with the certificate. Note that X.509 certificates

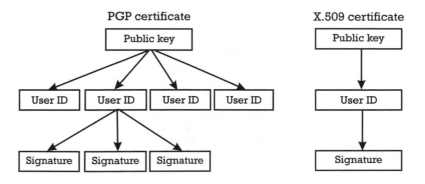

Figure 7.1 The structures of PGP and X.509 certificates.

normally do not include self-signatures (they include self-signatures only in the case of root CA certificates).

▶ *Validity period:* This field is used to determine the start and expiration date and time of the certificate. As such, it specifies the certificate's validity period or lifetime.

▶ *Preferred encryption algorithm:* This field is used to identify the encryption algorithm of choice for the certificate owner (e.g., CAST, IDEA, or 3DES).

One may think of a PGP certificate as a public key with one or more labels attached to it. For example, several user identifiers (user IDs) may be attached to a PGP certificate or public key, each of which contains different means of identifying the certificate owner (e.g., the certificate owner's name and corporate e-mail address or the certificate owner's first name and private e-mail address). Typically, a user ID includes the name of the user and one of his e-mail addresses put in angle brackets (< >), such as Rolf Oppliger <rolf.oppliger@esecurity.ch>. Also, one or several photographs may be attached to a PGP certificate or public key to simplify visual authentication processes. Again, this is a feature that is not known and does not exist in standard X.509 certificates.

In addition to their specific format, PGP certificates use a cumulative trust model. This basically means that there is no central CA that is trusted by every user, but that every user can decide for himself or herself whom to trust. More specifically, the association of a user ID with a PGP certificate or public key may be testified by one or several people, each of them generating a digital signature that is attached to the corresponding user ID in the PGP certificate. In fact, many people may sign a PGP certificate to attest to their own assurance that the public key included in the certificate actually belongs to the claimed user ID. The more people who sign a certificate, the more likely it will be trusted by somebody else. The resulting certification and trust infrastructure is highly distributed. It is sometimes also called a *web of trust.* The PGP web of trust is discussed in many references and books, including, for example, Chapter 8 of [4].

7.2.2 X.509 certificates

The ITU-T recommendation X.509 specifies both a certificate format and a certificate distribution scheme [8]. It was first published in 1988 as part of the X.500 directory recommendations. The X.509 version 1 (X.509v1) format was extended in 1993 to incorporate two new fields, resulting in the X.509

version 2 (X.509v2) format. In addition, and as a result of attempting to deploy certificates within the global Internet, X.509v2 was revised to allow for additional extension fields. The resulting X.509 version 3 (X.509v3) specification was officially released in June 1996. Meanwhile, the ITU-T recommendation X.509 has been approved by the ISO/IEC JTC1 [9].

The format of an X.509v3 certificate is specified in abstract syntax notation one (ASN.1[6]) and the resulting certificates are encoded according to specific encoding rules[7] to produce a series of bits and bytes suitable for transmission. Anyway, an X.509 public-key certificate contains the following 10 data items:

1. A version number (identifying version 1, version 2, or version 3);

2. A serial number (i.e., a unique integer value assigned by the issuer);

3. An object identifier (OID) that specifies the signature algorithm that is used to sign the public key certificate;

4. The DN of the issuer (i.e., the name of the CA that actually signed the certificate);

5. A validity period that specifies an interval in which the certificate is valid;

6. The DN of the subject (i.e., the owner of the certificate);

7. Information related to the public key of the subject (i.e., the key and the OID of the algorithm);

8. Some optional information related to the issuer (defined for versions 2 and 3 only);

9. Some optional information related to the subject (defined for versions 2 and 3 only);

10. Some optional extensions (defined for version 3 only).

All three versions of X.509 certificates contain the items 1 through 7 listed. Only version 2 and version 3 certificates may additionally contain items 8 and 9, whereas only version 3 may contain item 10.

---

6. ASN.1 is officially specified in ITU-T X.680 and ISO/IEC 8824.

7. There are three standardized encoding rules, namely the basic encoding rules (BER), the distinguished encoding rules (DER), and the packet encoding rules (PER). Obviously, anybody can specify and use his or her own set of encoding rules.

The trust model employed by ITU-T X.509 is hierarchical.[8] This basically means that a user must define a number of root CAs and corresponding root certificates (i.e., certificates that are trusted by default) from which trust may extend. Typically, a root certificate is self-signed, meaning that the root CA has issued its own certificate (i.e., the subject and issuer are identical). Note that from a theoretical point of view, self-signed certificates are not particularly useful. Anybody can claim something and issue a certificate for this claim. Consequently, a self-signed certificate basically says here is my public key; trust me.

Having established a number of root CAs and corresponding root certificates, a user can try to find a *certification path* (or *certification chain*) that leads from a root certificate to a leaf certificate (i.e., a certificate that is issued for a user or system). Formally speaking, a certification path or chain is defined in a tree or wood of CAs (root CAs and intermediate CAs) and refers to a sequence of one or more certificates that lead from a root certificate to a leaf certificate. Each certificate certifies the public key of its successor. Finally, the leaf certificate is typically issued for a person or a system. Let's assume that CA_{root} is a root certificate and B is an entity for which a certificate must be verified. In this case, a certification path or chain with n intermediate CAs (i.e., CA_1, CA_2, ..., CA_n) would look as follows:

$$CA_{root} \ll CA_1 \gg$$
$$CA_1 \ll CA_2 \gg$$
$$CA_2 \ll CA_3 \gg$$
$$\cdots$$
$$CA_{n-1} \ll CA_n \gg$$
$$CA_n \ll B \gg$$

The simplest model one may think of is a certification hierarchy representing a tree with a single root CA. However, more general structures and graphs (including mutually certifying CAs, cross-certificates, and multiple root CAs) are possible, as well. A PKI structure or graph among multiple CAs generally provides one or more certification paths between two entities.

---

8. Note, however, that ITU-T X.509 does not embody a hierarchic trust model. The existence of cross-certificates, as well as forward and reverse certificates, makes the X.509 model a mesh, analogous in some ways to PGP's web of trust. The X.509 model is often erroneously characterized as a hierarchic trust model because it is usually mapped to the directory information tree (DIT), which is hierarchic, more like name schemes.

ITU-T X.509 can be used in many ways. Consequently, every nontrivial group of users who want to work with X.509 certificates has to produce a profile that nails down the features that are left undefined in X.509. The difference between a specification (i.e., ITU-T X.509) and a profile is that a specification does not generally set any limitations on which combinations can and cannot appear in various certificate types, whereas a profile sets various limitations, for example, by requiring that signing and confidentiality keys be different. Many profiling activities are currently going on with regard to the legislation of digital and electronic signatures. We overview and address the profiling activities of the IETF next.

7.3   IETF PKIX WG

In 1995, the IETF recognized the importance of public key certificates, and chartered an IETF Public-Key Infrastructure X.509 (PKIX[9]) WG with the intent of developing Internet Standards needed to support an X.509-based PKI for the Internet community.[10] In the past, the IETF PKIX WG has initiated and stimulated a lot of standardization and profiling activities within the IETF. It is closely aligned with the activities within the ITU-T.

The operational model of the IETF PKIX WG consists of end entities,[11] CAs, and *registration authorities* (RAs).[12] The functions that the RA may carry out will vary from case to case but may include personal authentication, token distribution, certificate revocation reporting, name assignment, key generation, and key archival. In fact, a CA can delegate some of its authorities (apart from certificate signing) to an RA. Consequently, RAs are optional components that are transparent to the end entities. Finally, the certificates generated by the CAs may be made available in on-line directories and certificate repositories.[13]

---

9. http://www.ietf.org/html.charters/pkix-charter.html

10. In addition to the PKIX WG, the IETF also chartered another WG to address PKI issues. As mentioned above, this WG was called IETF Simple Public Key Infrastructure (SPKI) WG and was abandoned in 2001.

11. In the specifications of the IETF PKIX WG, the term *end entity* is used rather than the term *subject* to avoid confusion with the X.509v3 certificate field of the same name.

12. Other terms are used elsewhere for the functionality of an RA. For example, the term *local registration agent* (LRA) is used in ANSI X9 standards, *local registration authority* (also with the acronym LRA) is used in [3], *organizational registration agent* (ORA) is used in certain U.S. government specifications, and *registration agent* (RA) has also been used elsewhere.

13. The term *certificate repositories* is often used in the RFC documents of the IETF PKIX WG. Therefore, it is also used in this book.

According to this operational model, several informational, experimental, and standards track RFC documents in support of the original goals of the IETF PKIX WG have been approved by the IESG:

- Standards track RFC 2459 [15] profiles the format and semantics of X.509v3 certificates and X.509v2 certificate revocation lists (CRLs[14]) for use on the Internet. As such, it describes in detail the X.509v3 certificate format and its standard and Internet-specific extension fields, as well as the X.509v2 CRL format and a required extension set. Finally, the RFC also describes an algorithm for X.509 certificate path validation and provides ASN.1 specifications for all data structures that are used in the profiles.

- Standards track RFC 2510 [16] describes the various certificate management protocols that are supposed to be used in an X.509-based PKI for the Internet.

- More specifically, standards track RFC 2511 [17] specifies the syntax and semantics of the Internet X.509 certificate request message format (CRMF) that is used to convey a request for a certificate to a CA (possibly via an RA) for the purpose of X.509 certificate production. The request typically includes a public key and some related registration information.

- Informational RFC 2527 [18] presents a framework to assist writers of certificate policies and certificate practice statements (CPS) for CAs and PKIs. More specifically, the framework provides a comprehensive list of topics that potentially need to be covered in a certificate policy definition or CPS. Note that the framework needs to be customized in a particular operational environment.

- Informational RFC 2528 [19] profiles the format and semantics of the field in X.509v3 certificates containing cryptographic keys for the Key Exchange Algorithm (KEA).[15]

- Standards track RFC 2559 [20] addresses requirements to provide access to certificate repositories for the purpose of retrieving PKI information and managing that information. The mechanism is based

---

14. The notion of a CRL will be introduced and discussed in Section 7.4.1.

15. The KEA is a key exchange algorithm that was originally proposed by NIST for use together with the Skipjack encryption algorithm in Clipper and Fortezza chips. Refer to http://csrc.nist.gov/encryption/skipjack-kea.html for specification of the Skipjack and KEA algorithms.

on the Lightweight Directory Access Protocol (LDAP) as specified in RFC 1777 [21], defining a profile of LDAP for use within the X.509-based PKI for the Internet. In addition, RFC 2587 [22] defines a minimal schema to support PKIX in an LDAPv2 environment, as defined in RFC 2559.

▸ Standards track RFC 2585 [23] specifies the conventions for using FTP and HTTP to obtain certificates and CRLs from certificate repositories.

▸ Standards track RFC 2560 [24] specifies an Online Certificate Status Protocol (OCSP) that is useful in determining the current status of a digital certificate.

▸ Standards track RFC 2797 [25] specifies a certificate management protocol using the cryptographic message syntax (CMS). The resulting protocol has the acronym CMC.

▸ Standards track RFC 2875 [26] specifies two methods for producing an integrity check value from a Diffie-Hellman key pair.[16]

▸ Standards track RFC 3039 [27] forms a certificate profile for qualified certificates,[17] based on RFC 2459, for Internet use.

▸ The experimental RFC 3029 [28] describes a general data validation and certification server (DVCS) and the protocols to be used when communicating with it. In short, the DVCS is a TTP that can be used as one component in building reliable nonrepudiation services. It is designed to provide data validation services, asserting correctness of digitally signed documents, validity of public key certificates, and possession or existence of data. As a result of a validation process, the DVCS generates a data validation certificate (DVC).

▸ Finally, standards track RFC 3039 [29] elaborates on a Time-Stamp Protocol that can be used to provide a time stamping service. More specifically, it specifies the format of a request sent to a Time Stamping Authority (TSA) and of the response that is eventually returned.

---

16. This behavior is needed for such operations as creating the signature of a PKCS #10 certification request. These algorithms are designed to provide proof of possession rather than general-purpose signing.

17. The term *qualified certificate* is used to describe a certificate with a certain qualified status within applicable governing law.

In summary, the RFC documents itemized above specify an X.509-based PKI for the Internet community. This evolving PKI is sometimes also referred to as *Internet X.509 Public Key Infrastructure* (IPKI). As of this writing, the RFC documents that specify the IPKI refer to Proposed Standards.

The number of RFC documents that specify various aspects of the IPKI will certainly grow in the future, since a lot of work is done to further refine the IPKI and its operational protocols and procedures. In fact, the number of RFC documents specifying the IPKI will certainly have increased by the time you read this book. Refer to the IETF PKIX WG home page to get a complete and more comprehensive overview about the RFC and Internet-Draft documents that are currently available. The current trend in the industry is to make commercial PKI products "PKIX compliant," and this trend is likely to continue in the future.

7.4 Certificate revocation

According to RFC 2828 [6], certificate revocation refers to "the event that occurs when a CA declares that a previously valid digital certificate issued by that CA has become invalid." In practice, there are many reasons that may require certificate revocation. For example, a user's or a CA's private key may be compromised, or a user may no longer be registered and certified by a particular CA.

In general, certification and revocation of certification involve three different parties:

1. The certificate-issuing authority, such as the CA or attribute authority (AA);

2. The certificate repository, such as a networked directory service (which may be replicated several times);

3. The users of certificates.

In this setting, the certificate-issuing authorities do not necessarily provide on-line certificate status information about the certificates they have issued to users. Instead, they may operate off-line and update the certificate repositories only on a periodic basis. The certificate repositories, in turn, may operate on-line to be permanently available and accessible to the users. In general, it must be assumed that the certificate-issuing authorities are trusted, whereas the certificate repository and the users may not be. A user who contacts the certificate repository does not only want to retrieve a certificate, but also may want to get some kind of proof of validity for the certificates he or she retrieves.

From a theoretical point of view, there are four approaches to certificate revocation:

1. Having certificates expire automatically after a certain amount of time and requiring periodic renewals of certificates;

2. Listing all nonrevoked certificates in an on-line certificate repository, and accepting only certificates that are found there;

3. Having all certificate-issuing authorities periodically issue lists that itemize all certificates that have been revoked and should no longer be used;

4. Providing an on-line certificate status checking mechanism that informs users whether a specific certificate has been revoked.

Note that the approaches are not mutually exclusive, but can be combined to develop more efficient or more effective certificate revocation schemes. Also note that all approaches have advantages and disadvantages. For example, the first approach has the advantage of not requiring explicit certificate revocation (because the certificates expire after a certain amount of time). The disadvantages of this approach are due to the fact that certificate expiration only provides a slow revocation mechanism, and that it depends on servers' having accurate clocks. Someone who can trick a server into turning back its local clock can still use expired certificates (the security of the certificate revocation mechanism thus depends on the security of the timing service). Similarly, the second approach has the advantage that it is almost immediate, whereas the disadvantages are that the availability of authentication is only as good as the availability of the certificate repository, and that the security of the certificate revocation mechanism as a whole is only as good as the security of the certificate repository. Furthermore, users tend to cache certificates they have retrieved from the directory service for performance reasons, and the use of such a cache actually defeats the original purpose of the certificate repository (i.e., to provide timely status information). The third approach has the advantage that it is simple and straightforward, whereas the disadvantages are that the lists must be retrieved and taken into account and that the revocation of a certificate is enforced only after the publication and distribution of the next list. Finally, the fourth approach is immediate and provides a high level of security, but also reintroduces an on-line component.

For all practical purposes, the first and second approaches are the ones that are being followed for the revocation of attribute certificates, whereas the third and fourth approaches are the ones that are being followed for the revocation of public key certificates. For example, the ITU-T recommendation X.509 follows the third approach for the revocation of public key certificates.[18] More specifically, it recommends that each CA periodically issue a certificate revocation list (CRL) that itemizes all certificates that have been revoked and should no longer be used. The CRLs can be pushed or pulled by the communicating peers:

- If a CRL is pushed, the initiating peer (e.g., the client) provides the currently valid CRL to the responding peer (e.g., the server).

- Contrary to that, if a CRL is pulled, the responding peer retrieves the CRL from the certificate-issuing authority.

Applications that use certificates can either use the push model, the pull model, or both. For example, IKE, SSL/TLS, and S/MIME are all protocols that can push CRLs rather than requiring CRL retrieval from a repository.

In addition to the use of CRLs as proposed in the ITU-T recommendation X.509, the IETF PKIX WG is also following the fourth approach and has specified an On-line Certificate Status Protocol (OCSP) in standards track RFC 2560 [24] and a complementary DVCS in experimental RFC 3029 [28]. CRLs and OCSP are further addressed in the rest of this section. Afterward, we mention some alternative certificate revocation schemes that are primarily of theoretical interest.

7.4.1 CRLs

The classical and simplest solution to the certificate revocation problem is the use of CRLs. As mentioned above, this approach is followed in the ITU-T recommendation X.509 [8] and ISO/IEC 9594-8 [9]. In this approach, a CA periodically issues and digitally signs a message that lists all certificates that have been revoked and should no longer be used. This message is called a CRL and it is made available through the certificate repository. In addition to the revoked certificates, a CRL generally indicates the date and time of the next issue.

---

18. The X.509 CRL format is an ITU-T and ISO/IEC standard, first published in 1988 as version 1 (X.509v1 CRL). Similar to the ITU-T X.509 certificate format, the X.509v1 CRL was subsequently modified to allow for extension fields, resulting in the X.509 version 2 CRL (X.509v2 CRL) format.

Users who want to make sure that a particular certificate has not been revoked must query the certificate repository and retrieve the latest CRL. If the CRL does not include the certificate, the user can assume that the certificate has not been revoked (at least since the time the CRL was issued and digitally signed).

If a CRL is becoming too large, the use of delta CRLs may be appropriate. In short, a delta CRL lists all certificates that have been revoked and should no longer be used since the latest break point. Consequently, the set of all revoked certificates at a given point in time consists of all certificates listed in the most recent CRL plus all certificates listed in the delta CRLs that have been published meanwhile. Furthermore, other mechanisms are included in X.509 to allow a CA to split CRLs into multiple pieces (e.g., using CRL distribution points).

The major advantage of using CRLs (together with delta CRLs) is simplicity. A user of a certificate is required to retrieve the latest CRL from the appropriate CA or the repository and check whether the certificate has been revoked. Only if the certificate is not included in the CRL (and has not been revoked accordingly) is the user authorized to accept and use the certificate. Obviously, the consequence of this scheme is that the user has to periodically retrieve the latest CRLs from all the CAs he or she uses and accepts certificates from. This introduces some communication costs between the CA and the certificate repository, and high communication costs between the repository and the users (as CRLs may be very long). Furthermore, even though the use of CRLs can improve the fineness of the granularity with which certificates can be revoked, this granularity may still be coarser than people want (e.g., it may be a week or month, rather than an hour). In either case, a user does not receive succinct proof for the validity of a particular certificate.

Finally, note that a CRL is a negative statement. It is the digital equivalent of the little paper books of bad checks or bad credit cards that were distributed to cashiers in the 1970s and before. These have been replaced in the retail world by positive statements in the form of on-line validation of a single check, ATM card, or credit card. The digital equivalent to this on-line validation of a certificate is provided by the OCSP or a similar protocol.

7.4.2   OCSP

Instead of, or as a supplement to, checking against periodically issued CRLs, it may be necessary to obtain timely information regarding a certificate's current status. Examples include high-value funds transfer or large stock trades. Consequently, the IETF PKIX WG specified and standardized an OCSP in RFC 2560 [24]. In short, the OCSP enables a user to determine the status of an identified certificate. An OCSP client issues a status request to an OCSP responder and suspends acceptance of the certificate in question until the responder provides a response (whether the certificate in question is good, revoked, or is in an unknown state for the responder). A certificate-issuing authority can either respond to OCSP requests directly or have one (or several) delegated OCSP responder(s) providing OCSP responses to the requesting entities on its behalf.

As of this writing, the OCSP is not yet widely deployed on the Internet.[19] Nevertheless, it is possible and very likely that future CAs and certificate repositories will provide support for both certificate revocation mechanisms (i.e., CRLs and OCSP). It is equally possible and very likely that the value of an e-commerce transaction will determine whether a check in a CRL is sufficient, or whether an OCSP query must be invoked.

Finally, note that for financial transactions, the merchant often needs to know not just whether a certificate is valid, but whether the charge to be made against the account represented by the certificate is acceptable (e.g., because of credit-limit concerns). Thus, in such circumstances, timeliness of certificate status information may be irrelevant, because the merchant may need to contact the site responsible for the account (e.g., a bank for a bank credit-card charge), and that site would have very timely knowledge of certificate status information, because it probably does not rely on CRLs and OCPS.

7.4.3 Alternative schemes

The use of CRLs introduces some communication costs between the CA and the certificate repository, and high communication costs between the repository and the users (as CRLs may be very long). Furthermore, by using CRLs, a user does not receive succinct proof for the validity of a particular certificate. Protocols, such as the OCSP, can be used to address the second problem.

Some alternative certificate revocation schemes have been proposed that try to address both problems. For example, there is Silvio Micali's certificate revocation system (CRS) [30], Paul Kocher's certificate revocation trees

---

19. Note that browsers do not currently check the revocation status of any certificate at all. The only time a browser knows that a site certificate has been revoked is when it eventually expires. It is possible and very likely that this behavior will change in the future, and that certificate revocation checking will be adopted in one way or another.

(CRT) [31], and a certificate revocation and update scheme proposed by Moni Naor and Kobbi Nissim [32]. More recently, the design and optimization of certificate revocation schemes has become an active area of research. The results, however, are interesting mainly from a theoretical point of view (as of this writing, they are not relevant for all practical purposes).

A final word is due about the notion of certificate suspension. In many legislations for digital or electronic signatures, the user may suspend a certificate (in addition to revoking it). This is interesting from a user's point of view, because it allows him or her to temporarily disable a certificate. Note, however, that providing support for certificate suspension is also very difficult to say the least. It requires that the entire history of a certificate (i.e., the validity intervals for the certificate) is maintained and properly managed for a potentially very long period of time. While we are starting to understand certificate revocation, certificate suspension and its implications are still largely not understood today.

7.5 Certificates for the WWW

There are several types of certificates in use on the WWW. For example, every CA that issues certificates must have a certificate. This certificate, in turn, is either self-signed or signed by another CA. Next, every SSL/TLS-enabled Web server must have a server or site certificate to authenticate itself to browsers. Similarly, if certificate-based authentication is required by the server, each user must have a personal certificate. Finally, many software publishers use certificates to digitally sign code distributed over the Internet. As discussed next, the four types of certificates are named differently by different software vendors. For example, Figure 6.4 illustrates the Certificate Manager of Micrsoft's Internet Explorer. The Certificate Manager can be used to manage certificates that belong to the actual user of the browser, other people, intermediate CAs, and trusted CAs. In this terminology, the former two classes of certificates refer to personal certificates, whereas the latter two classes refer to CA certificates. As illustrated in Figures 6.5 and 6.6, the Opera browser does only distinguish between personal and CA certificates.

7.5.1 CA certificates

A CA certificate certifies that a public key actually belongs to a CA. As mentioned above, such a certificate may either be self-signed or signed by another CA.

‣ In the first case, the certificate is signed with the private key that belongs to the public key that is certified and that is attributed to the certificate owner (i.e., the CA). Note that every CA can issue a self-signed certificate, and that the assurance such a certificate provides is not very convincing (to say the least). In fact, a self-signed CA certificate says something like, "I am CA such and such. My public key is such and such. Trust me."

‣ In the second case, the certificate is signed with the private key of another CA. To verify the certificate, however, the public key of the other CA is needed. To make sure that this key is in an authentic and integer form, it should be provided as part of a public key certificate. Again, this certificate can be self-signed or signed by another CA. Consequently, the verification of such a CA certificate leads to a recursion. The recursion continues until a root certificate is found (i.e., a certificate that is trusted by default).

In practice, it is common to distribute software that makes use of CA certificates with a preconfigured list of trusted root certificates. Assurance then results from the way this list is managed by the software developer or distributor. For example, in Microsoft's Internet Explorer, the trusted root certificates that are preconfigured and come along with the software distribution can be found in the trusted root CA tab of the Certificate Manager (as illustrated in Figure 6.4). The list includes several dozens of commercially operating CAs. Similarly, in the Opera browser, the trusted root certificates can be found in the Certificate authorities panel (as illustrated in Figures 6.5 and 6.6). In either case, it is possible to import, export, and delete trusted root certificates.

The fact that browsers are packaged and shipped with lists of preconfigured and trusted root certificates must be considered with care. A user who does not alter this list in his or her browser will automatically and implicitly trust all certificates that are issued by any CA from that list. This is transparent to him or her. Sometimes this level of trust is appropriate, but sometimes it is not. For example, if you go through the list of trusted root certificates in your browser, you will see that there are some root certificates you would not immediately trust if you were asked off hand. To make things worse, trusted root certificates tend to have unreasonably long lifetimes.[20]

---

20. The long lifetimes are due to the fact that it is very uncomfortable to have trusted root certificates that expire. This has motivated certification service providers to use root certificates with very long lifetimes.

Some of them will expire not before 2028 or 2036. The preferred way to ship browsers would be to package them with empty lists and to have users import certificates from the CAs they trust. Unfortunately, this is not likely to happen anytime soon (mainly because it is uncomfortable for the user).

7.5.2 Server or site certificates

In the previous chapter we saw that the SSL and TLS protocols require that a server authenticates itself to a browser using a public key certificate. Such a certificate is called a *server* or *site certificate*. Every SSL/TLS-enabled Web server must be equipped with a server or site certificate, and there are many companies that provide such certificates.[21]

If a Web server provides a certificate that is issued by a CA found in the browser's list of trusted CA certificates, the certificate is silently accepted. If, however, a Web server provides a certificate that is issued by a CA not found in the list, the user is prompted whether he wants to accept it and proceed accordingly. For example, Figure 7.2 illustrates the Security Alert panel that Microsoft's Internet Explorer pops up when a server provides a certificate that is not signed by a trusted CA. In this example, the server certificate is valid (i.e., it has not expired yet) and the certificate matches the server's domain name. The only problem recognized by the browser is the fact that the certificate is digitally signed by an unknown and untrusted CA. In this situation, the user is asked whether or not he or she wants to proceed, and whether he or she wants to view the certificate's details, respectively.

Unfortunately, users tend to click Yes buttons whenever they appear simply to continue their work as soon as possible. There is hardly any user who carefully reads messages that appear in security alerts. Against this background, any browser that automatically displays some relevant details about server certificates is advantageous from a security point of view. For example, the Opera browser does so and automatically displays information about the server or site certificate, such as the certificate name and its issuer. Consequently, the user is automatically confronted with some information that may help to make more intelligent decisions about the validity of server or site certificates.

---

21. Some of these companies are mentioned at the end of the chapter.

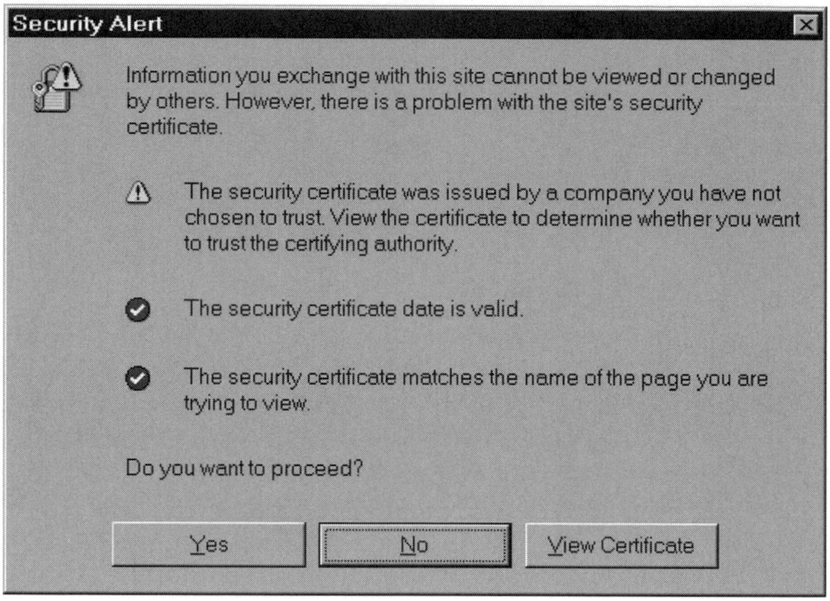

Figure 7.2 Microsoft Internet Explorer's Security Alert panel, which is displayed if the browser does not know or trust a server or site certificate. (© 2002 Microsoft Corporation.)

7.5.3 Personal certificates

Each user can have zero, one, or several personal certificate(s) to authenticate himself or herself to SSL/TLS-enabled Web servers that require client authentication. For example, in Microsoft's Internet Explorer, the Certificate Manager can be used to select a personal certificate.

As illustrated in Figure 7.3, this certificate can then be looked at in a special panel. In this example, the certificate is issued by VeriSign for Rolf Oppliger.[22] The certificate expired on December 16, 2001. Further information about the certificate is available by clicking at the Details and Certification Path tabs (as illustrated in Figures 7.4 and 7.5). The certificate's details show the fields of the X.509 certificate, whereas the certification path illustrates the certificate chain that is used to verify the certificate. In this example, the certificate of Rolf Oppliger is issued by the VeriSign Class 1 CA, and the certificate of this CA is issued by the VeriSign Class 1 Public Primary CA.

---

22. The certificate used in this example is used only for illustrative purposes.

Figure 7.3   Microsoft Internet Explorer's Certificate panel. (© 2002 Microsoft Corporation.)

7.5.4   Software publisher certificates

As will be discussed in Chapter 10, code signing is getting increasingly important to protect the authenticity and integrity of software distributed over the Internet. A digital signature computed for and distributed with software is sometimes also referred to as "digital shrink-wrap." It provides a feature similar to shrink-wrapped software packages (meaning that it is difficult to modify the software without giving the recipient a possibility to detect the modification).

Digitally shrink-wrapping software basically means that the software publisher must compute a digital signature for the software, and that the

Figure 7.4 The Details tab of Microsoft Internet Explorer's Certificate panel. (© 2002 Microsoft Corporation.)

software must be distributed together with the digital signature. Anybody in possession of the corresponding public key can verify the digital signature and authenticate the source of the software accordingly. Again, it is important to distribute the public keys that are necessary to verify the digital signatures in an authentic and integer form. This is where software publisher certificates come into play. A software publisher certificate basically certifies the authenticity and integrity of a software publisher's public key. Such certificates are typically issued by commercially operating certification service providers.

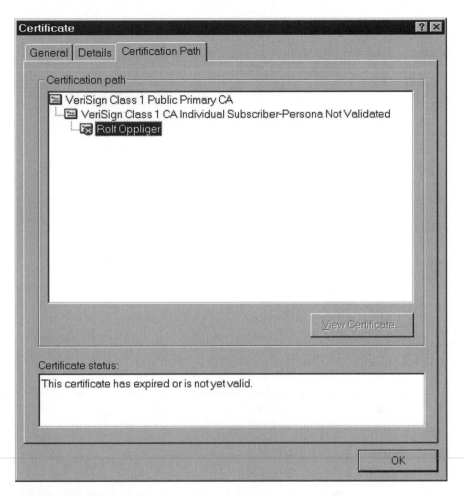

Figure 7.5 The Certification Path tab of Microsoft Internet Explorer's Certificate panel. (© 2002 Microsoft Corporation.)

7.6 Conclusions

Certificate management and PKIs are increasingly important topics for the Internet. In fact, many organizations face the problem of how to get the X.509v3 certificates they require for emerging technologies, such as IPsec, SSL/TLS, and S/MIME. In general, there are two possibilities:

1. The organization can establish a PKI of its own;

2. The organization can outsource the services and buy X.509v3 certificates from one or several commercial certification service providers.

If an organization wants to establish a PKI of its own, it can use one of the many commercial PKI solutions and products that are available on the market. Companies that offer PKI solutions and products include Entrust,[23] Baltimore Technologies,[24] and RSA Security.[25] You may refer to the trade press to get a more comprehensive and up-to-date overview about currently available PKI solutions and products.

If a company or organization wants to outsource certification services, it can buy corresponding X.509v3 certificates from one (or several) commercial certification service provider(s). Exemplary providers are VeriSign, Inc.[26] and Entrust.net.[27] In fact, an increasingly large number of commercial certification service providers are offering their services to the general public. Again, this trend is strengthened by legislation initiatives for digital or electronic signatures. Note, however, that the market for certification services is far from being mature, and that there are many ongoing changes.

In addition to the two possibilities mentioned, there is a whole range of intermediate possibilities. The general idea is to have the company or organization act as RA for its users and make use of a commercial certification service provider to actually issue certificates. This is interesting mainly because it is simple for the company or organization to register and authenticate its users, and also because almost everything can be batched from the certification service provider's point of view. A corresponding architecture was proposed in [33]. A similar architecture has been implemented and marketed in various offerings, such as VeriSign's OnSite Managed Trust Service.[28]

A more critical word should be said about the overall cost of public key cryptography in general, and PKIs in particular. Note that one of the original claims of public key cryptography was to minimize the initiation cost of a secure communication path between parties that share no prior administrative relationship. It was assumed that this would be the major reason why public key cryptography would dominate e-commerce applications in the first place. Note, however, that with no shared administrative structure to connect the parties, we must invent many things, such as certificate chaining, certificate revocation, and certificate directory services. In other words,

---

23. http://www.entrust.com/entrust
24. http://www.baltimore.com
25. http://www.rsa.com
26. http://www.verisign.com
27. http://www.entrust.net
28. http://www.verisign.com/products/onsite

we have to invent the very thing that public key cryptography claimed not to need, namely administrative overhead. This point was made by Aviel D. Rubin, Daniel Geer, and Marcus J. Ranum in [34]. In fact, they do not argue against public key cryptography in general, but they argue that much of the implied cost savings of public key cryptography over secret key cryptography is nothing more than an illusion. To further clarify the point, they argue that the sum of the cost for cryptographic-key issuance and the cost for cryptographic-key revocation is more or less constant (for both public key cryptography and secret key cryptography). Note that this argument is only an assertion and is not yet substantiated by any detailed analysis. Also note that much of the initial motivation for use of public key cryptography was not cost based, but rather security based. For example, the argument was made that there are many more vulnerabilities associated with schemes that make use of secret key cryptography only as compared with schemes that selectively make use of public key cryptography, especially when one crosses organizational boundaries. As an example, you may look at the Kerberos authentication system, especially in the case of inter-realm authentication. In spite of the fact that the argument is not substantiated by any detailed analysis and that the initial motivation for the use of public key cryptography and corresponding PKIs was security (not costs), the argument should still be considered with care. Note, for example, the problems we face when we try to establish and operate a PKI today. Some of the problems are caused by the need to revoke certificates. This problem makes it necessary to have an on-line component permanently available for an otherwise off-line CA. Ideally, certificate revocation is handled by an on-line component that is physically or logically separated from the off-line CA [35].

Finally, it should be kept in mind that the widespread use of public key certificates that include (or are logically linked to) globally unique names, such as DNs, may also provide the means to build a worldwide tracking system for user transactions. If a user acquires multiple certificates, each of which contains a different subject name with only local significance, he or she will not be able to be tracked. If, however, he or she acquires only one certificate and this certificate is used for multiple (or all) applications, he or she can be tracked very easily. Consequently, the widespread use of a single certificate per person may also contradict his or her privacy requirements.[29] Against this background, Stefan A. Brands developed a technological approach that can be used to replace X.509-based certificates [36]. The resulting certificates can be used to authenticate and authorize their owners;

29. This is particularly true for electronic ID cards that use unique personal certificates.

they do not, however, reveal any information that is not necessary to the certificate verifier. As such, the certificates may be called "minimum-disclosure" certificates. They provide a first example of a privacy enhancing technology (PET) in this area, and it is possible and very likely that we will see other PETs being developed and deployed in the future. We will come back to the notion of a PET in Chapter 12.

References

[1]   Feghhi, J., J. Feghhi, and P. Williams, *Digital Certificates: Applied Internet Security*, Reading, MA: Addison-Wesley, 1999.

[2]   Adams, C., and S. Lloyd, *Understanding the Public-Key Infrastructure*, Indianapolis, IN: New Riders Publishing, 1999.

[3]   Ford, W., and M. S. Baum, *Secure Electronic Commerce: Building the Infrastructure for Digital Signatures & Encryption*, 2nd ed., Upper Saddle River, NJ: Prentice Hall, 2000.

[4]   Oppliger, R., *Secure Messaging with PGP and S/MIME*, Norwood, MA: Artech House, 2001.

[5]   Oppliger, R., *Internet and Intranet Security, Second Edition*, Norwood, MA: Artech House, 2002.

[6]   Shirey, R., "Internet Security Glossary," Request for Comments 2828, May 2000.

[7]   Kohnfelder, L. M., "Towards a Practical Public-Key Cryptosystem," Bachelor's thesis, Massachusetts Institute of Technology, Cambridge, MA, May 1978.

[8]   ITU-T, Recommendation X.509: The Directory—Authentication Framework, 1988.

[9]   ISO/IEC 9594-8, *Information Technology—Open Systems Interconnection—The Directory—Part 8: Authentication Framework*, 1990.

[10]   Ellison, C., "Establishing Identity Without Certification Authorities," *Proceedings of USENIX Security Symposium*, July 1996.

[11]   Rivest, R. L., and B. Lampson, "SDSI—A Simple Distributed Security Infrastructure," April 1996.

[12]   Abadi, M., "On SDSI's Linked Local Name Spaces," *Proceedings of 10th IEEE Computer Security Foundations Workshop*, June 1997, pp. 98–108.

[13]   Ellison, C., "SPKI Requirements," Request for Comments 2692, September 1999.

[14]   Ellison, C., et al., "SPKI Certificate Theory," Request for Comments 2693, September 1999.

[15]   Housley, R., et al., "Internet X.509 Public Key Infrastructure Certificate and CRL Profile," Request for Comments 2459, January 1999.

[16]   Adams, C., "Internet X.509 Public Key Infrastructure Certificate Management Protocols," Request for Comments 2510, March 1999.

[17]   Myers, M., et al., "Internet X.509 Certificate Request Message Format," Request for Comments 2511, March 1999.

[18]   Chokhani, S., and W. Ford, "Internet X.509 Public Key Infrastructure Certificate Policy and Certification Practices Framework," Request for Comments 2527, March 1999.

[19]   Housley, R., and W. Polk, "Internet X.509 Public Key Infrastructure Representation of Key Exchange Algorithm (KEA) Keys in Internet X.509 Public Key Infrastructure Certificates," Request for Comments 2528, March 1999.

[20]   Boeyen, S., T. Howes, and P. Richard, "Internet X.509 Public Key Infrastructure Operational Protocols—LDAPv2," Request for Comments 2559, April 1999.

[21]   Yeong, Y., T. Howes, and S. Kille, "Lightweight Directory Access Protocol," Request for Comments 1777, March 1995.

[22]   Boeyen, S., T. Howes, and P. Richard, "Internet X.509 Public Key Infrastructure LDAPv2 Schema," Request for Comments 2587, June 1999.

[23]   Housley, R., and P. Hoffman, "Internet X.509 Public Key Infrastructure Operational Protocols: FTP and HTTP," Request for Comments 2585, May 1999.

[24]   Myers, M., et al., "X.509 Internet Public Key Infrastructure Online Certificate Status Protocol—OCSP," Request for Comments 2560, June 1999.

[25]   Myers, M., et al., "Certificate Management Messages over CMS," Request for Comments 2797, April 2000.

[26]   Prafullchandra H., and J. Schaad, "Diffie-Hellman Proof-of-Possession Algorithms," Request for Comments 2875, July 2000.

[27]   Santesson, S., et al., "Internet X.509 Public Key Infrastructure Qualified Certificates Profile," Request for Comments 3039, January 2001.

[28]   Adams, C., et al., "Internet X.509 Public Key Infrastructure Data Validation and Certification Server Protocols," Request for Comments 3029, February 2001.

[29]   Adams, C., et al., "Internet X.509 Public Key Infrastructure Time-Stamp Protocol (TSP)," Request for Comments 3161, August 2001.

[30]   Micali, S., "Efficient Certificate Revocation," Massachusetts Institute of Technology (MIT), Technical Memo MIT/LCS/TM-542b, 1996.

[31]   Kocher, P., "A Quick Introduction to Certificate Revocation Trees (CRTs)."

[32]   Naor, M., and K. Nissim, "Certificate Revocation and Certificate Update," *Proceedings of 7th USENIX Security Symposium*, January 1998.

[33]   Oppliger, R., A. Greulich, and P. Trachsel, "A Distributed Certificate Management System (DCMS) Supporting Group-Based Access Controls," *Proceedings of Annual Computer Security Applications Conference (ACSAC '99)*, 1999, pp. 241–248.

[34]   Rubin, A. D., D. Geer, and M. J. Ranum, *Web Security Sourcebook*, New York: John Wiley & Sons, 1997.

[35]   Lomas, M., "Untrusted Third Parties: Key Management for the Prudent," *Report on DIMACS Workshop on Trust Management*, 1996.

[36]   Brands, S. A., *Rethinking Public Key Infrastructures and Digital Certificates: Building in Privacy*, Cambridge, MA: MIT Press, 2000.

CHAPTER

8

Contents

8.1 Introduction

8.2 Microsoft .Net Passport

8.3 Kerberos-based AAIs

8.4 PKI-based AAIs

8.5 Conclusions

References

Authentication and Authorization Infrastructures

In this chapter, we address the notion of an authentication and authorization infrastructure (AAI) and discuss some technologies to build and operate an AAI. More specifically, we introduce the topic in Section 8.1, address Microsoft .NET Passport in Section 8.2, and elaborate on Kerberos- and PKI-based AAIs in Sections 8.3 and 8.4. Finally, we conclude with some final remarks in Section 8.5.

8.1 Introduction

In a 1993 edition of *The New Yorker*, Peter Steiner published a cartoon[1] that showed a dog explaining to another dog the major advantage of the Internet, namely that "on the Internet, nobody knows you're a dog." In subsequent years, the cartoon was used by many security companies as an argument that e-commerce requires a PKI to be successful in the first place. The statement was made that an Internet merchant must know the identity of his or her customers, and that the merchant would face a problem if he or she did not know that the, customers were dogs.

---

1. The cartoon was published on page 61 of the July 5, 1993, issue of *The New Yorker* (Vol. 69, No. 20). It is reproduced, for example, at http://www.unc.edu/courses/jomc050/idog.html for academic discussion, evaluation, and research.

213

One may argue whether this statement actually hits the point. Would an Internet merchant really face a problem if he or she did not know that the customers were dogs? To answer this question, it is helpful to have a look at the real world and to ask whether a real merchant would face the same problem. In the real world we would probably say yes. More interestingly, however, we would say yes, not because the merchant dislikes dogs, but because the probablity that the merchant would get money out of a dog is negligible. Consequently, as a result of risk analysis considerations, the merchant would typically refuse to serve a dog, out of fear of loosing money. There are (at least) two conclusions to draw:

1. Everything we do is subject to risk analysis.

2. The merchant may not care about the identity (or breed) of his or her customers if the risk of not getting paid is negligible.

This line of argumentation leads to the insight that e-commerce requires authenticity only in the foreground, and that authorization is much more important from a commercial point of view. More specifically, a merchant is typically more interested in the authorization of his or her customers than in their authenticity. This point was first made by Joan Feigenbaum in an invited talk she gave at the 1998 USENIX Workshop on Electronic Commerce [1]. It has led to many research and development activities that are collectively referred to as *trust management* (e.g., [2–8]).

Trust management is a rather artificial term, and its use is greatly overblown in the PKI industry. Following the line of argumentation introduced in [9] and further explored in Chapter 15 of this book, one may argue that trust management is not particularly important and that all that matters is risk management:

> Trust management is surely exciting, but like most exciting ideas it is unimportant. What is important is risk management, the sister, the dual of trust management. And because risk management makes money, it drives the security world from here on out. [9]

To clarify the point, we consider the situation in which a customer wants to order some goods from an on-line merchant. In this situation, there are two possible questions a customer may ask:

1. Does he or she trust the merchant (to handle the order properly)?

2. Does he or she carry the risk of having the merchant not properly handle the order?

Obviously, the first question is related to trust management, whereas the second one is related to risk management. In many situations, it is much simpler and more efficient to elaborate on risks than to discuss trust. In fact, trust is difficult to address and even more difficult to quantify. In either case, however, it is important to note that trust and risks are not independent, and that the two things basically try to measure the same (or at least closely related) things. For example, if we trust something we usually mean that the risks involved using it are small or negligible. Similarly, if we assume high risks we usually do not trust something or somebody.

If we agree that for all practical purposes authorization is more (or at least equally) important than authentication, we may want to extend the scope of a security infrastructure (e.g., a PKI) to address both authentication and authorization. This is where AAIs come into play. Similar to a PKI, an AAI may employ public key cryptography and public key certificates. Contrary to a PKI, however, an AAI need not necessarily be based on public key certificates. In fact, there is an increasingly large body of research and development that elaborates on other or complementary technologies to provide authentication and authorization services to communicating peers. This body of research and development is overviewed and briefly discussed in this chapter.

The simplest AAI one may think of is a password-based authentication system that is provided by a trusted third party (TTP), and that leaves authorization and access control decisions to participating server systems. This is basically the service that Microsoft .NET Passport provides. One may argue about the trustworthiness of Microsoft and the security properties of Microsoft .NET Passport, but for participants who only require a low level of security Microsoft .NET Passport provides a fairly simple and straightforward approach and solution for their AAI requirements.

The rest of this chapter starts with a thorough overview and discussion of Microsoft .NET Passport in Section 8.2. This discussion also takes into account that Microsoft is promoting .NET Passport very aggressively as a key technology for its user-centric application model and .NET initiative.

The design and development of authentication and key distribution systems has a long history in network security [10], and many more or less sophisticated authentication and key distribution systems are available in theory and practice (some of them have expired and are no longer supported by their original developers or vendors). One system that is particularly widely deployed on the Internet is the Kerberos authentication system (as briefly mentioned in Chapter 5). Kerberos may serve as a starting point to design and develop an AAI. In fact, there are several Kerberos-based AAIs that are overviewed and discussed in Section 8.3. Note that Microsoft .NET

Passport and Kerberos are not mutually exclusive, and that Microsoft has already announced that future releases of .NET Passport will also make use of and support Kerberos.

Microsoft .NET Passport and Kerberos-based AAIs depend on passwords that are selected by users. This basically means that the overall security of the resulting system is bounded by the security of passwords. Unfortunately, all statistical investigations reveal the fact that passwords selected by users have bad security properties (meaning, for example, that they can be guessed easily). Consequently, from a security point of view it is interesting to look into technologies that don't depend on users to select "good" secrets (for any meaningful definition of "good") and use computer-generated secrets instead. One such technology is public key crytography and public key certificates. As mentioned in the previous chapter, public key certificates and PKIs can be used to provide authentication infrastructures. Combined with some complementary technologies, they can also serve as a starting-point to additionally provide an authorization infrastructure and to come up with a comprehensive AAI accordingly. Such technologies are addressed in Section 8.4. Finally, the various technologies that can be used to build and operate an AAI are put into perspective in Section 8.5.

8.2   Microsoft .NET Passport

As part of its .NET initiative, Microsoft has introduced a set of XML-and SOAP-based Web services that collectively support what Microsoft has named a "user-centric" application model.[2] In this model, it is the user and not the hardware that needs to be authenticated and authorized to run the software, so user authentication and authorization become the core attributes.

As of this writing, Microsoft calls the services that implement the user-centric application model *.NET My Services*.[3] At the core of Microsoft .NET My Services is a user authentication service named *Microsoft .NET Passport* [11, 12]. The service was initially released in 1999 and is currently the most widely used service of its kind on the Internet and WWW.[4]

---

2. This is in contrast to a machine-centric application model in which software is licensed to run on a specific hardware device.
3. The services have formerly been code-named HailStorm.
4. As of July 2001, Microsoft claimed to have more than 165 million accounts. One reason for the large number is that all Hotmail accounts were converted to the .NET Passport system. Furthermore, it is not possible to delete an account once it is created (at least it is not obvious how one can delete it).

8.2.1 Overview

As mentioned in the introduction, Microsoft .NET Passport provides a password-based authentication service that makes use of a TTP. The TTP, in turn, is provided by Microsoft through its .NET Passport service, or via the servers that provide the service.

Microsoft uses the term *single sign-in* (SSI) to refer to the service that Microsoft .NET Passport provides. This is in contrast to the term *single sign-on* (SSO) that is otherwise used in the literature. It is not clear to what extent SSI differs from SSO in the terminology of Microsoft.[5] In this book, we use the terms SSI and SSO synonymously and interchangeably.

To make use of Microsoft .NET Passport and its service (i.e., the SSI service), a user must create a .NET Passport account to store his or her credentials. The credentials, in turn, must include his or her e-mail address (or phone number) and password. A corresponding .NET Passport registration screen is illustrated in Figure 8.1. Note that it is possible and very likely that the GUI will have changed when this book hits the shelves of the bookstores. So this figure, and some of the following figures, only serve illustrative purposes.

Each user may store additional, optional user profile information, such as demographic or preference data (for example, gender, occupation, and ZIP code) or their first and last name in his or her .NET Passport account. The screen that is used to request this additional information is illustrated in Figure 8.2. In addition, through .NET Passport express purchase service (as discussed below), the user can store credit-card information and addresses in his or her .NET Passport wallet and use this information to purchase products and services on-line. The corresponding screen to enter the user's payment information is illustrated in Figure 8.3. In summary, the .NET Passport user account can be used to store any information that is needed and must eventually be provided at multiple sites.

In essence, Microsoft .NET Passport provides a SSI service by hosting a central database that contains users' accounts, as well as the registration and sign-in/sign-out pages, that participating .NET Passport sites can cobrand. Using this service, a user can easily move between participating sites and services without the need to remember a specific set of credentials for each of them (this is basically the idea of an SSI or SSO service). Furthermore, there are several security levels that Microsoft .NET Passport

---

5. Note, for example, that the term *SSO* is used in the documentation that describes Microsoft's Kerberos implementation in Windows 2000 and XP.

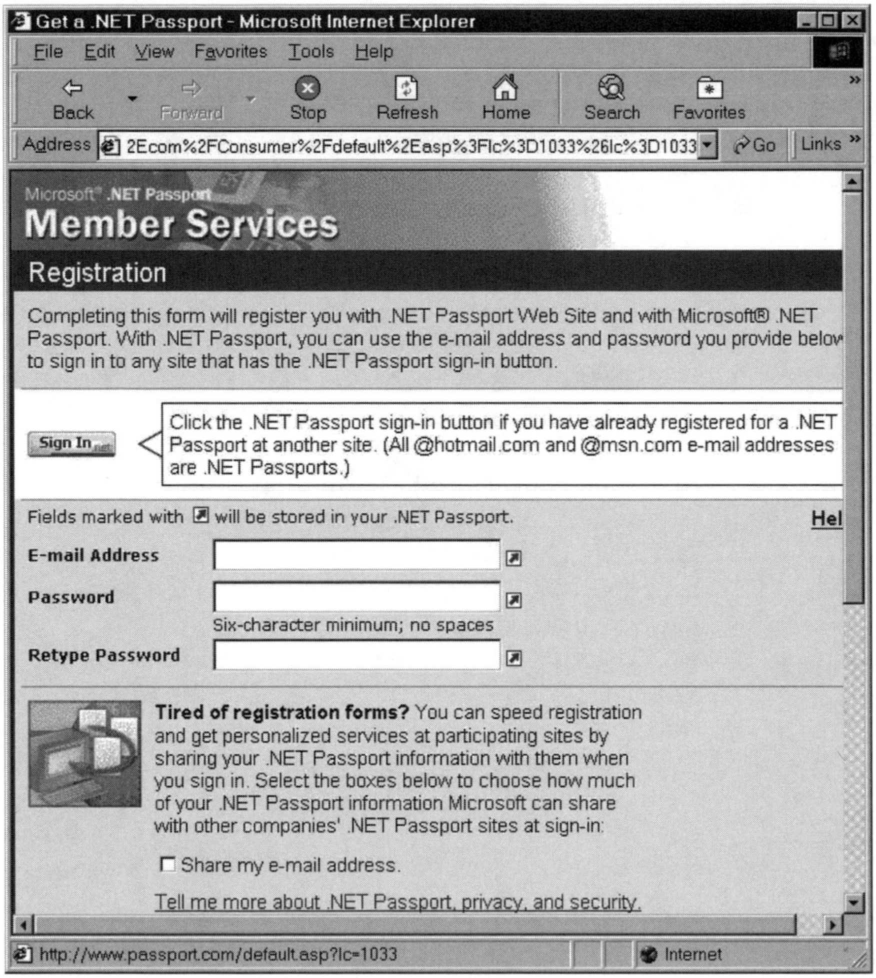

Figure 8.1 The .NET Passport registration screen. (© 2002 Microsoft Corporation.)

may provide (i.e., standard sign-in, secure channel sign-in, and strong credential sign-in). These security levels are described below.

Sites become participating .NET Passport sites by implementing the .NET Passport SSI service. Participating .NET Passport sites rely on .NET Passport to authenticate users rather than hosting and maintaining their own authentication schemes. However, .NET Passport does not authorize or deny a specific user's access to individual participating sites. Web sites that implement .NET Passport maintain control over permissions. As such, .NET Passport provides an authentication system or infrastructure and does not provide a complete and comprehensive AAI. This is similar to the Kerberos

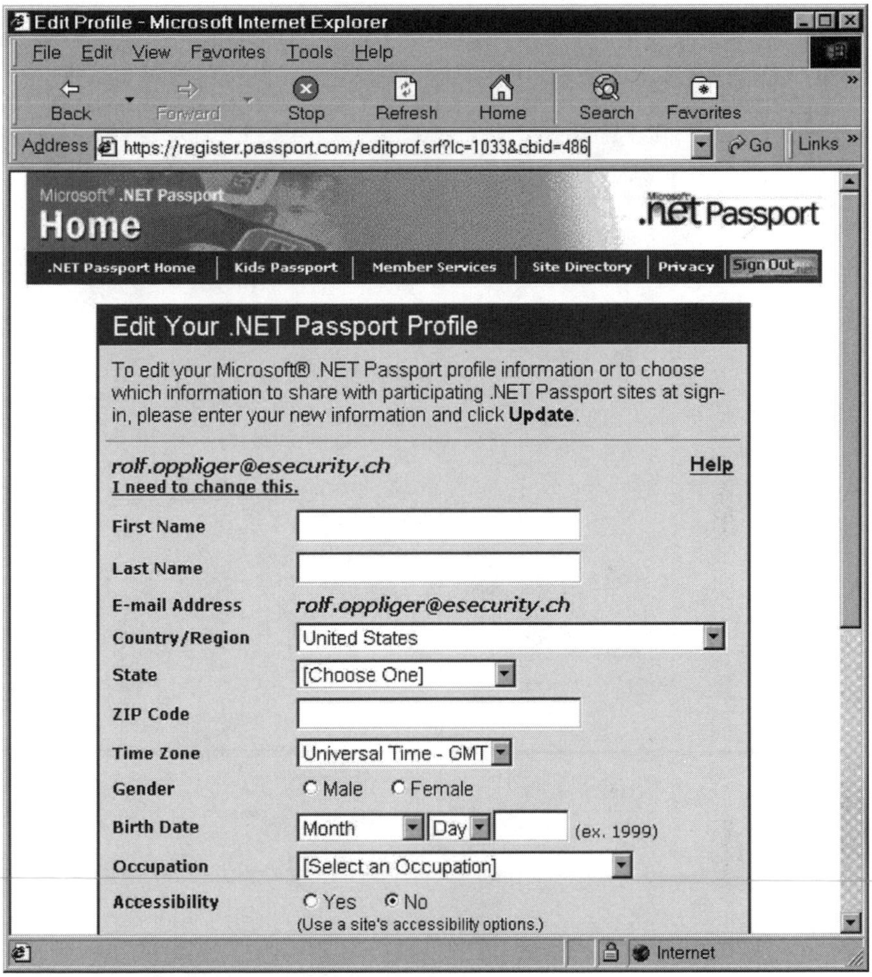

Figure 8.2   The .NET Passport screen to edit a user profile. (© 2002 Microsoft Corporation.)

system. Also similar to the Kerberos system, Microsoft .NET Passport can easily be extended to provide an AAI.

8.2.2   .NET Passport user accounts

Each .NET Passport user account may include the following components:

▸ The *.NET Passport Unique Identifier* (PUID) that is a 64-bit numeric value assigned by the .NET Passport service during the creation of the account. For obvious reasons, this component is required for every .NET Passport user account.

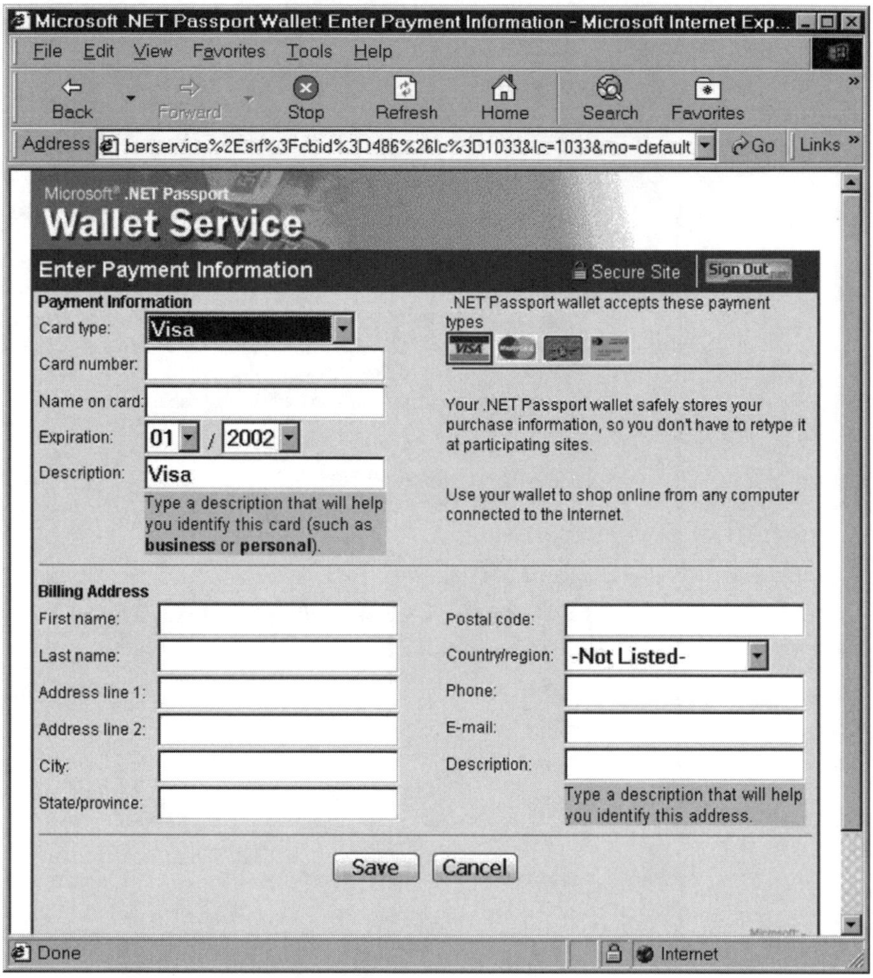

Figure 8.3 The .NET Passport screen to enter the user's payment information. (© 2002 Microsoft Corporation.)

> ▸ The *.NET Passport user profile* that may contain the following components:
>
> > ▸ The user's e-mail address or phone number;
> >
> > ▸ The user's first and last name;
> >
> > ▸ The user's demographic information such as postal code, country, and state or region.
>
> The user's e-mail address or phone number is the only required profile information.

▸ The *.NET Passport credentials* that contain the following components:

  ▸ The standard .NET Passport credentials consist of the user's e-mail address or phone number stored in the .NET Passport user profile and a password (or PIN) of at least six characters. An optional secret question and answer may be used to reset the password. The standard credentials are the minimum amount of information required for a user to have a .NET Passport account and to use the .NET Passport authentication service (i.e., for standard sign-in and secure channel sign-in).

  ▸ An additional four-digit security key that is used when the user accesses sites requiring strong credential sign-in. When created, the security key requires three associated secret questions and answers to reset it. The security key is created the first time the user accesses a site requiring strong credential sign-in.

▸ The optional *.NET Passport wallet*, used by the .NET Passport express purchase service. Each wallet may contain the following pieces of information:

▸ The user's credit-card numbers and the associated expiration dates, billing address, and friendly names.

▸ The user's shipping addresses and associated friendly names.

To operate the .NET Passport service, .NET Passport also stores some operational data about the user account. This includes the version number, whether the account contains a .NET Passport wallet, and so on.

Users create their account the first time they register for a .NET Passport. There are several ways to register. The most direct way is to register at the home page of .NET Passport[6] or by using the Microsoft Windows XP Registration Wizard. Also, a user may register by opening a Hotmail[7] account (i.e., Hotmail accounts are automatically registered as Passports) or he or she may register at a participating site. Participating sites automatically redirect users to a cobranded, centrally hosted .NET Passport registration page. In either case, the amount of information the user is asked for when registering for a Passport depends on the site where the user registers. For example, users directly registering at the .NET Passport home page are asked only for

6. http://www.passport.com
7. http://www.hotmail.com

the minimum information needed to create a Passport (i.e., an e-mail address and a password). If a participating site asks for additional, non-Passport information during registration, an arrow icon indicates the information that will be stored in the user's .NET Passport account. Information typed in fields not followed by this icon is not stored in the user's .NET Passport account (i.e., it is stored at the participating site only).

During Passport creation, users can choose what type of information they want to share with participating sites during sign-in (i.e., e-mail address, first and last names, all other .NET Passport user profile information). The site users register from can store all the information the site requested during Passport creation. Other participating .NET Passport sites, however, receive only the information the user has decided to share with participating .NET Passport sites. For example, users can decide not to share their e-mail address and their user profile information. In this case, when the user is authenticated, the participating Web sites receive only the user PUID. Furthermore, .NET Passport wallet information is shared only when users use the .NET Passport express purchase service.

We overview and briefly discuss the .NET Passport SSI and some complementary services, such as the .NET Passport Express Purchase and Kids .NET Passport services, next.

8.2.3 .NET Passport SSI service

The SSI service is the core service that .NET Passport provides. The service is implemented by a protocol and the protocol's message flows are illustrated in Figure 8.4. When a registered .NET Passport user clicks the standard sign-in link on a participating .NET Passport site, an initial HTTP request message is sent to this site (i.e., message 1). The participating site, in turn, sends back an HTTP redirect message for the cobranded .NET Passport sign-in page[8] located at the .NET Passport server (i.e., messages 2 and 3). From the user's point of view, the HTTP redirect for authentication is transparent.[9] A unique site ID is used to identify the participating site requesting the authentication. Furthermore, a return URL (generally the same URL as the one the user originally requested) is added to the .NET Passport URL in query string parameters.

8. The current version of .NET Passport also allows participating sites, using JavaScript, to display the .NET Passport sign-in module (called inline sign-in) within their own pages.
9. This transparency means that the user does not have to type in a new URL. The browser is automatically redirected to the authentication server.

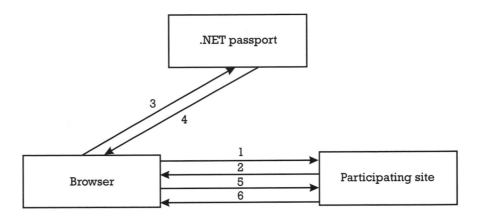

Figure 8.4 The .NET Passport Protocol's message flows.

Before displaying the appropriate .NET Passport sign-in page, .NET Passport checks the site ID and return URL. If they do not match an entry in the list of participating .NET Passport sites, the authentication is rejected (this ensures that only participating .NET Passport sites can request .NET Passport user authentication). The .NET Passport server then displays a page with a secure form that prompts the user to enter his or her .NET Passport credentials (i.e., his or her e-mail address and password). Again, this page might be cobranded by the participating site. In either case, the password is not displayed in the clear. When the user clicks the .NET Passport sign-in link, the credentials are transmitted to the .NET Passport server using the HTTP POST method on top of SSL (i.e., HTTPS). Consequently, the transmission of the user's credentials are strongly encrypted and protected against eavesdropping.

If the user's credentials match an entry in the .NET Passport database, he or she is authenticated. The PUID is extracted from the database along with the .NET Passport user profile information that he or she has agreed to share with participating sites at sign-in. The .NET Passport server then uses this information to create the following three cookies:

1. The *ticket cookie* that includes the PUID and a time stamp;

2. The *profile cookie* that includes the user profile information;

3. The *visited sites cookie* that includes a list of the sites the user has signed in to.

Cookies are encrypted using 3DES and a site encryption key that is shared between the .NET Passport server and the participating site (the key is identified through the site ID and must be distributed out-of-band). Using the site encryption key, the .NET Passport server encrypts the ticket and profile cookies, adds them as query string parameters to the return URL provided in the authentication request, and presents this URL to the user's browser so that it gets redirected to the participating site (i.e., messages 4 and 5).

The participating site extracts the encrypted ticket and profile cookies from the query string parameters and sends them to the .NET Passport Manager object running locally. The .NET Passport Manager object, in turn, decrypts the information and receives the PUID, the time stamp, and the user's profile information accordingly. The time stamp can be used to decide whether the user must reauthenticate. If the site's time window has expired, it displays the cobranded .NET Passport sign-in page with the user's e-mail address and the prompt to enter the user's password before proceeding. If everything is fine, the user is authenticated and the participating site displays the requested page (i.e., message 6). To personalize the user's experience in some way, the site might populate the page using information it has already gathered from the user or extracted from the profile cookie. The site can also use information from the profile cookie to create or upgrade its own database entry for that particular user. In either case, the requested page includes a sign-out link.

Note that there is no direct server-to-server communication of users' authentication and profile information between the .NET Passport server and the participating site. The information exchange always occurs through the client's browser using HTTP redirects and cookies. However, the Passport Manager on the participating site does periodically download a centrally hosted configuration file. This is an XML document that contains current URLs for the .NET Passport servers and the current .NET Passport profile configuration (or profile schema).

After signing in at one .NET Passport participating site, a user can sign in to any other participating site simply by clicking the corresponding .NET Passport sign-in link on that particular site. Again, the browser is silently redirected to the .NET Passport server and the site ID and return URL are sent for authentication. The .NET Passport server checks the validity of the site ID and the ticket cookie (i.e., PUID and time stamp) and silently returns encrypted ticket and profile cookies to the site to authenticate the user. Again, these cookies are encrypted using a key that is shared between the .NET Passport server and the participating site. In this way, after the first sign-in to any participating site has occured, the user can be authenticated by any other participating site with just one click. If, however, a participating site wants to ensure a recent authentication for added security, it can ask the

.NET Passport server to force a new authentication. Obviously, this requires the user to reenter his or her password regardless of the user's authentication state. Last but not least, users can also choose to be signed in automatically by saving their .NET Passport sign-in name and password on a given computer (i.e., the "sign-me in automatically" option). This option keeps a consumer signed in to .NET Passport at all times on that computer, even if the consumer disconnects from the Internet, closes the browser, or turns off the computer. From a security point of view, this option should be considered with care and is certainly not preferred.

Even though a user can use his or her .NET Passport account at multiple sites, the password is stored only in the .NET Passport database and is shared only with the .NET Passport servers that need it for authentication. If a legitimate user (or someone else) makes several incorrect attempts during sign-in, .NET Passport automatically blocks access to this users's account for a couple of minutes. This makes it significantly more difficult to launch a password cracker (i.e., a password-cracking program) to gain illegitimate access to a user's .NET Passport account.

When a user signs out by clicking the sign-out link on any participating site, the .NET Passport server checks the visited site's cookie to learn all the sites the user has signed in to during the session. For each of these sites, the .NET Passport redirects the browser to the site[10] and has the site locally execute a script. The script, in turn, is to delete all cookies that have been created at sign-in. Consequently, only the site that has created a cookie can also delete it.

Furthermore, unless users choose the option to automatically sign in to .NET Passport, all .NET Passport cookies are temporary cookies that are deleted when the browser session is closed. Even if a user does not sign out of .NET Passport or close his or her browser, .NET Passport cookies are time sensitive, meaning that they expire after a time period specified by .NET Passport or the participating site. This ensures that .NET Passport-related information is never stored in the user's computer system for an infinite amount of time.

.NET Passport includes three security levels that Microsoft intends to complement in future releases to support additional credential types (e.g., Kerberos tickets, public key certificates, and so on). Participating sites can request the level of secure authentication they require based on the sensitivity of the content or services they provide. In either case, the user's .NET Passport password is not sent to a participating site, and authentication

---

10. The URL for the script is provided by the site during the registration process.

and profile information is always sent encrypted using a key specific to the site.

8.2.3.1   Standard sign-in

Using .NET Passport standard sign-in, SSL is used only to secure the transmission of user credentials between the browser and the .NET Passport service (i.e., SSL is not used between the browser and the participating site). This is the security level described above. It is intended to be used by participating sites that don't require a high level of security. For example, Microsoft's Hotmail service employs .NET Passport standard sign-in.

8.2.3.2   Secure channel sign-in

.NET Passport standard sign-in is vulnerable to replay attacks because a participating site receives the encrypted ticket and profile cookies over an HTTP connection. The participating site then writes the cookies to the user's browser over the same connection. Consequently, an attacker listening to network traffic (between the browser and the participating site) could capture the encrypted tickets. The user's credentials are not at risk because the cookies are encrypted with a key that is known only to the .NET Passport server or the participating site, respectively. However, the attacker could replay the tickets against the participating site. He or she would then appear to be the user for the lifetime of the tickets.

In general, there are at least three possibilities to address and counter this vulnerability:

1.   Limit the lifetime of a ticket;

2.   Provide a possibility for an owner of a ticket to prove his or her legitimate ownership;

3.   Send and receive tickets only over secured channels.

The first approach is simple and straightforward. Each participating site of .NET Passport can make use of this possibility by selecting sufficiently short lifetimes for the tickets it issues. Obviously, the disadvantage is that users are frequently requested to reenter their credentials, ensuring that they are valid .NET Passport users. The second approach is not supported by .NET Passport. It was chosen, for example, by the developers of the Kerberos authentication system. In fact, Kerberos uses the notion of an authenticator to prove legitimate ownership of a ticket (this mechanism is explained in the next section). Finally, the third approach is supported by .NET Passport secure channel sign-in. In this mode, all communication takes place over secured channels (i.e., SSL or HTTPS channels) and are cryptographically protected accordingly. With .NET Passport secure channel sign-in, an attacker listening to the network traffic won't be able to get the tickets because the entire traffic is encrypted with a session key that is held only by the legitimate participants. From the user's point of view, the secure channel sign-in interface is the same as the standard sign-in interface except that the .NET Passport sign-in page is displayed using SSL.

8.2.3.3 Strong credential sign-in

As mentioned above, if a legitimate user makes several incorrect attempts during sign-in, .NET Passport automatically blocks access to that users's account for a couple of minutes (mainly to make it more difficult to launch password-cracking programs). In spite of this countermeasure, a determined and long-term brute-force attack is still possible and represents a potential risk. There are at least two approaches to addressing this problem:

1. Make the passwords stronger;

2. Block the account after a given number of unsuccessful attempts to sign-in.

Both approaches have drawbacks. Making passwords stronger adversely affects the usability of the .NET Passport service because of stringent password requirements, such as a minimal length, password expiration, and the requirement to use mixed-case, numeric, and symbol characters as part of the passwords. Similarly, blocking an account could easily be exploited in a denial-of-service attack.

Against this background, the designers of .NET Passport have chosen to use a two-stage sign-in process for protecting participating sites with more stringent security requirements. The first stage is identical to the secure channel sign-in process described above. The second stage, however, involves a second sign-in page that requires the user to enter a four-digit security key, or PIN. This page is displayed only through an SSL connection and incorporates a persistent failed-attempts counter for each user. The counter is reset upon each successful sign-in. In the event that five consecutive failed attempts are made, the user's security key is disabled. The user is still able to use the normal .NET Passport sign-in (i.e., standard sign-in or secure channel sign-in), but he or she has to go through a process to reset the security key. Since the security key is locked after five failed attempts to sign in and then must be reset to restore access, it is not vulnerable to an automated dictionary attack and therefore constitutes a strong credential. Consequently, the resulting authentication scheme is named *.NET Passport strong credential sign-in.*

.NET Passport strong credential sign-in is currently the highest level of security participating sites can request and will be used by sites for which preventing malicious access to a user's account is more important than ease of use.

8.2.4   Complementary services

There are two complementary services that can be provided in addition to the basic .NET Passport SSI service: the .NET Passport Express Purchase service and the Kids .NET Passport service. The two complementary services are briefly overviewed next.

8.2.4.1   .NET Passport express purchase service

Using the .NET Passport Express Purchase service and the optional .NET Passport wallet, a user can make use of his or her credit cards to purchase products or services online. In fact, .NET Passport Express Purchase uses the same redirection mechanism as described above. To post data, .NET Passport Express Purchase uses labels that comply with the electronic commerce modeling language (ECML).[11] When users click the .NET Passport Express Purchase link or button on a participating site's check-out page, they are redirected to their .NET Passport wallet page by means of a secure SSL connection. The site ID and return URL, supplied to .NET Passport by the participating site during registration for the .NET Passport Express Purchase service, are passed to the .NET Passport Wallet server as query string parameters during the redirection. Both the site ID and the return URL are checked by the .NET Passport Wallet server to identify the site and verify that it is a valid .NET Passport site (if the site is not valid, the request is rejected). If authenticated, users can select the credit card, billing address, and shipping address they want to use for the purchase.[12] By clicking the Continue button on the .NET Passport wallet page, they send their selected information to the participating site. This information is returned to the calling site only over an

---

11. Further information about the ECML can be found at http://www.ecml.org.

12. When a user chooses a stored credit card in a .NET Passport wallet, the complete credit card number is never displayed on the screen. The .NET Passport wallet pages display only the first six digits of the credit card number to help the user identify it, while preventing others from seeing the card's entire number.

SSL connection. Note that .NET Passport does not receive or track the purchase price or product information when processing .NET Passport Express Purchase transactions. Also, the .NET Passport Express Purchase service is not itself a credit card or debit card service. Participating sites are still required to process the transaction directly or through a third-party service.

8.2.4.2 Kids .NET passport service

In the United States the Children's Online Privacy Protection Act (COPPA) went into effect on April 21, 2000. COPPA requires that operators of online services or Web sites obtain parental consent prior to the collection, use, disclosure, or display of personal information from children.

Against this background, the designers of .NET Passport have provided a complementary service that makes the consent process easy for parents by providing one location for them to give consent for all participating Kids .NET Passport sites. The service has been named *Kids .NET Passport.*[13]

More specifically, .NET Passport users can register children under the age of 13 for special Kids .NET Passports that let parents and guardians control what information their children can share with participating Kids .NET Passport sites, and what those sites can do with that information. As with a standard .NET Passport account, a Kids .NET Passport account can store personal information (e.g., name, date of birth, e-mail address) that can be shared with participating sites. When a child with a Kids .NET Passport signs in at a particular site, .NET Passport checks the birth-date field in the profile. If the child is younger than 13, .NET Passport checks the account to determine whether the parent or guardian has granted consent for that site, and at what level (i.e., deny, limited, or full). The consent levels are summarized in Table 8.1. If the child's profile indicates that consent at one of the three levels has been granted for that site, the child is allowed to proceed.

Table 8.1 Consent Levels Used by the Kids .NET Passport Service

Deny	The site is not authorized to collect personal information from a child
Limited	The site is authorized to collect, store, and use personal information from a child, but it is not authorized to disclose it to a third party (unless it is necessary to operate the site)
Full	The site is authorized to collect, store, and use personal information from a child, and to disclose it to third parties

---

13. http://kids.passport.com

If, however, consent has not been granted, .NET Passport displays a notification message that the child must request consent from a parent or guardian before processing.

The Kids .NET Passport service works fine in theory. In practice, however, it is very unlikely that a child will use its Kids .NET Passport instead of simply requesting a normal .NET Passport. History has shown that kids turn out to be very innovative and ingenious when it comes to circumventing parental obstacles.

8.2.5 Security analysis

A short time after Microsoft launched the first version of its .NET Passport service in 1999, David P. Kormann and Aviel D. Rubin published[14] a paper entitled "Risks of the Passport Single Sign-on Protocol" [13]. In this paper, the AT&T researchers identified several risks and feasible attacks, and revealed a flaw in the interaction of Passport and Netscape Navigator that leaves a user logged in while informing him or her that he or she successfully logged out. Most of the identified risks and feasible attacks are related to key management. For example, most users don't care about server-side authenticity and don't properly verify server certificates. Consequently, various types of man-in-the-middle attacks are feasible. The same is true for DNS spoofing. Furthermore, .NET Passport is designed to have each participating site use one single key to generate cookies. This could be generalized to have each participating site use client-specific keys. The advantage of this would be that cookies are bound to clients and cannot be used universally. Most importantly, .NET Passport is a centralized system that has a single point of failure (i.e., the central database is an attractive target, since its knowledge allows an attacker to spoof any user that has an account in the system).

In their security analysis, Kormann and Rubin also argued that .NET Passport is a ticketing system that lacks a basic component of many such systems (e.g., Kerberos), namely, authenticators, to prove the legitimate ownership of tickets. Instead of authenticators, .NET Passport employs SSL connections to securely transfer tickets. It is too early to tell whether there are any risks and feasible attacks that will result from this alternative technology.

As mentioned previously, .NET Passport is one of the simplest authentication service one can think of that is based on user-selected passwords.

---

14. The paper was first published on the Web and was later published in [13].

In the following section, we elaborate on alternative and more sophisticated designs that are based on one of the oldest authentication systems still in use today (i.e., Kerberos).

8.3 Kerberos-based AAIs

Microsoft .NET Passport implements a simple and straightforward approach to provide password-based authentication. There is, however, another authentication system that is also based on user passwords and that is in widespread use (even in the Microsoft world). This system is called Kerberos and it was briefly mentioned in Chapter 5. Kerberos can be used to provide a starting point of an AAI. In fact, the Kerberos system is used in the Windows 2000 and XP operating systems for SSO.

8.3.1 Kerberos

The authentication and key distribution system Kerberos[15] [10, 14–16] was originally developed at MIT to protect the emerging network services provided by Athena Project [17–19]. The aim of the Kerberos system was to extend the notion of authentication to the computing and networking environment at MIT.

The first three versions of the Kerberos system were used only at MIT. The first version that was made publicly available was Kerberos version 4 (Kerberos V4), and this version has achieved widespread use beyond MIT.[16] Officially released in December 1992, MIT Kerberos V4 is in its final state. In fact, MIT does not anticipate ever making a new Kerberos V4 software release in the future.

Some sites require functionality that Kerberos V4 does not provide, while others have a computing and networking environment or administrative procedures that differ from those at MIT. In addition, in 1990, Steven Bellovin and Michael Merrit published a paper describing some shortcomings and limitations of Kerberos V4 [20]. Against this background, work on Kerberos version 5 (V5) also fueled by discussions with Kerberos V4 users and administrators about their experience with the Kerberos model in general, and the MIT reference implementation in particular. In

---

15. In Greek mythology, Kerberos is the name of the three-headed watchdog of Hades, whose duty it was to guard the entrance of the underworld.
16. Outside the United States and Canada, the eBones distribution of Kerberos V4 is used and widely deployed. The eBones distribution is available at `http://www.pdc.kth.se/kth-krb`.

September 1993, Kerberos V5 was officially specified in RFC 1510 [21], and as such it was submitted to the Internet standards track. Again, MIT provided a publicly and freely available Kerberos V5 reference implementation.

It should be noted that Kerberos V4 and V5, although conceptually similar, are substantially different from one another, and are even competing for dominance in the marketplace. In short, Kerberos V4 has a greater installed base, is simpler, and has better performance than V5, but works only with IP addresses; whereas Kerberos V5 has a smaller installed base, is less simple and thus less efficient, but provides more functionality than V4. For the purpose of this book, we simplify the Kerberos system and protocol considerably. This simplified form of Kerberos is equally valid for Kerberos V4 and V5. Further and more detailed information can be obtained from Chapter 2 of [10] and [22]. Also, the Kerberos home pages at MIT[17] and the Information Sciences Institute (ISI)[18] of the University of Southern California provide good sources of information. In particular, there is a document originally written by Bill Bryant in 1988. Entitled "Designing an Authentication System: A Dialogue in Four Scenes," the document introduces and discusses the considerations and decisions that led to Kerberos V4 design. The document is recommended reading and can be downloaded from the MIT Kerberos home page[19] and many other sites related to network security.

Kerberos is based on authentication and key distribution protocols that were originally proposed in [23, 24] and later modified to use time stamps [25]. In the Kerberos model and terminology, an administration domain is called a *realm*. It is assumed that every company or organization that runs the Kerberos system establishes a realm that is uniquely identified by a realm name. Also, Kerberos is based on the client-server model. Users, clients, and servers implementing and providing specific network services are considered *principals*, and each principal is uniquely identified by a principal identifier.

The aim of Kerberos is to allow a client acting on behalf of a user to authenticate (i.e., prove its identity) to a service (i.e., an application server) without having to send authentication information in the clear across the network. Also, user authentication should be empowered by passwords, but the use of the passwords should be minimized (i.e., they should be used only

---

17. http://web.mit.edu/kerberos/www
18. http://nii.isi.edu/info/kerberos
19. http://web.mit.edu/kerberos/www/dialogue.html

once during the single sign-on processes). To achieve these goals, the Kerberos system requires the existence of a TTP that acts as a key distribution center (KDC). The KDC, in turn, consists of two logically separated components:

- An *authentication server* (AS);

- A set of *ticket-granting servers* (TGSs).

Note that the AS and the TGSs are only logically separated components and that they may be processes running on the same machines. Also note that the machines that provide these services must be carefully protected and located in physically secure environments. If an intruder is able to subvert either the AS or any of the TGSs, he or she may compromise the entire system at will.

The KDC maintains a database that includes an entry for every principal registered in the Kerberos realm. The information a Kerberos KDC stores for each principal P includes (but is not restricted to) the following two items:

- The principal identifier of P;

- The key K_p that is shared between P and the KDC (e.g., a password if P is a user).

For obvious reasons, the confidentiality of the keys (i.e., K_p for each principal P) must be protected. The Kerberos system therefore encrypts all keys with a KDC master key. This encryption allows a system manager to remove copies of the KDC database from the master server, and send copies thereof to slave servers without going to extraordinary lengths to protect the privacy of the copies. Slave servers are required in large realms to provide a highly available Kerberos authentication service. Note that Kerberos does not store the KDC master key in the same database, but manages that key separately.

In principle, Kerberos implements a ticketing system. This basically means that a central authority (i.e., the KDC) issues tickets that clients and servers can use to mutually authenticate themselves and to agree on a shared secret. The shared secret, in turn, can then be used for subsequent data authentication and encryption. In either case, a Kerberos ticket is a data record that is issued by the Kerberos KDC. Among other things, the ticket contains the following:

- The session key that will be used for authentication between the client and the server;

‣ The name of the principal to whom the session key was issued;

‣ An expiration time after which the session key is no longer valid.

The ticket is not sent directly to the server, but instead sent to the client, who forwards it to the server as part of an authentication exchange. A Kerberos ticket is always encrypted with the server key, known only to the AS and the intended server. Because of this encryption, it is not possible for the client to modify the ticket without detection. There are two types of tickets:

‣ *Ticket-granting tickets* (TGTs) are issued by the Kerberos AS and can be used to request service tickets from a TGS;

‣ *Service tickets*, or *tickets* in short, in turn, are issued by a TGS and can be used to authenticate to specific server systems.

During the duration of a typical session, a TGT is usually obtained first. The TGT (instead of the user's password) is then locally stored on the client and used to request service tickets for each and every server system the client must authenticate to.

Figure 8.5 illustrates the Kerberos system and the corresponding protocol steps. The six steps can be be formalized as follows:

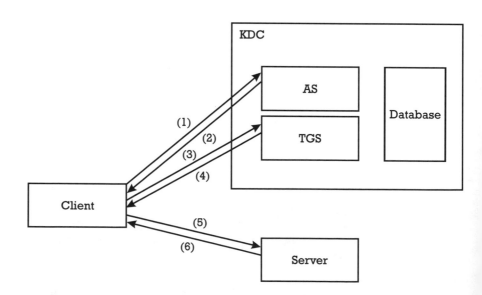

Figure 8.5   The Kerberos system and the corresponding protocol steps.

$$
\begin{array}{llll}
1 : C & \longrightarrow & AS & : \; KRB\_AS\_REQ(U, TGS, L_1, N_1) \\
2 : AS & \longrightarrow & C & : \; KRB\_AS\_REP(U, T_{c,tgs}, \{TGS, K, T_{start}, T_{expire}, N_1\}K_U) \\
3 : C & \longrightarrow & TGS & : \; KRB\_TGS\_REQ(S, L_2, N_2, T_{c,tgs}, A_{c,tgs}) \\
4 : TGS & \longrightarrow & C & : \; KRB\_TGS\_REP(U, T_{c,s}, \{S, K', T'_{start}, T'_{expire}, N_2\}K) \\
5 : C & \longrightarrow & S & : \; KRB\_AP\_REQ(T_{c,s}, A_{c,s}) \\
6 : S & \longrightarrow & C & : \; KRB\_AP\_REP(\{T'\}K') \\
\end{array}
$$

Furthermore, the six steps can be grouped in three exchanges:

1. The *AS exchange* between the client and the AS (steps 1 and 2);

2. The *TGS exchange* between the client and the TGS (steps 3 and 4);

3. The *AP exchange* between the client and the application server (steps 5 and 6).

Obviously, the AS exchange must be performed only once during the log-in process, whereas the TGS exchange and the AP exchange must be performed for each server the client wants to access (if the server requires authentication).

When a user U wants to sign on a Kerberos realm, he or she has a client C send a KRB_AS_REQ (Kerberos authentication server request) message to the AS of the Kerberos KDC in step 1. The message basically includes the principal identifier for U, the identifier for a TGS, a desired lifetime L_1 for the TGT, and a randomly chosen nonce N_1.

After having received the KRB_AS_REQ message, the AS looks up and extracts the secret keys for both U and the TGS. If required, the AS preauthenticates the request, and if preauthentication fails, a corresponding error message is returned to C. Otherwise, the AS randomly selects a new session key K, and returns a KRB_AS_REP (Kerberos authentication server reply) message to C in step 2. The message includes U, a TGT $T_{c,tgs} = \{U, C, TGS, K, T_{start}, T_{expire}\}K_{tgs}$, and $\{TGS, K, T_{start}, T_{expire}, N_1\}K_U$. The TGT's start and expiration times T_{start} and T_{expire} are set in accordance with the realm's security policy in a way that fits the specified lifespan L_1 of the KRB_AS_REQ message.

After having received the KRB_AS_REP message in step 2, C applies a well-known one-way hash function h to the user-provided password pwd_U to compute the user's master key $K_U = h(pwd_U)$.[20] Equipped with this key, C can decrypt $\{TGS, K, T_{start}, T_{expire}\}K_U$, and extract TGS, K, T_{start}, and T_{expire}

---

20. Kerberos V4 did not prompt the user to enter the password until after C has received the KRB_AS_REP message. This is because Kerberos V4 was serious in following the generally good security rule of having C know the user's password only for the minimum time possible. But waiting the few seconds to retrieve the

accordingly. C is now in the possession of a TGT that is valid from T_{start} to T_{expire}. It can use this TGT to request a service ticket from the TGS for every registered server S in the realm. Note that in a TGT, a lifetime is used like a password expiration time. Limiting the lifetime of a TGT thus limits the amount of damage that can be caused by a compromise of the TGT. In Kerberos, there is generally no possibility to revoke a TGT once it has been issued. Thus, limiting the TGT lifetime implicitly sets a deadline after which the TGT becomes obsolete.

Before initiating a TGS exchange, C must determine in which realm of the application server he or she will request whether a ticket has been registered. If C does not already possess a TGT for that realm, C must obtain one. This is first attempted by requesting a TGT for the destination realm from the local Kerberos server (using the KRB_TGS_REQ message recursively). The Kerberos server may return a TGT for the desired realm, in which case C can proceed. Alternatively, the Kerberos server may also return a TGT for a realm which is closer to the desired realm, in which case this step must be repeated with a Kerberos server in the realm specified in the returned TGT. If neither is returned, the request must be retried with a Kerberos server for a realm higher in the hierarchy. This request will itself require a TGT for the higher realm, which must be obtained by recursively applying these directions. Once the client obtains a TGT for the appropriate realm, it determines which Kerberos servers serve that realm, and contacts one. The list might be obtained through a configuration file or a corresponding network service.

In step 3, C sends a KRB_TGS_REQ (Kerberos ticket-granting server request) message to the TGS. The message includes the principal identifier S for the server, a requested lifetime L_2 for the service ticket, a nonce N_2, the TGT $T_{c,tgs}$, and an authenticator $A_{c,tgs}$ to prove legitimate ownership of the TGT. $A_{c,tgs}$ can be regarded as the principal identifier of C and a time stamp, both of them encrypted with the session key K: $A_{c,tgs} = \{C, T\}K$. Note that $T_{c,tgs}$ can have a comparably long lifetime, and could be eavesdropped upon and replayed. The purpose of the authenticator is thus to show that C holds the secret key, and to thwart this kind of attack. Also note that the use of authenticators generally requires that principals on the network keep

---

KRB_AS_REP message before asking the user for the password really does not enhance security significantly, and in fact Kerberos V5 has the user enter the password before C sends the KRB_AS_REQ message. The reason for the designers of Kerberos V5 to change the order was that V5 requires C to prove that it knows the user's password before the AS sends the KRB_AS_REP message, which makes it less easy to obtain a quantity with which to launch an offline password guessing attack.

reasonably synchronized time. The times can be off by some amount. The allowable time skew is independently set at each server, and therefore some servers may be configured to be fussier than others about times being close. The allowed time skew is usually set to be accurate within 5 minutes without undue administrative burden. In practice, that assumption has turned out to be more problematic than expected. Distributed time services, once deployed, make much tighter synchronization possible.

The KRB_TGS_REQ message is processed in a manner similar to that of the KRB_AS_REQ message, but there are some additional checks to be performed. In step 4, the TGS returns a KRB_TGS_REP message (Kerberos ticket-granting server reply) that shares its format with the KRB_AS_REP message. It includes the principal identifier for the user, a ticket $T_{c,s}$ for the requested server S, and an expression (i.e., $\{S, K', T'_{start}, T'_{expire}, N_2\}$) encrypted with K. Again, the client can use K to decrypt the expression and to extract the identifier for the server, the new session key K' (which the client uses to talk to the server), a lifetime for the ticket, and the nonce N_2.

When the KRB_TGS_REP is received by C, it is processed in the same manner as the KRB_AS_REP processing described above. The primary difference is that the ciphertext part of the response must be decrypted with the session key that is shared with the TGS rather than with the user's master key.

It turns out that there is neither functionality nor security gained by having Kerberos require an authenticator as part of the KRB_TGS_REQ message. If someone who did not know the session key K transmitted $T_{c,tgs}$ to the TGS, the TGS would return a message encrypted with K, which would be of no use to someone who did not know the session key. The reason the designers of Kerberos did it this way is to make the protocol for talking to the TGS be the same as for talking to the other servers. When talking to other servers, the authenticator does indeed provide security, because it authenticates the knowledge of the corresponding session key.

The AP exchange of the Kerberos V4 protocol is used by network applications either to authenticate a client to a server, or to mutually authenticate a client and a server to each other. The client must have already acquired credentials for the server using the AS or TGS exchange.

In step 5, C sends a KRB_AP_REQ (Kerberos application request) message to the server S. The message includes $T_{c,s}$, $A_{c,s} = \{C, T'\}K'$, and some additional bookkeeping information. Authentication is based on the server's current time of day, the ticket $T_{c,s}$, and the authenticator $A_{c,s}$.

To make sure that the KRB_AP_REQ message is not a replay of a request recent enough to look current given the time skew, S should keep all time stamps received within the maximum allowable time skew and check that each received time stamp is different from any of the stored values. Any authenticator older than the maximum allowable time skew would be rejected anyway, so there is no need to remember values older than the threshold value. Kerberos V4, however, does not bother saving time stamps. Saving time stamps does not help if S is a replicated service in which all the instances of the service use the same master key. The threat of an eavesdropper replaying the authenticator C sent to one instance of S to a different instance of S could have been avoided if Kerberos had done something like put the network layer of the instance of S in the authenticator, too.

If no error occurs, and if mutual authentication is required, S has to return a KRB_AP_REP (Kerberos application reply) message to C in step 6. Again, this message is encrypted with the session key K' that is shared between C and S. Since this key was in the ticket encrypted with the server's secret key, possession of this key is proof that S is the intended principal. More accurately, S has to increment the time stamp included in the KRB_AP_REQ message authenticator and re-encrypt it with K'.

As described thus far, Kerberos provides mutual authentication services for the client and server. However, a by-product of the Kerberos authentication protocol is the exchange of a session key K' that is shared between the clients and the servers. This key can then be used by the application to protect the confidentiality and integrity of communications. Typically, communications between the client and server is transparently encrypted and decrypted using the DES and the session key K'.

There are at least two problems that should be considered with care when it comes to large-scale deployment of the Kerberos system:

1. The fact that one part of the KRB_AS_REP message is encrypted with K_U can be used to launch a verifiable password guessing attack against the user's password. More accurately, it is possible to guess a password candidate, derive a candidate K_U from this value, and decrypt the relevant part of the KRB_AS_REP message with this key. It is then verifiable whether the password candidate was properly guessed. There are several strategies to protect against this type of attack, but unfortunately, all require the use of public key cryptography or similar constructs.

2. The fact that the Kerberos KDC shares a secret key with each prinicpal in the realm allows the administrator of the KDC to spoof any principal. This is a consequence of the fact that the Kerberos system uses only secret key cryptography.

Furthermore, every network application must be modified to make use of the Kerberos system. The process of modifying a network application to make use of Kerberos is commonly referred to as "Kerberizing" it. In general, Kerberizing network applications is the most difficult part of installing Kerberos. Fortunately, the MIT reference implementations of the Kerberos system include Kerberized versions of some popular network applications, such as Telnet and the Berkeley r-tools. Other applications have been Kerberized by vendors and are included in their supported products. The availability of Kerberized applications has improved with time, and is expected to further improve in the future. However, a site would still have to arrange itself to add Kerberos support to any application developed in-house.

One of the commonly agreed upon design principles for authentication and key distribution systems is the use of a standardized API, such as the *Generic Security Services API* (GSS-API) specified by the IETF Common Authentication Technology (CAT) WG. The use of the GSS-API for Kerberos V5 is specified in RFC 1964 [26]. Also, more work is needed to standardize and eventually simplify the GSS-API, such as demonstrated by GSS-API version 2 [27] or the Simple Public-Key GSS-API Mechanism [28].

Note that the Kerberos system provides authentication, data confidentiality, and data integrity services. By itself, it provides no information as to whether or not the client is authorized to access the server and to use the corresponding services. In general, there are three possibilities to address authorization within the Kerberos model:

1. The Kerberos KDC could maintain authorization information for each service and issue tickets to authorized users only.

2. A dedicated service could maintain authorization information by keeping access lists for each service and allowing the client to obtain sealed certification of list membership. The client would then present the sealed certification in addition to a Kerberos ticket to the requested service.

3. Each service could maintain its own authorization information, with the optional help of a service that stores access lists and provides certification of list membership.

The Kerberos model is based on the assumption that each service knows best who its users should be and what form of authorization is appropriate for them. Consequently, the third approach is employed in the Kerberos system. Next we will see that the main difference between Kerberos and

Kerberos-based AAIs, such as SESAME and Windows 2000, is that the former employs the second approach to address authorization.

8.3.2 SESAME

The Secure European System for Applications in a Multivendor Environment (SESAME) was a European research-and-development project aimed at developing an AAI and system for distributed computing and networking environments [29–31]. It achieved this by including and combining an extended Kerberos V5 authentication service and a privilege attribute service that can be used to provide authorization and corresponding access control services.

Recall that in the Kerberos system a client requests a TGT from the AS, and that the client can use this TGT to request service tickets from the TGS. In the SESAME system, a similar approach is used for authorization and access control. If a client wants to use a service, he or she must not only be authenticated by the AS, but also have his or her other privilege attributes certified by an additional component, a so-called *privilege attribute server* (PAS). In SESAME, the term *privilege attribute certificate* (PAC) is used to refer to a certified set of privilege attributes. In principle, a PAC consists of both the user's privileges and corresponding control information. The user's privileges are data such as the user's identity, role, organizational group, and security clearance, whereas the control information says where and when the PAC can be used and whether it can be delegated or not. Note that a PAC is conceptually similar to an attribute certificate. In short, the client and the PAS must exchange KRB_PAS_REQ and KRB_PAS_REP messages between the AS exchange (using the KRB_AS_REQ and KRB_AS_REP messages) and the TGS exchange (using the KRB_TGS_REQ and KRB_TGS_REP messages). In these messages, the client is provided with a PAC that is relevant for the user on whose behalf it is acting.

Refer to Chapter 6 of [10] or [31] to get a more comprehensive overview and discussion of the SESAME system. With the deployment of similar mechanisms in Windows 2000, interest in SESAME and SESAME-enabled applications has disappeared in the past.

8.3.3 Windows 2000

More recently, Microsoft has implemented the Kerberos V5 authentication service with extensions for public key authentication[21] for the Windows

---

21. These extensions are specified by the IETF CAT WG under the acronym PKINT.

2000 operating system. The Kerberos KDC is integrated with other Windows 2000 security services running on the domain controller and uses the domain's active directory as its security account database.[22]

In addition to the functionality specified in [21], Windows 2000 implements an authorization mechanism in the Kerberos system in a specific and unique way. When the Kerberos protocol is used for authentication, a list of security identifiers (SID) identifying a principal and the principal's group memberships is transported to the client in the authorization data field of a ticket. Authorization data, in turn, are gathered in two steps:

1. The first step takes place when the KDC in a Windows 2000 domain prepares a TGT.

2. The second step is accomplished when the KDC prepares a service ticket for the server in the domain.

When a user requests a TGT, the KDC in the user's account domain queries the domain's active directory. The user's account record includes the user's SID as well as SIDs for any security group to which the user belongs. The list of SIDs returned by the KDC is placed in the authorization data field of the TGT.[23] In a multiple-domain environment, the KDC also queries the Global Catalog for any universal groups that include the user or one of the user's domain security groups. If any are found, their SIDs are also added to the list in the TGT's authorization data field.

When a user requests a service ticket, the KDC in the server's domain copies the contents of the TGT's authorization data field to the ticket's authorization data field. Furthermore, if the server's domain is different from the user's account domain, the KDC queries the active directory to find out whether any security groups in the local domain include the user or one of the user's security groups. If any are found, their SIDs are also added to the list in the service ticket's authorization data field.

8.4   PKI-based AAIs

In the previous chapter, we had a look at public key certificates and PKIs. We also discussed why public key certificates that can be used to authenticate

---

22. For consistency, the Microsoft documentation uses the term *domain* instead of *realm*. Furthermore, the distinction between an AS and a TGS is not made. Both components are collectively referred to as a KDC.

23. Note that this use of the authorization data field to actually carry authorization information is consistent with revisions to the Kerberos V5 protocol specification [21] submitted to the IETF.

users and customers solve only half of the problems related to e-commerce. In addition to authentication, e-commerce providers must have an opportunity to properly authorize users and customers. Consequently, an e-commerce provider must have an opportunity to attain some authorization information about his or her users and customers.

An X.509v3 public key certificate can convey authorization information about its owner. The information can, for example, be encoded in one of the X.509v3 standard or extension fields. Note, however, that there are at least two reasons why caution should be taken in using X.509v3 public key certificates for conveying authorization information:

1. The authority that is most appropriate for verifying the identity of a person associated with a public key (i.e., a CA) may not be appropriate for certifying the corresponding authorization information. For example, in a company, the corporate security or human resources departments may be the appropriate authorities for verifying the identities of persons holding public keys, whereas the corporate finance office may be the appropriate authority for certifying permissions to sign on behalf of the company.

2. The dynamics of the two types of certificates may be fundamentally different. For example, the persons authorized to perform a particular function in a company may vary monthly, weekly, or even daily. Contrary to that, public key certificates are typically designed to be valid for a much longer period of time (e.g., one or two years). If it becomes necessary to revoke and reissue public key certificates frequently because of changing authorizations (which are encoded into the public key certificates), this may have a severe impact on the performance characteristics of the resulting certificate management scheme.

Recognizing that public key certificates are not always the best vehicle to carry authorization information, the U.S. American National Standards Institute (ANSI) X9 committee developed an alternative approach known as *attribute certificates*. Meanwhile, this approach has been incorporated into both the ANSI X9.57 standard and the X.509-related standards and recommendations of the ITU-T, ISO/IEC, and IETF.

According to RFC 2828 [32], an attribute certificate is "a digital certificate that binds a set of descriptive data items, other than a public key, either directly to a subject name or to the identifier of another certificate that is a public-key certificate." The latest version of the ITU-T recommendation

X.509 also specifies the format of an attribute certificate (currently in version 1). An X.509 attribute certificate also has a subject field, but the attribute certificate is a separate data structure from that subject's public key certificate. A subject may have multiple attribute certificates associated with each of its public key certificates, and an attribute certificate may be issued by a different authority (i.e., the AA) than the authority that issued the associated public key certificate (i.e., the CA).

In essence, an attribute certificate binds one or more pieces of additional information to the certificate owner. As such, the attribute certificate may contain group membership, role, clearance, or any other form of authorization or access control-related information associated with its owner. In conjunction with authentication services, attribute certificates may provide the means to securely transport authorization information to applications and application programs. Consequently, attribute certificates are particularly well suited to control access to system resources, and to implement role-based authorization and access controls accordingly [33]. Note that attribute certificates are conceptually similar to PACs used in SESAME and Microsoft's Windows 2000 operating system.

Anyone can define and register attribute types and use them in attribute certificates. The certificate is digitally signed and issued by an AA. AAs, in turn, are assumed to be certified by CAs, so that a single point of trust— namely, a trusted public key of a root CA—can eventually be used to validate the certificates of AAs, other CAs, and end users.

An X.509 attribute certificate contains a sequence of data items and has a digital signature that is computed from that sequence. In addition to the digital signature, an attribute certificate contains the following nine pieces of information:

1. A version number (typically specifying version 1);

2. A subject (either a DN or a serial number of an X.509 public key certificate);

3. An issuer (i.e., the DN of the issuing AA);

4. An object identifier for the algorithm that is used to sign the attribute certificate;

5. A serial number (i.e., a unique integer assigned by the issuer);

6. A validity period specified by a pair of time values (i.e., a start time and an expiration time);

7. A sequence of attributes describing the subject;

8. An optional field that may be used to identify the issuer if a DN is not sufficient;

9. An arbitrary number of optional extensions.

Apart from differences in content, an attribute certificate is managed the same way as a public key certificate. For example, if an organization already runs a directory service for public key certificates and related status information, this service can also be used to distribute attribute certificates.

Also similar to public key certificates, attribute certificates can be used in either the push or pull model:

▸ In the push model, the certificates are pushed from the client to the server.

▸ In the pull model, the certificates are pulled by the server from an on-line network service (either the certificate issuer or a directory service that is fed by the certificate issuer).

A PKI-based AAI that makes use of attribute certificate infrastructure should support both models, because some applications work best when a client pushes the certificates to the server, whereas for other applications it is more convenient for the client simply to authenticate to the server and for the server to request the client's certificates from a corresponding network service or certificate repository.

There exist a number of standards and standardized procedures to issue, manage, and possibly revoke certificates. This is particularly true for public key certificates, but is also becoming true for attribute certificates. With regard to attribute certificates, however, most security protocols must be modified to make use of them. For example, the SSL and TLS protocols are able to handle public key certificates to address authentication and key exchange; they are not yet able to handle attribute certificates to address authorization. Nevertheless, it would be convenient to have an SSL/TLS client submit a list of relevant attribute certificates to access an intranet server. To make this happen, the SSL and TLS protocols must be extended[24] and the extended protocols must be implemented and deployed. Consequently, there is still a long way to go until we see attribute certificates deployed in practice.

---

24. There are some preliminary work specifying the use of attribute certificates in the SSL and TLS protocols.

8.5 Conclusions

In this chapter, we addressed the notion of an AAI, and elaborated on some technologies to build and operate such an infrastructure. In addition to the technologies explained in this book, there is also work going on to have middleware provide a comprehensive set of security services. Most importantly, CORBA security is a hot topic today; you may refer to [34] for a corresponding overview and dicusssion from a developer's point of view. All technologies compete for market share and it is not at all clear what technology will be used in the future. What is urgently needed is more experience in practical deployment and application integration, particularly in heterogeneous environments and on a large scale. As such, the field of designing and implementing AAIs is open for further research and development.

There is some fear in the industry that Microsoft .NET Passport may be successful in providing a viable alternative to PKI-based AAIs, especially in the short term. Consequently, some competitors of Microsoft (e.g., Sun Microsystems, Cisco Systems, and RSA Security) have launched a Liberty Alliance Project.[25] The project refers to an organization that has been chartered "to create an open, federated, single sign-on identity solution for the digital economy via any device connected to the Internet." Membership is open to all commercial and noncommercial organizations. As of this writing, the Liberty Alliance Project has provided only some press releases. Consequently, it is to early too say whether the project will be successful, and whether its solution will provide a viable alternative to Microsoft .NET Passport. It is also possible and likely that we will see other projects and organizations be launched to compete Microsoft .NET Passport and the Liberty Alliance Project.

References

[1] Feigenbaum, J., "Towards an Infrastructure for Authorization," Position paper, *Proceedings of USENIX Workshop on Electronic Commerce—Invited Talks Supplement*, 1998, pp. 15–19.

[2] Maurer, U. M., and P. E. Schmid, "A Calculus for Secure Channel Establishment in Open Networks," *Proceedings of European Symposium on Research in Computer Security (ESORICS)*, 1994, pp. 175–192.

[3] Maurer, U. M., "Modelling a Public-Key Infrastructure," *Proceedings of European Symposium on Research in Computer Security (ESORICS)*, 1996, pp. 325–350.

---

25. www.projectliberty.org

[4]   Kohlas, R., and U. M. Maurer, "Confidence Valuation in a Public-key Infrastructure Based on Uncertain Evidence," *Proceedings of Public Key Cryptography '00*, 2000, pp. 93–112.

[5]   Kohlas, R., and U. M. Maurer, "Reasoning About Public-Key Certification: On Bindings Between Entities and Public Keys," *IEEE Journal on Selected Areas in Communication*, Vol. 18, No. 4, 2000, pp. 591–600.

[6]   Blaze, M., J. Feigenbaum, and J. Lacy, "Decentralized Trust Management," *Proceedings of IEEE Conference on Security and Privacy*, 1996, pp. 164–173.

[7]   Blaze, M., J. Feigenbaum, and M. Strauss, "Compliance-Checking in the PolicyMaker Trust-Management System," *Proceedings of Financial Cryptography*, 1998, pp. 251–265.

[8]   Blaze, M., et al., "The KeyNote Trust-Management System Version 2," Request for Comments 2704, September 1999.

[9]   D. Geer, "Risk Management Is Where the Money Is," Digital Commerce Society of Boston, November 1998, at `http://catless.ncl.ac.uk/Risks/ 20.06.html#subj1`.

[10] Oppliger, R., *Authentication Systems for Secure Networks*, Norwood, MA: Artech House, 1996.

[11] Microsoft Corporation, "Microsoft .NET Passport Technical Overview," White Paper, September 2001.

[12] Microsoft Corporation, "Microsoft .NET Passport Security and Privacy Overview," White Paper, October 2001.

[13] Kormann, D. P., and A. D. Rubin, "Risks of the Passport Single Signon Protocol," *Computer Networks*, Vol. 33, 2000, pp. 51–58.

[14] Steiner, J. G., B. C. Neuman, and J. I. Schiller, "Kerberos: An Authentication Service for Open Network Systems," *Proceedings of the USENIX UNIX Security Symposium*, August 1988.

[15] Kohl, J., and B. C. Neuman, *The Kerberos Network Authentication Service*, Cambridge, MA: Massachusetts Institute of Technology (MIT), December 1990.

[16] Schiller, J. I., "Secure Distributed Computing," *Scientific American*, November 1994, pp. 72–76.

[17] Champine, G. A., D. E. Geer, and W. N. Ruh, "Project Athena As a Distributed Computer System," *IEEE Computer*, Vol. 23, September 1990, pp. 40–50.

[18] Champine, G. A., *MIT Project Athena—A Model for Distributed Computing*, Burlington, MA: Digital Press, 1991.

[19] Miller, S. P., et al., "Kerberos Authentication and Authorization System," Section E.2.1 of the Project Athena Technical Plan, Cambridge, MA: Massachusetts Institute of Technology (MIT), December 1987.

[20] Bellovin, S. M., and M. Merritt, "Limitations of the Kerberos Authentication System," *ACM Computer Communication Review*, Vol. 20, 1990, pp. 119–132.

[21] Kohl, J., and B. C. Neuman, "The Kerberos Network Authentication Service (V5)," Request for Comments 1510, September 1993.

[22] Tung, B., *Kerberos: A Network Authentication System*, Reading, MA: Addison-Wesley, 1999.

[23] Needham, R. M., and M. D. Schroeder, "Using Encryption for Authentication in Large Networks of Computers," *Communications of the ACM*, Vol. 21, December 1978, pp. 993–999.

[24] Needham, R. M., and M. D. Schroeder, "Authentication Revisited," *ACM Operating Systems Review*, Vol. 21, 1987, p. 7.

[25] Denning, D. E., and G. Sacco, "Timestamps in Key Distribution Protocols," *Communications of the ACM*, Vol. 24, 1981, pp. 533–536.

[26] Linn, J., "The Kerberos Version 5 GSS-API Mechanism," Request for Comments 1964, June 1996.

[27] Linn, J., "Generic Security Services Application Program Interface, Version 2," Request for Comments 2078, January 1997.

[28] Adams, C., "The Simple Public-Key GSS-API Mechanism," Request for Comments 2025, October 1996.

[29] Parker, T. A., "A Secure European System for Applications in a Multi-Vendor Environment (The SESAME Project)," *Proceedings of the 14th National Computer Security Conference*, 1991.

[30] McMahon, P. V., "SESAME V2 Public Key and Authorisation Extensions to Kerberos," *Proceedings of the Internet Society Symposium on Network and Distributed System Security*, February 1995, pp. 114–131.

[31] Ashley, P., and M. Vandenwauver, *Practical Intranet Security—Overview of the State of the Art and Available Technologies*, Norwell, MA: Kluwer Academic Publishers, 1999.

[32] Shirey, R., "Internet Security Glossary," Request for Comments 2828, May 2000.

[33] Oppliger, R., G. Pernul, and C. Strauss, "Using Attribute Certificates to Implement Role-Based Authorization and Access Control Models," *Proceedings of 4. Fachtagung Sicherheit in Informationssystemen (SIS 2000)*, October 2000, pp. 169–184.

[34] Lang, U., and R. Schreiner, *Developing Secure Distributed Systems with CORBA*, Norwood, MA: Artech House, 2002.

Contents

9.1 Introduction

9.2 Electronic cash systems

9.3 Electronic checks

9.4 Electronic credit-card payments

9.5 Micropayment systems

9.6 Conclusions

References

Electronic Payment Systems

In this chapter, we overview and briefly discuss some electronic payment systems that can be used in e-commerce to transfer monetary value from one entity to another. After a short introduction in Section 9.1, we elaborate on electronic cash systems, electronic checks, electronic credit-card payments, and micropayment systems in Sections 9.2 to 9.5. Finally, we draw some conclusions in Section 9.6.

Note that electronic payment systems are subject to frequent changes and that it is not clear at the moment where the market is heading to and what electronic payment systems we will see in the future. Against this background, the chapter is kept short on purpose and provides many references to material that can be used for further study. More information is also available, for example, in three complementary books published in Artech House's computer security series. More specifically, [1] provides a comprehensive overview about the electronic payment systems that dominate the marketplace today, whereas [2] and [3] delve into the technical details of the Java Card and the smart cards that conform to the specifications developed by Europay, MasterCard, and Visa International (i.e., EMV cards). The books are recommended reading for anybody working in the field.

9.1 Introduction

The exchange of goods conducted face-to-face between two or more entities dates back to before the beginning of recorded

249

history. Eventually, as trade became more complicated and inconvenient, human beings invented some increasingly abstract forms of representation for value. Consequently, we (or rather our predecessors) have experienced a progression of value transfer systems, starting from barter arrangements, through commodity money, coins and bank notes, payment orders, checks, and credit cards. This development is likely to continue in the future.

More recently, the progression of value transfer systems has culminated in *electronic payment systems*. In fact, the growing importance of electronic commerce (e-commerce) and corresponding applications has resulted in the introduction of a variety of different and partly competing electronic payment systems (again, you may refer to [1] for a comprehensive overview and discussion). Within currently available electronic payment systems, payments are done electronically, but the mapping between the electronic payments and the transfer of real value is still guaranteed by banks through financial clearing systems. These clearing systems are built on the closed networks of financial institutions (i.e., banks) that are considered comparatively more secure than open networks, such as the Internet.

It is important to note that all abstract forms of representation for value and corresponding value transfer systems suffer from well-known (and probably also some unknown) security problems. For example, money can be counterfeited, signatures on checks can be forged, and checks can be bounced. Electronic payment systems retain the same or similar security problems and may eventually pose additional risks. For example, unlike paper, digital data (representing monetary value) can be copied perfectly and arbitrarily often, digital signatures can be counterfeited perfectly by anybody who has access to the private key, and a customer's name can be associated with every payment, effectively eliminating the anonymity of conventional cash. Thus, without new security mechanisms and techniques being developed, implemented, and deployed, widespread use of electronic payment systems and corresponding e-commerce applications is not likely to take off.

All currently available electronic payment systems differ in details, but have the same basic purpose of facilitating the transfer of monetary value between multiple parties. In general, electronic payments involve a *buyer* (the party that wants to use the money to buy goods or services) and a *merchant* (the party that wants to sell goods or services and accepts money accordingly). In the terminology of (electronic) payment systems, a buyer is often called a *payer*, and a merchant is often called a *payee*. The two pairs of terms are used synonymously and interchangeably in this book.

The intent of an electronic payment system is to safely and securely transfer monetary value from the payer to the payee. The transfer is accomplished by one (or several) electronic payment protocol(s). These protocols are general in nature and must not depend on the actual transport media in use. As a matter of fact, a payment protocol may be implemented as part of a Web application using HTTP, as part of an e-mail application using SMTP, or as part of any other application protocol. In either case, it must be ensured that the data involved in an electronic payment protocol execution is safe and secure, even if the medium is not. In the case that the medium is attacked, nothing more than a useless data stream must be obtained by the attacker. To provide this kind of safety and security, most electronic payment systems make use of some more or less sophisticated cryptographic techniques.

Note, however, that there is no obligation to use cryptographic techniques. For example, it has been possible for a long time to make credit-card payments without requiring the customer and merchant to be colocated. Credit-card companies have allowed orders to be taken either by post or telephone. These orders are collectively referred to as *mail order/ telephone order* (MOTO) transactions, and special rules have been imposed by the credit-card companies on how these transactions are to be processed. In fact, cardholders are asked to provide some additional information, such as their names and addresses, that are used to verify their identity. Also, if goods that require physical delivery are being ordered, they must be sent to the address associated with the cardholder. Although there are many possibilities for fraud and misuse associated with MOTO transactions, they are still very popular today (for certain applications the benefits simply outweigh the risks).

Using credit cards to make payments across computer networks (e.g., the Internet) has similar associated risks as are experienced with MOTO transactions. Attackers eavesdropping on network traffic may intercept data and capture credit-card and associated verification information. What makes the risks considerably higher than MOTO transactions is the open nature of computer networks and the speed in which transactions can be conducted in these networks.[1]

Against this background, there are only a few electronic payment systems for the Internet that don't make use of cryptographic techniques. For example, one of the earliest credit-card-based payment system was marketed by a company called First Virtual Holdings (FV).[2] In October 1994, the company commenced operation of a noncryptographic payment system called the *VirtualPIN*. The goal of the VirtualPIN system was to allow the

---

1. The major security problems are still related to the way the credit-card information is handled on the client and server sides.
2. The First Virtual Holdings, Inc., does not exist anymore.

selling of low-value information goods across the Internet without the need for special-purpose client hardware or software to be put in place.

In the VirtualPIN system, both the customers and merchants had to register with FV before any transactions could take place.

> • A customer registering with FV had to forward credit-card information and an e-mail address to the FV server and in exchange received a pass phrase, called a VirtualPIN. This initial part of the exchange could take place across the Internet, with the user filling out a form and inventing the first part of a pass phrase. The FV server acknowledged this and added a suffix to the pass phrase to actually form the VirtualPIN. The customer then made a telephone call to FV to tender credit-card information. This allowed FV to establish a link between the VirtualPIN and the pass phrase on the one hand and the customer's credit-card information on the other hand without ever using this information on the Internet.

> • Merchants had to go through a similar registration procedure in which they gave bank account information to FV and then were given a merchant VirtualPIN.

After a customer had properly registered with FV, he or she could browse any Web site on which a FV merchant was selling goods. The customer selected the item(s) he or she wished to purchase and was asked to enter the VirtualPIN (representing his or her FV account identifier). The VirtualPIN was then forwarded to the merchant, and the merchant checked that it was valid by querying a corresponding FV server. If the customer's VirtualPIN was not blacklisted, the merchant delivered the information to the customer and forwarded information about the transaction, including the customer's VirtualPIN, to the FV server. No payment was made at this point, since the system was based on a try-before-you-buy philosophy. Consequently, the next step was for the FV server to send an e-mail message to the customer asking whether he or she accepted or rejected the goods. In addition, the customer could also indicate that a fraud was going on (as a third option). Upon receipt of this message, the FV server would immediately blacklist the customer's VirtualPIN. At the end of every 90 days, the customer's credit-card account was debited for the charges that had accumulated during the time period, and the corresponding merchant's checking account was credited with payments for the items sold. FV performed the accounting for both the customer and merchant, taking a percentage of each transaction as a commission fee.

It is obvious that if a VirtualPIN was compromised by an attacker eavesdropping on network data traffic, bogus purchases could be made from then until the VirtualPIN was blacklisted. Since payment authorization requests were sent to the customer by e-mail, this time period could range from a few minutes to perhaps a couple of days. Furthermore, degradation-of-service and denial-of-service attacks on the e-mail system could be used to prolong this period substantially. Consequently, the actual security of the FV payment system was not based on the VirtualPIN and the pass phrase, but rather on the customer's ability to revoke each payment within a certain period of time. In other words, there was no definite authorization during payment. Until the end of the clearing period (typically 90 days as mentioned above), the merchant had to take the entire risk.

A similar credit-card-based system has been developed and is being marketed successfully by PayPal.[3] The system is, for example, used to settle purchases made on Internet auction sites, such as eBay.[4] Contrary to FV and PayPal, however, most contemporary electronic payment systems are more complex and use more sophisticated cryptographic techniques. Most of these systems require at least one financial institution, such as a bank, that links the data exchanged in the payment protocol to corresponding transfers of monetary value. Typically, banks participate in electronic payment protocols in two roles:

▸ As an *issuer* (interacting with the customer or payer);

▸ As an *acquirer* (interacting with the merchant or payee).

In addition, there may be some form of *arbiter* to settle disputes. In most electronic payment systems, the presence of an arbiter is not explicit. Even if the necessary pieces of evidence are produced, disputes must be handled outside the actual payment systems. In many cases, dispute handling is not even specified. This is about to change, since contemporary research in electronic payment systems and the provision of nonrepudiation services also addresses dispute handling.

In general, electronic payment systems are classified according to the relationship between the time the payment initiator (i.e., the customer) considers the purchase as finished and the time the corresponding monetary value is actually taken from his or her account. Consequently, one can distinguish between prepaid, pay-now, and pay-after payment systems:

---

3. http://www.paypal.com
4. http://www.ebay.com

▸ In a *prepaid payment system*, a certain amount of money is taken away from the customer (for example, by debiting his or her bank account) before any purchase is made. This amount of money can afterward be used for payments. Smart card-based electronic purses and wallets, electronic cash, and certain bank checks (i.e., certified checks) fall into this category.

▸ In a *pay-now payment systems*, the customer's account is debited exactly at the time of the purchase. Certain debit cards fall into this category.[5]

▸ Finally, in a *pay-after payment system*, the merchant's bank account is credited the amount of the purchase before the customer's account is debited. Normal credit cards fall into this category.

Note that any prepaid payment system is conceptually similar to physical cash. Consequently, they are sometimes also referred to as *cashlike payment systems*. Also note that the later two payment systems (i.e., pay-now and pay-after payment systems) are also similar in nature. In either case the payer must have some sort of account with the bank, and a payment is always done by sending some form, such as a check or credit-card slip, from the customer to the merchant. Consequently, these two categories of payment systems are sometimes collectively referred to as *checklike payment systems*. Note that a key difference between cashlike and checklike payment systems is also due to the fact that providing anonymity in a cashlike payment system is possible and conceptually simple, whereas anonymity in a checklike payment system is inherently more difficult to provide (this is because the merchant must have some kind of guarantee that he or she will actually receive his or her money anytime in the future).

In the field of electronic payment systems, the notions *on-line* and *off-line* refer to a specific property of the corresponding payment protocol. Although the payment protocol is functionally a protocol between two parties (i.e., the customer and the merchant) many payment systems require that the merchant contact a TTP acting as a central authority (e.g., a bank, a credit-card company, or an acquirer) before accepting a payment. If that is the case, the system is called an *on-line payment system*. In this case, the communication between the merchant and the central authority may be

---

5. For example, Switch debit cards are very common in the United Kingdom. They are issued by banks and are used like credit cards, although the money is deducted from the customer's bank account immediately. Further information about Switch debit cards can be found at the home page of Switch Card Services Ltd. at http://www.switch.co.uk/switch.htm.

using any communication medium (not necessarily the Internet). If such a contact with a TTP is not required during the payment protocol, the system is called an *off-line payment system*. In an offline payment system, merchants are required to contact their acquirer on a regular basis for clearing all received payments.

In general, on-line payment systems are more appropriate to adequately secure the merchant and the bank against customer fraud, since every payment must be approved. The primary disadvantage of on-line authorization is the associated per-transaction cost, imposed by the requirement for a highly reliable and efficient clearing system at the customer's bank. Consequently, offline payment systems have been designed (and still continue to be designed) to lower the cost of transactions by delaying the clearing to a batch process. Off-line systems, however, suffer from the potential of double spending, whereby the electronic currency is duplicated and spent repeatedly. Thus, off-line protocols concentrate on preventing or detecting and limiting fraud, and in catching the fraudulent party in the second case. Off-line systems that detect and limit fraud are generally suitable only for low-value transactions where accountability after the fact is sufficient to deter abuse.

In the remaining part of this chapter, we overview and briefly discuss the working principles of electronic cash systems, electronic checks, electronic credit-card payments, and micropayment systems. For each category we mention some exemplary systems by name.

9.2 Electronic cash systems

Almost all statistical investigations show that consumers make extensive use of cash. Depending on the country involved, somewhere between 75% and 95% of all financial transactions are paid with cash, even though the value of these transactions are for the most part quite low. As mentioned above, prepaid or cashlike payment systems provide an electronic analog for physical cash.

In short, a bank issues *electronic cash* (e-cash), and customers use e-cash to purchase goods or services from merchants that accept this form of payment. Consequently, there are three parties involved in an e-cash system:

1. An e-cash issuing bank;

2. A customer (or payer);

3. A merchant (or payee).

Typically, the customer and merchant have accounts with the same bank. However, the customer and merchant may also have accounts with different banks. In this case, the banks are referred to as the customer's bank or issuer and the merchant's bank or acquirer.

Given this cast, an e-cash transaction typically takes place in three distinct and independent phases:

1. In the first phase, the customer withdraws some e-cash. He or she therefore requests his or her bank (i.e., the issuer) to transfer some monetary value from his or her account to the e-cash issuing bank. Following this value transfer, the bank issues[6] and sends a corresponding amount of e-cash to the customer. The customer, in turn, stores the e-cash locally (e.g., on his or her hard disk or smart card).

2. In the second phase, the customer uses the e-cash to purchase some goods or services. In particular, he or she selects goods or services and transfers the corresponding amount of e-cash to the merchant. The merchant, in turn, delivers the goods or services to the customer.

3. In the third phase, the merchant redeems the e-cash he or she has just received from the customer. He or she therefore transfers the e-cash to the issuing bank. Alternatively, the merchant may also transfer the e-cash to his or her bank (the merchant's bank), and this bank may, in turn, redeem the money from the e-cash issuing bank. In this case, the issuing bank transfers money to the merchant's bank for crediting the merchant's account.

It is commonly agreed that e-cash should satisfy some general properties. For example, e-cash should be independent in the sense that its existence must not depend on a particular system platform or location. Probably one of the distinguishing features of physical cash (at least in the case of coins) is anonymity, meaning that cash must not provide information that can be used to trace previous owners. One can reasonably argue that e-cash must also provide this form of anonymity. Consequently, e-cash should be transferable from one person to another, and this transfer should occur without leaving any trace of who has been in possession of the e-cash before. In this case, however, it must be ensured that each owner can spend the

---

6. In general, e-cash is issued by having the bank mint digital coins. The digital coins, in turn, are minted by digitally signing an item, such as a serial number for the coin, with a private key that is characteristic for the actual denomination of the coin.

e-cash only once and that double spending can be prevented or at least be detected in one way or another. Furthermore, e-cash should be available in several denominations and be divisible in a way similar to physical cash. Finally, e-cash should be available in such a way that it can be securely stored on various media, such as hard disks or smart cards.

Not all e-cash systems that have been proposed in the past satisfy all of these properties. For example, the anonymity property is still very controversial today, since it leads to the undesired possibility of illegal money laundering, or hiding of black market and blackmail money. This has led to development of fairly anonymous e-cash systems, in which the customer's anonymity may leak under certain conditions. The development of fairly anonymous e-cash systems is an active area of research today.

There are many electronic cash systems developed in theory and practice. Examples include David Chaum's e-cash system [4–6],[7] an electronic cash system that was developed in a European research-and-development project called Conditional Access for Europe (CAFE) [7, 8], NetCash[8] developed at the University of Southern California [9], the Mondex electronic cash card,[9] EMV cash cards [3], as well as cards that conform to the Common Electronic Purse Specification (CEPS). All of these systems and their corresponding protocols are overviewed and further described in Chapter 6 of [1].

9.3 Electronic checks

Since the use of checks is widely deployed in the real world (at least in the United States), electronic checks may also provide an interesting payment scheme for e-commerce applications. A payment system for electronic checks includes the following parties:

---

7. The system was originally marketed by a Dutch company called DigiCash. DigiCash was acquired by eCash Technolgies, Inc. in August 1999, and eCash Technolgies, Inc. was acquired by InfoSpace, Inc. in February 2002. As of this writing, it is not clear if and in what form the e-cash system developed by Chaum will be marketed in the future.

8. http://www.isi.edu/gost/info/netcash

9. The concept of the Mondex card was developed in 1990 at NatWest, a major banking organization in the United Kingdom. After several field trials, a separate company, called Mondex International Ltd., was formed in 1996 to promote the technology through a series of further trials in many different locations around the world. Today, Mondex International is a subsidiary of MasterCard International. As of this writing, little is publicly known about the security features used in the Mondex electronic cash cards. Consequently, the cards have not been subject to public scrutiny.

> ▸ A customer and a customer's bank;

> ▸ A merchant and a merchant's bank;

> ▸ A clearinghouse to process checks among different banks.

From a technical point of view, electronic checks are rather simple. An electronic check may simply consist of a document that is digitally signed with the customer's private key. The receiver (the merchant or the merchant's bank) uses the customer's public key to verify the digital signature accordingly. More specifically, an electronic check transaction is executed in three phases:

1. In the first phase, the customer purchases some goods or services and sends a corresponding electronic check to the merchant. The merchant, in turn, validates the check with his or her bank for proper payment authorization. If the check is valid, the merchant accomplishes the transaction with the customer (and delivers the goods or services).

2. In the second phase, the merchant forwards the electronic check to his or her bank for deposit. This action may take place at the discretion of the merchant.

3. In the third phase, the merchant's bank forwards the electronic check to the clearinghouse for cashing it. The clearinghouse, in turn, cooperates with the customer's bank, clears the check, and transfers the money to the merchant's bank, which updates the merchant's account accordingly. The customer's bank also updates the customer with the corresponding withdrawal information.

Compared with paper checks and some other real-world payment systems, electronic checks provide several advantages. For example, electronic checks can be issued without needing to fill out, mail, or deliver checks. They also save time in processing the checks. With paper checks, the merchant typically collects all the checks and collectively deposits them at the bank. With electronic checks, the merchant can instantly forward the checks to the bank and get them credited to his or her account. As such, electronic checks can greatly reduce the time from the moment a customer writes a check to the time when the merchant receives the deposit. In addition, electronic check systems can be designed in such a way that the merchant gets proper authorization from the customer's bank before accepting a check. This is very similar to the concept of a cashier's check.

In the past, the research community has formulated some electronic check systems for the Internet. Examples include NetBill developed at Carnegie Mellon University [10, 11] and NetCheque, developed at the University of Southern California [12, 13].[10] More importantly, however, the Financial Services Technology Consortium (FSTC[11]) has developed an eCheck system[12] that makes use of a financial services markup language (FSML). Most parts of the system are covered by U.S. patents that have been granted to the FSTC.[13] It is possible and very likely that the FSTC eCheck system will be the electronic check system of choice for all financial institutions working in this area.

You may refer to Chapter 5 of [1] for further information regarding NetBill, NetCheque, and the FSTC eCheck system.

9.4 Electronic credit-card payments

In the past, credit-card payment systems have become the payment instrument of choice for Internet users and customers. There are several security requirements that these systems must address. For example, a mechanism must be provided to authenticate the various parties involved, such as customers and merchants, as well as participating banks. Another mechanism must be provided to protect the credit-card and payment information during transmission over the Internet. Finally, a process must be instituted to resolve credit-card payment disputes between the various parties involved.

Several electronic credit-card payment systems have been designed to address these requirements. Most of these schemes have additional properties. For example, in some schemes (including, for example, the SET scheme as addressed below) the credit-card information can be prevented from disclosure to the merchant, whereas the information about the products or services purchased can be prevented from disclosure to the banks. Note that

---

10. http://www.isi.edu/gost/info/NetCheque
11. The FSTC is a group of American banks, research agencies, and government organizations that have come together to assist in enhancing the competitiveness of the U.S. financial services industry. Further information about the FSTC can be found at http://www.fstc.org.
12. The FSTC eCheck system is described in a white paper that is electronically available at http://www.echeck.org/library/wp/ArchitectualOverview.pdf.
13. The relevant patents are U.S. 5677955 entitled "Electronic Funds Transfer Instruments," U.S. 6021202 entitled "Method and System for Processing Electronic Documents," and U.S. 6209095 entitled "Method and System for Processing Electronic Documents."

this property is not inherent in traditional credit-card systems. Consequently, an electronic credit-card payment scheme may provide a higher level of security than a traditional credit-card payment scheme. Also, an electronic credit-card payment scheme can be designed to obtain almost instant payments to the merchants from credit-card sales. For traditional credit-card schemes, it takes a significant amount of time for the merchant to deliver the credit-card receipts to the bank, and for the bank to settle the payments (this advantage is similar to that of electronic checks).

There are five parties involved in a secure electronic credit-card payment scheme:

- A credit-card holder;

- A merchant;

- A merchant's bank;

- A certificate management center;

- A credit-card issuing bank.

The credit-card holder uses his or her credit-card to purchase products or services from the merchant. The merchant, in turn, interacts with his or her bank, called the merchant's bank, the acquirer bank, or simply the acquirer. In an electronic credit-card payment scheme, the acquirer typically refers to a financial institution that has an account with a merchant and processes credit-card authorizations and corresponding payments. In this setting, a payment gateway is a device operated by the acquirer to handle merchant payment messages. A very important party for a secure electronic credit-card payment system is the certificate management center that issues and revokes public key certificates to the parties involved.

There are usually two networks involved in an electronic credit-card payment scheme:

- A public network (typically the Internet);

- A private network owned and operated by the banking community.

The basic assumption is that data transmissions across the private network are sufficiently secure, whereas data transmissions across the public network are inherently insecure and must be cryptographically protected. Consequently, an electronic credit-card payment protocol mainly focuses on the communications that take place over the Internet and does not address communications that take place over the private network.

In the recent past, several electronic credit-card payment schemes have been designed, proposed, and implemented (most of them are overviewed and discussed in Chapter 4 of [1]). Examples include the iKP (where $i =$ 1, 2, or 3) family of Internet-keyed payments protocol developed by IBM in the early 1990s [14], the Secure Electronic Payment Protocol (SEPP) developed by a consortium chaired by MasterCard, the Secure Transaction Technology (STT) developed by another consortium chaired by Visa International and Microsoft, and—most importantly—a scheme and set of protocols named *Secure Electronic Transaction* (SET) developed as an industry standard in 1996 [15, 16]. In the second half of the 1990s, it was commonly agreed and expected that SET would become the technology of choice for electronic credit-card-based payments over the Internet. This expectation has not become true and support for SET has never really took off in the commercial world. One reason for this fact is that the SET protocols are complex and difficult to implement. Furthermore, the deployment of SET requires an existing and fully operational PKI (which is hard to achieve as discussed in Chapter 7). Meanwhile, Visa International and MasterCard have both started to work on alternative technologies that will eventually replace SET. As a temporary and intermediate solution, Visa International and MasterCard both use the last three digits of the number that is printed on the back of each credit-card as a proof of physical ownership. Visa International is using the term *card verification code* (CVC) to refer to this number, whereas MasterCard is using the term *card verification value* (CVV). Taking all the recent developments in account, it is not at all clear how the market for electronic credit-card payments will evolve in the future.

9.5 Micropayment systems

An important factor in the evaluation of electronic payment systems is the cost of the overhead involved in collecting payments as compared to the actual amount of money being transferred. Apart from the overhead costs incurred in the extra transactions required to implement the payment protocol, there is also another set of costs that banks may charge for their services. These bank service or transaction fees may be charged when an account or credit-card is accessed and may contribute a large component to the overall costs of a payment system.

Of the conventional payment instruments of cash, check, and credit card, the one most suited for low-value transactions is cash. Nevertheless, the use of cash is limited in that no transaction can involve less than the value of the smallest coin (e.g., one cent). There are some e-commerce applications where this limitation poses a serious problem. Examples include obtaining a quotation of the current price of a share on the stock market or making a single query in a database system. In conventional commerce, the solution to this problem has been to use a subscription mode of payment, where the customer pays in advance and can access the product or service for a fixed period of time. While this ensures that the provider is paid, it seals off what is in many cases a large customer base of people who may only wish to use a service occasionally. To make things worse, it also restricts the ability of people to simply try out a service.

Following this line of argument, it is clear that the subscription mode of payment does not adequately solve all requirements for electronic payments in e-commerce, and that there is need for payment systems that efficiently transfer very small amounts of money, perhaps less than one cent, in a single transaction. These payment systems are collectively referred to as *micropayment systems*, and their design and optimization has attracted many researchers in the past. To achieve the required efficiency, micropayment systems must not involve computationally expensive cryptographic operations. The basic idea is to replace the use of public key cryptography with keyed one-way hash functions. The main advantage of this replacement is efficiency, whereas the main disadvantage is the inability to provide nonrepudiation services. However, since micropayments typically do not exceed a few cents, the merchant may carry the risk that a customer later denies having committed to a payment.

Against this background, there are many micropayment systems that have been designed and implemented in the past. Examples include Millicent developed by Digital Equipment Corporation (DEC) [17, 18], SubScrip developed at the University of Newcastle in Australia [19], PayWord and MicroMint developed by Ronald L. Rivest and Adi Shamir [20], Agora [21], and NetCents [22]. Most of these systems are overviewed and discussed in Chapter 7 of [1]. None of these systems has become a commercial success and is widely deployed on the Internet. This is not likely to change anytime soon, because services continue to be paid with advertisements and subscription fees.

9.6 Conclusions

In the recent past, the growing importance of e-commerce and e-commerce applications has resulted in the design and development of many different and partly incompatible electronic payment systems. In this chapter, we overviewed and briefly discussed some electronic cash systems, electronic checks, electronic credit-card payments, and micropayment systems.

From an academic point of view, the design and development of electronic payment systems is an interesting and challenging field of study. That's why we have a big variety of complementary or competing systems. From an application developer's point of view, however, this variety is very uncomfortable, because it requires that a specific application supports many systems. Furthermore, the application must be developed in a way that allows future systems to be supported with an effort that is as small as possible.

Against this background, one may hope that a certain degree of convergence will occur in the industry (where systems that address the same needs will compete and one will emerge as victor). As with any payment system, a major factor in its success is consumer trust and acceptance. Any system backed by big-name banking organizations or indeed the banking industry as a whole will easily build this level of consumer trust and acceptance. Consequently, it was hoped that SET would emerge as a standard way of doing credit-card payments over the Internet. Unfortunately, reality has shown a different story and SET is still not widely deployed today. Contrary to SET, it is possible and very likely that the FSTC eCheck system will be the electronic check system of choice in the financial world. With regard to electronic cash systems and micropayment systems it is very difficult to predict the future.

In addition to the electronic payment systems mentioned in this chapter, there is also a trend in the industry to have payment systems depend on the security features of some complementary networks. For example, mobile networks are widely deployed in Europe. These networks generally implement some strong authentication technologies. This is particularly true for GSM networks. Consequently, GSM networks and their services— such as the short messaging service (SMS)—provide an interesting infrastructure to implement electronic payments and to charge GSM subscribers accordingly. For example, the Paybox system[14] works this way and is widely deployed in Germany. Payment systems like Paybox are particularly important for mobile commerce (m-commerce) and m-commerce applications.

Last but not least, there are also some banking and other regulations pertaining to handling electronic payments. For example, who is authorized to issue electronic money? Can every bank issue its own currency and mint

---

14. http://www.paybox.de

its own digital coins? If so, how is fraud prevented, and who's in charge of monitoring the banking operations to protect the customers? Note that conventional payment instruments have, in the past at least, been operated by banks who are subject to regulation by their national central bank. Typically, a bank must be licensed to operate, and in the course of obtaining this license, will subject itself to scrutiny. As of this writing, it is not clear what regulations should be imposed on electronic payment systems, and how the above-mentioned concerns should be addressed.

References

[1]   O'Mahony, D., M. Peirce, and H. Tewari, *Electronic Payment Systems for E-Commerce, Second Edition*, Norwood, MA: Artech House, 2001.

[2]   Hassler, V., et al., *Java Card for E-Payment Applications*, Norwood, MA: Artech House, 2002.

[3]   Radu, C., *Deploying Electronic Payment Systems*, Norwood, MA: Artech House, 2002.

[4]   Chaum, D., "Blind Signatures for Untraceable Payments," *Proceedings of CRYPTO '82*, August 1982, pp. 199–203.

[5]   Chaum, D., "Security without Identification: Transaction Systems To Make Big Brother Obsolete," *Communications of the ACM*, Vol. 28, No. 10, October 1985, pp. 1030–1044.

[6]   Chaum, D., "Achieving Electronic Privacy," *Scientific American*, August 1992, pp. 96–101.

[7]   Chaum, D., A. Fiat, and M. Naor, "Untraceable Electronic Cash," *Proceedings of CRYPTO '88*, August 1988, pp. 319–327.

[8]   Chaum, D., and T. Pedersen, "Wallet Databases with Observers," *Proceedings of CRYPTO '92*, August 1992, pp. 89–105.

[9]   Medvinsky, G., and B. C. Neuman, "NetCash: A Design for Practical Electronic Currency on the Internet," *Proceedings of ACM Conference on Computer and Communications Security*, 1993.

[10]   Cox, B., J. D. Tygar, and M. Sirbu, "NetBill Security and Transaction Protocol," *Proceedings of USENIX Workshop on Electronic Commerce*, July 1995.

[11]   Sirbu, M., and J. D. Tygar, "NetBill: An Internet Commerce System Optimized for Network Delivered Services," *IEEE Personal Communications*, August 1995, pp. 6–11.

[12]   Neuman, B. C., and G. Medvinsky, "Requirements for Network Payment: The NetCheque Perspective," *Proceedings of IEEE Compcon*, March 1995.

[13] Neuman, B. C., and G. Medvinsky, "Internet Payment Services," *Proceedings of MIT Workshop on Internet Economics*, March 1995, pp. 401–415.

[14] Bellare, M., et al., "iKP—A Family of Secure Electronic Payment Protocols," *Proceedings of USENIX Workshop on Electronic Commerce*, July 1995.

[15] Loeb, L., *Secure Electronic Transactions: Introduction and Technical Reference*, Norwood, MA: Artech House, 1998.

[16] Merkow, M. S., and J. Breithaupt, *Building SET Appliactions for Secure Transactions*, New York: John Wiley & Sons, 1998.

[17] Manasse, M., "The Millicent Protocols for Electronic Commerce," *Proceedings of the 1st USENIX Workshop on Electronic Commerce*, July 1995.

[18] Glassman, S., et al., "The Millicent Protocol for Inexpensive Electronic Commerce," *Proceedings of 4th International World Wide Web Conference*, December 1995, pp. 603–618.

[19] Furche, A., and G. Wrightson, "SubScrip—An Efficient Protocol for Pay-Per-View Payments on the Internet," *Proceedings of International Conference on Computer, Communications and Networks (ICCCN '96)*, October 1996, pp. 603–618.

[20] Rivest, R. L., and A. Shamir, "PayWord and MicroMint," *RSA Laboratories' CryptoBytes*, Vol. 2, No. 1, Spring 1996, pp. 7–11.

[21] Gabber, E., and A. Silberschatz, "Agora: A Minimal Distributed Protocol for Electronic Commerce," *Proceedings of the 2nd USENIX Workshop on Electronic Commerce*, 1996.

[22] Poutanen, T., H. Hinton, and M. Stumm, "NetCents: A Lightweight Protocol for Secure Micropayments," *Proceedings of the 3rd USENIX Workshop on Electronic Commerce*, August 1998.

CHAPTER

10

Contents

10.1 Introduction

10.2 Binary mail attachments

10.3 Helper applications and plug-ins

10.4 Scripting languages

10.5 Java applets

10.6 ActiveX controls

10.7 Security zones

10.8 Implications for firewalls

10.9 Conclusions

  References

Client-side Security

In this chapter, we focus on client-side security in general, and the security implications of executable (or active) content in particular. After a brief introduction in Section 10.1, we elaborate on binary mail attachments in Section 10.2, helper applications and plug-ins in Section 10.3, scripting languages in Section 10.4, Java applets in Section 10.5, and ActiveX controls in Section 10.6. In Section 10.7, we elaborate on security zones as implemented, for example, in Microsoft Internet Explorer. In Section 10.8, we discuss the implications of executable content for firewalls, and in Section 10.9, we draw some conclusions. It is reasonable to expect that client-side security problems as outlined in this chapter will become a more and more important topic in the future.

10.1 Introduction

One of the most dangerous things that can be done with a computer system connected to a network (e.g., the Internet) is to download an arbitrary piece of software and execute it locally. This is because many operating systems place no limits on what a program can do once it starts running. Consequently, when a user downloads an arbitrary piece of software and executes it locally, the user places himself or herself entirely in the hands of the corresponding programmer or software developer (note, however, that this is true not only for downloaded programs, but also for any program that is executed locally).

In practice, most programs that are downloaded behave as expected. But the point is that they don't have to and some don't. Some programs have bugs and programming errors that cause computer systems to crash. Other programs have bugs that may be exploited by hackers. Still other programs are malicious and may do damaging things, such as erasing hard disks or transmitting confidential data to some arbitrary locations on the Internet.

In general, the ultimate goal of a (software) attacker is to be able to execute a program of his or her choice on a computer system of his or her choice without the corresponding victim's knowledge. Once this ability is achieved, any other attack is usually feasible and may be mounted. The easiest way for an attacker to accomplish this goal is to provide a user of the computer system with some program code to execute with his or her privileges.

One would think that an easy way to protect a computer system against this type of attack is to inspect all downloaded programs to see if they contain malicious software. Unfortunately, it's impossible to determine what a computer program will do without actually running it. What's possibly even more worrisome is the fact that it's often impossible to determine what a program is doing while or after it is running. Programs may have many ways of hiding the functions they actually implement.

Even sophisticated operating systems with memory protection and other security features, such as the Windows or Linux operating systems, offer users little protection against malicious programs that they download and execute locally. That's because once the program is running, it typically inherits all the privileges and corresponding access rights from the user who invoked it. No commercially deployed operating system allows users to create a restricted area in which potentially malicious programs can be executed (similar to the Java sandbox addressed below). To make things worse, Internet users have been told for years to download various programs and execute them locally without asking any further questions. For example, browsers as well as helper applications and plug-ins are typically distributed by having users download, execute, and install particular software modules. The same is true for bug-fixes, patches, and system upgrades. This user behavior automatically leads to security problems.

In general, executable or active content embraces a large collection of technologies that make the Internet (including the WWW) more interesting and interactive, but also more dangerous. In short, executable or active content is downloaded into client software where it is executed locally. Sometimes the local execution requires a user initiative, but sometimes it doesn't. Examples of executable or active content include binary mail attachments, data files for word processors and other office automation programs, Java applets, ActiveX controls, as well as programs written in scripting languages, such as JavaScript or VBScript.

Well-written executable or active content may enhance Internet sites and corresponding Web pages with animations, interactive games, and serious applications, such as database browsers or groupware applications. In fact, the entire idea of network computing was centered around the idea of well-written (and well-intended) executable or active content. However, one question that arises immediately is how to decide whether executable or active content is well-written (and well-intended). If the content is buggy or not well-written, it may contain security holes that may compromise the user's privacy or the integrity of the data stored on the computer system. Even more worrisome, executable or active content written for malicious purposes may attempt to damage the computer system or seek to gain illegitimate access to the local network. Unfortunately, it has been shown that deciding whether an arbitrary piece of software is malicious or includes malicious code is difficult (to say the least) [1].

From a theoretical point of view, the security problems related to executable or active content occur because there is no fundamental difference between a program (representing an active component) and data (representing a passive component) with regard to its internal representation within a computer system. In fact, they are both internally represented as a series of zeros and ones. Furthermore, in the traditional approach to designing and building computer systems,[1] programs and data are treated equally and stored in the same memory.[2] This allows a program to modify both data and programs (eventually modifying itself). For example, most computer viruses take advantage of the fact that they can manipulate and directly modify program code. But in spite of these theoretical considerations, we have become accustomed to the clear distinction between active programs and passive data. Unfortunately, this distinction has been blurred in the recent past. Things that we used to assume are safe, such as data files for word processors, can now contain and use a macro virus to attack our systems. As a matter of fact, macro viruses that infect data files (or rather, the macro programming features of these data

---

1. This approach is generally attributed to John von Neumann. You may refer to the URL http://www-groups. dcs.st-andrews.ac.uk/history/Mathematicians/Von_Neumann.html to get a comprehensive overview about John von Neumann's work.
2. Note that this approach applies to *Von Neumann architecture machines*, but it does not necessarily apply to other machines. For example, in a *Harvard architecture machine*, programs and data are stored in separate memories. The reason for this separation is efficiency; it has, however, also a positive side effect on security.

files) are spreading very rapidly throughout the Internet and the WWW. To make things worse, Web pages can contain executable or active content that is entirely transparent and invisible to Web users.

The WWW in general, and the deployment of executable or active content in particular, have also changed the way software is being distributed and sold globally. Instead of having users physically walk into trusted neighborhood retail stores and buy shrink-wrapped software packages, they download the software they want from corresponding Web sites (i.e., Web-based software distributors). The point that must be kept in mind is that there are all kinds of distributors. Some of them are good and distribute software that is perfectly secure and safe, whereas others are not so good and distribute software that is either not secure and safe (because it contains, for example, bugs and programming errors) or—even worse— malicious (because it contains, for example, a Trojan horse). The point is that it is hard to tell the difference without actually running the software (it may even be difficult to tell the difference after the software has run). To make matter worse, there is hardly any traceability or accountability in the Web-based software distribution model. This makes liability issues very difficult to address and resolve.

Against this background, it is important to note that the WWW and its possibility to distribute executable or active content has shifted the main security problem from protecting the server against potentially malicious clients to protecting the client against potentially malicious servers. One way to protect the client is to use secure software distribution systems that provide something conceptually similar to a digital shrink-wrap. For example, a group of researchers at Bell Communications Research (Bellcore) developed and ran a secure software distribution system called Bellcore's Trusted Software Integrity System (BETSI) in the early 1990s [2, 3]. BETSI used PGP and distinguished between authors and users:

> *Authors* were people or companies (e.g., Microsoft) who wished to securely distribute software on the Internet (i.e., software publishers).

> *Users* were people who wished to download software that has authenticity and integrity guarantees.

Authors had to register with BETSI in advance. Once they were registered, they could communicate securely with a BETSI server because they shared authentic and valid copies of one another's PGP public keys. If an author had a file (e.g., a software package) he or she wanted to securely distribute, he or she created an integrity certificate request for it. The request contained information, such as the author's name, the file's name, and the MD5 hash value of the file. The author then digitally signed the request with his or her private PGP key and sent the result to the BETSI server. The BETSI server, in turn, verified the message and its PGP signature. If the message was valid, BETSI sent back to the author an integrity certificate that was digitally signed. The integrity certificate basically claimed that the named author was registered and that he or she had properly requested a certificate linking a certain hash value to a specific file (or filename). The author then verified the integrity certificate and was free to make it publicly available (e.g., together with the file).

On the other side, each BETSI user was required to have PGP, an implementation of MD5, and an authentic PGP public key from the BETSI server. When he or she downloaded a file, he or she also got an integrity certificate for this file. He or she could then verify that the file had not been (intentionally or unintentionally) modified, by verifying the integrity certificate with BETSI's public key and computing the hash value of the corresponding file. If the integrity certificate was valid, the user could be sure that the file was authentic and had not been modified.

Unfortunately, the use of BETSI or any other secure software distribution system has never really taken off in the commercial world. This is slowly beginning to change with the use and deployment of code signing technologies and systems (as discussed later in this chapter). These technologies and systems are conceptually similar to BETSI.[3]

In the following sections, we overview and briefly discuss the potential problems related to the various classes of executable or active content. In particular, we elaborate on binary mail attachments, helper applications and plug-ins, scripting languages, Java applets, and ActiveX controls.

10.2 Binary mail attachments

A *binary mail attachment* is an attachment to an e-mail message that contains some binary data. The binary data, in turn, may encode anything, such as random data, structured data (e.g., data for a word processing program), or even executable code. As such, binary mail attachments encoding executable code represent the simplest class of executable or active content. The sender of an e-mail message simply attaches a program respresenting executable code to a message, and the recipient—manually or automatically—executes the program upon reception.

---

3. This is the reason why BETSI is discussed in the first place.

It is common practice today to use binary mail attachments to distribute simple animation programs over the Internet. In general, these programs are executed on the recipients' side without thinking about security implications. For example, it would be a fairly simple exercise for a software developer to write a program that automatically deletes all files a user running the program has access to and is authorized to delete. In fact, several programs that illustrate this possibility have already been demonstrated on the Internet. In theory, these programs are well suited to increase the awareness of the problem of binary mail attachments to e-mail users. In practice, however, these programs are not very effective and users continue to redistribute binary mail attachments they like to their colleagues and friends. This is worrisome, to say the least.

More recently, many Internet security incidents reported in the media have been caused by malicious software (e.g., Internet worms) that is able to replicate itself. You may remember the Love Letter worm that hit the Internet in 2000.[4] Since then, many Internet worms have employed binary mail attachments that are sent to arbitrary e-mail addresses found in electronic address books. If a recipient of such a mail open the attachment, it is usually executed by some preconfigured program.[5] Sometimes it is not even necessary that the recipient open the attachment because his or her user agent is configured in a way that invokes a program that matches the MIME type of the message and automatically displays (i.e., previews) it. This possibility should be kept in mind when configuring a user agent to preview incoming messages.

In summary, the use of a binary mail attachment should be considered with care. Every user should understand that the attachment he or she receives must not originate from the claimed source, and that it is executed with his or her privileges. As such, it can do anything he or she is authorized to do (including, for example, the deletion of data files). Once this is understood, it is possible and likely that users will get more concerned about the security implications of binary mail attachments, and that they will actually try to avoid them.

10.3 Helper applications and plug-ins

In the early days of the WWW, most browsers could only render and display ASCII and HTML text, as well as images in either the GIF or the JPEG format.

---

4. http://www.cert.org/advisories/CA-2000-04.html
5. The program is preconfigured to be used for a specific MIME type.

While these four data types provided a good basis and starting point for the Web to emerge, there were many kinds of types that couldn't be translated into these data types. Consequently, Web developers had to think about possibilities to extend the ability of browsers to understand, render, and display other data types.

An obvious possibility is the use of so-called *helper applications* (also known as *external viewers*). In short, a helper application is an application program that is run automatically by the Web browser if a data type other than ASCII, HTML, GIF, or JPEG is received.[6] The important thing to note is that the helper application is an application program of its own that also runs in its own address space. As such, helper applications provide a flexible and extensible way through which practically any kind of information can be downloaded, rendered, and displayed.

Motivated by the work that had been done in the field of helper applications, Netscape Communications developed a similar system called *plug-ins*.[7] In short, a plug-in is a software module that is loaded directly into the address space of the Web browser and is automatically run when a document of a particular data type is downloaded. One of the simplest uses for plug-ins is to replace helper applications. Instead of requiring that data be specially downloaded, saved in a file, and processed by a helper application, the data can be loaded directly into the browser's memory space and processed by the appropriate plug-in. As of this writing, most popular helper applications have been rewritten as plug-ins, including, for example, the Adobe Acrobat reader to display PDF files, the RealAudio player to play sound files, or the Macromedia Shockwave player to play animated video sequences. In either case, plug-ins are manually downloaded by users and usually stored in a specific directory called `Plugins`.[8] The browser scans the `Plugins` directory when it starts up to discover what plug-ins are available.

In spite of their advantages in terms of functionality and browser extensibility, helper applications and plug-ins can also be the source of security problems. For example, if a user downloads a helper application or plug-in, he or she should make sure that the software is authentic and has

---

6. Parts of this section also apply to user agents for e-mail. In fact, many user agents can be configured to run an application program if data of a specific MIME type is received.

7. Plug-ins have been developed by Netscape Communications. Although Microsoft Internet Explorer can also run plug-ins, they are deprecated in favor of ActiveX controls.

8. Most installations of Microsoft Internet Explorer have an empty `Plugins` directory, mainly because plug-ins are deprecated in favor of ActiveX controls.

not been tampered with. Consequently, a secure software distribution system, such as BETSI or something conceptually similar, is urgently needed. Also, if a user downloads data that is locally executed by a helper application or plug-in, he or she must make sure that the data is not malicious and does not try to exploit a vulnerability in the execution environment. This is difficult to achieve (to say the least). In general, the more powerful a helper application or plug-in is, the more possibilities an attacker usually has to find and exploit vulnerabilities (and to eventually attack the browser accordingly).

One of the most powerful application programs is an interpreter for a general-purpose programming language. Given the appropriate input, an interpreter can typically open, read, modify, or delete any file on a computer system. To make things worse, many programming languages allow programs to open network connections, enabling them to scan for vulnerabilities and security loopholes on other computers. Because they are so powerful, interpreters for general-purpose programming languages should never be used or configured as helper applications.[9] This includes Microsoft Word and Excel (unless the macros feature is turned off), since they are both equipped with the Visual Basic scripting language.

Against this background, the following programs should never be used or configured as helper applications:

> Any other program that includes Microsoft's Visual Basic scripting language;

> Many other scripting languages, such as Perl, Python, and Tcl/Tk;

> UNIX shells, such as sh, csh, tcsh;

> The DOS command shell COMMAND.COM;

> Any PostScript interpreter other than GhostView.[10]

If somebody configures a browser to automatically run one of these programs as a helper application when a document of a certain MIME type is downloaded, he or she is implicitly trusting the authors of the corresponding Web pages to be friendly with his or her computer. This

---

9. Obviously, the same is true for the use and configuration of interpreters for general-purpose programming languages as plug-ins. This is, however, less dangerous because the interpreters would have to be provided as plug-ins.

10. Note that there are PostScript commands to open, read, and delete files, as well as to execute arbitrary commands. However, these commands are disabled by default when GhostView is run in safe mode.

level of trust may not always be justified and is very dangerous (to say the least).

In 1996, a group of researchers at the University of California at Berkeley developed and piloted a technology to limit the risks of untrusted helper applications in the Solaris operating system [4]. The basic idea is to limit the access that a helper application has to the system calls at the operating system level. They used the term *sandboxing* to represent the idea that a program can play around in its own confined area, without having access to anything outside. As such, the approach is conceptually similar to the sandbox approach used to secure the execution environment for Java applets (as addressed in Section 10.5).

10.4 Scripting languages

There are many possibilities to extend the functionality or interactivity of a browser. In the previous section, we saw that helper applications and plugins provide an immediate solution. Similarly, there are some full-fledged programming languages that can be used to implement programs that are executed on the client side. The most important programming language in use today is Java. It can be used to implement Java applets that are executed in a browser's Java virtual machine (JVM). Unfortunately, the capabilities of most programming languages can only be exploited by technically skilled programmers. The creation of Java applets from scratch, for example, is beyond the capabilities of many Webmasters. Also, a full-blown Java applet is overkill for most applications. If a Webmaster only needs to verify that the value typed in by a user is a syntactically correct telephone number, it would be overkill to develop an applet for this purpose (it would also be overkill to make use of a helper application or plug-in). In this situation, the use of a scripting language provides a simple solution.

There is an increasingly large set of scripting languages available today. Some of these languages primarily address the server side,[11] whereas others primarily address the client side. Among the second class, the most widely used and deployed scripting languages are *JavaScript*,[12] *JScript*,[13]

---

11. Server-side scripting languages and their security implications are addressed in Chapter 11.

12 JavaScript is a simple scripting language that Netscape Communications developed to make animation and other forms of interaction more convenient. It was first named LifeScript.

13. JScript is the Microsoft version of JavaScript. It has been available in Microsoft Internet Explorer since version 3.0.

and *VBScript*.[14] Not all scripting languages are supported by all browsers. For example, VBScript only runs on Microsoft Internet Explorer.

Scripting languages are most often used to control and modify the appearance of a browser. For example, they can make visual elements of browsers appear or disappear, or they can make messages appear in the status lines of browsers. In fact, some of the earliest JavaScript applications displayed moving banners across the browser's status line. Also, scripting languages can be used to create new windows, check or fill out fields in forms, jump to new URLs, process image maps locally, change the content of an HTML file, compute mathematical results, or perform other functions.

The security of a scripting language primarily depends on the power of its commands or methods. For example, if a language has no method to access a file, there is no possibility to maliciously (mis)use code to manipulate a file. Similarly, if the language has no method to establish a network connection to a remote site, there is no possibility to maliciously (mis)use code to export a file. Both of these statements are true for JavaScript. Consequently, JavaScript can be considered a comparably secure scripting language. Unfortunately (from a security point of view), JavaScript is changing rapidly, and Netscape Communications has developed a capabilities-based system that relies on digital signatures to determine which privileges JavaScript code should have. In this system, the security implications are similar to the ones related to Java applets and ActiveX controls (as discussed below).

The most serious threats of scripting languages are related to DoS attacks and privacy violations:

▸ As mentioned above, scripting languages can be used to do many things that are computationally expensive (e.g., create new windows, compute mathematical functions). Consequently, these languages can be (mis)used to mount DoS attacks against browsers and corresponding clients.[15]

▸ Because scripting language code runs inside a browser, it potentially has access to the same information that is available to the browser. If the code—maliciously or not—leaks parts of this information,

---

14. VBScript is a dialect of Visual Basic and draws on the popularity of that programming language in Microsoft Windows environments.
15. Similar attacks can also be mounted against e-mail user agents that support scripting languages.

privacy violations may occur. Many examples of such privacy violations have been reported in the media, and it is possible and very likely that more privacy violations will be found and reported in the future.

More worrisome, scripting languages can be used to mount electronic versions of social engineering attacks.

▸ For example, the following JavaScript code segment can be used to pop up a window and prompt the user to reenter his or her dial-up password:

```
<SCRIPT LANGUAGE="JavaScript">
  password = prompt("You have lost your dial-up connection.\n
                     Please reenter your password","");
</SCRIPT>
```

It is possible and very likely that many users type in their passwords if such a window pops up on the screen.

▸ Similarly, the status line of a browser normally displays the URL that will be retrieved if the user clicks on an HTML link. By using JavaScript, a user can also be made to believe that one URL actually points someplace else. For example, the following HTML link will display http://www.realshop.com when the mouse is moved over the link, but clicking on the link will actually have the browser jump to the Web site located at http://www.fakedshop.com:

```
Click <A href="http://www.fakedshop.com"
     onMouseover="window.status='http://www.realshop.com';
     return true">here</A> to enter the real shop.
```

Obviously, the two technologies (and many others) can be combined to maliciously mislead users at will.

In summary, one must say that scripting languages, such as JavaScript, JScript, and VBScript, provide interesting possibilities to attack client systems (or the users of these systems), and that these systems should therefore be configured in a way that these languages are disabled. Unfortunately, this is not always possible and an increasingly large number of applications requires support for these languages. Against this background, the use and deployment of code and object signing technologies to authenticate code written in scripting languages is getting more and more important.

10.5 Java applets

Java is an object-oriented, general-purpose programming language[16] that has a syntax similar to C^{++}, dynamic binding, garbage collection, and a simple inheritance model [5]. The language was designed and developed by Sun Microsystems in the early 1990s. The original intent was to use the programming language in the world of consumer electronics. More specifically, it was assumed that it would become important in the future to have consumer electronics devices that could download software over a computer network, that this software had to be written in a specific programming language, and that Java would be an appropriate choice to do so. Instead of being compiled for a specific microprocessor, Java is designed to be compiled into a processor-independent bytecode and this bytecode is then interpreted in a Java virtual machine (JVM). This approach (i.e., the use of bytecode) would allow a manufacturer of consumer electronics to change the microprocessor(s) without losing compatibility with the existing software base.

After its initial release in the world of consumer electronics, it was recognized that Java ideally matched the requirements of a programming language for the emerging WWW. In fact, Java could be used to write a program that could be compiled into a platform-independent bytecode, and this bytecode could then be interpreted in a JVM. The JVM, in turn, could be embedded inside either the operating system or the browser. The second possibility was demonstrated in 1995, when Sun Microsystems released the first version of its Java-capable browser (i.e., HotJava) and Netscape Communications licensed Java to include a JVM in Netscape Navigator. A Java bytecode segment that is downloaded over a computer network and interpreted in a JVM on the browser is called a *Java applet*. Sometimes, it makes sense to compile the Java bytecode into the native machine code of the particular platform on which the JVM is running. In this case, a just-in-time (JIT) compiler is used.

The notion of software that can be dynamically downloaded over a computer network, if needed, gave birth to a new paradigm in the computer industry. The new paradigm was named *network computing* and most vendors launched press releases about the importance and future plans to support network computing and to build *network computers* (based on Java or any other network-capable programming language). Sometimes, network computers were also called *thin clients* and this term is still in use today. Meanwhile, network computing and network computers have disappeared,

---

16. The programming language was originally called Oak.

but the programming language that originally started the hype (i.e., Java) has remained and is likely to stay in the future.

It is commonly agreed today that Java is a programming language that has "good" characteristics related to security and safety, meaning that Java programs typically contain fewer bugs and programming errors than programs written in other general-purpose programming languages, such as C or C++. This is because Java provides automatic memory management (including, for example, garbage collection), exception handling, and built-in bounds checking on all strings and arrays. Furthermore, Java doesn't have pointers, only has single inheritance, and is strongly typed. All of these features are important for a programming language that is used to write secure and safe code.

10.5.1 Security architecture

First of all, it is important to note that Java was not originally designed to be a secure and safe programming language. Instead, it was designed to be a programming language for consumer electronics devices, and it was assumed that Java programs would be downloaded from device manufacturers and approved content providers. But when Java was repositioned for the WWW, security immediately became a concern. By design, the Web allows any user to download anything from any site, whether it is from an approved content provider or not. If Web users can download and run a program by simply clicking on a hypertext link on a Web page, then there needs to be some mechanisms for protecting users and their computer systems against buggy, hostile, or malicious code.[17] Against this background, the developers of Java came up with a security architecture that includes a sandbox, a security manager, a bytecode verifier, and a class loader.

Sandbox: In the computer security literature, a runtime environment that is restricted and does not provide support for potentially dangerous things, such directly calling operating system functions or establishing network connections, is sometimes called a sandbox. Most browsers in use today provide sandboxes for the execution of Java applets. The first browsers

---

17. For example, a group of researchers at Princeton University found a number of security problems in the Java programming language in 1996. The team christened themselves the *Secure Internet Programming* (SIP) group and has published several bulletins informing users of the problems they found. Further information is available at http://www.cs.princeton.edu/sip.

implemented sandboxes that were very restrictive and didn't allow browsers to do useful things (e.g., reading or writing configuration files). In the recent past, however, software vendors have come up with browsers that allow Java applets to temporarily step out of their sandbox to provide more functionality under controlled circumstances. If, for example, a Java applet is digitally signed and originates from a trusted software developer, it may be authorized to step out of the sandbox and access the local file system or establish network connections to remote sites. This is where code signing technologies and systems come into play (refer to Section 5.3).

Security Manager: The sandbox of a browser is typically controlled by a security manager object (i.e., an instance of the `SecurityManager` class). Consequently, each browser may have a security manager of its own.[18] The security manager is called before any potentially dangerous operation is executed. It must determine whether the operation is allowed or not.

Class Loader: Because most of the security checks in the Java programming environment are written in the Java language itself, it's important to ensure that a malicious piece of code can't disable these checks. For example, one way to launch such an attack would be to have a malicious Java program disable the standard `SecurityManager` class or replace it with a more permissive version. Such an attack could be carried out by a downloaded piece of machine code or a Java applet that exploited a bug in the Java runtime system. To prevent these types of attack, the Java class loader examines classes to make sure that they do not violate the runtime system.

Bytecode Verifier: To further protect the Java runtime environment, Java employs a bytecode verifier. The verifier is to ensure that downloaded bytecode could only have been created by compiling a valid Java program. For example, it is supposed to assure that a downloaded program doesn't violate access restrictions or object types, and doesn't forge pointers. The bytecode verifier is implemented as a series of ad hoc checks.

The Java sandbox, security manager, bytecode verifier, and class loader are further addressed in [6] and many other references on Java security. They collectively implement a security policy.

---

18. In practice, however, most browsers have the same or very similar security managers.

10.5.2 Security policy

The Java security policy is complicated by the fact that the Java programming language is dual-use:

- On the one hand, Java is a general-purpose programming language for creating any application software.

- On the other hand, Java is also a programming language for creating applets that perform some particular tasks on the user's machine.

Obviously, these different purposes require fundamentally different security policies. For example, Java's original implementors envisioned three different security policies that could be enforced by browsers:

1. Do not run Java programs at all.

2. Run Java programs with different privileges depending on their actual sources. For example, Java applets downloaded from remote Web sites would run with severe restrictions, whereas Java programs loaded off the local file system would be considered trustworthy and would have no such restrictions (they would have full access to all the system resources).

3. Run Java programs with no restrictions at all.

All three policies were implemented in Sun Microsystems' HotJava browser, and the choice was left to the user. Most users chose the second policy. All browsers in use today allow the user to enable or disable Java, and to more severely restrict Java applets that are downloaded from remote sites than applets that are loaded from the local file system.

10.5.3 Code signing

The basic idea of *code signing* is that a software developer, publisher, or distributor digitally signs a software module, and that a user—or a client software acting on behalf of the user—verifies the digital signature before it actually executes the software module. The digital signature verifies the claimed source of the software module and the identity of the software developer, publisher, or distributor that is responsible and may be held accountable for its behavior accordingly. The use of digital signatures to verify the claimed source of software is conceptually similar to the use of shrink-wraps for physical software packages. Consequently, people sometimes use the term *digital shrink-wrap* to refer to them. In the introduction, we saw that BETSI provided a simple code signing system that worked that way. Since then, many vendors have developed code signing technologies and systems of their own. They all work similarly but use different terms. For example, Netscape Communications uses the term *object signing system* to refer to its code signing system, whereas Microsoft Corporation uses the term *Authenticode*. In fact, Authenticode describes a series of file formats for signing Microsoft 32-bit `.exe`, `.cab`, `.dll`, and `.ocx` files.[19] A digitally signed file contains the original unsigned file, the digital signature, and an X.509v3 digital certificate for the public key needed to verify the Authenticode signature.

Obviously, code signing technologies and systems can be used by browsers to have Java applets step out of their sandboxes under controlled circumstances. In fact, most code signing technologies and systems in use today allow users to dynamically assign specific sets of privileges to Java applets. The sets of privileges primarily depend on the trustworthiness of the corresponding software developers, publishers, or distributors. This basically means that not all software developers, publishers, and distributors are equally trustworthy and that there is some heuristic to determine and actually measure their trustworthiness. This heuristic must be provided by the user.

Code signing is an important building block of the security of browsers that support Java applets. As mentioned above, its implementation occurs in two phases:

1. In the first phase, code signing was implemented in a way that is conceptually similar to BETSI. The aim was to allow a user to determine and verify the claimed source of a Java applet. If the source was trustworthy, the applet would step out of the sandbox and have full access to the computer system and its local resources (similar to a Java application). If, however, the source was not trustworthy, the applet would still run in the sandbox. In this case, the trustworthiness of a software publisher was a binary decision (i.e., it was either trustworthy or not) and depended on the software publisher's certificate. This basically meant that the user could determine a set of certificates he or she was willing to accept and to consider as trustworthy. If a Java applet was digitally signed by

---

19. Authenticode cannot be used to sign Windows `.com` files or 16-bit `.exe` files.

a software publisher that had such as certificate, it was allowed to step out of the sandbox and fully access the computer system and its local resources. This phase was implemented in Microsoft Internet Explorer 3.0 and Netscape Navigator 4.0.

2. In the second phase, however, more granularity was added to the code signing systems employed for Java applets. More specifically, it was allowed that a Java applet could step out of the sandbox and access the computer system and its resources in some predefined way (i.e., the applet did not necessarily have full access to the computer system and its local resources). Giving applets capabilities in this way satisfies the principle of least privilege, meaning that an applet can be given exactly the privileges it needs to perform its task, but nothing more. All major browsers support this phase in their latest releases. From a security point of view, this is advantageous and good news. Unfortunately, however, the configuration and proper use of a highly granular code signing system has also turned out to be difficult in practice.

All code signing systems in use today employ X.509v3 software publisher certificates[20] issued by (commercial or noncommercial) certification service providers such as, for example, VeriSign, Inc.

10.6 ActiveX controls

Unlike Java, which is a programming language of its own, the term *ActiveX* was coined by Microsoft to refer to a repackaging of some existing technologies. More specifically, ActiveX is a stripped-down version of Microsoft's object linking and embedding (OLE) and component object model (COM) architectures, two highly successful Windows programming components that allow multiple programs to interact, exchange data, and share each other's windows. As such, ActiveX is a system and a corresponding API for downloading executable code over the Internet. The code is bundled into a single file called *ActiveX control*. In general, a file carrying an ActiveX control has the extension .ocx.

ActiveX controls are small programs that can be written in any programming language, including, for example, C, C^{++}, Visual Basic,

---

20. Netscape Communications uses the term *object signing certificate* to refer to a software publisher certificate.

or Java. They are automatically downloaded and installed as needed, then automatically deleted when no longer needed. Consequently, an ActiveX control is conceptually similar to a plug-in (as discussed in Section 10.3). In spite of the conceptual similarities, there are, however, also two fundamental differences between ActiveX controls and plug-ins:

1. Plug-ins are usually used to extend a browser so that it can accommodate a new document type, whereas most ActiveX controls used to date have brought a new functionality to a specific Web site.

2. Plug-ins must be manually installed, whereas ActiveX controls are downloaded and run automatically.

Both differences lead to a situation in which ActiveX controls behave like Java applets from a user's point of view (although the technologies are completely different).

The syntax for incorporating an ActiveX control into an HTML document is similar to that for incorporating a Java applet. In fact, the <OBJECT> tag is used to identify the name of the ActiveX control, the URL of the directory that contains it, an ID attribute that contains a unique hexadecimal serial number, and some other parameters. The serial number allows an ActiveX control to be downloaded automatically from one of several ActiveX control archives and repositories that are located anywhere on the Internet. Like inline images and Java applets, ActiveX controls developed and maintained at one site can be incorporated into HTML documents on another site. Also like Java applets, the ActiveX control is passed as runtime information in a series of <PARAM> tags. This allows the developer to customize the behavior of an ActiveX control.

In general, there are two kinds of ActiveX controls: the ones that contain native machine code and the ones that contain Java bytecode. The first kind are written in programming languages, such as C, C^{++}, or Visual Basic. The control's source code is compiled into an executable that is downloaded to the browser and executed on the client machine. Contrary to that, the second kind are written in Java or any other programming language that can be compiled into Java bytecode. These controls are downloaded to the browser and executed in the browser's JVM. Note that the two different kinds of ActiveX controls have fundamentally different security implications.

1. The ActiveX technology is simply a means to download and run native machine code on the client machine. It is up to the programmer to decide whether to follow the ActiveX APIs, whether

to use the operating system APIs, or whether to attempt direct manipulation of the computer system's resources. In general, there is no way to properly audit the ActiveX control functions on contemporary operating systems.

2. ActiveX controls that are downloaded as Java bytecode can be subject to all of the same restrictions that normally apply to Java applets. Consequently, these controls can be run by the browser within a sandbox. Alternatively, a browser can grant these controls specific privileges, such as the ability to read and write within a specific directory or to initiate network connections to specific IP addresses. Perhaps most importantly, the actions of such an ActiveX control can be properly audited (if the Java runtime environment allows such auditing).

In spite of the fact that ActiveX support has been ported to a variety of platforms (in addition to Microsoft Windows), ActiveX controls that are downloaded as machine code are processor and operating system dependent. These controls are typically compiled for a particular processor and with a particular set of APIs. Contrary to that, ActiveX controls that are written in Java can be processor and operating system independent.

In practice, ActiveX controls that are downloaded as machine code are predominant. From the point of view of software developers and Web users, they have three important advantages:

1. Developers can use the programming languages and compilers with which they are familiar.

2. Developers can draw on their existing repository of application programs, OLE components, and libraries, allowing them to bring ActiveX controls to market faster.

3. ActiveX controls can do anything (meaning that they are not restricted by a sandbox).

Obviously, the third point illustrates that ActiveX controls are risky from a security point of view. If the ActiveX controls can do anything, they can also trash files (or entire file systems), reformat hard disks, probe firewalls, install viruses, or do anything an attacker may dream of. Once an ActiveX control is running on a system, it has the ability to do anything that any other full-fledged program can do. While this makes ActiveX controls powerful, it also makes them potentially very dangerous. An ActiveX control written for malicious purposes may compromise the users' privacy or damage computer systems in overt or subtle ways.

The inherent risks of ActiveX controls have been demonstrated on several occasions. The most prominent demonstration occurred in February 1997, when Lutz Donnerhacke, a member the German Chaos Computer Club (CCC), demonstrated an ActiveX control that could initiate electronic funds transfers using the European version of the Quicken software for home banking. With this version of Quicken, it is possible to initiate a transfer directly from one bank account to another. Donnerhacke's ActiveX control started up a copy of Quicken on the user's computer and recorded an electronic funds transfer in the user's checking account ledger. Written in Visual Basic as a demonstration tool for a German television station, the ActiveX control did not attempt to hide its actions. Consequently, it is possible and very likely that sooner or later similar ActiveX controls will occur that are made more stealthy. Again, it will be important to decide whether an ActiveX control is authentic and has not been tampered with. And again, this is where code signing technologies and systems come into play.

As mentioned above, Authenticode is a code signing technology and system developed and marketed by Microsoft. The system can be used to let users verify the identity of the author of a particular ActiveX control, and to let them determine whether the control has been modified since the first time it was distributed. ActiveX controls can be digitally signed and controlled using Authenticode. Microsoft Internet Explorer, for example, can be configured to disregard any ActiveX control that isn't properly signed, to run only ActiveX controls that have been signed by specific software publishers, or to accept ActiveX controls signed by any registered software publisher.

Authenticode signatures can be used for different purposes depending on whether the ActiveX control is distributed in binary machine code or JVM bytecode:

> For ActiveX controls distributed in binary machine code, an Authenticode signature can be used to enforce a simple decision: either download the control or not.

> For ActiveX controls distributed in JVM bytecode, an Authenticode signature can additionally be used to determine which access permissions are given to the Java bytecode when it is running in the JVM.

If an ActiveX control mixes binary machine code and JVM bytecode, or if both binary machine code and JVM bytecode controls are resident on the same Web page, the capabilities-controlled access permitted by the Java system is disabled. Also, Authenticode signatures are only verified when a control is downloaded from the Internet. If the control resides on the local file system, it is assumed to be trustworthy and safe to run. In this case, the ActiveX control is given unrestricted access to the system.

Obviously, code signing as implemented by the Authenticode technology is an important tool for certifying the authenticity and integrity of an ActiveX control. However, code signing does not provide safety as is implied by Microsoft Internet Explorer's control panel (see Figure 10.2). It is important to note that code signing does not provide users with a safe environment where they can run their program code. Instead, it provides users with some audit trail, so that if a program misbehaves, it should be possible to interrogate the signed program code and decide whom to sue. Unfortunately, security through code signing is not that simple and has three shortcomings.

1. The damage that an ActiveX control does may not be immediately visible. In fact, an ActiveX control may be used to install a trapdoor (a hidden access to secret data or services).

2. The Authenticode technology does not protect a user against bugs and malicious software (e.g., computer viruses and Trojan horses).

3. The Authenticode software (and its validation routines), as well as the audit trails, are vulnerable in the sense that once a signed ActiveX control is running, it may erase the audit trail that would allow the user to identify the author (unless the prompt option had been chosen, where the user would be told beforehand who had signed it).

Earlier in this chapter, we said that the aim of code signing technologies is to trace back a malicious piece of software downloaded into a browser to its original publisher, who may be held accountable and be subject to litigation. We should mention that the degree to which a user of maliciously signed code can litigate against a software vendor heavily depends on the supporting legal structure, the type of certificate the vendor used to digitally sign the code, and a number of other factors. For example, on June 17, 1997, Fred McLain released an ActiveX control called Exploder Control on one of his personal Web pages.[21] When downloaded to a computer that has a power

---

21. http://www.halcyon.com/mclain/ActiveX/welcome.html

conservation BIOS, the Exploder Control shuts down Windows 95, and turns off the computer. Later, McLain obtained an Individual Software Publisher Digital ID from VeriSign, signed his ActiveX control, and reposted it on the Web page. McLain was soon to lose his certificate. Because he violated his contractual agreements associated with his software publisher certificate when he used it to sign malicious code, VeriSign unilaterally revoked the software publisher certificate. Note, however, that this was a futile act since very few people bother to retrieve and actually check CRLs at all. Consequently, hardly anyone knew that McLain's software publisher certificate was revoked. Also note that McLain's Exploder Control incited a flurry of controversy about the usefulness and effectiveness of code and object signing technologies and systems. In either case, it showed that without certificate revocation checking, these technologies and systems are almost always without any value.

10.7 Security zones

As mentioned above, Microsoft Internet Explorer (since version 4.0) implements and makes use of a highly granular code signing technology and system (i.e., Authenticode) to extend privileges to executable or active content (e.g., Java applets, ActiveX controls). We also mentioned previously that a highly granular code signing system has the disadvantage that the configuration and proper use of it is difficult in practice.

Against this background, Microsoft developed and implemented a model that allows a user to divide the Internet into security zones and to configure each security zone individually. In this model, the term *security zone* refers to a group of Web sites in which a user has the same level of trust. Some zones may be trustworthy (e.g., the intranet zone), whereas some other zones may not be trustworthy at all (e.g., the Internet zone). In either case, the trustworthiness of a zone directly influences its security configuration (i.e., the more trustworthy a zone is, the more things will typically be allowed). The aim of security zones is to simplify the configuration and proper use of a security-related system (e.g., a code signing system).

As illustrated in Figure 10.1, Microsoft Internet Explorer comes along with four security or Web content zones that can be configured individually:

1. The *Internet* zone contains all Web sites that are not assigned to any other security zone.

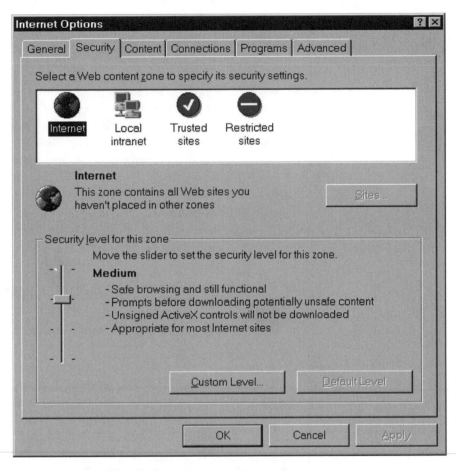

Figure 10.1 Microsoft Internet Explorer's Security menu to configure security zones. (© 2002 Microsoft Corporation.)

2. The *local intranet* zone contains all Web sites that are located on the intranet. As such, it is assumed that these sites are protected by a firewall and that they can be assigned far-going access privileges accordingly.

3. The *trusted sites* zone contains Web sites that are located on the Internet, but can still be considered to be trustworthy. The Web sites of partner companies and customers are good candidates for trusted sites. Similar to the sites from the local intranet zone, these sites can be assigned far-going access privileges.

4. Contrary to that, the *restricted sites* zone contains Web sites that are not considered trustworthy. In fact, this zone represents the "black

list.'' Consequently, these sites must be severely restricted in terms of access privileges assigned to them.

As also illustrated in Figure 10.1, a security level must be assigned to each of these four zones individually. Either one of the four predefined levels can be chosen using the slider, or the detailed behavior for the level must be customized pressing the Custom Level... button. For example, Figure 10.2 illustrates the Security Settings menu that pops up if the user presses the Custom Level... button for the Internet zone. Again, there is a possibility to make use of some default values and to reset the custom settings to High, Medium, Medium-low, or Low. If the user wants to individually define his or her custom setting for the Internet zone, he or she can do so by clicking the corresponding checkboxes. Figure 10.2 illustrates some checkboxes to configure the use of signed and unsigned ActiveX controls. There are many

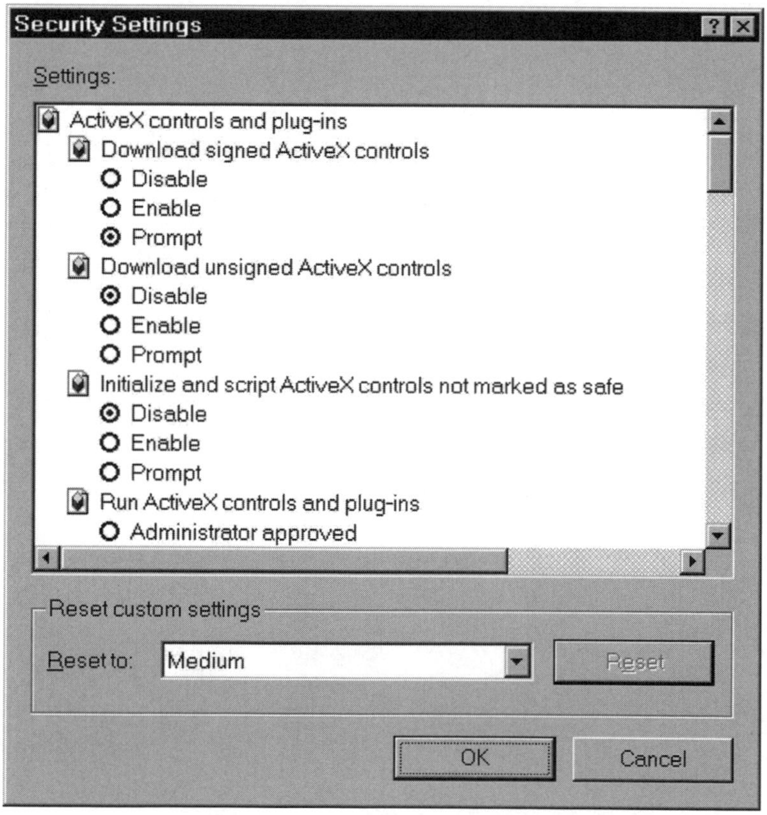

Figure 10.2 Microsoft Internet Explorer's Security Settings menu to configure the Internet zone. (© 2002 Microsoft Corporation.)

other questions that must be answered if one wants to define a custom setting from scratch. This is not something that average Web users want to do.

In either case, the idea of defining and using security zones to simplify the configuration and proper use of a browsers' security settings is something useful. It is possible and likely that future browsers (and other client software packages) will make use of it. It is, however, an open question, whether four security zones (as implemented, for example, in Microsoft Internet Explorer) is an optimal choice.

10.8 Implications for firewalls

As discussed in this chapter, executable or active content is potentially dangerous and should be avoided in the first place. Unfortunately, this is not always possible and an increasingly large number of Web sites are making use of executable or active content. If these sites are located on the Internet, the corresponding HTTP request messages must pass the (corporate) firewall. Consequently, one may think about strategies and technologies to block executable or active content at the firewall.

Against this background, it is important to note that executable or active content has changed the firewall's role and importance in the overall security landscape (security architecture). The role of a firewall has been to logically separate the insiders (i.e., the "good" guys) from the outsiders (i.e., the "bad" guys). With the use of executable or active content, this logical separation is difficult, because insiders running executable or active content may effectively become inside assistants for outsiders. In fact, insiders may not even know that they are being (mis)used by outsiders to attack computer systems from the inside.

In the past, several strategies and technologies to block executable or active content at the firewall have been developed, implemented, and partly deployed. For example, in the case of a proxy-based firewall, *response content filtering* may be used [7]. In response content filtering, the proxy server looks into the content of an HTTP response message. Typically, content filters are designed specifically for a certain type of executable content, and are invoked only if the MIME content type matches one of the content types for which the filter has been configured.

The following examples illustrate some possible response blocking and content filtering mechanisms:

> • *Java applet blocking* mechanisms prevent Java applets from being downloaded to computer systems located behind the firewall.

A simple strategy takes advantage of the fact that all Java class files begin with the 4-byte hex signature CA, FE, BA, and BE (according to the JVM specification). The strategy is to prevent all inbound files beginning with this signature from being forwarded by the firewall. By proxying protocols, such as HTTP and FTP, such transfers can be detected and blocked. Another commonly suggested strategy is to reject all browser requests via HTTP and FTP for files with names ending in .class. This strategy once enjoyed most of the advantages of the previous strategy, even though there was never any requirement in the JVM specification that class files actually have the suffix .class. Unfortunately, both strategies cannot block other executable or active content, such as JavaScript code or ActiveX controls. Because of JavaScript's inline nature, blocking JavaScript code at the firewall turns out to be difficult.

▸ *HTML tag filtering* mechanisms allow certain HTML tags to be removed from HTML documents (applicable for documents of MIME type text/html). This is used in the same way as other filtering mechanisms to prevent the exploitation of known security holes and bugs. For example, it is possible to filter out embedded objects from HTML documents, such as Java applets, ActiveX controls, or JavaScript code. In the case of Java applets, for example, it is possible to scan the HTML documents for <APPLET> tags and rewrite them in a more benign form. The firewall toolkit originally developed by Trusted Information Systems, Inc. (TIS) has been extended accordingly [8]. Similarly, it is possible to scan the HTML documents for tags that are used to incorporate JavaScript code and ActiveX controls.

▸ *Virus scanning* allows downloaded programs to be scanned for known computer viruses (applicable for documents of MIME type application/octet-stream). By restricting the application of this technology, HTML and ASCII text transfer performance remains unaffected by computer virus scanning.

▸ Similar to virus scanning, various forms of *code scanning* allow specialized analysis of executable content, such as Java applets and ActiveX controls, inspecting which function calls are made and determining whether they are allowed or not. For example, a software called SurfinGate (developed by Finjan Software[22])

---

22. http://www.finjan.com

performs this sophisticated type of filtering. Unfortunately, it is not easily decidable whether a specific code segment is malicious or not (we have already mentioned this fact at several places throughout the book).

All mechanisms require use of an application-level gateway or proxy server (i.e., they can not be implemented with a packet filter alone). For example, `httpf` is a widely deployed open source implementation of a filtering proxy server that is licensed under the GNU General Public License (GPL).[23] Obviously, a filtering proxy server is not able to protect a client system against malicious code that is already located on the system.

Last but not least, it is important to note that encrypted data streams cannot be parsed or scanned by an application-level gateway or proxy server. This poses some interesting problems with regard to the simultaneous use of cryptographic security protocols, such as IPsec or SSL/TLS, and scanning and filtering technologies. It is certainly a good practice to scan all data streams that are not encrypted. Consequently, we see complementary virus scanners running at firewalls, mail exchange servers, and end systems. This plurality has a positive effect on the overall protection against malicious code.

10.9 Conclusions

In this chapter, we focused on client-side security in general, and the security implications and risks of executable (or active) content in particular. Fortunately, although the cost of malicious code has been estimated in the billions of dollars, the attacks that have occurred are much less serious than what has been (and is) possible. In fact, a variety of hostile and malicious Java applets and ActiveX controls have been demonstrated, but only a few serious attacks have actually occured.[24] This will probably change as knowledge on programming executable or active content becomes more common and widespread.

Most incidents that have occurred in practice have launched DoS attacks. Note that any programming or scripting language or environment that allows systemwide resources to be allocated, and then places no limitations on the allocation of these resources, is subject to these types of

---

23. Further information about `httpf` is available at `http://httpf.sourceforge.net`.
24. Note, however, that this is only an assumption, and that it may be the case that attacks have occured and nobody has recognized them.

attacks. But the languages addressed in this chapter seem to be especially suitable for DoS attacks, apparently because their authors have not considered these attacks to be serious threats, and because it is very difficult (if not impossible) to protect against them. There is a programming language for mobile code (i.e., Telescript) that controls the use of systemwide resources by giving each process a limited supply of funds (so-called teleclicks), and requiring a process to expend a certain quantity of teleclicks in order to accomplish specific results, such as spawning new copies of itself. This approach can at least be used to protect against certain DoS attacks. It is conceptually similar to the use of a micropayment system (i.e., teleclicks represent the currency). However, the languages addressed in this chapter do not make use of this (or a similar) concept. In fact, code segments written in these languages can easily clog large amounts of system resources, and there are only a few possibilities for a user who is under attack to regain control of his or her system. To make things worse, there is nothing even resembling process control within most Web browser environments. The only way to interrupt a running piece of code is generally to kill and shut down the browser.

In summary, client-side security is unsatisfactory and the design, implementation, deployment, and use of security technologies that can be used to better protect against malicious executable or active content must be left for further study. Unfortunately, the problem is hard and it is possible and very likely that appropriate solutions will not be found anytime soon. In the meantime, users who care about security are well advised to disable executable or active content in their browsers (if possible and appropriate).

References

[1]   Thompson, K., "Reflections on Trusting Trust," *Communications of the ACM*, Vol. 27, No. 8, August 1984, pp. 761–763.

[2]   Rubin, A. D., "Location-Independent Data/Software Integrity Protocol," Request for Comments 1805, June 1995.

[3]   Rubin, A. D., "Trusted Distribution of Software over the Internet," *Proceedings of Internet Society Symposium on Network and Distributed System Security*, February 1995, pp. 47–53.

[4]   Goldberg, I., et al., "A Secure Environment for Untrusted Helper Applications," *Proceedings of USENIX Security Symposium*, July 1996, pp. 1–13.

[5]   Flanagan, D., *Java in a Nutshell, Second Edition*, Sebastopol, CA: O'Reilly & Associates, 1997.

[6]   Oaks, S., *Java Security*, Sebastopol, CA: O'Reilly & Associates, 1998.

[7]   Luotonen, A., *Web Proxy Servers*, Upper Saddle River, NJ: Prentice Hall, 1998.

[8]   Martin, D. M., S. Rajagopalan, and A. D. Rubin, "Blocking Java Applets at the Firewall," *Proceedings of Internet Society Symposium on Network and Distributed System Security (SNDSS '97)*, February 1997.

CHAPTER

11

Contents

11.1 Introduction

11.2 CGI

11.3 Server APIs

11.4 FastCGI

11.5 Server-side includes

11.6 ASP

11.7 JSP

11.8 Conclusions

References

Server-side Security

After having looked at client-side security issues in the previous chapter, we now elaborate on security issues related to the server side. Remember from the Preface that most server-side security problems and corresponding exploits that make press headlines are due to software bugs and flawed configurations of Web servers. Consequently, if one really cares about the security of the server side, one has to start with a proper installation and configuration of the Web server software. Because there are many books and manuals that give step-by-step instructions about how to properly install and securely configure a specific Web server, we are not going to repeat them in this book. For example, you may refer to [1, 2] for a general overview, or [3, 4] for more specific information about the Apache Web server.

In the recent past, it has become popular to design and build multitier Web-based applications to make the user's experience more interesting and interactive. In fact, there is an increasingly large number of acronyms that refer to the same idea but use slightly different technologies. The aim of this chapter is to put these technologies into perspective, and to discuss their security implications. After a short introduction in Section 11.1, we elaborate on CGI, server APIs, FastCGI, SSIs, ASP, and JSP in Sections 11.2 to 11.7 (the acronyms are explained in the corresponding sections). We conclude with some final remarks in Section 11.8.

11.1 Introduction

As already mentioned in the introductory chapter of this book, HTTP is a very simple request/response protocol that can be used by a client (i.e., browser) to retrieve some information from a Web server. The requested information, in turn, is represented by static or dynamically created Web pages (written, for example, in HTML or XML).

> ▸ If the information is represented by static Web pages, the situation is comparatively simple and the Web pages can be directly retrieved from the server's document tree.

> ▸ If, however, the information is represented by dynamically created Web pages, the situation is more complicated and the pages must be generated by a specific application program in response to an incoming HTTP request message. In this case, the application program must be invoked by or communicate somehow with the Web server.

Obviously, the second possibility is much more powerful and is at the core of a multitier Web-based application architecture as illustrated in Figure 11.1. In this architecture, a user employs a browser to access a Web server (sometimes also called a Web frontend) and to request specific funtionality. The Web server, in turn, interacts with an application server to provide this funtionality. The browser and the Web server usually employ HTTP or HTTPS to communicate, whereas the Web server and the application server may employ any application protocol to communicate.[1] In a typical setting, the browser would be located on the Internet, the Web server would be located on a firewall's DMZ, and the application server would be located on the intranet.

The major advantage of a multitier Web-based application architecture is that normal browsers can be used on the client side. This is in contrast to

Figure 11.1 A multitier Web-based application architecture.

---

1. Following the current trend in industry, the application server is likely to have a Web services interface. In this case, the Web server and the application server may also use HTTP and HTTPS to communicate.

traditional client/server applications that require (a) clients and servers to use a specific application protocol, and (b) specific client software to be distributed, installed, configured, and maintained. In practice, requirement (b) is particularly challenging and difficult to address on a large scale.

Unfortunately, there are also some security problems and challenges related to multitier Web-based application architectures. For example, in the typical setting mentioned above, it is usually difficult to design and properly implement a firewall that is able to proxy the application protocol between the Web server and the application server in a sufficiently secure way. Most of the security problems and challenges, however, are due to the fact that the Web server (together with the application server) may be misused to do things other than what it was originally designed for. Because the Web server provides more functionality (than to simply return static Web pages), this functionality can also be attacked. The probablity that this functionality is vulnerable and may be exploited primarily depends on the technology in use to dynamically create the Web pages.

Historically, the first technology to dynamically create Web pages was the Common Gateway Interface (CGI) and programming or scripting languages that made use of it. CGI was first implemented in the NCSA server and has many benefits, such as simplicity, language and architecture independence, process isolation, and the fact that it is specified as an open standard. From a security point of view, process isolation is particularly important, because it means that applications run in separate processes, and that buggy application server software may not crash the entire Web server or access the server's internal state information. CGI, however, also has some significant drawbacks and problems. One of the more important problems is performance. Since a new process is created for every HTTP request message and thrown away when the request is served, efficiency is fairly poor.

In response to the performance problem of CGI, some vendors designed and developed proprietary application programming interfaces (APIs) for their Web server software. In fact, the most important server APIs are NSAPI from Netscape Communications, ISAPI from Microsoft, and the Apache Web server API.[2]

Applications linked into a server API may run significantly faster than CGI scripts. In fact, the CGI initialization problem is improved, because the application runs in the server process and is persistent across requests. On the other side, however, Web server APIs also sacrifice many benefits of CGI.

---

2. Further information about the Apache Web server is available at http://www.apache.org. Its API is, for example, overviewed in Chapter 14 of [4].

In fact, they are more complex, proprietary, tied into the server architecture, and programs must be written in a language supported by the API. Most importantly, Web server APIs do not provide process isolation (as discussed above). Since the applications run in the server's address space, buggy or maliciously written application program code may compromise the security of the Web server as a whole. This can also be used to attack other application programs.

Given the advantages and disadvantages of both CGI and vendor-specific APIs, the FastCGI interface was developed and proposed as a viable solution. Contrary to CGI, FastCGI processes are persistent and the Web server may use TCP connections to communicate with the FastCGI script (instead of environment variables and a mechanism for interprocess communication). Furthermore, there are many other technologies that have been designed, developed and marketed in the past. For example, Server-Side Includes (SSIs) are directives that are directly executed by the Web server. Similarly, Microsoft is pushing a technology called Active Server Pages (ASP) and Sun Microsystems is pushing a similar but more open technology called JavaServer Pages (JSP). All of these technologies work in similar ways and have similar security problems. They are overviewed, briefly discussed, and put into perspective next.

11.2 CGI

Having Figure 11.1 in mind, CGI refers to the interface between the Web server and the program running on the application server. This application program is usually called a *CGI script*.[3] Roughly speaking, CGI processing works as follows:

1. A Web server receives an HTTP request message that invokes a CGI script.

2. The Web server creates a new server-side process to take care of this request.

3. The server-side process takes the input provided by the browser and passes it to the appropriate application program or CGI script.

4. The CGI script computes the output and returns it back to the server-side process.

---

3.   The term *script* is used because most of these programs are written in a simple scripting language, such as Perl.

5. The server-side process returns the CGI script's output to the client.

6. The server-side process exits and the Web server waits for new incoming HTTP request messages.

Information is exchanged between the server-side process and the CGI script using environment variables that are sent and received using a mechanism for inter-process communication (e.g., pipes in a UNIX environment). Consequently, a CGI script must be able to read from standard input (i.e., stdin) and write to standard output (i.e., stdout). As long as this requirement is fullfilled, it can be written in any programming or scripting language. Consequently, most CGI scripts are written in interpreted scripting languages that are supposed to be fast and easy to use. Examples include Perl,[4] the Tool Control Language (Tcl), Java, or Python.[5] As of this writing, Perl is by far the most popular and widely deployed language for CGI programming or scripting.

The most important environment variables used for CGI programming are summarized in Table 11.1. Note that not all environment variables are set

Table 11.1 CGI Environment Variables (in Alphabetical Order)

Environment Variable	Meaning
AUTH_TYPE	User authentication method used
CONTENT_LENGTH	Length of input data
CONTENT_TYPE	Internet media type of input data
GATEWAY_INTERFACE	CGI version
HTTP_ACCEPT	List of MIME types accepted by the client
HTTP_USER_AGENT	Software and version of browser
HTTP_REFERER	URL of referring document
MOD_PERL	Defined if running under mod_perl
PATH_INFO	URL part after the script identifier
PATH_TRANSLATED	PATH_INFO translated into filesystem
QUERY_STRING	Query string from URL (if present)
REMOTE_ADDR	IP address of the client
REMOTE_HOST	DNS name of the client
REMOTE_IDENT	Remote user identification (unreliable)
REMOTE_USER	Name of the authenticated user
REQUEST_METHOD	HTTP request method (e.g., GET)
SCRIPT_NAME	Virtual path of the script
SERVER_NAME	DNS name of the server
SERVER_PORT	Port number of the server
SERVER_PROTOCOL	Name and version of the protocol
SERVER_SOFTWARE	Server software name and version

4. http://www.perl.com
5. http://www.python.org

for all HTTP request messages, and that a browser may also send new HTTP headers. If a browser sent a new HTTP header to the Web server, the server (or the server-side process) would package the header into a new CGI environment variable. The environment variable, in turn, would be prefixed with "HTTP_" and any dash character (-) would be changed to an underscore character (_). The Web server (or the server-side process) need not handle all possible HTTP headers.

In addition to the environment variables summarized in Table 11.1, some SSL/TLS-enabled Web servers also set additional environment variables when SSL or TLS is used. For example, Table 11.2 summarizes the additional environment variables set by an SSL/TLS-enabled Apache Web server (i.e., Apache-SSL or Apache with mod_ssl). Other SSL/TLS-enabled Web servers may set other environment variables. In either case, the environment variables may be used by the CGI scripts to provide security services. For example, a CGI script that provides access to a database with confidential material may abort, unless a certain type of cipher suite is used.

According to Table 11.1, the server-side process running on the Web server may provide to the CGI script some information that is encoded in the QUERY_STRING environment variable. This information is usually provided by the user and is the user's sole means for passing input data to the CGI script. It may contain, for example, a list of keywords for a search engine or an SQL expression for use by a database gateway.

In either case, a browser may send a query string to a Web server (or CGI script, respectively) in two different ways:

Table 11.2   Some Additonal Environment Variables for SSL/TLS (in Alphabetical Order)

Environment Variable	Meaning
HTTPS	Set if HTTPS is being used
HTTPS_CIPHER	SSL/TLS cipherspec
HTTPS_KEYSIZE	Number of bits in the session key
HTTPS_SECRETKEYSIZE	Number of bits in the secret key
SSL_CIPHER	The same as HTTPS_CIPHER
SSL_CLIENT_DN	Distinguished name in client's certificate
SSL_CLIENT_<x509>	Component of client's distinguished name
SSL_CLIENT_I_DN	Distinguished name of issuer of client's certificate
SSL_CLIENT_I_<x509>	Component of client's issuer's distinguished name
SSL_PROTOCOL_VERSION	SSL protocol version
SSL_SERVER_DN	Distinguished name in server's certificate
SSL_SERVER_<x509>	Component of server's distinguished name
SSL_SERVER_I_DN	Distinguished name of issuer of server's certificate
SSL_SERVER_I_<x509>	Component of server's issuer's distinguished name
SSL_SSLEAY_VERSION	Version of the SSLeay library

▶ The browser can append the query string to the CGI script's URL. For example, a resulting URL may look as follows:[6]

```
http://www.esecurity.ch/cgi-bin/
do_search?search=eSECURITY+Technologies
```

This example assumes that the CGI script `do_search` is installed in the `cgi-bin` directory of the Web server hosting `www.esecurity.ch`. In this case, the query string refers to the substring `search=eSECURITY+Technologies`. Because it is part of the URL, it has to follow the URL syntax rules, such as replacing spaces with the plus character (+). The CGI script, in turn, must reconstruct the query string by examining the environment variable QUERY_STRING. This way of sending query strings to CGI scripts uses the standard HTTP GET method and is typically used by older CGI scripts.

▶ The browser can send the query string using the HTTP POST method. This method is usually called in response to the user filling out and submitting an HTML form. For example, a simple code segment that includes an HTML form may look as follows:

```
<FORM ACTION="/cgi-bin/do_search" METHOD=POST>
Search string: <INPUT TYPE="text" NAME="search"><P>
<INPUT TYPE="submit" VALUE="Search">
</FORM>
```

When this HTML code segment is received by the browser, a corresponding fill-out form is displayed. Figure 11.2 illustrates how this form is displayed using, for example, the Opera browser. If the user typed in the search string "eSECURITY Technologies" and pressed the Search button, the browser would use the HTTP POST method (as indicated by the form's METHOD attribute) to submit the contents of the form to the Web server. The Web server, in turn, would write the following query string to the process it just started:

```
search=eSECURITY+Technologies
```

The CGI script `/cgi-bin/do_search` can now read the query string from standard input and process it accordingly.

---

6.   Note that this URL is a fictitious example only.

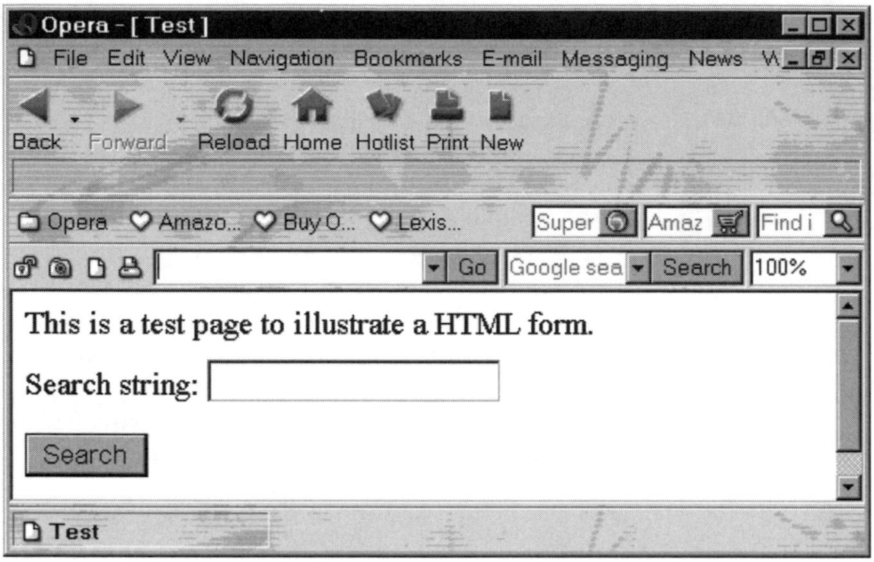

Figure 11.2 A simple HTML fill-out form displayed using the Opera browser. (© 2002 Opera Software.)

From a security point of view, the HTTP POST method is preferred because the query string does not appear in the requested URL. Note, however, that a determined attacker can still eavesdrop on the data traffic and extract any information he or she wants.

In addition, there are many concerns related to the security of CGI scripts. For example, many CGI scripts that had been distributed with Web server software packages in the past were later found to be flawed or buggy. The corresponding security flaws or software bugs could be exploited to attack the machines that hosted the CGI scripts. Fortunately, this problem is no longer relevant, because most Web server software packages are distributed either without CGI scripts or with CGI scripts that are not executable by default (i.e., they are configured with read privileges only). In either case, if a CGI script is found to be flawed or buggy, it must be removed from the Web server as soon as possible (it can also be corrected or replaced with a more secure script that provides the same or a similar functionality).

The adiministrator of a Web server has to make several decisions with regard to the installation and secure configuration of CGI scripts:

‣ First, he or she has to carefully design the user account used to run the Web server and to implement the principle of least privilege. Note that whatever restrictions apply to a Web server also apply to the CGI scripts. For example, if a Web server runs as root on a UNIX system it can potentially leak the password files. This can be changed, for example, by using a shadowed password file and to run the Web server as a user with only a few privileges (e.g., a user called nobody).

> Second, he or she has to decide whether the server uses script-aliased CGI or non-script-aliased CGI.

>> Using *script-aliased CGI* means that a CGI script can only be executed if it is installed in an explicitly configured directory, typically the subdirectory cgi-bin in the root directory of the Web server.

>> Using *non-script-aliased CGI* means that a CGI scripts can be executed if its filename extension corresponds to the one defined in the server's configuration settings. In this case, it does not really matter where a CGI script is installed and it can also be located in a user's directory.

> Having only one directory to look for CGI scripts is better and less error prone. Consequently, script-aliased CGI should be the preferred option (if possible and appropriate).

> Third, he or she has to decide what CGI scripts to install. Obviously, he or she should only install CGI scripts that are needed by at least one legitimate user. CGI scripts that are not used by anybody only represent a potential vulnerability to the security of the Web server and should be removed.

In either case, interpreters, shells, and other scripting engines must never be installed in a directory where they may be invoked by a request with user-supplied input data. This is particularly true for the directory that hosts the CGI scripts (i.e., the cgi-bin directory). Unfortunately, there are examples in which software vendors have shipped Web servers with a Perl interpreter installed in the CGI directory (mainly to make it simpler to install and configure CGI scripts written in Perl). This is very dangerous. Imagine, for example, what happens if a Perl interpreter perl.exe and a Perl script search.pl are installed in the CGI directory of the Web site www.victim.com. In this case, any user can invoke the script by simply requesting the following URL:

```
http://www.victim.com/cgi-bin/perl.exe?search.pl
```

This is convenient. This configuration, however, does not only allow the Perl script search.pl to be executed, but to run arbitrary Perl commands on the Web server. For example, anybody can request the following URL from the Web server:

```
http://www.victim.com/cgi-bin/perl.exe?-e+%27unlink+%3C*%3E%27
```

Following the rules for unescaping URLs, the Web server transforms this expression into the shell command `perl -e unlink '<*>'`, which represents a Perl command to delete all files in the current directory. Whether the command is successful depends on whether the server's user permissions allow it to make the delete operations.

In practice, many security problems occur simply because the Web server administrators and CGI script programmers assume that users behave properly and play by the rules. This means that they often assume that users type in only valid input data, that file names only contain legal characters, that users don't peek at secret CGI parameters contained inside hidden form fields, and similar things. There are, however, many ways in which users may not play by the rules and try to exploit weaknesses or vulnerabilities. An example is given above. Another example crops up in Perl scripts designed to send an e-mail message to an address entered in a fill-out form. In UNIX, it's comparably easy to do this by opening a pipe to the `mail` command and printing the body of the e-mail message to this pipe. Assuming that `param` is a function that extracts named fields from the CGI query string, a Perl script segment may look as follows (the example is taken from [1]):

```
$address = param('address');
$subject = param('subject');
$message = param('message');
open(MAIL,"| /bin/mail -s '$subject' $address");
print MAIL $message;
close MAIL;
```

The script segment first uses `param` to recover the e-mail address, subject line, and body of the message. It then opens a pipe to the `mail` command, using the `-s` flag to specify a subject line and passing the recipient's e-mail address on the command line. The script prints the body of the message to the pipe and closes it. When the pipe is closed, the mail command delivers the message. The script is intended to be called from a fill-out form that may look as follows:

```
<FORM ACTION="/cgi-bin/handle_mail" METHOD=POST>
To: <INPUT TYPE="text" NAME="address"> <P>
Subject: <INPUT TYPE="text" NAME="subject"> <P>
Message: <TEXTAREA NAME="message" ROWS=5></TEXTAREA> <P>
```

```
<INPUT TYPE="submit" VALUE="Send Mail">
</FORM>
```

If the user typed `rolf.oppliger@esecurity.ch` into the To: field, and Test into the Subject: field, the CGI script would run the following command:

```
/bin/mail -s 'Test' rolf.oppliger@esecurity.ch
```

In this case, everything works as anticipated and the e-mail message is sent to `rolf.oppliger@esecurity.ch`. Unfortunately, the script has a problem: it blindly trusts that the e-mail address and subject line supplied by the user are valid. Now consider what happens when a malicious user types the string `rolf.oppliger@esecurity.ch; cat /etc/passwd` into the e-mail address field. In this case, the shell command the script now executes looks as follows:[7]

```
/bin/mail -s 'Test' rolf.oppliger@esecurity.ch; cat /etc/passwd
```

The effect of this is to run the anticipated mail command and then execute `cat/etc/passwd`. This command prints the content of the password file to standard output, which is transferred to the requesting browser. Of course, there's no reason that the same or a similar technique couldn't be used to read the contents of any file on the server host, including HTML documents that are normally protected by access control mechanisms and encrypted in transmit through the SSL or TLS protocol. In fact, variants of this exploit can be used to do many (malicious) things on the Web server. Consequently, the most important thing to do from a security point of view is to validate user-supplied input data, and to perform some pattern-matching checks accordingly. If something suspicious if found, the input data must be modified or refused.

Simson Garfinkel and Eugene H. Spafford compiled a list of general principles and rules for safe CGI programming [5]. The principles and rules are summarized in Table 11.3; they should be kept in mind when designing and implementing CGI scripts. In the same book, the authors also provide rules for C, Perl, and Hypertext Proprocessor (PHP) programmers. These rules are not summarized here.

Last but not least, it is important to note that on some platforms and systems a wrapper may be used to more securely run CGI scripts. Historically, the term *wrapper* was first coined by Wietse Venema for a

---

7.   On UNIX systems, the semicolon is a metacharacter used to separate multiple commands.

Table 11.3 General Principles and Rules for Safe CGI Programming*

No.	Principle or Rule
1	Carefully design the program before you start.
2	Show the specification to another person.
3	Write and test small sections at a time.
4	Check all values provided by the user.
5	Check arguments that you pass to operating system functions.
6	Check all return codes from system calls.
7	Have internal consistency-checking code.
8	Include lots of logging.
9	Some information should not be logged.
10	Make the critical portion of your program as small and as simple as possible.
11	Read through your code.
12	Always use full pathnames for any filename argument, for both commands and data files.
13	Rather than depending on the current directory, set it yourself.
14	Test your completed program thoroughly.
15	Be aware of race conditions.
16	Don't have your program dump core except during your testing.
17	Do not create files in world-writable directories.
18	Don't place undue reliance on the source IP address in the packets of connections you receive.
19	Include some form of load shedding or load limiting in your server to handle cases of excessive load.
20	Put reasonable time-outs on the real time used by your CGI script while it is running.
21	Put reasonable limits on the CPU time used by your CGI script while it is running.
22	Do not require the user to send a reusable password in plaintext over the network connection to authenticate herself.
23	Have your code reviewed by another competent programmer (or two, or more).
24	Whenever possible, reuse code.

*According to [5].

tool he named TCP wrapper.[8] The tool is heavily used on UNIX platforms. It provides some level of access control based on the source and destination of a TCP connection request and logging for successful and unsuccessful connections. More specifically, the TCP wrapper starts a filter program before the requested server process is started, assuming that the connection request is permitted by the access control lists. All messages about connections and connection attempts are logged via the syslog daemon (i.e., `syslogd`). Similar to the TCP wrapper, a wrapper may be used to more securely run another program (e.g., a CGI script). The execution of the other program can be made more secure because the wrapper can be configured in a way that fully controls it and changes its permissions

---

8.   The tool can be downloaded from `ftp://ftp.porcupine.org/pub/security`.

accordingly. For example, the suEXEC wrapper can be used on UNIX systems running the Apache Web server (since version 1.2). The wrapper provides the ability to run CGI script under user IDs different from the user ID of the calling Web server (normally, when a CGI script executes, it runs as the same user who is running the Web server). Further information about the suEXEC wrapper is available at `http://httpd.apache.org/docs/suexec.html`. Also, its installation and configuration is further addressed in [4].

11.3 Server APIs

As mentioned above, some vendors of Web server software packages have tried to overcome the performance problems of CGI scripts by compiling and linking application programs directly into the Web server software via proprietary APIs (i.e., NSAPI, ISAPI, and Apache Web server API). As a result, the application programs have access to the Web server's internal data structures and functions. This makes them faster and more powerful than CGI scripts. Unfortunately, it also gives them the ability to crash the Web server if they are not properly written (unlike CGI programs, user data is sent to the server directly in memory structures rather than through environment variables and mechanisms for interprocess communication). Consequently, compiling and linking application programs directly into a Web server is mostly about avoiding the cost of restarting a CGI script over and over again. It saves the overhead of process invocation at the cost of some reprogramming.

From a security point of view, it is important to note that an application program that is compiled and linked into the Web server software inherits the privileges and access rights of the Web server. This is in contrast to a CGI script that may be configured to run with less privileges and access rights. Consequently, server API scripts must be very carefully designed and implemented. According to [1], compiling and linking application programs into the a Web server is like roping mountain climbers together. If everyone is competent, it saves much. If anyone on the rope is a fool, all perish.

In summary, the use of server API scripts is a bad idea from a security point of view. If one has a choice, one should use CGI scripts (rather than server API scripts). Most of the time, however, one won't have a choice because a Web server must be optimized for performance. In this case, principles and rules for safe programming are even more important than for CGI.

11.4 FastCGI

Given the advantages and disadvantages of both CGI and vendor-specific server APIs, the *FastCGI* interface was designed and developed as an alternative solution.[9] FastCGI is conceptually similar to CGI, but there are two major differences:

1. The server-side processes that invoke FastCGI scripts are persistent. This basically means that after finishing a request, a server-side process waits for a new request instead of exiting.

2. In addition to environment variables and pipes, TCP connections may be used between a Web server and a FastCGI script. This allows FastCGI scripts to run locally (i.e., on the same machine as the Web server) using a pipe, or remotely (i.e., on another machine) using a TCP connection.

FastCGI's ability to run applications remotely (over TCP connections) provides some major benefits as compared to CGI. For example, it is possible to have a Web server located on a DMZ of a firewall configuration using remote FastCGI to dynamically retrieve information from an internal database application server. Furthermore, it is possible to employ FastCGI to build Web servers that provide load balancing for their related application servers.

From a security point of view, remote FastCGI is particularly challenging because a FastCGI script that is invoked must make sure that it is connected to the right Web server. Otherwise it may be made to provide potentially sensitive information to a remote system (note that this is not the case with CGI scripts because CGI scripts are assumed to run locally). Consequently, server authentication is a major issue for FastCGI. In currently available FastCGI implementations, server authenticity is provided through the servers' IP addresses. This is certainly not the preferred choice and more recent FastCGI implementations employ the provision of server authenticity in the SSL/TLS protocol. Due to the interest in newer server-side technologies, such as ASP and JSP, it is not likely that FastCGI will be widely deployed on the WWW anytime soon.

---

9. Further information about FastCGI is available at `http://www.fastcgi.com`.

11.5 Server-side includes

Server-side includes (SSIs) are directives that are written into HTML files, and that are executed by the Web server when the corresponding HTML files are delivered. For performance reasons, a Web server must be told whether it has to look for SSIs or not. This is usually done in the configuration settings of the Web server.

In general, an SSI may look as follows (the operator and arguments are summarized in Table 11.4):

`<!-#operator arg1="x" arg2="y"... ->`

For exampple, the SSI `<!-#fsize arg1="/etc/passwd"->` would return the bytesize of the password file.

From a security point of view, most SSI operators look innocent and are not dangerous to use. For example, the `echo` operator can only be used to provide information about the current date and time, or about the current file. Similarly, the `fsize` operator returns specific information (i.e., the bytesize) of a file. There is, however, one dangerous operator: `exec`. Note that this operator can take a string argument and pass it to the operating system for execution. Consequently, it can be (mis)used in many ways. For example, an insider can use the `exec` operator to invoke any operating system command. Also, there may be situations in which an outsider can provide input that is passed to the `exec` operator. In fact, one can easily imagine a situation in which an outsider is asked to enter a user name and

Table 11.4 Operators and Arguments for SSIs

Operator	Arguments (meaning)
echo	$DOCUMENT_ NAME (echoes current filename)
	$DOCUMENT_ PATH (echoes path to the current filename)
	$DATE_ LOCAL (echoes current date and time on local host)
	$DATE_ GMT (echoes current date and time in Greenwich time)
	$LAST_ MODIFIED (echoes lastmod data on current filename)
	plus all the variables that are available to CGI scripts
include	virtual /x/y (includes file /x/y relative to document root)
	file /x/y (includes file /x/y relative to current directory)
fsize	x (echoes bytesize of file x)
flastmod	x (echoes last mod date of file x)
cong	errmsg (configures generic error message for SSI failure)
	sizefmt (configures fsize format)
	timefmt (configures time format)
exec	cgi (string treated as path to a CGI script)
	cmd (string passed to /bin/sh and executed directly)

this user name is passed as an environment variable to an operating system command for execution. For example, the following SSI uses the finger command on a UNIX system to display some information about the user specified in the $QUERY_STRING environment variable [6]:

```
<!-#exec cmd="finger $QUERY_STRING"->
```

In this example, an arbitrary command can be encoded by an outsider entering a user name by adding a semicolon and the command after the user name. If, for example, the outsider entered oppliger; ls -al in the HTML form requesting the user name, the SSI would execute finger oppliger and ls -al. Obviously, there are many similar examples one may think of. There are, at least, two recommendations to make:

1. Once again, it is very important to validate user-supplied input data.

2. If possible, access to the exec operator should be denied.

An Apache Web server is usually configured to enable SSI by putting in the server options the directive Options Includes. By replacing Options Includes with Options IncludesNOEXEC, one can enable SSIs but deny access to the exec operator.

Due to the fact that SSIs are still rarely used today, there are only a few studies and investigations about the security implications of SSIs (e.g., [7]). This is unfortunate and will likely change, if SSIs are more widely deployed.

11.6 ASP

The term *Active Server Pages* (ASP) refers to a proprietary server-side scripting technology used by Microsoft to dynamically create Web pages. Roughly speaking, an ASP page is an HTML page that contains some server-side scripts that are processed by the Web server before the HTTP response message is sent back to the browser. As such, the ASP technology is conceptually similar to the use of SSIs.

More specifically, when a browser requests an ASP file (i.e., a file with the extension .asp) from a Web server, the server processes the ASP file from top to bottom and executes any server-side script it finds in the file. The scripts, in turn, can be written in either the VBScript or JScript scripting languages. The server then formats a standard Web page (e.g., an HTML or XML page) and returns it to the browser. Consequently, anybody familar with VBScript or JScript programming is potentially able to create ASP files.

In the past, ASP has been involved in many security problems. Most of these security problems, however, have been due to the fact that ASP is deeply interwined with the Microsoft Windows operating systems and Web servers (i.e., Microsoft IIS and Personal Web Server). Consequently, attackers usually employ ASP pages to exploit vulnerabilities and bugs either in the operating system or the Web server software. If they did not use ASP pages, they would search and eventually find other possibilities to exploit the same vulnerabilities and bugs. Nevertheless, it is arguably correct to say that VBScript and JScript are powerful scripting languages that simplify the attacker's job considerably.

11.7 JSP

Similar to ASP, Sun Microsystems developed a technology called *JavaServer Pages* (JSP[10]) to be used in the Java world.[11] Again, the aim of JSP is to provide support for the design and implementation of multi-tier Web-based applications. Contrary to ASP, however, JSP relies on the Java programming language and inherits its ability to run on multiple platforms accordingly. Most importantly, JSP runs on most Web servers in use today, including, for example, Apache and Micrsoft IIS.

More specifically, JSP is implemented as a Java API that is part of the *Java 2 Platform, Enterprise Edition* (J2EE). Readers familiar with servlets[12] will notice that JSP does not provide anything conceptually new, and that everything that can be done with a JSP page can also be done by writing a servlet. In fact, servlets have access to exactly the same set of Java APIs as JSP, and JSP pages are compiled into servlets.

JSP can be used to separate the static content of a Web page from the logic to generate the dynamic parts of it. Consequently, Web publishers can use familiar tools to create and edit Web pages, and simply embed calls to the necessary application components where needed. All they need to know is how to invoke the logic. A JSP programmer can then build and maintain the logic components.

---

10. http://java.sun.com/products/jsp/

11. The JSP technology is implemented, for example, as part of the Jakarta project at the Apache Software Foundation. The resulting Tomcat implementation is free and open-source. It also implements servlets. Further information about Tomcat can be found at http://jakarta.apache.org/tomcat.

12. http://java.sun.com/products/servlet

11.8 Conclusions

In this chapter, we overviewed and discussed the security implications of some technologies that can be used to design and build multitier Web-based applications (i.e., CGI, server APIs, FastCGI, SSIs, ASP, and JSP). Since the current trend to build Web-based applications and services is likely to continue, we will see many other server-side technologies being created and aggressively marketed in the future. This is unfortunate, because many server-side technologies do the same or at least very similar things. Note that most things we said for CGI scripts also apply for server APIs, ASP, and JSP. Most importantly, an application developer must never trust any string the user types in.

From a security point of view, the most dangerous thing about technologies that can be used to design and build multitier Web-based applications is that they all provide additional functionalities to Web servers, and that these additional functionalities can be attacked directly or (mis)used to indirectly attack other things. Several examples were given in this chapter. It is possible and very likely that many other examples will be reported in the future. Consequently, it is very important that Web-based applications and services are designed, implemented, and deployed with security in mind and in a way that security requirements are properly met. This is mainly a design issue and the designers of Web-based applications and services should be educated in security or collaborate with security professionals or engineers. There are simply too many things that can go wrong. This is particularly true if Web-based applications and services are provided on the Internet (using, for example, reverse proxy mechanisms). Last but not least, it is important to note that software engineering principles are becoming more and more important for Web-based applications and services.

References

[1]   Stein, L. D., *Web Security: A Step-by-Step Reference*, Reading, MA: Addison-Wesley, 1998.

[2]   Larson, E., and B. Stephens, *Administrating Web Servers, Security, & Maintenance Interactive Workbook*, Upper Saddle River, NJ: Prentice Hall, 1999.

[3]   Aulds, C., *Linux Apache Web Server Administration*, Alameda, CA: Sybex, 2000.

[4]   Laurie, B., and P. Laurie, *Apache: The Definitive Guide, Second Edition*, Sebastopol, CA: O'Reilly & Associates, 1999.

[5]   Garfinkel, S., with E. H. Spafford, *Web Security, Privacy & Commerce, Second Edition*, Sebastopol, CA: O'Reilly & Associates, 2001.

[6]   Rubin, A. D., D. Geer, and M.J. Ranum, *Web Security Sourcebook*, New York: John Wiley & Sons, Inc., 1997.

[7]   Karro, J., and J. Wang, "Protecting Web Servers from Security Holes in Server-Side Includes," *Proceedings of Annual Computer Security Applications Conference (ACSAC '98)*, December 1998, pp. 103–111.

CHAPTER

12

Contents

12.1 Introduction

12.2 Early work

12.3 Cookies

12.4 Anonymous browsing

12.5 Anonymous publishing

12.6 Voluntary privacy standards

12.7 Conclusions

References

Privacy Protection and Anonymity Services

In this chapter, we focus on the increasingly important field of privacy protection and anonymity services for the WWW. More specifically, we introduce the topic in Section 12.1, elaborate on some early work (mainly in the field of providing anonymity services for electronic mail) in Section 12.2, discuss cookies and their privacy implications in Section 12.3, address technologies to anonymously browse and anonymously publish on the Web in Sections 12.4 and 12.5,[1] elaborate on voluntary privacy standards in Section 12.6, and draw some conclusions in Section 12.7. Note that parts of this chapter are taken from [1]. Also note that many countries have data privacy or data protection laws that must be considered and taken into account when personal data are stored, processed, or transmitted. These laws and their implications are not addressed in this book. You may refer to [2] to get some further information about the legal situation in your country. Last but not least, [3] provides another source of information.

12.1 Introduction

Many users think that browsing the Web is an anonymous activity. This is because it is not immediately visible to them

---

1. In some literature, these technologies are also referred to as privacy enhancing technologies (PETs).

that there are many computer systems behind the scences that busily collect information about or related to them. For example, each Web server has a log file that is usually configured to add an entry for every single HTTP request message that is received and processed. For example, a fictitious entry may look as follows:

```
proxy.esecurity.ch - - [13/May/2002:15:04:31 +0200]
  "GET /esecurity.html HTTP/1.0"
  200 1369"http://www.esecurity.ch/"
  "Mozilla/4.0 (compatible; MSIE 5.5; Windows NT 5.0)"
```

In this example, a client machine with DNS name proxy.esecurity.ch anonymously[2] requested the resource http://www.esecurity.ch/esecurity.html using HTTP version 1.0 in the afternoon of May 13, 2002. The Web server accepted the request (indicated by status code 200) and sent back the 1369 bytes long HTML file esecurity.html. In addition to the information needed to serve the request, the client also sent to the server and the server logged some information related to the client platform and software in use. In this example, the client was running Windows 2000 and Microsoft Internet Explorer version 5.5.

Any interested reader may refer to the analyzing service of Privacy.net[3] to learn about the information his or her browser provides when it connects to a Web server.[4] For example, Figure 12.1 illustrates a corresponding Web page rendered by the Opera browser. In this example, the server correctly recognizes that the client is running an Opera browser version 6.0 (english version) running on a Windows NT 4.0 platform. Also, the server learns about the browser settings related to JavaScript, cookies, plug-ins, and many other features that are not even illustrated in Figure 12.1. Note, for example, that the browser reveals the fact that it is running the Shockwave Flash plug-in version 5.0. From a security point of view, this fact reveals that the browser may be attacked using a vulnerability and corresponding exploit related to this specific version of the Shockwave Flash plug-in. From a privacy point of view, this fact also reveals that the browser is also used to display animated Web sites.

2. The fact that the request was anonymous is represented by the empty user name that would follow the client name in the log file.
3. http://privacy.net/analyze
4. German speaking readers may also refer to http://www.datenschutz.ch for an analysis of the browser's privacy settings.

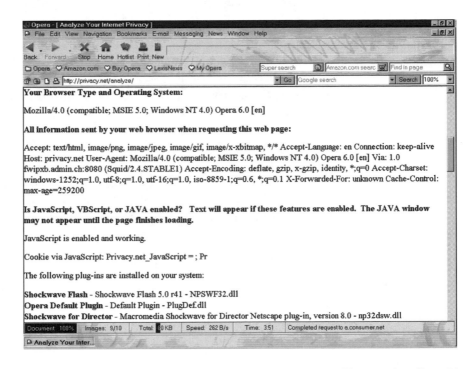

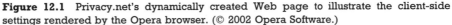

Figure 12.1   Privacy.net's dynamically created Web page to illustrate the client-side settings rendered by the Opera browser. (© 2002 Opera Software.)

Even more information is available to local network administrators and Internet service providers (ISPs). Their internetworking devices are usually configured to log relevant information. Most importantly, their HTTP proxy servers keep track of every Web site and URL that is requested by a user. Consequently, the local network administrators and ISPs are the ones that are most likely able to establish user profiles. These profiles may threat the privacy of users and it is an ongoing (legal) discussion about how far they can go.

The mechanism of choice to establish user profiles is traffic analysis. According to RFC 2828 [4], the term traffic analysis refers to the "inference of information from observable characteristics of data flow(s), even when the data is encrypted or otherwise not directly available. Such characteristics include the identities and locations of the source(s) and destination(s), and the presence, amount, frequency, and duration of occurrence." Outside the military, the threat of traffic analysis has largely been ignored. But traffic analysis is becoming a significant threat to the privacy of Web users, and the browsing behavior of Web users is increasingly subject to observation. As Web-based applications and services become more prevalent, this behavior includes the shopping habits and spending patterns of individual users, as well as other personal data that have traditionally been considered private. Similarly, the Web is becoming an important source for information and intelligence gathering. In a competitive environment, a company may wish to protect its current research topics. However, monitoring HTTP data traffic may reveal the company's primary focus. By keeping Web browsing characteristics private, the company's interests are adequately protected. We saw in Chapter 9 that some electronic payment systems (e.g., anonymous electronic cash systems) allow secure financial transactions over the Internet while preserving the untraceability and anonymity that normal cash allows. However, if electronic cash is transmitted over a channel that identifies both the payer and the payee, the transaction may no longer stay anonymous.

Unfortunately, traffic analysis is a threat that is very difficult to protect against, given the architecture of the Internet and WWW.[5] For example, simply encrypting IP packets between a browser and a Web server (e.g., using the SSL/TLS protocol) does not protect against traffic analysis (i.e., the analysis still reveals that the browser and the Web server are sending IP packets forth and back). Consequently, other security mechanisms are required to protect communicating peers against traffic analysis and to provide corresponding anonymity services.

According to [5], there are three types of anonymous communication properties that can be provided individually or in combination:

1. Sender anonymity;

2. Receiver anonymity;

3. Unlinkability of sender and receiver (i.e., connection anonymity).

In short, *sender anonymity* means that the identity of the party who sent a particular message is hidden, while its receiver and the message itself might not be. Similarly, *receiver anonymity* means that the identity of the receiver is hidden, while its sender and the message itself might not be. Finally, *unlinkability of sender and receiver* (also referred to as *connection anonymity*) means that though the sender and receiver can each be identified individually as participating in some communication, they cannot be identified as communicating with each other.

---

5. In leased lines and circuit-switched networks, traffic padding may be used to protect against traffic analysis.

All three types of anonymous communication properties may be relevant for the WWW. For example, sender anonymity is relevant if somebody wants to publish anonmyously on the Web. Refer to Section 12.5 for corresponding technologies. Similarly, receiver anonymity is relevant if somebody wants to browse anonymously through the Web. Refer to Section 12.4 for corresponding technologies. Last but not least, connection anonymity is relevant if somebody wants to hide the fact that he or she is participating in some Web traffic. In Section 12.4.4, we will learn about a technology called onion routing that can be used to implement anonymous connections.

12.2 Early work

There is some early work in providing anonymity services for electronic mail (e-mail). For example, `anon.penet.fi` was a simple and easy-to-use anonymous e-mail forwarding service (a so-called *anonymous remailer*) that was operated by Johan Helsingius in Finland.[6] In short, the `anon.penet.fi` anonymous remailer was provided by a simple SMTP proxy server that stripped off all header information of incoming e-mail messages before forwarding them toward their destination. In addition, if not already assigned, an alias (i.e., a pseudonym) for the sender of an e-mail message was created. In the outgoing message, the real e-mail address of the sender was replaced by the alias that allowed the recipient(s) of the message to reply to the sender without knowing his or her real identity or e-mail address.

In essence, `anon.penet.fi` provided sender anonymity by simply keeping the mapping between real e-mail addresses and their aliases secret. The downside of this simple approach was that any user of `anon.penet.fi` had to trust the service provider not to reveal his or her real identity or e-mail address. This level of trust may or may not be justified.[7] In either case, it is difficult for a user to decide whether this level of trust is appropriate for any given service provider. Today, there are several anonymous remailers available for public use on the Internet.[8]

---

6. According to a press release on February 20, 1995, over 7,000 messages were forwarded daily, and the alias database contained more than 200,000 entries.

7. On February 8, 1995, based on a burglary report filed with the Los Angeles police, transmitted by Interpol, the Finish police presented Helsingius a warrant for search and seizure. Bound by law, he complied, thereby revealing the real e-mail address of a single user.

8. A list of currently available anonymous remailers is maintained, for example, at `http://anon.efga.org/ Remailers`.

A more sophisticated approach to provide anonymity services for e-mail was developed and proposed by David Chaum in the early 1980s [6]. In fact, Chaum introduced the notion of a *Chaum mixing network* that—as its name suggests—is a network consisting of a set of *Chaum mixes* (or *mixes*). Each Chaum mix is an anonymous remailer that has a public key pair and is able to decrypt messages with its private key accordingly. In addition to forwarding incoming e-mail messages, a Chaum mix may also try to hide the relationship between incoming and outgoing messages by reordering, delaying, and eventually padding them to disable or at least complicate traffic analysis.

When a user wants to send a message in a Chaum mixing network, he or she must first choose a route through a series of Chaum mixes $M_1, \ldots, M_n$ to the intended recipient, and then prepare a layered message for delivery. In fact, the first layer includes the name of the recipient and the message encrypted with the public key of the recipient. The second layer includes M_n and the first layer encrypted with the public key of M_n. The third layer includes M_{n-1} and the second layer encrypted with the public key of M_{n-1}. This continues until the last layer includes M_1 and the last but one layer encrypted with the public key of M_1. This last layer represents the message that is actually sent out. For example, if $n = 3$ and the recipient is B, the message that is sent out may look as follows:

$$M_1, \{M_2, \{M_3, \{B, \{message\}k_B\}k_{M_3}\}k_{M_2}\}k_{M_1} \qquad (12.1)$$

If this message reaches M_1, the Chaum mix uses its private key (i.e., $k_{M_1}^{-1}$) to decrypt $\{M_2, \{M_3, \{B, \{message\}k_B\}k_{M_3}\}k_{M_2}\}k_{M_1}$. The result is split into two parts (i.e., M_2 and $\{M_3, \{B, \{message\}k_B\}k_{M_3}\}k_{M_2}$) and the first part is used to route the second part to M_2. Similar to M_1, M_2 uses its private key (i.e., $k_{M_2}^{-1}$) to decrypt $\{M_3, \{B, \{message\}k_B\}k_{M_3}\}k_{M_2}$. Again, the result is split into two parts (i.e., M_3 and $\{B, \{message\}k_B\}k_{M_3}$) and the first part is used to route the second part to M_3. M_3, in turn, decrypts $\{B, \{message\}k_B\}k_{M_3}$ using its private key (i.e., $k_{M_3}^{-1}$). The result is B and $\{message\}k_B$ and as such it can be forwarded to B. Finally, B uses his or her private key (i.e., k_B^{-1}) to decrypt the message.

If a Chaum mixing network were used to transmit e-mail messages only through one single Chaum mix, this mix would have to be trusted not to reveal the senders' and receivers' identities (since it sees both of them). In this case, the situation would be comparable to the service provided by `anon.penet.fi`. Consequently, most people would prefer to forward e-mail messages through two or more Chaum mixes in an attempt to protect themselves against a single mix that may see both the sender and the receiver identities of a particular message. In other words, using two or more mixes keeps the sender anonymous to every mix but the first and the receiver anonymous to every mix but the last. Also, a user's identity is best hidden if he runs his own Chaum mix and directs all of his outgoing e-mail messages through it.

If one were worried about an adversary powerful enough to monitor several Chaum mixes in a network simultaneously, one would also have to worry about timing and other correlation attacks. In an extreme case, consider the situation in which a Chaum mixing network is idle until a message is sent out and forwarded to its recipient. Then even though an adversary can't decrypt the layered encryption, he or she can still locate the route just by watching the active parts of the network and analyzing the data traffic accordingly. Chaum mixing networks have been designed to resist such attacks using queues to batch, reorder, and process incoming messages. In fact, each mix may keep quiet—absorbing incoming messages but not retransmitting them—until its outbound buffer overflows, at which point the mix emits a randomly chosen message to its next hop. However, due to the real-time constraints of some applications, the batching, reordering, and processing of data messages in queues is not always possible. As discussed below, this is particularly true for the WWW.

One question arises immediately with regard to the use of anonymous remailers and corresponding services: how can the recipient of an (anonymous) e-mail message reply to the sender? The answer is that the recipient can't unless explicitly told how to do so. A simple technique is to tell the recipient to send a reply to a certain newsgroup, such as `alt.anonymous.messages`, with a specific subject field, such as `12345example`. The reply can then be grabbed by the sender from the appropriate newsgroup. This approach of replying is yet untraceable but also expensive and unreliable. A more sophisticated technique uses the knowledge of how to build an untraceable forward route from the sender to the recipient, to build an inverse untraceable backward route from the recipient to the sender. In general, the forward and backward routes are independent (they can be completely identical, partially identical, or completely disjunct). According to this technique, the sender computes a block of information that is used to anonymously return a response message from the recipient to the sender. This additional block of information is sometimes also referred to as a *return path information* (RPI) block. The RPI block must be sent with the original message and some padding data from the sender to the recipient. It is then used by the recipient to build a corresponding backward route or return path. This technique was prototyped by IBM Research in a system called BABEL [7].

Anonymous remailers are fairly well understood today. Unfortunately, the lessons leart cannot be directly applied to the WWW, because the characteristics of e-mail and the WWW are inherently different:

- First, the WWW is an interactive medium, while e-mail is store-and-forward. This basically means that a delay of several hours is acceptable for e-mail (most of the time).

- Second, e-mail is a push technology, meaning that the sender of an e-mail message initiates a data transfer, possibly without the knowledge or consent of the recipient (the existence of e-mail bombing attacks illustrates this point fairly well). By contrast, the WWW is a pull technology, meaning that the recipient must explicitly request data being transferred from the sender.

The first difference implies that full featured Chaum mixing networks are unacceptable (or at least difficult to use) for HTTP data traffic. Nevertheless, the second difference also offers some possibilities to improve security (in terms of anonymity). For obvious reasons, the security of an anonymity-providing system, such as a Chaum mixing network, increases as the number of available and publicly accessible cooperating nodes (i.e., Chaum mixes) increases. In the realm of e-mail, operators of anonymous remailers have often come under fire when their services were abused by people sending threatening letters or unacceptable spam (refer to `anon.penet.fi` discussed earlier in this chapter). In fact, the undesirability of handling irate users causes the number of anonymous remailers to stay considerably low, potentially impacting the anonymity of the overall system. By contrast, a Web server can't initiate a connection with an unwilling browser and send it data when no request was made. This consensual nature of the Web should cause fewer potential node administrators to become discouraged, and therefore lead to corresponding increases in cooperating nodes.

Last but not least, it is important to note that Web proxy servers are often well suited to implement anonymity services because of their caching capabilities (to improve network performance). The very fact that data is being cached at some proxy servers makes it less likely that requests are forwarded all the way to the destination server. This makes traffic analysis more complicated, and harder to accomplish.

12.3 Cookies

The customization of Web-based applications and services requires the availability of state information related to users and their browsing habits and behaviors. Unfortunately, HTTP is stateless and neither provides support for sessions, nor it knows what HTTP request and response messages actually "belong" to the same user. Consequently, one approach to make state information available to a Web-based application or service would be to authenticate the user for each request and to store information for this particular user on the server side (e.g., in a database). Note, however, that there are at least two disadvantages related to this approach:

1. User must authenticate himself or herself for every request.

2. The Web server must store a lot of information and host a huge database accordingly.

Alternatively, one can download state information to the browser and have the browser resubmit the information when it returns to the same Web server. In this case, the state information is stored and managed in a highly decentralized way. This is basically the way the HTTP state management mechanism specified in RFC 2965 [8] works. The mechanism has a long history (in Internet time) and has gone through numerous discussions related to privacy. The interested reader is referred to [9] for a corresponding overview and discussion.

In short, the HTTP state management mechanism uses *cookies* that are sent forth and back between the Web server and the browser. In fact, the Web server provides cookies and the browser stores and resubmits these cookies. More specifically, RFC 2965 [8] introduces two new HTTP headers (i.e., the Cookie and the Set-Cookie header) that can be used to carry cookies and corresponding state information from one session to another. In fact, the Set-Cookie header is used by the Web server to send a cookie to the browser, and the Cookie header is used by the browser to return the cookie to the Web server when it reconnects to it. The syntax and semantics of the headers are fully specified in [8]. For example, a simple Set-Cookie response header may look as follows:

```
Set-Cookie: USER_NAME=Rolf; path=/; expires=Saturday, 18-May-02
23:12
```

The Web server sets a cookie that holds a user name in a corresponding variable (i.e., USER_NAME), and the browser stores the cookie locally. If the browser requested a resource in path "/" on the same server (before May 18, 2002), it would send the following Cookie request header to the Web server:

```
Cookie: USER_NAME=Rolf
```

At this point in time, the Web server knows that the requesting user has been previously assigned the name Rolf. If there were other attributes stored in the cookie, the server could customize its behavior for this particular user accordingly. Consequently, cookies can be long and encode a lot of information. Furthermore, cookies can be encrypted. In this case, the key needed to encrypt and decrypt the cookies must be known only be the Web server. This simplifies key management considerably.

In either case, cookies can be used to track the path of a user when he or she browses through a Web site (they have been designed for this purpose) or a collection of Web sites.[9] Users may object to this behavior as an intrusive accumulation of private information, even if their identities may not be evident.[10] Consequently, a user should be able to enable or disable the HTTP state management mechanism, and to either reject or refuse the use of cookies accordingly. This is possible in all major browsers in use today. For example, Figure 12.2 illustrates the Microsoft Internet Explorer's Security Settings menu that can be used to enable or disable cookies. There is made a distinction between persistent cookies (i.e., cookies that are stored in a specific file) and transient cookies (i.e., cookies that only live for the ongoing session and that are not stored in a file). This distinction is not necessarily made by all browsers. In Figure 12.2, both types of cookies are enabled by the current user. Similarly, Figure 12.3 illustrates the Preferences menu of the Opera browser. In the Privacy section of this menu, there is a Cookies panel that can be used to customize the use of cookies.

If a browser does not allow a user to disable cookies, it is always possible to periodically delete the file in which the cookies are stored. For example, on a UNIX system, the browser can be prevented from storing and saving cookies by replacing the cookies file with a link to /dev/null. Similarly, on Windows and Macintosh systems, there are commercial programs that promise to sweep cookie files clear.

Note that the HTTP state management mechanism and the corresponding cookies are designed to maintain state information between two endpoints of an HTTP session (i.e., a browser and a Web server). They cannot be used for storing state information between the browser and a proxy server, or between different proxy servers in a proxy chain.[11]

---

9. In the second case, a third-party tracking service must be used. Such services are provides by companies like DoubleClick, Inc. (http://www.doubleclick.com).

10. Identities may be evident if users fill out forms that contain identifying information.

11. Note that a common way to use (or misuse) cookies is to store authentication information so that a reauthentication does not have to occur every time in future requests, but the appropriate authentication information is directly available in a corresponding cookie. To prevent spoofing attacks in this setting, it i

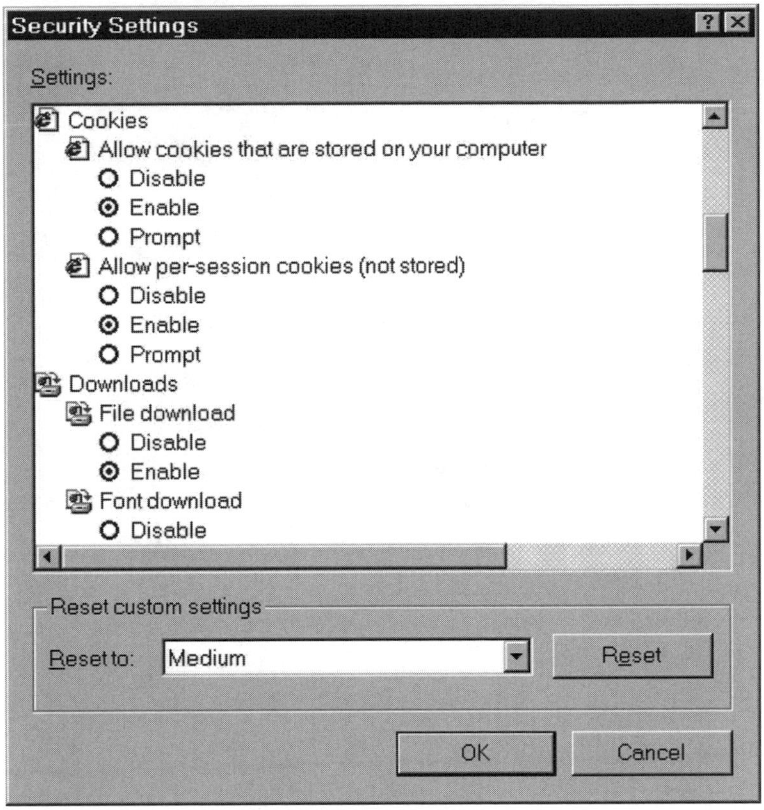

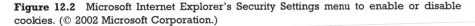

Figure 12.2 Microsoft Internet Explorer's Security Settings menu to enable or disable cookies. (© 2002 Microsoft Corporation.)

Also note that there are other technologies that may compromise the privacy of users (in addition to cookies). For example, *Web bugs*[12] are very small images placed on Web pages or e-mail messages to facilitate third-party tracking of users and collection of statistics. In fact, a typical Web bug consists of a 1-pixel-by-1-pixel transparent GIF image. To detect it, one

---

common practice to encode, not just the username into the cookie, but also the IP address where the first request came from. Now consider the case in which the route to the server is dynamically changing in a way that a request is not guaranteed to come from the same IP address (of the proxy server) as the earlier request. In this case, the cookie may be rendered invalid. In this situation, a feature to support proxy cookies would be useful [10]. Such a feature will hopefully emerge at some later point in time (obviously, the more secure approach is not to store any static authentication information in a cache in the first place).

12. The term *Web bugs* was coined by the Privacy Foundation (http://www.privacyfoundation.org) that released a corresponding report in September 2000.

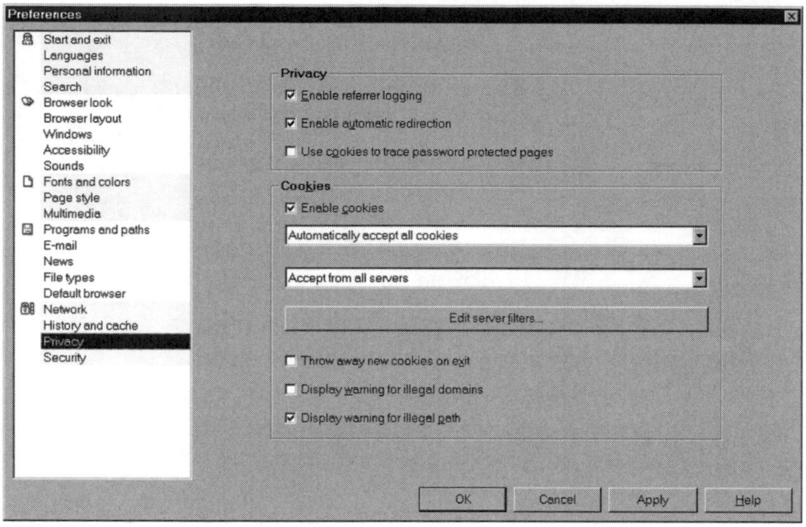

Figure 12.3 Opera's Preferences menu to configure the use of cookies. (© 2002 Opera Software).

must view the source of the Web page or e-mail message. Note what happens if the following HTML statement is included in a Web page or e-mail message:

```
<img src="http://www.esecurity.ch/tracking.gif"
    width=1 height=1 border=0>
```

If a browser renders the Web page or an HTML-enabled user agent displays the e-mail message, the image `tracking.gif` is retrieved from `http://www.esecurity.ch` and is displayed in a pixel. As such, the image is invisible to the unassisted eye and it usually goes unnoticed (unless one looks at the source). Because the browser or user agent retrieves the image from `http://www.esecurity.ch`, the Web server writes a corresponding entry in its log file. Consequently, the Web server's log file reveals who and from where the image file was retrieved.

12.4 Anonymous browsing

In this section, we overview and discuss some technologies that can be used to protect the privacy of Web users and to provide support for anonymous browsing accordingly. In particular, we overview and briefly discuss anonymizing HTTP proxy servers, JAP, Crowds, onion routing, and the Freedom Network.

12.4.1 Anonymizing HTTP proxy servers

In short, an anonymizing HTTP proxy server is an HTTP proxy server that removes all parts of an HTTP request message that—directly or indirectly—reveals information about the browser, but are not really required by the Web server to serve the request and to respond appropriately. Most importantly, an anonymizing HTTP proxy server can hide the browser's IP address. If the Web server sends back the requested resource, it can be forwarded by the anonymizing HTTP proxy server to the browser. Similarly, the Web server need not learn anything about the client platform and browser in use.

Most anonymizing HTTP proxy servers work with nested URLs.[13] A nested URL is an URL in which the document part refers to another URL. For example, in a nested URL of the form

```
http://proxy.../http://www.esecurity.ch
```

the document part (i.e., `http://www.esecurity.ch`) refers to another URL. By retrieving the nested URL, the browser first connects to the HTTP proxy server running at `proxy...`, and this proxy server connects to the Web server at `http://www.esecurity.ch`. Similar to anonymous remailers, the use of anonymizing HTTP proxy servers can also be chained and a cascade of corresponding servers may be used. This is important if there is no single proxy server a user is willing to trust.

The following example illustrates a nested URL that is forwarded by two proxy servers (i.e., `proxy1...` and `proxy2...`) before it is finally delivered to the Web server:

```
http://proxy1.../http://proxy2.../http://www.esecurity.ch
```

Obviously, each proxy server in the chain removes its part of the nested URLs. This means that the Web server finally sees only the resource that is requested and the IP address of the last proxy server in the chain. There is no possibility for the Web server to determine what browser originally requested the resource, or on what proxy chain the request message was delivered. Each proxy server, however, holds some local state information about the established connections (on either side of the proxy). Consequently, any response message from the Web server can be sent back to the browser using exactly the same proxy chain (in reverse order).

If an anonymizing HTTP proxy server is not chained, it can be complemented by the SSL/TLS protocol to improve its ability to provide

---

13. Most existing HTTP proxy servers (e.g., Apache) provide support for nested URLs.

anonymity services to its users. In fact, the anonymizing HTTP proxy server can either tunnel or proxy the SSL/TLS-protected data traffic between the browser and the Web server. In the second case, the connection between the proxy server and the Web server may or may not be protected using the SSL/TLS protocol (in addition to the use of the SSL/TLS protocol between the browser and the proxy server).

There is an increasingly large number of companies and organizations that operate anonymizing HTTP proxy servers and provide corresponding anonymity services for Web users. Two examples include Anonymizer.com[14] and IDzap, LLC.[15] Most of these services have versions in which they support the SSL/TLS protocol in one way or another.

12.4.2 JAP

A group of researchers at the University of Technology Dresden adapted the notion of a Chaum mixing network for the WWW and designed and developed a corresponding system that can be used to anonymoulsy browse through the Web. The system is named JAP and its open source software is entirely written in the Java programming language.[16]

In essence, the JAP system implements a Chaum mixing network for HTTP. Each Chaum mix is represented by a piece of software (i.e., an anonymizing HTTP proxy server) that a JAP user must install and configure locally. This software acts as a local JAP proxy server to the browser.

When the user wants to anonymoulsy request a resource from a Web server using the JAP system, the browser must forward the request to the local JAP proxy server. The JAP proxy server, in turn, must encrypt the request message multiple times (once for every JAP proxy server on the request message's delivery path to the Web server). The encrypted message is then sent through the defined chain of intermediate JAP proxy servers to the Web server, and the Web server sends back the requested resource. The procedure is identical to the one described in Section 12.2 for the delivery of anonymous messages in a Chaum mixing network.

12.4.3 Crowds

In the late 1990s, a group of researchers at AT&T Research designed and prototyped a sophisticated system to provide anonymity services for Web

---

14. http://www.anonymizer.com
15. http://www.idzap.com
16. http://anon.inf.tu-dresden.de

users [11, 12]. The system was named *Crowds*. This is because the system operates by grouping users into a large and geographically diverse group (a so-called crowd). The basic idea of Crowds is to probabilistically chain multiple anonymizing HTTP proxy servers, and to encrypt all data that is sent forth and back between the proxy servers. The fact that the chaining is probabilistic differentiates Crowds from many other systems, including, for example, the JAP system mentioned above.

In the Crowds systems, each user is represented by a process—a so-called *jondo*[17]—that runs on his or her system. When this process is started, it contacts a server called the *blender* to request admittance to the crowd. If admitted, the blender reports to the jondo the current membership status of the crowd and information that enables the jondo to actually participate in the system. The user, in turn, must configure the jondo to serve as proxy server by specifying its hostname and port number in his or her browser as the proxy for all services (i.e., Gopher, HTTP, and SSL). Afterwards, any request originating from the browser is sent directly to its jondo. Upon receiving the first request, the jondo establishes a random path of jondos to and from the Web server. More precisely, the jondo picks a jondo from the crowd (possibly itself) at random, and forwards the request to it. When this jondo receives the request, it flips a biased coin to determine whether or not to forward the request to another jondo. If the result is to forward, then the jondo selects a random jondo and forwards the request to it. Otherwise the jondo submits the result to the Web server for which the request was destined originally. Consequently, each request travels from the user's browser, through a number of jondos, and finally to the Web server. Subsequent requests initiated at the same jondo follow the same path (except perhaps going to a different Web server), and server response messages traverse the same path as the request messages, only in reverse.

All communications between any two jondos is encrypted using a key known only to the two jondos. Encryption keys are established as jondos join the crowd. Therefore, some group membership procedures must be defined and put in place. These procedures determine who can join the crowd and when they can join, and inform members of the crowd membership accordingly. In fact, there are many schemes and corresponding group membership protocols that can potentially be used to manage crowd memberships. While providing robust and reliable distributed solutions, many of these schemes have the disadvantage of incurring significant overhead and providing semantics that are arguably too strong for the

---

17. The term *jondo* is pronounced "John Doe." It refers to the image of a faceless participant of the system.

application at hand. In the Crowds system, a simpler and centralized solution is used. As mentioned above, membership in a crowd is controlled and reported to crowd members by the blender. To make use of the blender (and thus the crowd), the user must establish an account with the blender (i.e., an account name and password that the blender stores). When the user starts a jondo, the jondo and the blender use this shared secret (the password) to authenticate each other's communication. As a result of this communication, the blender may accept the jondo into the crowd, add the new jondo (i.e., its IP address, port number, and account name) to its list of current members, and report this list back to the jondo. In addition, the blender may also generate and report back a list of shared keys, each of which can be used to authenticate another member of the crowd. The blender then sends one key of the new jondo to each other jondo that is intended to share it (encrypted under the account password for that jondo) and informs the other jondos of the new member. At this point all members are equipped with the data they need for the new member to participate in the crowd.

Each member maintains its own list of crowd members. This list is initialized to that received from the blender when the jondo joins the crowd, and is updated when the jondo receives notices of new or deleted members from the blender. The jondo can also (autonomously) remove jondos from its list of crowd members, if it detects that the corresponding jondos have failed. This allows for each jondo's list to diverge from others' lists if different jondos have detected different failures in the crowd.

Obviously, a major disadvantage of this centralized approach to group membership management is that the blender is a TTP for the purposes of key distribution and membership reporting. Techniques exist for distributing trust in such a TTP among many replicas, in a way that the corruption of some fraction of the replicas can be tolerated [13]. In its present, nonreplicated form, however, the blender is best executed on a trusted computer system (e.g., with log-in access available only at the console). Note, however, that even though the blender is a TTP for some functions, HTTP traffic is not generally routed through the blender, and thus a passive attack on the blender does not immediately break Web transaction security. Moreover, the failure of the blender does not interfere with ongoing transactions. It is planned that in future versions of Crowds, jondos will establish mutually shared keys using the Diffie-Hellman key exchange, where the blender serves only to authenticate and distribute the Diffie-Hellman public values of the Crowds members. This will eliminate the present reliance on the blender for key generation. Another possibility would be the use of Kerberos or any other authentication and key distribution system.

In practice, firewalls present a problem for the deployment of Crowds. Remember from the description given above that jondos are identified by their IP addresses and port numbers. Most corporate firewalls do not allow incoming connections on ports other than a few well-known ones. Thus, a firewall will generally prevent a jondo outside the firewall from connecting to another jondo inside the firewall. It is conceivable that if Crowds becomes widespread, and there is demand for a special reserved port, that firewalls will open this port and allow jondos to communicate accordingly. Until then, Crowds will be most useful across academic institutions, as a service provided by ISPs to private subscribers, and within very large organizations (because they traditionally do not use firewalls).

Crowds 1.0 is implemented in Perl 5.0. According to their developers, Perl was chosen for its rapid prototyping capabilities and its portability across UNIX and Microsoft platforms. Obviously, the performance of Crowds could be improved by implementing the system in a compiled language, such as C or C^{++}.[18] Further information and the corresponding software can be obtained from the Crowds home page.[19]

12.4.4 Onion routing

Also in the late 1990s, a group of researchers at the U.S. Naval Research Laboratory (NRL) adapted the idea of using a Chaum mixing network to provide anonymous connections[20] in a system called *onion routing* [14, 15].[21] The onion routing system is conceptually different from the JAP system. While onion routing works at the network layer and is independent from the application protocol in use, the JAP system is specifically designed for HTTP.

In onion routing, the term *onion* refers to a layered encrypted message, whereas the term *onion router* refers to a Chaum mix that acts as a node in a corresponding onion routing network. Instead of making TCP connections

---

18. Note, however, that another bottleneck of the system is the communication that must take place. This bottleneck cannot be resolved using a compiled language.

19. http://www.research.att.com/projects/crowds

20. Anonymous connections are similar to TCP connections, but they are also resistant against passive and active attacks (including traffic analysis). Anonymous connections are bidirectional, have small latency, and can be used anywhere a TCP connection can be used. Note that a connection may be anonymous, although communication need not be (e.g., if the data stream is not encrypted).

21. Note that the onion routing system is conceptually similar to the PipeNet proposal that was posted by Wei Dai to the Cypherpunks mailing list in February 1995. Contrary to the onion routing system, however, the PipeNet proposal has not been implemented so far.

directly to a responding machine (the so-called *responder*), an initiating application (the so-called *initiator*) makes an anonymous connection through a sequence of onion routers. Contrary to normal routers, onion routers are connected by longstanding and permanent TCP connections. Although the technology is called onion routing, the routing that occurs does so at the application layer (and not at the Internet layer). More specifically, the system relies upon IP routing to route data through longstanding TCP connections. Therefore, although the series of onion routers in an anonymous connection is fixed for the lifetime of that connection, the route that data actually travels between individual onion routers is determined by the underlying IP network. Consequently, onion routing is conceptually similar to loose source routing with IP. Anonymous connections are multiplexed over longstanding connections. For any anonymous connection, the sequence of onion routers in a route is strictly defined at connection setup, and each onion router can only identify the previous and next hops along the route. Data passed along the anonymous connection appears different at each onion router, so data cannot be tracked en route and compromised onion routers cannot cooperate.

In onion routing, an application does not directly talk to a router nor to an onion router. Instead, there must be proxies that interface between the applications and the onion routing network. For example, to access a Web site through an onion routing network, one has to set the browser's HTTP proxy to an onion network entry point (a so-called application proxy). In fact, the initiator establishes a TCP connection to an application proxy. This proxy defines a (perhaps random) route through the onion routing network by constructing a layered data structure (an onion) and sending that onion through the network. Similar to a Chaum mixing network, each layer of the onion is encrypted with the public key of the intended onion and defines the next hop in the route. An onion's size is fixed, so each onion router adds some random padding data to replace the removed layer. The last onion router forwards data to the responder's application proxy, whose job is to pass data between the onion routing network and the responder. In addition to carrying the next hop information, each onion layer also contains seed material from which cryptographic keys will actually be derived (for encrypting or decrypting data sent forward or backward on the anonymous connection).

After sending the onion, the initiator's application proxy starts sending data through the established anonymous connection. As data moves through the anonymous connection, each onion router removes one layer of encryption, so it finally arrives as plain text. Obviously, the layering occurs in the reverse order for data moving backward from the receiver to the initiator. Stream ciphers are used for data encryption and decryption. Similar to the original idea of a Chaum mixing network, onion routers may also randomly reorder data items they receive before forwarding them (but preserve the order of data in each anonymous connection).

As mentioned previously and contrary to the original intent of a Chaum mixing network, the batching technique is out of the question for the support of interactive applications, such as HTTP. This means that coordinated observation of the network links connecting onion routers could eventually reveal an anonymous connection's route and leak the source and destination IP addresses accordingly. Therefore, it's important to ensure that the links between the onion routers can't be simultaneously eavesdropped upon. The easiest way to achieve this is to put onion routers on different network segments in different buildings with different administrators—ones who would be unlikely to collude. Also note that by layering cryptographic operations in the way described above, an advantage is gained over conventional-style link layer encryption. Even though the total cryptographic overhead for passing data is the same as for link layer encryption, the protection is better. In link layer encryption, the chain is as strong as the weakest link, and one compromised node can reveal everything. In onion routing, however, the chain is as strong as its strongest link, and one honest onion router is enough to maintain the anonymity of the connection. Even if link layer encryption were used together with end-to-end encryption, compromised nodes could still cooperate to reveal route information. This is not possible in an onion routing network, since data always appears differently to each onion router.

For TCP-based application protocols that are proxy aware, such as HTTP, Telnet, and SMTP, there are application proxies for Sun Solaris. Interestingly, for certain application protocols that are not proxy aware, most notably rlogin, it has been possible to design interface proxies as well. In either case, the best protection results from having a connection between an application proxy and an onion router that is trusted one way or another. For example, one possibility is to place an onion router on the firewall of a corporate intranet. In this case, the onion router would serve as an interface between the machines behind the firewall and the external network (most notably the Internet).

In summary, onion routing is a technology that deserves further study and wider deployment. Unfortunately, the onion router prototype network went off-line in January 2000, so it is not likely that we will see the technology widely deployed on the Internet or WWW anytime soon. Further information about onion routing and the onion router prototype network is available at the onion routing home page.[22]

12.4.5 Freedom network

More recently, a Canadian company called Zero-Knowledge Systems[23] has developed and is marketing a technology that is conceptually similar to onion routing. In fact, Zero-Knowledge Systems has coined the term *Freedom network* to refer to its Chaum mixing network, and the term *Freedom server* to refer to a Chaum mix. The Freedom Network is designed so that each packet is sent through at least three separate Freedom servers, each one operated by a different orgnaizations. It will be interesting to see how successful the Freedom Network will be deployed on the global Internet or WWW.

12.5 Anonymous publishing

The technologies overviewed and discussed so far address the problem of how to protect the privacy of Web users, and how to provide support for anonymous browsing. In this section, we address the problem of how to anonymously publish on the Web. The current WWW architecture provides little support for anonymous publishing. In fact, the architecture fundamentally includes identification information in the URL that is used to locate resources, and it seems difficult to avoid revealing this information (at least if it is required that resources published anonymously be accessible from standard Web browsers without the need of specialized client software or anonymity tools). Also note that the browser privacy problem is orthogonal to the anonymous publishing problem, and that the two problems compose well: if full anonymity is needed, techniques for anonymous browsing must work in tandem with an infrastructure supporting anonymous publishing.

12.5.1 JANUS and the rewebber service

JANUS was a joint research project of the Forschungsinstitut für Telekommunikation (FTK) of Dortmund, Hagen, and Wuppertal in Germany. One of the major results of the project was an anonymous publishing service that was first provided by the Fernuniversität Hagen and later taken over by

---

22. http://www.onion-router.net
23. http://www.zeroknowledge.com

a spin-off company called ISL Internet Sicherheitslösungen GmbH. More recently, the service name was changed from JANUS to Rewebber.[24]

In its current form, the Rewebber service provides anonymity services for both browsers and Web publishers (or Web servers, respectively):

> • In order to provide anonymity services for a browser, the Rewebber service acts as an anonymizing HTTP proxy server. It accepts requests from arbitrary browsers, removes all data that may reveal information about the requesting user, and forwards the requests to the Web servers. Similarly, the servers' responses are relayed back to the appropriate browsers. Furthermore, the Rewebber service supports the SSL/TLS protocol.

> • In order to provide anonymity services for a Web publisher and to support anonymous publishing accordingly, the Rewebber service makes use of encrypted URLs that are part of nested URLs. This is explained in more detail below.

In Section 12.4.1, we elaborated on anonymizing HTTP proxy servers and their ability to process nested URLs. It is important to note at this point that not all parts of a nested URL must be unencrypted. In fact, it is possible to encrypt parts of a nested URL in a way that they can be decryted by the anonymizing HTTP proxy server that processes the nested URL. For example, imagine what happens if the document part in `http://proxy.../http://www.esecurity.ch` would be encrypted. In this case, the document part would look like random data and the resulting nested URL would look like `http://proxy.../url_encrypted/rez73529j63...` In this example, the prefix `url_encrypted` indicates that the string that follows (i.e., `rez73529j63...`) actually refers to an encrypted URL. The anonymizing HTTP proxy server (serving the request) would then take the appropriate cryptographic key to decrypt the relevant parts of the encrypted URL and retrieve the corresponding resource from the Web server, accordingly. In our example, the anonymizing HTTP proxy server would decrypt `rez73529j63...` and retrieve the requested resource from `http://www.esecurity.ch`. If the resource contained some URLs, these URLs would also have to be encrypted before the response is returned back to the browser. Obviously, URL rewriting techniques can be used at this point.

Note that URL decryption must only be possible for the anonymizing HTTP proxy server, whereas URL encryption needs to be possible for

---

24. The service is currently available at `www.rewebber.com`.

everybody. Consequently, URL encryption and decryption look like a suitable application for public key cryptography.[25] Consequently, the Rewebber service holds an RSA public key pair that is used to encrypt and decrypt URLs. The public key is published and documented, for example, in the Rewebber service's FAQ document.

In some literature, anonymizing HTTP proxy servers holding a public key pair that can also be used to transparently encrypt and decrypt URLs are also called *rewebbers*. Similarly, the encrypted parts of URLs are called *locators*. These terms are also used in the remaining part of this chapter.

In summary, rewebbers (like, for example, the one provided by the Rewebber service) provide a simple but efficient way to provide support for anonymous publishing on the Web. There are, however, at least three limitations and shortcomings that should be kept in mind when one considers the use of this technology:

1. A rewebber provider must be trusted not to reveal unencryted or decrypted URLs.

2. Web publishers must make available and somehow publish encrypted URLs (i.e., URLs that are encrypted with the public key of the Rewebber service).

3. Users must enter encrypted URLs.

These limitations and shortcomings are addressed in a more sophisticated technology that is overviewed and briefly discussed next.

12.5.2 TAZ servers and the rewebber network

Two researchers at the University of California at Berkeley generalized the use of rewebbers and developed a technology that employs rewebber chains in a so-called rewebber network and a mechanism to resolve logical names of resources into encrypted URLs to anonymously publish on the Web [16].

Let us assume that there is a rewebber network (i.e., a network consisting of rewebbers), and that the public keys of the rewebbers are publicly available in some certified form. Let's further assume that—in order to make traffic analysis more difficult—the rewebbers transparently encrypt

---

25. Note, however, that URL encryption need not be possible for everybody. One could also think about a system in which URLs are sent over an SSL/TLS connection to a server that dynamically encrypts them. In this case, URL encryption and decryption could also be implemented with secret key cryptography.

and decrypt files using a secret key cryptosystem. In the prototype implementation, a DES version called DESX[26] is used.

If a Web publisher wants to anonymously publish a resource (e.g., an HTML file) on the Web, he or she randomly selects a chain of rewebbers $R_1, R_2, \ldots, R_n$ leading from the browser to the Web server that holds and makes available the file, as well as a set of n DESX keys. He or she then uses the DESX keys and the rewebbers' public keys to constructs a nested URL. Formally speaking, the nested URLs may look as follows:

$$http://R_1/\{K_{R_1}, http://R_2/\{K_{R_2}, \ldots http://R_n/\{K_{R_n}, URL\}k_{R_n} \ldots\}k_{R_2}\}k_{R_1} (12.2)$$

In this formula, each R_i $(1 \leq i \leq n)$ refers to a rewebber. According to the last layer, the nested URL is first sent to the rewebber (i.e., R_1). This rewebber uses its private key (i.e., $k_{R_1}^{-1}$) to decrypt $\{K_{R_1}, http://R_2/\{K_{R_2}, \ldots http://R_n/\{K_{R_n}, URL\}k_{R_n} \ldots\}k_{R_2}\}$ and the result is split into two parts.

- The first part (i.e., K_{R_1}) is stored to later decrypt any data that is sent back from the Web server.

- The second part (i.e., $http://R_2/\{K_{R_2}, \ldots http://R_n/\{K_{R_n}, URL\} k_{R_n} \ldots\}k_{R_2}$) is sent to the next rewebber in the chain (i.e., R_2).

Similar to R_1, R_2 decrypts the message with its private key (i.e., $k_{R_2}^{-1}$) and splits the result into two parts. The first part (i.e., K_{R_2}) is stored to later decrypt any data that is sent back from the Web server, and the second part is sent to the next rewebber in the chain. This continues until R_n finally decrypts K_{R_n} and URL. Once more, K_{R_n} is stored to later decrypt any data that is sent back from the Web server, and the resource referenced with URL is retrieved from this Web server. On the reverse path from the Web server back to the requesting browser, the multiple-encrypted resource is decrypted with each $K_{R_i}(1 \leq i \leq n)$ by the corresponding rewebber.

Rewebber chains and networks have the advantage that they don't make it necessary that there be a single rewebber that is ultimatively trusted. Instead, in a rewebber chain only the rewebber closest to the browser ever sees the decrypted data, and only the rewebber closest to the server knows from where it is really getting data. In order to link the two, the cooperation of every rewebber in the chain would be necessary. This avoids the existence

---

26. The DESX encryption algorithm refers to a technique intended to extend the strength of DES that was originally proposed by Ronald L. Rivest.

of a single point of failure, and allows the distribution of trust throughout a network.

Since a rewebber network makes heavy use of URL encryption and locators, the above-mentioned problems of how to publish encrypted URLs and how to make users type them in correctly occur immediately. One possible solution to these problems is the creation of a logical namespace combined with a machanism to automatically resolve a logical name into an encrypted URL. The resolution mechanisms can be implemented by special servers. In [16], the logical namespace is represented by a new top level domain .taz (TAZ standing for "temporary autonomous zone") and the servers are called *TAZ servers*. Consequently, the function of a TAZ server is to offer publishers an easy way to point potential readers to their material, as well as offering readers an easy way to access it. A TAZ server consists essentially of a public database mapping virtual hostnames ending in .taz to locators for rewebbers. The emphasis on *public* is to stress that nothing in this database must be kept secret. Unlike an anonymous remailer like anon.penet.fi (which associates an alias e-mail address with a real one), TAZ servers merely associate .taz addresses with locators. Most importantly, the TAZ server administrator cannot decrypt the locators that are stored in the database. These facts are essential to building trust.

12.5.3 Publius

More recently, a group of researchers from AT&T Research and New York University designed and developed a "robust, tamper-evident and censorship-resistant" Web publishing system named *Publius*[27] [17].

In short, the Publius system consists of Web publishers (people who want to anonymously publish static content[28] on the Web), Web servers that host random-looking content, and retrievers who browse the Publius system. There is a static, system-wide list of available servers.

Any content published with the Publius system is encrypted by the publisher and spread over some Web servers. More specifically, the publisher randomly chooses a key K from a secret key cryptosystem and encrypts the content with this key. In addition, he or she splits the key K into n shares,

---

27. Publius was the pen name used by the authors of the *Federalist Papers*, Alexander Hamilton, John Jay, and James Madison. This collection of 85 articles, published pseudonymously in New York State newspapers form October 1787 through May 1788, was influential in convincing New York voters to ratify the proposed United States constitution.
28. In its current form, the Publius system does not provide support for dynamicaly created content.

such that any k of them can reproduce the original key K, but $k - 1$ give no hints as to the key. There are cryptographic schemes known as *secret-sharing schemes* that can be used for this purpose (e.g., [18]). Each selected Web server then receives the encrypted Publius content and one of the shares. At this point, the server has no idea what it is hosting; it simply stores some random looking data. To browse content, a retriever must get the encrypted Publius content from some server and k of the shares. This retrieval step is also supported by the Publius system in a way that is transparent to the user. More information about the system is available at `http://cs1.cs.nyu.edu/~waldman/publius.html`.

12.6 Voluntary privacy standards

Given the current situation on the Internet and WWW, many people have the feeling that their privacy is silently going away. In this situation, there are two classes of people:

▸ On the one hand, there are people who argue that government regulation is needed.

▸ On the other hand, there are people who argue that industry-regulated privacy standards are needed (mainly because government regulation tends to be too rigid, too costly to implement, and more difficult to repeal).

Industry-regulated privacy standards look particularly promising. Without government regulation, however, these privacy standards will always be voluntary. The most important voluntary privacy standards refer to privacy seals and P3P. They are briefly overviewed and discussed next.

12.6.1 Privacy seals

In short, the idea of a *privacy seal* is to have an independent organization or company act as a trusted party that looks at the privacy practices of a Web site and decides whether the site conforms to a given set of criteria. Only if the site conforms to the criteria, is it allowed to display the corresponding privacy seal. The criteria differ in details. Most of them, however, require that a privacy policy be posted, and that—according to this policy—consumers be informed about the personal information that is being collected and how it will be used. As of this writing, there are two privacy seals that are widely deployed on the WWW: BBBOnLine and

TRUSTe. In addition, there is an increasingly large number of privacy seals and programs that compete for market share.[29]

12.6.1.1 BBBOnLine

In the U.S., the Council of Better Business Bureaus has a long tradition serving as a standard-bearer for reliability and as a vehicle for consumer complaints. More recently, the Council of Better Business Bureaus founded a subsidiary named *BBBOnLine*[30] to promote trust and confidence on the Internet. BBBOnline, in turn, launched the BBBOnline Privacy seal and the corresponding privacy program.

12.6.1.2 TRUSTe

According to its Web site,[31] *TRUSTe* is an independent, nonprofit organization dedicated to establishing a trusting environment where users can feel comfortable dealing with companies on the Internet. The organization was founded in 1997 by the Electronic Frontier Foundation (EFF[32]) and the CommerceNet Consortium.[33]

The privacy seal of TRUSTe is also known as trustmark [19]. It is awarded to Web sites that adhere to established privacy principles and agree to comply with TRUSTe's oversight and consumer resolution process. A displayed trustmark signifies to on-line users "that the Web site will openly share, at a minimum, what personal information is being gathered, how it will be used, with whom it will be shared, and whether the user has an option to control its dissemination." Based on such disclosure, users can make informed decisions about whether or not to release their personally identifiable information (e.g. credit-card numbers) to the Web site.

12.6.2 P3P

In addition to the increasingly large numer of privacy seals, the W3C launched the *Platform for Privacy Preferences Project* (P3P[34]) to provide a platform for trusted and informed online interactions [20]. The idea is that a

---

29. Two examples are the Gold Privacy Seal (http://www.goldprivacyseal.com) and the site Guardian Privacy Seal (http://www.siteguardian.org/guardian.nsf/sealinfo!OpenPage).
30. http://www.bbbonline.com
31. http://www.truste.org
32. http://www.eff.org
33. http://www.commercenet.com
34. http://www.w3.org/P3P

Web site may publish and make available a privacy statement in a format that is readable and understandable by a browser. The browser, in turn, can be configured to automatically decide whether it agrees with the privacy statement, and whether it wants to provide information to the Web site accordingly. To make this possible, P3P provides a formal language that the browser and Web site can use to talk to each another. As such, P3P is conceptually similar to PICS as discussed in Section 14.3. (in fact, P3P can also be seen as an outgrowth of PICS). There is some industry support for P3P. Most importantly, Microsoft Internet Explorer version 6.0 provides limited support for P3P.[35]

In spite of the fact that P3P provides an interesting technology that is also being adapted by the industry, it remains a voluntary privacy standard that is difficult to enforce. How do you, for example, enforce that all Web sites publish P3P statements, that the sites play by the rules, and that the P3P statements they publish correspond to the truth? Note that anybody can claim (in a P3P statement or using another language) that he or she plays by the rules. The difficult question is to decide whether this claim is justified. P3P is not particularly helpful in making this decision.

12.7 Conclusions

In this chapter, we addressed the increasingly important field of privacy protection and anonymity services. More specifically, we overviewed and discussed some *privacy enhancing technologies* (PETs) that can be used to anonymously browse through the Web and/or anonymously publish on the Web, as well as some voluntary privacy standards (i.e., privacy seals and P3P). Unfortunately, it is not clear what technologies and/or standards will be used and widely deployed in the future. In fact, the handling of personal information is a hotly debated topic. The need to maximize users' privacy is at odds at a fundamental level with businesses' need to minimize fraud. The first goal seeks to maximize users' anonymity, whereas the second goal requires users to be strongly and unequivocally identified and authenticated. Somehow, a compromise must be struck for this dilemma. As of this writing, this compromise has not been found yet.

Last but not least, it's important to note that many countries have data privacy or data protection laws that make it a legal obligation for people

---

35. Microsoft Internet Explorer's P3P implementation is controlled through the Privacy tab of the Internet Options control panel. Support is limited, because it mainly addresses the use of cookies.

storing, processing, and transmitting personal data to adequately protect the privacy of the data. This is particularly true for European countries. In fact, the European Commission's Directive on Data Protection went into effect in October 1998, and prohibits the transfer of personal data to non-European Union nations that do not meet the European adequacy standard for privacy protection. While the U.S. and the European Union share the goal of enhancing privacy protection for their citizens, the United States takes a different approach to privacy from that taken by the European Union. The United States uses a sectoral approach that relies on a mix of legislation, regulation, and self-regulation. The European Union, however, relies on comprehensive legislation that, for example, requires creation of government data protection agencies, registration of databases with those agencies, and in some instances prior approval before personal data processing may begin. As a result of these different privacy approaches, the Directive could have significantly hampered the ability of U.S. companies to engage in many trans-Atlantic transactions. In order to bridge these different privacy approaches and provide a streamlined means for U.S. organizations to comply with the Directive, the U.S. Department of Commerce (DoC) in consultation with the European Commission developed a *safe harbor* framework. The framework is an important way for U.S. companies to avoid experiencing interruptions in their business dealings with the EU or facing prosecution by European authorities under European privacy laws. As of this writing, it is too early to tell whether the safe harbor framework will be successfully deployed on the marketplace.

References

[1]	Oppliger, R., "Privacy Protection and Anonymity Services for the World Wide Web (WWW)," *Future Generation Computer Systems (FGCS)*, Vol. 16, Issue 4, February 2000, pp. 379–391.

[2]	Rotenberg, M., *The Privacy Law Sourcebook 2001: United States Law, International Law, and Recent Developments*, Electronic Privacy Information Center (EPIC), 2001.

[3]	Garfinkel, S., and D. Russell, *Database Nation: The Death of Privacy in the 21st Century*, Sebastopol, CA: O'Reilly & Associates, 2001.

[4]	Shirey, R., "Internet Security Glossary," Request for Comments 2828, May 2000.

[5]	Pfitzmann, A., and M. Waidner, "Networks Without User Observability," *Computers & Security*, Vol. 2, No. 6, pp. 158–166.

[6]   Chaum, D., "Untraceable Electronic Mail, Return Addresses and Digital Pseudonyms," *Communications of the ACM*, Vol. 24, No. 2, February 1981, pp. 84–88.

[7]   Cülcü, C., and G. Tsudik, "Mixing Emails with BABEL," *Proceedings of ISOC Symposium on Network and Distributed System Security*, February 1996, pp. 2–16.

[8]   Kristol, D. M., and L. Montulli, *HTTP State Management Mechanism*, Request for Comments (RFC) 2965, October 2000.

[9]   Kristol, D. M., "HTTP Cookies: Standards, Privacy, and Politics," *ACM Transactions on Internet Technology*, Vol. 1, No. 2, November 2001, pp. 151–198.

[10]   Luotonen, A., *Web Proxy Servers*, Upper Saddle River, NJ: Prentice Hall, 1998.

[11]   Reiter, M. K., and A. D. Rubin, "Crowds: Anonymity for Web Transactions," *ACM Transactions on Information and System Security*, Vol. 1, No. 1, 1998.

[12]   Reiter, M. K., and A. D. Rubin, "Anonymous Web Transactions with Crowds," *Communications of the ACM*, Vol. 42, No. 2, February 1999, pp. 32–38.

[13]   Reiter, M. K., "Distributing Trust with the Rampart Toolkit," *Communications of the ACM*, Vol. 39, No. 4, April 1996, pp. 71–74.

[14]   Syverson, P. F., M. G. Reed, and D. M. Goldschlag, "Private Web Browsing," *Journal of Computer Security, Special Issue on Web Security*, Vol. 5, No. 3, 1997, pp. 237–248.

[15]   Goldschlag, D. M., M. G. Reed, and P. F. Syverson, "Onion Routing for Anonymous and Private Internet Connections," *Communications of the ACM*, Vol. 42, No. 2, 1999, pp. 39–41.

[16]   Goldberg, I., and D. Wagner, "TAZ Servers and the Rewebber Network: Enabling Anonymous Publishing on the World Wide Web," *First Monday* (electronic journal), Vol. 3, No 4, available on-line at `http://www.rstmonday.dk/issues/issue3_4/goldberg/index.html`.

[17]   Waldman, M., A. D. Rubin, and L. F. Cranor, "Publius, A Robust, Tamper-Evident and Censorship-Resistant Web Publishing System," *Proceedings of 9th USENIX Security Symposium*, August 2000.

[18]   Shamir, A., "How To Share a Secret," *Communications of the ACM*, Vol. 22, 1979, pp. 612–613.

[19]   Benassi, P., "TRUSTe: An Online Privacy Seal Program," *Communications of the ACM*, Vol. 42, No. 2, February 1999, pp. 56–59.

[20]   Reagle, J., and L. F. Cranor, "The Platform for Privacy Preferences," *Communications of the ACM*, Vol. 42, No. 2, February 1999, pp. 48–55.

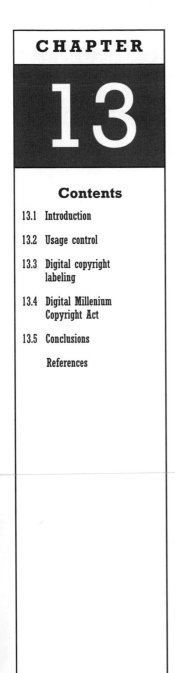

CHAPTER

13

Contents

13.1 Introduction

13.2 Usage control

13.3 Digital copyright labeling

13.4 Digital Millenium Copyright Act

13.5 Conclusions

References

Intellectual Property Protection

In the digital world we live in today, intellectual copyright protection is becoming an increasingly important topic. This is because digital data is particularly simple to copy and redistribute (or resell) without any loss of quality. In this chapter, we address intellectual copyright protection. More specifically, we introduce the topic in Section 13.1, elaborate on usage control and digital copyright labeling techniques in Section 13.2 and 13.3, overview and briefly discuss the U.S. Digital Millennium Copyright Act (DMCA) in Section 13.4, and draw some conclusions in Section 13.5. Note that this chapter only provides a brief introduction and overview about the topic, and that additional and complementary resources are necessary to work in this area.

13.1 Introduction

Intellectual property protection is a legitimate goal. The need for intellectual copyright protection has been around since the creation of technologies that allow anybody to make copies of specific content [1]. Three examples from the analog world illustrate this point:

1. The invention of the printing press was followed by concerns regarding the need for intellectual copyright protection. Note that the printing press provided

the ability to produce multiple copies of a document at relatively low cost (as compared to the value of the document being copied). Fortunately, piracy of documents by way of printing press could easily be stopped because of the effort that was required, the special equipment that was needed, and the fact that the resulting copies were not exactly the same as the original documents.

2. The invention of various recording technologies for audio and video streams was followed by concerns regarding the need for intellectual copyright protection. In the case of vinyl records, making copies also required special equipment, and copies were not as good as the original records (sometimes this argument was also used to promote special editions). With the advent of magnetic tape (for both audio and video recording), however, the piracy potential increased tremendously, mainly because the copying effort was small and the equipment was ubiquitous. Fortunately (at least from the content provider's point of view), the barrier to widespread piracy of such content is the progressively degraded quality of the content with each generation of copies. A copy of a copy of a copy of an original item contains all the noise and defects introduced and amplified at each step.

3. The possibility to make photostatic copies of paper documents has also caused some concerns regarding the need for copyright protection. Again, even the highest-quality copy of a document is degraded, or at least changed, because in some cases photocopiers make things more readable, increase contrast, or introduce other improvements that are nonetheless changes from the original document.

Today, the same thing happens to technologies that allow anybody to make copies of digital data. Digital data, in turn, may encode anything (e.g., text, graphics, images, audio, video, or software) and the technologies to copy the data remain the same in either case. In fact, the digital representation and distribution of data has increased the potential for misuse and theft, and has significantly intensified the problems associated with copyright protection and enforcing these rights. The problems are rooted from the intrinsic characteristics of digital data, namely that making and distributing a copy is easy, inexpensive, and fast, and that each copy is identical to the original.

The market for digital data is expected to grow very rapidly. Today, we see digital photographs, MP3 music files, DVD movies, pay TV, electronic books (e-books), and many other things that are marketed and deployed on a global scale. In the future, it is expected that anything that carries information will be digitized and sold in digital form. According to [2], the market for digital media is projected to be in the billions of dollars per year. This number may not be precise, but it may give a feeling about the scale.

Against this background, content providers and distributors of digital data are afraid of online services, and they are looking for technical approaches to address the challenge of intellectual copyright protection and enforcing these rights. In fact, intellectual copyright protection has found increased attention on electronic marketplaces, such as the WWW.

There are basically two technical approaches to address the challenge of intellectual copyright protection:

1. *Usage control* requires some hardware or software that is able to control the usage of the protected material. More specifically, it means that any usage of the protected material, such as viewing, playing, or printing, must be controlled and approved by authorized rendering hardware or software.

2. *Digital watermarking techniques* embed digital marks into protected material to designate copyright-related information, such as origin, owner, content, or recipient. These marks can then be used to identify the legitimate owner of the intellectual property, and to enforce his or her copyrights.

The two approaches are not mutually exclusive and complement each other. They are overviewed and briefly discussed next. Of course, they both require a legal framework that makes it an offence to circumvent (or try to circumvent) any technology put in place. This is particularly true for digital watermarking technologies. Also, this is where the DMCA comes into play.

13.2 Usage control

As mentioned above, usage control requires some hardware or software that is able to control and approve the usage of the protected material. In the past, the computer and software industries have developed and deployed many technologies that are based on usage control. For example, we all remember the ongoing competition between software vendors trying to protect their software products with new and innovative protection schemes on the one hand, and software pirates trying to bypass or circumvent the schemes on the other. A similar competition is going on between pay TV companies that scramble or encrypt data streams and pirates trying to illegitimately descramble or decrypt the data streams. More recently, the DVD industry has developed, implemented, and deployed a Contents Scramble System (CSS) that allows them to protect films distributed on DVDs. In 1999, the 15-year-old Jon Johansen created the DeCSS program so that he could view CSS-protected DVDs on a Linux machine. In fact, DeCSS was published as part of an open source development project to build Linux DVD players called LiViD, or Linux Video. More recently, several CSS Descramblers have become available and you may refer to `http://www.cs.cmu.edu/~dst/DeCSS/Gallery` for a corresponding overview.

All of these examples suggest that usage control is seldom successful and even more seldom successfully deployed on the large scale.[1] Nevertheless, many people intuitively think that usage control is a powerful technology that can be very strong and made difficult to bypass or circumvent. For example, usage control was also recommended by the Working Group on Intellectual Property Rights for the U.S. National Information Infrastructure in 1995 [3]. Unfortunately, usage control has many (legal and practical) problems, and most of these problems are related to the restrictive nature of usage control.

In theory, there are many possibilities to design, implement, and deploy technologies for usage control on the WWW. For example, a technology could use a PICS-like rating scheme specifically designed for intellectual property protection. As of this writing, however, there is neither such a scheme available, nor any publicly announced plans to standardize such a scheme. Another technology could use proprietary software modules that implement usage control. For example, a few years ago a group of IBM researchers developed a usage control scheme that was intended to be used to sell copyrighted material on the WWW [4]. The material would be packaged in a so-called *cryptolope*, and this cryptolope could only be opened by a helper application that controls operations, such as save, print, copy, and view. Similar work is reported in [5]. Unfortunately, such technologies make it difficult to use commercial off-the-shelf software on the user side. Against this background, it is not likely that we will see usage control on the WWW widely deployed anytime soon.

---

1. Many other examples can be found in Bruce Schneier's monthly newsletter *Crypto-Gram* (`http://www.counterpane.com/crypto-gram.html`).

13.3   Digital copyright labeling

Instead of trying to restrict and control the usage of some copyright protected material, one may also allow its unlimited copying and use, but make sure that some copyright-related information is available to anybody who cares and who is interested in the legitimate ownership of the intellectual property. This is where *digital copyright labeling techniques* or *digital watermarking* technologies come into play.

13.3.1   Introduction

In the real world, the term *watermarking* refers to a technique that can be used to impress into paper a specific text or image mark (called a *watermark*). From daily life, we are all familiar with watermarks of varying degrees of visibility that may be added to presentation media as a guarantee of authenticity, quality, and ownership.

Similarly, in the digital world, the term *digital watermarking* refers to a technique that can be used to impress into digital data a specific text, image mark or label. Quite naturally, such a mark or label is called a *digital watermark.* The aim of a digital watermark is to embed a digital mark into protected material to designate copyright-related information, such as origin, owner, content, or recipient. Unlike usage control, digital copyright labeling does not limit the number of copies allowed, but may deter people from illegal copying by allowing the determination of the legitimate owner of the protected material and the corresponding copyright (in the case of ownership labeling), or by allowing an illegitimately redistributed copy to be traced back to its original recipient (in the case of recipient labeling). Consequently, digital copyright labels may provide evidence for copyright infringements after the event. They may also serve as a kind of deterrent to illicit copying and dissemination by making the misuse of protected material traceable and providing evidence of illegal acts accordingly. Note that the use of digital copyright labeling techniques also requires a legal system that allows the copyright holders to sue people who breach their rights. Also note that the use of digital copyright labeling techniques is not contrary to usage control; it is, rather, complementary by providing another defense against misbehavior on the protected material that may have escaped from the domain of usage control. More specifically, digital copyright labeling techniques may also be used by sophisticated usage control technologies to encode control information into the digital data streams.

In general, there are two types of labels for identifying and protecting copyrights as related to multimedia documents:

1. A document can be marked with a label that uniquely identifies the copyright holder (*ownership labeling*).

2. A document can be marked in a manner that allows its distribution to be uniquely traced (*recipient labeling*).

In the literature, ownership labels are often referred to as watermarks, whereas recipient labels are often referred to as *fingerprints*. Consequently, fingerprinting a document means introducing individual marks into each copy sold or distributed that make the copy unique. This is similar to the way fingerprints make people unique [6]. Once an illegal copy turns up, the content provider can see from the fingerprint which of the original copies was illegally redistributed. Consequently, the corresponding party can be sued for having illegitimately redistributed his or her copy.

Although digital copyright labeling is relatively new as a means of protecting intellectual property rights, the theories and techniques behind it have been around for quite a long time. Refer to [7, 8] for a comprehensive overview about the theories and techniques that can be used for digital watermarking. By applying multiplexing techniques as in data communications, some digital watermarking techniques can also be used to embed multiple marks (watermarks or fingerprints) and extract them separately. This feature will be important for identifying ownership and other intellectual property rights in works composed of many copyright assets, such as multimedia documents and presentations, as well as groupware and workflow documents.

The specific requirements of each watermarking technique may vary with the application, and there is no universal watermarking technique that satisfies all requirements for all applications. Consequently, each watermarking technique has to be designed within the context of the entire system in which it is being deployed. There are several parameters that are used to categorize watermarking techniques. The resulting categories are briefly overviewed next.

13.3.2 Categories of watermarking techniques

In this subsection we briefly overview some categories of watermarking techniques that apply for images. Other forms of multimedia documents, such as audio or video, generally require watermarking techniques that can be categorized according to slightly different criteria.

13.3.2.1 Visible and invisible watermarks

A digital watermark can be visible or invisible:

> ▸ A *visible digital watermark* is intended to be perceptible by the user. As such, it typically contains a visual message or a company logo indicating ownership of the image.

> ▸ Contrary to that, an *invisible digital watermark* is intended to be imperceptible but is detected or extracted by an appropriate piece of software. Consequently, an invisibly watermarked image is similar but not identical to the original unmarked image.

Users prefer to have a watermarked document behave no differently and suffer no perceptible quality degradation from the original. Consequently, users generally prefer invisibly watermarked images.

13.3.2.2 Fragile and robust watermarks

A digital watermark can be fragile or robust:

> ▸ A *fragile digital watermark* is generally corrupted by any (image-processing) transformation. For example, watermarks for image integrity checks, in which a change must be detected or spatially localized, are necessarily fragile.

> ▸ Contrary to that, a *robust digital watermark* resists common (image-processing) transformations. More precisely, the watermark that is embedded in the data must be recoverable despite intentional or unintentional modifications of the image. For example, a watermark technique for images should be robust against such image-processing operations as filtering, requantization, dithering, scaling, and cropping.

Robustness is a key requirement often imposed by applications. For example, watermarks that are used for ownership assertion should be robust. Unfortunately, the requirements of truly robust watermarks are difficult to meet in practice, and the development of robust watermarking techniques is a difficult problem. In fact, a single technique satisfying all requirements imposed on robust watermarking is quite difficult to achieve and is the subject of current research and development.

13.3.2.3 Public and private watermarks

A digital watermark can be public or private:

▸ A *public digital watermark* can be detected and read by anyone not having access to certain secret information. All the user needs is an appropriate detector software.

▸ Contrary to that, a *private digital watermark* can only be detected and read by someone who has access to an appropriate detector software and certain secret information, such as a pass phrase, a pseudorandom number generator seed, or the original image.

Obviously, private digital watermarking techniques are superior, from a security point of view. The secret information improves security but also renders detection of the watermark difficult or impossible without the secret information. This information must be communicated and distributed to a user or third party via secure channels if the watermark detection process is not always carried out by the image owner. Thus, a private watermarking scheme cannot be used for annotation or to inform a potential user of its proprietary status; only the content owner has the secret information that is required to detect the watermark. With a private scheme, the watermark can be used only to demonstrate ownership of content once its owner discovers its illicit use. Contrary to that, public watermarking techniques are attractive for many applications. For example, if we want to detect copyright violations in an image archive or in images published on the Web, we can use mobile agents, such as Webcrawlers, to perform identity checks for as many images as we can locate. Private watermarking techniques that require the original or a reference image in the watermarking detection procedure are less suitable for such applications (they require the mobile agents to locally store images).

Depending on whether secret or public keys are used for private digital watermarking, secret key and public key watermarking techniques may be distinguished (similar to secret and public key cryptography):

▸ A *secret key digital watermarking technique* uses the same user key for watermark insertion and extraction or detection. Consequently, secret key digital watermarking schemes require secure communication channels between the image owner and the image receiver, or user, to pass the keying information.

▸ Contrary to that, a *public key digital watermarking technique* uses separate keys for watermark insertion and extraction or detection. A private key is known only by the image owner and is typically used for watermark insertion, whereas a public key is known to everybody and is typically used for watermark extraction or detection.

Public key digital watermarking techniques are particularly important for digital fingerprinting and traitor tracing for broadcast encryption [9 – 11].

13.3.3 Attacks

The proponents of digital copyright labeling have made broad claims regarding the security of their watermarking techniques, often without specifying which attacks they are expected to survive. Many of these claims have been disproved. In fact, some recent analytical results show that for many watermarking techniques, removal is not a difficult problem [12]. Consequently, it is required that a terminology similar to the one used in cryptanalysis is developed for the analysis of watermarking techniques.

According to [13], there are four classes of possible attacks against watermarking techniques:

1. *Robustness attacks* aim to diminish or remove the presence of a mark in a watermarked image without harming the image beyond rendering it useless. Typical signal-processing attacks revolve around commonly used operations, such as data compression, filtering, resizing, printing, and scanning. An example is the collusion attack, in which differently watermarked versions of the same image are combined to generate a new image, thereby reducing the overall strength of the watermark.

2. *Presentation attacks* are slightly different from robustness attacks in the sense that they don't necessarily remove the mark from the watermarked image. Instead, the image is manipulated so that the detector can't find the mark anymore. An exemplary presentation attack was developed at Cambridge University to foil automated Webcrawlers. The attack involves chopping a watermarked image into small parts that are then reassembled on a Web page with appropriate HTML tags. A Webcrawler sees only the individual image blocks, which are too small to contain any watermark. Obviously, this attack causes no image quality degradation, as the pixel values are preserved.

3. In some watermarking schemes, the mark's detected presence can have multiple interpretations. Consequently, an attacker can

engineer a situation that neutralizes the strength of any evidence of ownership presented. Against this background, *interpretation attacks* aim to forge invalid or multiple interpretations from watermark evidence. For example, an attacker can attempt to introduce another watermark in an already watermarked image, thereby creating an ownership deadlock. Typically, such an attack requires in-depth analysis of the specific watermarking technique under attack.

4. Finally, *legal attacks* go beyond the technical merits or scientific evidence presented by watermarking techniques. As such, they make use of existing and future legislation on copyright laws and digital information ownership, the different interpretations of the law in various jurisdictions, the credibility of the owner and of the attacker, and the ability of an attacker to cast doubt on the watermarking scheme in the courtroom.

Understanding these attacks may help propose watermarking techniques that are more robust not only in the strength of their marks but also in their ability to guard against possible attacks. In either case, it is not known today whether the design and implementation of digital watermarks that are sufficiently robust against attacks is feasible at all.

13.4 Digital Millenium Copyright Act

Usage control and digital watermarking techniques do not provide a complete solution to the problems of intellectual property protection in the digital world. Consequently, many content providers and vendors started to lobby Congress for protective legislation during the 1990s. The effort resulted in the *Digital Millennium Copyright Act* (DMCA) that passed the Congress on October 12, 1998.[2] Two weeks later, the President of the United States signed the Act into law.[3]

The DMCA was originally designed to implement the Copyright Treaty[4] that was signed in December 1996 at a World Intellectual Property Organization (WIPO) conference held in Geneva. However, the DMCA goes far beyond the requirements of the WIPO, and adds criminal and civil provisions against the development, sale, trafficking, or even discussion of

---

2. http://www.loc.gov/copyright/legislation/hr2281.pdf
3. The DMCA was signed by the former President Clinton.
4. The text of the WIPO Copyright Treaty is available, for example, at http://www.gseis.ucla.edu/iclp/ wipo1.html.

methods and tools to reverse-engineer or circumvent any technology used to protect copyright. As an effect on the DMCA, it is no longer possible in the academic community to openly study and discuss usage control and digital watermarking technologies.

As of this writing, the DMCA is under legal challenge in several U.S. courts. Grounds for the challenges include the claim that it imposes prior restraint on speech and writing, which is a violation of the First Amendment to the U.S. Constitution. Nevertheless, the DMCA has strong influence on other countries, and many governments are trying to put in place similar legislation.

13.5 Conclusions

With the ongoing digitization of data and data streams on the WWW, intellectual property protection is becoming an increasingly important topic and field of study. In this chapter, we overviewed and briefly discussed usage control and digital copyright labeling. Both technological approaches are not complete in the sense that they solve all problems related to intellectual property protection. Consequently, there is room for alternative or complementary technologies and the entire field is open for research and development.

As of this writing, digital copyright labeling techniques and digital watermarks look particularly promising. Though commercial use has begun, there are still some barriers preventing digital copyright labeling techniques and digital watermarks from becoming effective and widespread. The major technical challenge is to develop a foolproof protection system while keeping the copyright labels hidden. Absolute robustness is impossible, but there is much room for improvement. None of the existing systems can claim that their labels will survive all major signal-processing operations and transformations. Like cryptography, this technology will be useful as long as it makes tampering with or removing labels a time-consuming and costly task. Just as DNA tests did in order to be accepted as legal evidence in court, digital copyright labeling techniques must establish their status in the legal system in order to fulfill their mission. As of this writing, the legal status of digital watermarking is still untested, and therefore unresolved. It took more than 20 years for the digital signature to establish itself as common commercial practice and inspire legislative action after the concept was first published, so there may be a long way to go. In fact, the question of how long we have to wait for digital watermarks and fingerprints to be adopted legally and socially remains to be answered [14].

References

[1]   Acken, J. M., "How Watermarking Adds Value to Digital Content," *Communications of the ACM*, Vol. 41, No. 7, July 1998, pp. 75–77.

[2]   Garfinkel, S., with E. H. Spafford, *Web Security, Privacy & Commerce, Second Edition*, Sebastopol, CA: O'Reilly & Associates, 2001.

[3]   Lehman, B. A., and R. H. Brown, *Intellectual Property and the National Information Infrastructure*, Report of the Working Group on Intellectual Property Rights, Section C, Part II, 1995.

[4]   Lotspiech, J., U. Kohl, and M. A. Kaplan, "Cryptographic Envelopes and Digital Library," IBM Research Report RJ 10069, 1997.

[5]   von Faber, E., E. Hammelrath, and F. P. Heider, "The Secure Distribution of Digital Contents," *Proceedings of Annual Computer Security Applications Conference (ACSAC '97)*, December 1997, pp. 16–22.

[6]   Wagner, N. R., "Fingerprinting," *Proceedings of the IEEE Symposium on Security and Privacy*, 1983, pp. 18–22.

[7]   Petitcolas, F., and S. Katzenbeisser (Eds.), *Information Hiding Techniques for Steganography and Digital Watermarking*, Norwood, MA: Artech House, 2000.

[8]   Bloom, J., M. Miller, and I. Cox, *Digital Watermarking*, San Francisco, CN: Morgan Kaufmann Publishers, 2001.

[9]   Pfitzmann, B., and M. Schunter, "Asymmetric Fingerprinting," *Proceedings of EUROCRYPT '96*, pp. 84–95.

[10] Chor, B., A. Fiat, and M. Naor, "Tracing Traitors," *Proceedings of EUROCRYPT '94*, pp. 257–270.

[11] Pfitzmann, B., "Trials of Traced Traitors," *Proceedings of Workshop on Information Hiding*, 1996, pp. 49–64.

[12] Craver, S., et al., "Resolving Rightful Ownership with Invisible Watermarking Techniques: Limitations, Attacks, and Implications," *IEEE Journal on Selected Areas in Communications*, Vol. 16, No. 4, May 1998, pp. 573–586.

[13] Craver, S., B.-L. Yeo, and M. Yeung, "Technical Trials and Legal Tribulations," *Communications of the ACM*, Vol. 41, No. 7, July 1998, pp. 45–54.

[14] Zhao, J., E. Koch, and C. Luo, "In Business Today and Tomorrow," *Communications of the ACM*, Vol. 41, No. 7, July 1998, pp. 67–72.

CHAPTER

14

Contents

14.1 Introduction

14.2 Content blocking

14.3 Content rating and self-determination

14.4 Conclusions

References

Censorship on the WWW

In this chapter, we address censorship on the Internet and WWW. In particular, we introduce the topic in Section 14.1, address two technical approaches—content blocking as well as content rating and self-determination—in Sections 14.2 and Section 14.3, and draw some conclusions in Section 14.4. By doing so, we are going to stay on the technical side and not delve into the (sometimes heated) discussions about the political and legal justification for censorship on the Internet and WWW. These discussions are going on in almost every country that is connected (or is about to connect) to the Internet. You may refer to [1, 2] for a discussion about the legal considerations and implications of censorship.

14.1 Introduction

Nowadays, the Internet in general, and the WWW in particular, is often criticized for providing an information infrastructure that can also be (mis)used for the distribution of content that is illegal or offensive, such as propagandistic material from the radical left or right-wing, child-pornographic images and video sequences, instructions to build bombs or make drugs, and information for terrorists. Most people agree that the Internet should not provide support for the distribution of such content, and several proposals have been made to prevent the Internet from being (mis)used for these purposes. The proposals fall into two categories: On the one hand, there is content blocking, and on the other hand, there is content rating and self-determination.

▸ The idea of *content blocking* is to make ISPs ultimatively responsible for the content they provide or make available and accessible to their subscribers.

▸ Contrary to that, the idea of *content rating and self-determination* is to make ISP subscribers responsible for the content they access. To make it possible for them to decide whether they want to access specific content, this content must be rated according to some known rating scheme.

In the case of content blocking, ISPs must find ways to cut off Internet and Web sites that provide or make available and accessible to their subscribers dubious content. Contrary to that, ISPs have no obligations in the case of content rating and self-determination. In this case, it is up to the content providers to have their content rated, and it is up to the Internet users and ISP subscribers to behave accordingly (e.g., to configure their browsers in a way that dubious content is not rendered). Consequently, the idea of content blocking is driven by the service providers, whereas the idea of content rating and self-determination is driven by the content providers and ISP subscribers.

In the following two sections we address the technologies that are used to implement content blocking as well as content rating and self-determination.

14.2 Content blocking

In the recent past, several approaches have been proposed to block content identified by some parties as illegal or offensive. According to a report published by the Australian government in 1998 [3], such content can either be blocked at the packet or application level (as further explained in Chapter 3):

▸ In short, blocking content at the packet level requires (screening) routers to examine the source IP address of an incoming IP packet, compare it with a black list, and either forward (if the IP address isn't itemized in the black list) or drop (if the IP address is itemized in the black list) the packet.

‣ Blocking content at the application level requires application-level gateways and proxy servers that examine resources or resource information in order to decide whether the corresponding application protocol request, such as an HTTP GET method invocation, should be served or not. For example, a common approach for blocking content at the application level is to specify URLs that should not be served and place them in corresponding black lists that are distributed and installed on proxy servers. Before serving an HTTP request, a proxy server would then make sure that the requested URL is not itemized in the black list. Obviously, the granularity of such blocking decisions can be made much finer than in the case of blocking content at the packet level.

According to this brief description, packet-level blocking is sometimes also referred to as *IP address blocking*, whereas application-level blocking is also called *URL blocking*. Both technologies as well as their advantages and disadvantages are overviewed and briefly discussed next.

14.2.1 IP address blocking

The technologies used to implement IP address- or packet-level blocking are similar to the ones discussed in Chapter 3, when we elaborated on packet filtering and stateful inspection technologies. In short, any kind of access control list (ACL) must be specified in order to distinguish packets that should be forwarded and packets that should be dropped. This distinction is mainly based on the information that is usually found in IP packet headers, such as source and destination IP addresses.

In general, IP address- or packet-level blocking could be carried out by any ISP. In practice, however, it is more efficient to have IP address- or packet-level blocking carried out by the relatively small number of Internet backbone service providers (BSPs). Since packet-level blocking involves a comparison of each IP packets source address with a supplied black list of IP addresses (the ones that are blocked), it can easily be implemented using ACL features of the screening routers operated by the BSPs.

As of this writing, the effectiveness of IP address- or packet-level blocking is a hotly debated topic. The proponents of the technology claim that it is a possible way to effectively block illegal or offensive content on the Internet or WWW. Contrary to that, the opponents of the technology refer to the four following technical issues that collectively limit its effectiveness:

1. IP address- or packet-level blocking is indiscriminate in the sense that the decision to block an IP address actually means that all (virtual) Web sites configured to use this address are blocked and made invisible to Internet users and ISP subscribers. This poses some practical and legal problems for companies that host virtual Web sites. Positively speaking, it would also be an incentive for them to remove the offensive material.

2. IP address- or packet-level blocking may also affect other TCP/IP services than HTTP. Note that a decision to block a particular Internet or Web site because of some illegal or offensive content generally means that all other services, such as FTP, SMTP, or NNTP, will also be blocked. The reason for that is that IP address- or packet-level blocking decisions are mainly based on IP addresses. Although it is possible to include port numbers (that specify services) in the decision rules, this is seldom done (mainly because it negatively influences the performance of the screening routers). Also, if it were done, the port numbers could be changed even more easily than IP addresses.

3. IP address- or packet-level blocking devices can often be bypassed and circumvented. For example, it is possible for an Internet or Web site to regularly change its IP address, thereby bypassing the access control enforced by a black list entirely. Similarly, specific network technologies, such as IP tunneling, can be used to circumvent any IP address or packet-level blocking device.

4. IP address- or packet-level blocking requires some computational power on the routing (and filtering) devices. Consequently, routers may need to be upgraded to implement IP address- or packet-level blocking. Note that a top-of-the-line router from Cisco, appropriately configured, can carry out packet-level blocking at line speeds, whereas some older style routers may need to be replaced or upgraded to meet the requirements of contemporary internet working performance.

In either case, support for IP address- or packet-level blocking complicates the packet filtering rules that are implemented and enforced by a firewall. Finally, there are also some nontechnical issues to consider. For example, not all Internet traffic passes through a BSP. Many multinational organizations have TCP/IP networks (i.e., intranets) that use leased lines. The employees of these organizations would not be subject to IP address- or packet-level blocking as enforced by BSPs. Also, there are increased operational costs associated with the creation, maintenance, and distribution of black lists, as well as the configuration of the corresponding screening routers' ACLs. As of this writing, there are only a few statistics available about these costs.

14.2.2 URL blocking

URL- or application-level blocking requires the existence of application-level gateways and HTTP proxy servers that examine resources or resource information to decide whether a specific request should be served or not. Consequently, ISPs prevent their clients from accessing the Internet directly for some application protocols, such as HTTP, by forcing them to access the Internet through a proxy server, which performs blocking and may store (or rather cache) frequently accessed material. This actually requires the user to configure his or her browser to make use of the ISP's proxy server (as discussed in Chapter 3). The proxy server can then compare requests from the browser with a supplied black list of Internet and Web sites.

As of this writing, URL- or application-level blocking is most commonly used in corporate intranets to control access to specific Web sites, such as `www.playboy.com` or `www.penthouse.com`. There are only a few countries that try to enforce URL- or application-level blocking technologies for their citizens.

Again, the discussion about the effectiveness of URL or application-level blocking is controversial. Proponents of the technology claim that it is a possible way to effectively block illegal or offensive content on the WWW, whereas opponents of the technology refer to the following technical issues that collectively limit the effectiveness of the technology:

- First, URL- or application-level blocking can be bypassed or circumvented in many ways.

    - For example, a user can access an Internet or Web site by specifying its descriptive DNS name, or its equivalent IP address. A black list that only checks DNS names can therefore be bypassed unless it also includes the equivalent IP address(es), which double (or multiply) the size of the corresponding black list.

    - Similarly, it is possible to regularly change the IP address or DNS name of the computer system that hosts the Web server, or run several Web servers on a specific computer system and change the port number periodically.

All of these and similar changes will cause a URL- or application-level blocking strategy to fail (since the URLs change). The changes can be made explicit and communicated to the users, or they can be made implicit by having corresponding URL translation services run on server machines. The latter approach is conceptually similar to the TAZ network introduced in Chapter 12 with regard to anonymous publishing on the WWW.

▸ Second, push technologies bypass URL- or application-level blocking entirely, since content is delivered to users without specifically being requested. Note that a proxy server that implements URL- or application-level blocking generally filters requests for specific content. If the content is delivered without a corresponding request, it will not be blocked by the proxy server.

▸ Third, the policy of forcing users to access the Internet through a single proxy server (that implements URL- or application-level blocking) reduces the reliability and decreases performance of Internet connectivity, as it introduces a single point of failure and bottleneck. There are also some application protocols that have problems working through a proxy server at all. For example, we saw in Chapter 3 that UDP-based application protocols are inherently difficult to handle with proxy servers (because they don't use connections in the first place).

Similar to IP address- or packet-level blocking, URL- or application-level blocking generally complicates the configuration of firewalls and causes some additional costs. Many ISPs, Web site hosting organizations, and educational institutions (e.g., universities) do not employ proxy servers at all, and a requirement to do so may be a financial burden for some of them. In addition to the hardware costs, there are the ongoing costs of maintaining and administering the proxy servers, and supporting the clients that are forced to use them. Finally, there is the enormous and expensive task of creating, updating, and distributing the black lists. In addition, the following two nontechnical issues must also be considered with care:

1. ISPs may be placed in a dilemma. Note that if an ISP is asked to adopt the role of a moral arbiter, it will be placed in a difficult position by its subscribers for either going too far or not going far enough.

2. A black list is a valuable commodity in its own right and black lists should be maintained in secure environments accordingly. Note

that a black list is a valuable target for a hacker, and once uncovered will be published on the Internet, thereby creating a "must see" list for curious users. This may have the negative side effect of publicizing the sites on black lists more widely than if the black lists did not exist at all.

An alternative to blocking content is deleting content. Blocking prevents an Internet or Web site from being accessed, whereas deletion refers to the physical removal of a resource after it has been published on the Web. The deletion of a resource (or a set of resources) can only be carried out by its (their) owner(s) or the corresponding Web site administrator(s) or law enforcement officers. Note, however, that after a resource has been deleted, it may still exist on the following locations:

▶ Personal computers that have originally downloaded the resource and saved it;

▶ Proxy servers that have served the download operation and have cached the corresponding resource;

▶ Mirror sites that have downloaded the resource for further distribution.

In summary, both IP address- or packet-level blocking and URL- or application-level blocking are technically possible, but can easily be circumvented. Also, as mentioned above, mandating their use may result in black lists (either for IP addresses or URLs) becoming hot properties, with the net result and effect that the blacklisted Internet and Web sites may even become more popular than if they were not blacklisted at all. Note, however, that this is more a psychological problem than a technical one. Also note that the same argument can also be used to argue against content rating and self-determination (and to promote law enforcement as being the only practical solution).

14.3 Content rating and self-determination

Rather than censoring what content is being distributed and made accessible on the Internet and WWW, the idea of *content rating and self-determination* is to enable users to judge the content of a Web site based on some objective criteria and to control access to the content accordingly. This idea actually conforms to the general argument of human beings' being ultimately responsible for their own behaviors and activities.

Content rating is not something conceptually new. For some media, such as cinema movies, we are already accustomed to content rating, whereas for other media, such as television and the Web, the effectiveness and efficiency of content rating and self-determination schemes remain to be shown.[1] In either case, it must be ensured that content rating schemes can neither be circumvented nor manipulated. For all practical purposes, this turns out to be difficult.

The *Platform for Internet Content Selection* (PICS) is an initiative created by the industry to promote content rating and self-determination [4, 5]. Coordinated by the W3C, PICS aims at providing an infrastructure for associating labels with content.[2] It is value neutral in the sense that it does not specify the content of labels. It only specifies a label format and describes how the corresponding labels may be transmitted. As such, it is a platform on which content rating services and filtering software packages can actually be built. Computer systems can process PICS labels in the background, automatically shielding users from undesirable content or directing their attention to sites of particular interest.

The PICS specification provides the means to implement a content rating service. It consists of the following components:

‣ A syntax for describing a content rating service, so that computer programs can present the service and its labels to the users.

‣ A syntax for labels, so that computer programs can automatically process them. A label describes either a single document or a group of documents (provided by an Internet or Web site). A label may include a cryptographic hash value of the associated document or may even be digitally signed.

‣ An embedding of labels (or lists of labels) into the RFC 822 transmission and HTML document formats. In the first case, RFC 822-style headers are used, whereas in the second case, the HTML META tag is used for embedding one or more labels in the header of an HTML document.

‣ An extension of HTTP, so that clients can request labels to be transmitted with a document.

---

1. Note that in many countries (e.g., Australia) television shows have ratings.
2. http://www.w3.org/PICS

▸ A query-syntax for an online database of labels (a label bureau as discussed below).

There are products that implement the PICS specifications, and the W3C maintains a list of PICS-compatible filtering products and services (i.e., client software, HTTP servers, proxy servers, label bureaus, and rating services).

In general, PICS can be used and provides support for both self-labeling (by an autonomous content provider or on-line publisher) and third-party labeling (by a label bureau):

▸ A content provider or on-line publisher who wants to label his or her content must first choose which rating vocabulary to use. The W3C recommends the use of a vocabulary already used by others, to make it easy for Internet users to understand the corresponding labels. Again, a list of self-rating vocabularies is available, but W3C does not endorse any particular vocabulary. Typically, the content provider or on-line publisher chooses a self-labeling service, connects to the corresponding Web site, and describes the resource to be published by filling out an online questionnaire. After completing the questionnaire, the service gives the content provider or online publisher a text label in a special format, which is then inserted into the corresponding HTML file.

▸ In addition to the self-labeling service, an independent rating agency need not get cooperation from every content provider or Web publisher whose material it labels. As with self-labeling described above, the independent labeler first needs to invent or adopt a vocabulary. The rater then uses a software tool to create labels that describe particular URLs. Instead of pasting those labels into documents, the independent rater distributes the labels through a separate server, which is called a *label bureau*. Filtering software will know to check at that label bureau to find the labels, much as consumers know to read particular magazines for reviews of appliances or automobiles.

Several PICS-compliant rating services are in operation today, allowing content providers and Web publishers to self-label their content.[3] The most important rating scheme and service is RSACi, developed by

---

3. Contrary to that, there are hardly any independent label bureaus in operation today.

the Recreational Software Advisory Council (RSAC).[4] According to the information found on its Web site, RSAC "is an independent, nonprofit organization based in Washington, D.C, that empowers the public, especially parents, to make informed decisions about electronic media by means of an open, objective, content advisory system."

The RSACi system provides consumers with digitally signed information about the level (ranging from 0 up to 4) of violence, nudity, sex, and offensive language in software games and Web sites. The corresponding RSACi levels are summarized in Table 14.1. Most importantly, RSACi is supported by Microsoft Internet Explorer. As illustrated in Figure 14.1, the corresponding Content Advisor can be enabled on the "Content" tab of the Internet Options menu. If it is enabled, the user is prompted to enter a supervisor password (as illustrated in Figure 14.2). The aim of the supervisor password is to prevent children from changing the settings of the Content Advisor.

The Content Advisor panel is illustrated in Figure 14.3. For all criteria of the RSACi system (i.e., violence, nudity, sex, language), the user can specify a maximum level that is acceptable. The Ratings tab, as illustrated in Figure 14.3, can be used for this purpose. In addition, there are other tabs that can be used to customize the Content Advisor.

There are several points to consider with care regarding the use of content rating and self-determination technologies, such as employed by PICS and RSACi:

Table 14.1 The RSACi Levels for Violence, Nudity, Sex, and Language

Level	Violence Rating Descriptor	Nudity Rating Descriptor	Sex Rating Descriptor	Language Rating Descriptor
4	Rape or wanton, gratuitous violence	Frontal nudity (qualified as provocative display)	Explicit sexual acts or sex crimes	Crude, vulgar language or extreme hate speech
3	Aggressive violence or death to humans	Frontal nudity	Nonexplicit sexual acts	Strong language or hate speech
2	Destruction of realistic objects	Partial nudity	Clothed sexual touching	Moderate expletives or profanity
1	Injury to human being	Revealing attire	Passionate kissing	Mild expletives
0	None of the above or sports related	None of the above	None of the above or innocent kissing; romance	None of the above

---

4. http://www.rsac.org

Figure 14.1 Microsoft Internet Explorer's Content tab of the Internet Options menu. (© 2002 Microsoft Corporation.)

1. Not every label is trustworthy. For example, the creator of a computer virus can very easily distribute a misleading label claiming that the software is safe. Checking for labels merely converts the question of whether to trust a piece of software to where to trust the label that is associated with it (and since both can be provided by the same person, they can be identical). One obvious solution is to use copyright protection labeling or cryptographic techniques to determine whether a document has been changed since its label was created and to ensure that the label is the work of its purported author.

2. Mandatory self-labeling need not lead to censorship, so long as individuals can decide which labels to ignore. Unfortunately, people

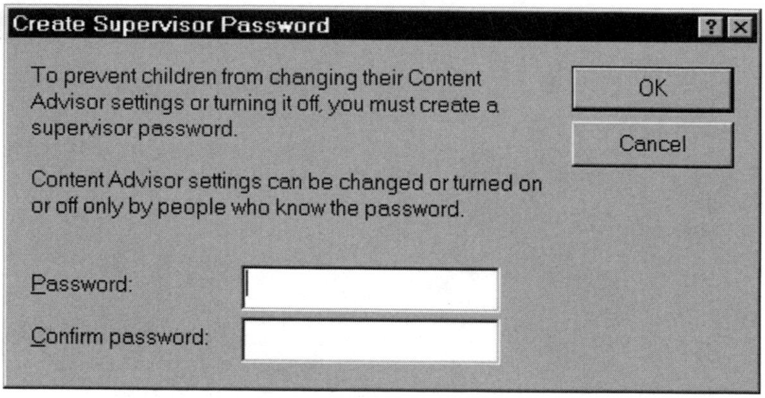

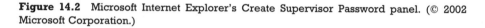

Figure 14.2 Microsoft Internet Explorer's Create Supervisor Password panel. (© 2002 Microsoft Corporation.)

may not always have the choice. As mentioned above, Singapore and China are experimenting with national firewalls that are going to implement some content blocking strategies. Nevertheless, it is fair to say that improved individual controls remove one rationale for central control but do not prevent its imposition.

3. Any content rating system, no matter how well conceived and executed, will tend to stifle noncommercial communication. Rating requires human time and energy; many sites of limited interest will therefore probably go unrated. Because of safety concerns, some people will block access to materials that are unrated or whose labels are untrusted. For such people, the Internet will function more like broadcasting, providing access only to sites with sufficient mass-market appeal to merit the cost of labeling.

As an added inducement to content rating, it is worthwhile to mention that some future applications may use labels for searching as well as filtering. Thus, rating a Web site's documents will make it easier both for some audiences to avoid the documents and for others to intentionally find them. Consequently, content rating is another example of a dual-use technology.

As of this writing, it is too early to say whether content rating and self-determination will be successful and successfully deployed on the marketplace. PICS and RSACi are supported by Microsoft Internet Explorer. There is, however, less strong support by other software vendors and content providers. In fact, there is hardly any Web site that has its content rated according to any scheme (not necessarily RSACi). Consequently, it is

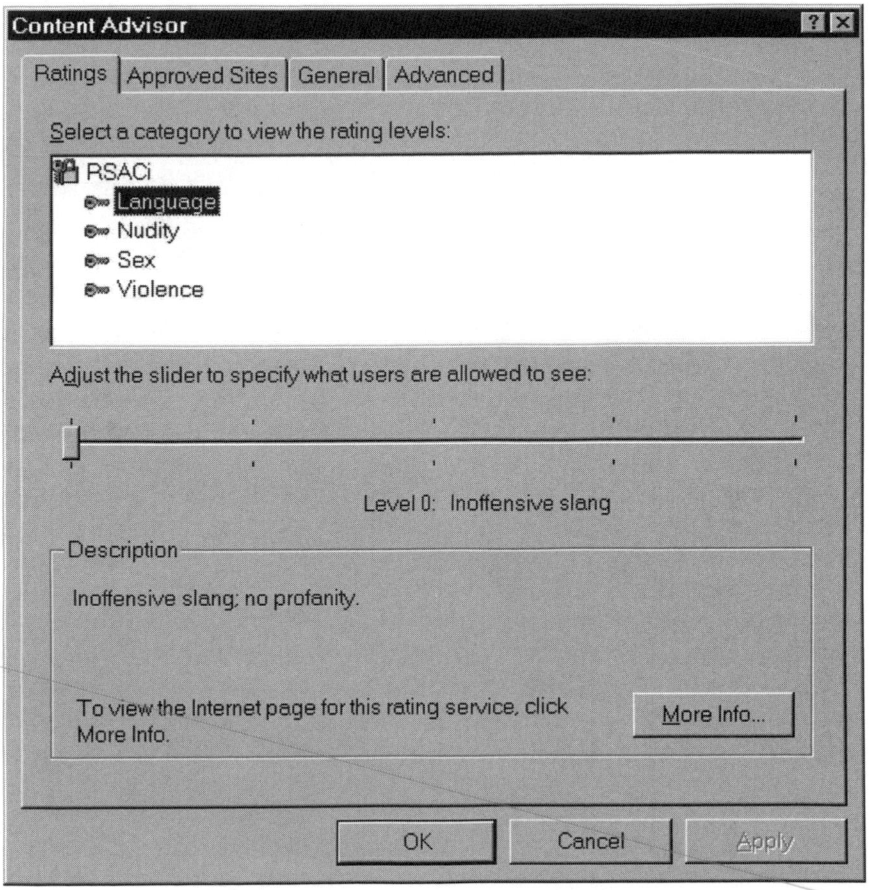

Figure 14.3 Microsoft Internet Explorer's Content Advisor panel. (© 2002 Microsoft Corporation.)

possible and more likely than not that the notion of content rating and self-determination will silently disappear in the future.

14.4 Conclusions

In general, censorship refers to the official suppression of information as published in specific media, such as newspapers, films, and books. In the past, many states have developed a highly refined system of censorship. Although most information is allowed to flow freely, certain kinds of information are censored nationwide. In particular, we mentioned propagandistic material from the radical left or right-wing and child-pornographic images or video sequences as examples.

More recently, the question has arisen whether there is need for censorship on the Internet and the WWW. If this question is answered with a yes, the next question to ask is about technologies that can eventually be used to enforce censorship on the Internet and the WWW. This question was addressed in this chapter. In fact, we addressed two technologies, namely content blocking as well as content rating and self-determination.[5]

The issue of content blocking is a difficult and, at times, emotional issue. Based on a thorough analysis of content blocking technologies, the previously mentioned Australian report concluded that content blocking implemented purely by technological means will be ineffective, and neither of the two approaches (IP address- or packet-level blocking and URL- or application-level blocking) should be mandated [3]. Instead, the report argues that ISPs could be encouraged to offer differentiated services to their subscribers, based on access to the Internet through a proxy server. The following two services may be considered:

1. A clean service for which the proxy server includes a list of permitted URLs. Requests for URLs found on the list should be served, whereas requests for URLs outside the list should be refused.

2. A best-effort service for which the proxy server includes a list of refused URLs. Requests for URLs found on the list should be refused, whereas requests for URLs outside the list should be served.

Obviously, the distinction between a clean service and a best-effort service is similar to the distinction between the two stances of a firewall policy (what is not explicitly allowed is refused and what is not explicitly refused is allowed). In either case, ISPs may incur some costs in setting up differentiated services. These costs could either be passed on to clients in increased fees, or an ISP may see some competitive advantage in providing such an environment to clients. Alternatively, the governments may consider providing some incentives to ISPs to offer such differentiated services.

---

5. Note that the proponents of content rating and self-determination technologies often argue that their technologies do not enforce censorship (but, rather, some more sophisticated access control). In either case (and whatever the claims of the corresponding proponents are), content rating and self-determination technologies are being designed for building censorship software, and, as such, represent technologies that can be used to enforce censorship.

In either case, international cooperation is needed to determine jurisdiction. Locally hosted content that is either illegal or considered to be offensive is best handled by a direct approach to the ISP or the organization that hosts the material, requesting that the ISP or hosting organization take appropriate action. However, most content on the Internet resides on foreign servers. In fact, the content in question may be entirely legal in the jurisdiction in which it is being hosted, as a result of differences in international regulation. Consequently, the authors of [3] propose international forums to create the necessary infrastructure, so that organizations that host content could determine the jurisdiction of the client software making the request. Having determined the jurisdiction, the server could find out whether the requested content was legal in the client's jurisdiction.

Finally, at the time of this writing it is not clear whether any form of censorship on the Internet or WWW—either content blocking or content rating and self-determination—will be accepted by Internet users at all. Statistical investigations will have to clarify this point. Also, statistical investigations must be done to quantify the costs that are involved in any censorship technology.

References

[1]   Foerstel, H. N., (ed.), *Banned in the Media: A Reference Guide to Censorship in the Press, Motion Pictures, Broadcasting, and the Internet*, Westport, CT: Greenwood Publishing Group, 1998.

[2]   Price, M. E., (ed.), *The V-Chip Debate: Content Filtering from Television to the Internet*, Mahwah, NJ: Lawrence Erlbaum Associates, 1998.

[3]   McCrea, P., B. Smart, and M. Andrews, "Blocking Content on the Internet: A Technical Perspective," Report prepared for the Australian National Office for the Information Economy, available on-line at http://www.cmis.csiro.au/Reports/blocking.pdf, June 1998, .

[4]   Resnick, P., "Filtering Information on the Internet," *Scientific American*, March 1997, pp. 106–108.

[5]   Resnick, P., and J. Miller, "PICS: Internet Access Controls Without Censorship," *Communications of the ACM*, Vol. 39, No. 10, October 1996, pp. 87–93.

Contents

15.1 Introduction

15.2 Formal risk analysis

15.3 Alternative approaches
      and technologies

15.4 Conclusions

      References

Risk Management

In this chapter, we summarize some general remarks about risk management and how the Internet and the WWW have changed (or are about to change) the way we think about it. More specifically, we introduce the topic in Section 15.1, elaborate on formal risk analysis in Section 15.2, address some alternative approaches and technologies for risk management in Section 15.3 and draw some conclusions in Section 15.4. Some parts of this chapter are taken from Chapter 21 of [1].

15.1 Introduction

In practice, it is often important to know the risks one faces when adopting a new technology. This is particularly true for the Internet and the WWW. A company or organization that considers establishing a presence on the Web is very likely (and well advised) to question the vulnerabilities, threats, and related risks.

According to RFC 2828 [2], these terms (and some related terms) can be defined as follows:

▸ A *vulnerability* is a flaw or weakness in a system's design, implementation, or operation and management that could be exploited to violate the system's security policy.[1]

---

1. According to this definition, one could argue that a system without a security policy is not vulnerable because there is nothing that could be

- A *threat* is a potential for violation of security, which exists when there is a circumstance, capability, action, or event that could breach security and cause harm.

- A *risk* is an expectation of loss expressed as the probability that a particular threat will exploit a particular vulnerability with a particular harmful result.

- *Risk analysis* (or *risk assessment*) is a process that systematically identifies valuable system resources and threats to those resources, quantifies loss exposures (i.e., loss potential) based on estimated frequencies and costs of occurrence, and (optionally) recommends how to allocate resources to countermeasures so as to minimize total exposure.

- Last but not least, *risk management* is a process of identifying, controlling, and eliminating or minimizing uncertain events that may affect system resources.

The individual steps in a risk management process are illustrated in Figure 15.1. On the left side, a vulnerabilities analysis must be performed. This analysis has to reveal the vulnerabilities that are relevant for a given situation (i.e., a given IT environment). On the right side, a threats analysis must be performed. A threats analysis, in turn, requires an explicit threat model; that is, a model that elaborates on who is capable and motivated to attack the system in question. In the absence of such a model, one cannot hope to estimate the threats and the corresponding risks. Note that it is something completely different to secure a corporate intranet against foreign intelligence services than it is to secure a corporate intranet against casual attacks. Based on the results of a vulnerabilities analysis and a threats analysis, a risk analysis can be performed. The risk analysis quantifies loss exposures based on estimated frequencies and costs of occurrence.

From a more general point of view, everything we do in daily life—either professionally or privately—is driven by risk management considerations. If there is no vulnerability or threat (and, consequently, no risk), we generally do not spend any time or money in security and safety. If, however, there are risks and these risks are severe or appear severe to us in terms of expected losses, we are generally willing to spend large amounts of

---

exploited to violate the policy. On the other hand, one could also argue that there is a policy for every system, even if it exists only in the owner's mind.

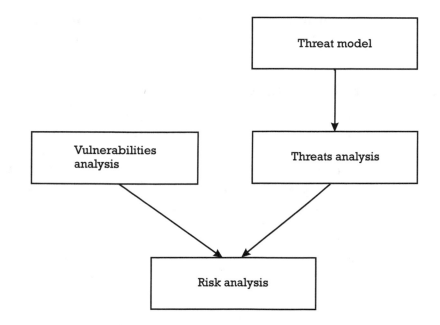

Figure 15.1   The individual steps in a risk management process.

time or money in security and safety. The point is that we are not always aware that some risk management considerations are being performed in our brains. For example, if somebody tells you to jump from a building, the expected loss (i.e., the loss of life) is generally too high to be tolerable. Consequently, you are not going to jump (at least we hope so). If, however, someone asks you for the current time, there is no loss to expect.[2] Consequently, you would tell this person the current time. All these risk management considerations are done subconsciously (as a learned behaviour) and we may not even be aware of them. Also, the same risks are perceived differently by different people. Consequently, risk perception is also an important topic that complements risk management.

In the IT world, we are not yet fully accustomed to making risk management considerations. This is because the field is still new, dynamically changing, and not well understood. Also, there are hardly any statistical investigations we can use to make some long-term claims about relevant risks. Consequently, we have to deliberately consider each

---

2.   There may still be a loss to expect, namely, if the questioner for the current time only wants to distract you so you can be robbed more easily.

risk individually. If this is done, it is usually done in a labor-intensive process called *formal risk analysis.*

15.2 Formal risk analysis

In the past, several frameworks, models, methods, and methodologies to formally perform risk analyses have been developed and proposed [3, 4]. For example, the British Central Computer and Telecommunications Agency (CCTA) came up with a methodology called *CCTA Risk Analysis and Management Methodology* (CRAMM) and a tool of the same name. The tool is being marketed by a company called Logica.[3] Similarly, a methodology called MARION—an acronym derived from the French term *méthodologie d'analyse des risques informatiques et d'optimation par niveau*—was developed by the French *club de la sécurité informatique francais* (CLUSIF[4]).

Unfortunately, the performance of a formal risk analysis has turned out to be difficult in practice. There are mainly two reasons:

1. A formal risk analysis process requires the establishment of an inventory for all assets (e.g., to decide whether they are valuable). Unfortunately, this is a very difficult and labor-intensive task. To make things worse, the inventory is a moving target that changes continually and must be periodically updated.

2. A formal risk analysis always requires the quantification of loss exposures based on estimated frequencies and costs of occurrence. Either value—the estimated frequencies and the costs of occurrence—is hard to quantify (i.e., it requires a lot of knowledge and skills).

    – How do you, for example, quantify the estimated frequency for a system being hacked? Does this value depend on the operating system in use? Does it depend on the actual configuration? Does it depend on software patches being installed or not installed?

    – Similarly, how do you quantify the costs of occurrence? Note that no system or network resource need be *damaged* during the system hack. Nevertheless, the loss of reputation as well as the owner's or investors' confidence may still be large and worrisome.

---

3. http://www.logica.com
4. https://www.clusif.asso.fr

Against this background, one may argue that probability theory is currently an inappropriate approach to quantify loss exposures in the IT world. This may change once we have enough data to make probability-based assessments of the overall risk. In either case, we do not have an alternative approach so far.

Because of these difficulties, it is common today to perform only qualitative risk analyses. A *qualitative risk analysis*, in turn, differs from a quantitative or formal risk analysis in the quantification step. Infact, a qualitative risk analysis only addresses risks that are existent (independent from potential loss exposures). For example, if a Web site is connected to the Internet, a qualitative risk analysis would only identify the risk of being hacked (possibly specifying the risk to below, medium, or high), whereas a quantitative or formal risk analysis would additionally try to quantify the estimated frequency and the costs of occurrence to eventually compute a quantitative value for the risk under consideration. In either case, risk analysis must start with an analysis of vulnerabilities and threats.

In many companies and organizations it is not even possible to perform a qualitative risk analysis, and some simpler risk management approaches and technologies must be used instead. Some alternative approaches and technologies are addressed next.

15.3 Alternative approaches and technologies

Given the difficulties of performing formal risk analyses, IT security professionals are looking into alternative approaches and technologies to manage the relevant risks. The two most promising approaches and technologies are security scanning to perform vulnerability analyses, and intrusion detection to identify and respond to potentially malicious activities. One major difference between security scanning and intrusion detection is related to their temporal use. A security scanner is running in real time when it is started (i.e., it is rarely run all of the time). Contrary to that, intrusion detection tools and products are designed to run in real time and to constantly monitor systems and networks for possible attacks [5]. Security scanning and intrusion detection are hot topics today. They are overviewed and briefly discussed next.

15.3.1 Security scanning

The term *security scanning* refers to the process of performing vulnerability analyses, and the term *security scanner* refers to a tool that can be used to automatically perform such analyses. In essence, a security scanner holds a database that includes known vulnerabilities[5] of operating systems and corresponding configurations. Each system can be probed and tested to detect and identify the vulnerabilities that are relevant.

Security scanning tools and security scanners can be partitioned into host-based scanners and network-based scanners:

> • A *host-based scanner* runs on a system and looks into the configuration of the system from the inside. For example, a host-based scanner can check whether files that contain user authentication information (e.g., user passwords) can be read by nonprivileged processes.

> • Contrary to that, a *network-based scanner* runs on a system and looks into the configurations of other systems from the outside. For example, a network-based scanner can check which systems are accessible and which services are running on the ports of these systems.

Ideally, a scanner is host-based and network-based, meaning that it can investigate on and take into account information that is available on either side. As of this writing, there are many security scanners commercially or freely available on the Internet. The most widely used and deployed security scanners on the Internet are developed and marketed by Internet Security Systems, Inc.[6] In addition, there are many security scanners publicly and freely available on the Internet. Examples include the Computer Oracle and Password System (COPS[7]) and the Security Administrator Tool for Analyzing Networks (SATAN[8]). Also, the Nessus security scanner was developed in an open source project of the same name.[9]

More recently, Microsoft Corporation has launched the Strategic Technology Protection Program (STPP). As part of the STPP, the Microsoft Baseline Security Analyzer (MBSA) has been designed and developed as a tool to assess one or more Windows-based computer systems for known vulnerabilities and to determine whether or not they are up-to-date with the latest security-related patches and hotfixes. The tool is publicly and freely

---

5. Note that known vulnerabilities are vulnerabilities that have been found by experience on other systems, and that there is no list of known vulnerabilities that is guaranteed to be complete.
6. http://www.iss.net
7. http://www.sh.com/cops
8. http://www.sh.com/satan
9. http://www.nessus.org

available. Having software providers provide tools like the MBSA is certainly the right way to go. The disadvantage is that attackers can use the same tools to discover breakable computer systems.

15.3.2 Intrusion detection

According to [6], an *intrusion* refers to "a sequence of related actions by a malicious adversary that results in the occurrence of unauthorized security threats to a target computing or networking domain," and the term *intrusion detection* refers to the process of identifying and responding to intrusions.

There are many tools that can be used to automate intrusion detection. These tools are commonly referred to as *intrusion detection systems* (IDSs). Although the research community has been actively designing, developing, and testing IDSs for more than a decade, corresponding products have only recently received wider market interest. Furthermore, the IETF has chartered an Intrusion Detection Exchange Format (IDWG) WG "to define data formats and exchange procedures for sharing information of interest to intrusion detection and response systems, and to management systems which may need to interact with them." Refer to the IDWG's home page[10] to get more information about the relevant Internet-Drafts and RFC documents.

There are basically two technologies that can be used to implement an IDS: attack signature recognition and anomaly detection.

1. Using attack signature recognition, an IDS uses a database with known attack patterns (also known as attack signatures) and an engine that uses this database to detect and recognize attacks. The database can either be local or remote and the engine can either work in real time or not. In either case, the quality of the IDS is as good as the database and its attack patterns as well as the engine that makes use of this database. The situation is similar and quite comparable to the antivirus software (i.e., the database must be updated on a regular basis).

2. Using anomaly detection, an IDS uses a database with a formal representation of "normal" (or "normal looking") user activities and an engine that makes use of this database to detect and recognize attacks. For example, if a user almost always starts up his or her

---

10. http://www.ietf.org/html.charters/idwg-charter.html

e-mail user agent after having successfully logged onto a system, the IDSs' engine may get suspicious if he or she starts a Telnet session to a trusted host first. The reason for this activity may be an attacker misusing the account to gain illegitimate access to a remote system. Again, the database can be either local or remote, and the quality of the IDS is as good as the database and its statistical material.

Again, it is possible to combine both technologies in an IDS. More information about intrusion detection technologies and IDSs that employ these technologies and are commercially available can be found in many books (e.g., [5–10]).

15.4 Conclusions

Security engineers and professionals often elaborate on and argue about the importance, usefulness, and suitability of specific security technologies without having the relevant vulnerabilities, threats, and corresponding risks in mind. For example, using a secure messaging scheme, such as PGP or S/MIME, is almost useless if you have nothing to lose and all you want to do is forward electronic versions of the latest jokes to a friend. The use of a secure messaging scheme, however, is very useful if you want to transfer an electronic order to an e-commerce service provider. Consequently, all we do in terms of security should be driven by risk management considerations.

Historically, the usual way to manage risks in the IT world started with a formal risk analysis. This has changed and we start seeing two trends:

1. Formal risk analyses are being replaced or complemented with alternative approaches and technologies (e.g., security scanners and IDSs).

2. Preventive security mechanisms are being complemented by detective and reactive security mechanisms.

The first trend occurs simply because formal risk analyses are difficult and labor-intensive and because they poorly scale to large IT environments. Contrary to that, the second trend occurs because preventive security mechanisms, such as firewalls and the use of cryptographic security protocols, have turned out to be incomplete, meaning that they do not patch all vulnerabilities and do not protect against all possible threats. As a first order approximation you may think of all systems and applications to be vulnerable and exploitable by specific attacks. This is true even if the systems and applications use some sophisticated preventive security mechanisms. In fact, it is possible and likely that security breaches and vulnerability exploits will always occur and compromise the security of our systems and applications. The role of the preventive security mechanisms is only to lower the likelihood that a serious exploit will happen.

Against this background, we have to think about detection and response. How do you, for example, make sure that exploits and attacks are detected in the first place? Note that, contrary to the real world, a victim may not necessarily be aware of the fact that he or she has become a victim in the digital world. Data can be copied electronically without leaving any traces. Similarly, what do you do if an exploit or attack is actually detected? How do you respond to exploits and attacks? In either case, you need detective and reactive security mechanisms. One may argue that detective and reactive security mechanisms are becoming more important because of the incomplete nature of the preventive security mechanisms we have in place today.

More recently, Bruce Schneier provided some arguments for the importance of detection and response and why they are important in the insecure IT world in which we live today [11]. Anybody who is in charge of designing security for an intranet environment should carefully think about the role of detection and response in that environment. These components are becoming increasingly important these days.

References

[1]   Oppliger, R., *Internet and Intranet Security, Second Edition*, Norwood, MA: Artech House, 2002.

[2]   Shirey, R., "Internet Security Glossary," Request for Comments 2828, May 2000.

[3]   Parker, D. B., *Fighting Computer Crime: A New Framework for Protecting Information*, New York: John Wiley & Sons, 1998.

[4]   Peltier, T. R., *Information Security Risk Analysis*, Boca Raton, FL: CRC Press, 2001.

[5]   Escamilla, T., *Intrusion Detection: Network Security Beyond the Firewall*, New York: John Wiley & Sons, 1998.

[6]   Amoroso, E., *Intrusion Detection: An Introduction to Internet Surveillance, Correlation, Trace Back, Traps, and Response*, Sparta, NJ: Intrusion.net Books, 1999.

[7]   Northcutt, S., D. McLachlan, and J. Novak, *Network Intrusion Detection: An Analyst's Handbook*, 2nd ed., Indianapolis, IN: New Riders Publishing, 2000.

[8]   Cooper, M., et al., *Intrusion Signatures and Analysis*, Indianapolis, IN: New Riders Publishing, 2001.

[9]   Proctor, P. E., *Practical Intrusion Detection Handbook*, Englewood Cliffs, NJ: Prentice Hall, 2000.

[10]   Bace, R. G., *Intrusion Detection*, Indianapolis, IN: New Riders Publishing, 1999.

[11]   Schneier, B., *Secrets and Lies: Digital Security in a Networked World*, New York: John Wiley & Sons, 2000.

Conclusions and Outlook

In this book, we have addressed many technologies, mechanisms, and services that are available and that can be used to secure the WWW and its applications. Some of these technologies, mechanisms, and services are in widespread use today (e.g., the SSL/TLS protocol), whereas others are still on the drawing boards of security professionals and architects. For example, the questions of how to properly secure Web services are still being studied and will (hopefully) emerge into a comprehensive set of security-related standards.[1]

Taking into account the security technologies, mechanisms, and services that are available and that can be used to secure the WWW and its applications, one may argue that the security problems of the WWW will soon go away. This is an optimistic point of view. There is, however, also a pessimistic point of view. The pessimistic point of view basically argues that—in spite of the many security technologies, mechanisms, and services that are available today—the security problems of the WWW won't go away and may even get worse.

In fact, there are two natural enemies of security, and both apply to the WWW:

1. Complexity;

2. Speed.

---

1. As briefly mentioned in Chapter 5, there is a WS-Security specification that is the first in a series of security standards related to Web services.

The more complex a system is, the more difficult it generally is to keep it secure. This rule of thumb certainly applies to IT. Consequently, the mere fact that operating systems and application software are getting more and more complex implies that, they are also getting more and more difficult to secure. This is a very uncomfortable fact of life, and the only countermeasure is to simplify software considerably. Against this background, Web services look promising. It is, however, too early to tell whether Web services will be successfully deployed in the marketplace.

Similarly, the faster a system is designed, implemented, and deployed, the more likely it contains design flaws, vulnerabilities, bugs, and programming errors that may be exploited by a determined attack. Again, this is an uncomfortable fact of life, and the only countermeasure is to slow down the software development processes. Unfortunately, there is currently no sign that the computer and communications industries will ever attempt to slow down the software development processes. In fact, we see product development cycles being shortened, presales software testing being replaced with postsales software testing using beta versions, and security considerations being postponed to later versions of software products. In addition, the speed of information dissemination, news, and people exploiting bugs are also getting faster and faster. The net effect of all these trends is that software is released and shipped that has bad quality and questionable security properties.

Given this background, it is possible and very likely that future software used on the WWW will also be buggy and vulnerable, and that, exploits will therefore continue to occur. Once again, this is a strong argument for detection and response (as addressed in Chapter 15).

The question that arises immediately is, what can be done to increase the overall security of existing and future Web applications and services. The first line of defense is education. Protocol and application designers, software developers, programmers and users who are educated in security matters are more likely to make reasonable and intelligent decisions with regard to the security of their computer systems and networks. In fact, it must be understood that security requires more than simply going through the bullets of a checklist.[2] It requires a proper understanding of the technologies, vulnerabilities, threats, risks and possible countermeasures. There is always a trade-off to make, and this trade-off can only be made if the situation and its implications are properly understood.

---

2.   This is the reason this book does not include checklists.

As mentioned above, many protocol or software developers postpone security considerations to some later version. This is dangerous. For example, when Tim Berners-Lee defined the first version of HTTP, he gave little thought to security. In fact, he argued that the aim of the WWW built on top of HTTP was to publish information for the public. So why bother about security in the first place? According to this line of argumentation, HTTP included only a few security features that were known to be weak, such as the HTTP basic authentication scheme. When people started to use HTTP to build intranet and e-commerce solutions, however, it was realized that it is important to strongly authenticate users, to control access to data, to protect the confidentiality and integrity of data in transmission, and to provide nonrepudiation services to the parties involved. Consequently, several extensions to HTTP have been proposed, including, for example, the HTTP digest authentication scheme, the S-HTTP, as well as the SSL and TLS protocols. Unfortunately, the use and deployment of these secondary technologies has turned out to be slow (as compared to the primary technology, HTTP).

Consequently, some basic security features should always be incorporated into a first version of a protocol or software product. This is where security professionals and engineers come into play. Security engineering is a relatively young discipline that is inherently difficult and error-prone. In fact, there are many examples of flawed security features that are built into protocols and products by engineers who are not security experts. Building a highly secure system or protocol is indeed a hard problem. Also note that security engineering is different from any other type of engineering. Most engineering looks at making things work in the presence of natural forces and accidents. Security engineering has to make things work, not only in the presence of natural forces and accidents, but despite the most ingenious attempts by malicious attackers to prevent the system from working. The fact that contemporary e-commerce applications involve multiple parties and multiple protocols further increases the complexity of the security problem. The field is wide open for research and development.

Abbreviations and Acronyms

AA	attribute authority
AC	attribute certificate
ACL	access control list
AES	advanced encryption standard
AFS	Andrew file system
AFT	authenticated firewall traversal
AH	authentication header
ANSI	American National Standards Institute
AOL	America Online
API	application programming interface
ARPA	Advanced Research Projects Agency
AS	authentication server
ASCII	American Standard Code for Information Interchange
ASN.1	abstract syntax notation 1
ASP	Active Server Pages
ATM	asynchronous transfer mode; automated teller machine

BCP	best current practice
Bellcore	Bell Communications Research
BER	basic encoding rules
BITS	Bump-in-the-stack
BITW	Bump-in-the-wire
BSP	backbone service provider
CA	certification authority
CAFE	Conditional Access for Europe
CAT	common authentication technology
CBC	cipher block chaining
CC	common criteria
CCC	Chaos Computer Club
CCP	compression control protocol
CCTA	Central Computer and Telecommunications Agency
CD	compact disk; committee draft
CDP	certificate discovery protocol
CEC	Commission of the European Communities
CEPS	Common Electronic Purse Specification
CERIAS	Centre for Education and Research on Information Assurance and Security
CERN	European Laboratory for Particle Physics[1]
CERT	computer emergency response team
CERT/CC	CERT coordination center
CFB	cipher feedback
CGI	common gateway interface
CHAP	challenge-response handshake authentication protocol

---

1.   The acronym is taken from the French name of the laboratory

CLI	command line interface
CMS	cryptographic message syntax
COCOM	coordinating committee for multilateral export controls
COM	component object model
COPPA	Children's Online Privacy Protection Act
COPS	Computer Oracle and Password System
CPS	certificate practice statement
CRAMM	CCTA Risk Analysis and Management Methodology
CRC	cyclic redundancy checksum
CRHF	collision resistant hash function
CRL	certificate revocation list
CRMF	certificate request message format
CRS	certificate revocation system
CRT	certificate revocation tree
CSI	Computer Security Institute
CSS	Contents Scramble System
CUG	closed user group
CV	control value
CVC	card verification code
CVV	card verification value
DAC	discretionary access control
DAP	directory access protocol
DARPA	Defense Advanced Research Projects Agency
DCA	Defense Communications Agency
DCE	distributed computing environment
DCMA	Digital Millennium Copyright Act
DDoS	distributed denial of service

DER	distinguished encoding rules
DES	data encryption standard
DFA	differential fault analysis
DISA	Defense Information Systems Agency
DIT	directory information tree
DMV	Department of Motor Vehicles
DMZ	demilitarized zone
DN	distinguished name
DNA	deoxyribonucleic acid
DNS	domain name system
DNSsec	domain name system security
DoC	U.S. Department of Commerce
DoD	U.S. Department of Defense
DoS	U.S. Department of State
DOI	domain of interpretation
DOS	disk operating system denial of service
DPA	differential power analysis
DSA	digital signature algorithm
DSS	digital signature standard
DVCS	data validation and certification server
E-cash	electronic cash
ECB	electronic code book
ECC	elliptic curve cryptosystem
ECML	Electronic Commerce Modeling Language
E-commerce	electronic commerce
ECP	encryption control protocol
EDI	electronic data interchange

EFF	Electronic Frontier Foundation
EFT	electronic funds transfer
EGP	exterior gateway protocol
EIT	Enterprise Integration Technologies
E-mail	electronic mail
ESM	encrypted session manager
ESP	encapsulating security payload
EU	European Union
FAQ	frequently asked questions
FDDI	fiber distributed data interface
FIPS	Federal Information Processing Standard
FIRST	Forum of Incident Response and Security Teams
FNC	Federal Networking Council
FSML	Financial Services Markup Language
FSTC	Financial Services Technology Consortium
FSUIT	Federal Strategy Unit for Information Technology
FTP	File Transfer Protocol
FV	First Virtual
FYI	for your information
GII	global information infrastructure
GISA	German Information Security Agency
GPL	General Public License
GRE	generic routing encapsulation
GSS-API	generic security service API
GUI	graphical user interface
HTML	hypertext markup language
HTTP	Hypertext Transfer Protocol

IAB	Internet Architecture Board
IANA	Internet Assigned Numbers Authority
IBM	International Business Machines Corporation
ICMP	Internet Control Message Protocol
IDEA	international data encryption algorithm
IDS	intrusion detection system
IEC	International Electrotechnical Committee
IEEE	Institute of Electrical and Electronic Engineers
IESG	Internet Engineering Steering Group
IETF	Internet Engineering Task Force
IGP	Interior Gateway Protocol
IIOP	Internet Inter-ORB Protocol
IIS	Internet Information Server
IKE	Internet key exchange
IKMP	Internet Key Management Protocol
IMAP	Internet Message Access Protocol
IP	Internet Protocol
IPC	interprocess communications facility
IPKI	Internet X.509 public key infrastructure
IPng	IP next generation
IPPCP	IP Payload Compression Protocol
IPRA	Internet Policy Registration Authority
IPsec	IP security
IPSP	IP Security Protocol
IPST	IP Secure Tunnel Protocol
IRSG	Internet Research Steering Group
IRTF	Internet Research Task Force

ISAKMP	Internet Security Association and Key Management Protocol
ISAPI	Internet server API
ISDN	integrated services digital network
ISI	Information Sciences Institute
ISO	International Organization for Standardization
ISOC	Internet Society
ISP	Internet service provider
IT	information technology
ITSEC	information technology security evaluation criteria
ITU-T	International Telecommunication Union—Telecommunication Standardization Sector
IV	initialization vector
J2EE	Java 2 Platform, Enterprise Edition
JIT	just-in-time
JSP	JavaServer Pages
JTC1	Joint Technical Committee 1
JVM	Java virtual machine
kbps	kilobit per second
KDC	key distribution center
KDS	key distribution server
KEA	key exchange algorithm
KEK	key encryption key
KTC	key translation center
LAN	local-area network
LDAP	lightweight directory access protocol
LLC	logical link control
LRA	local registration agent; local registration authority

LSB	least significant bit
L2F	layer 2 forwarding
L2TP	Layer 2 Tunneling Protocol
MAC	message authentication code
MAN	metropolitan-area network
MBone	multicast backbone
MBSA	Microsoft Baseline Security Analyzer
MD	message digest
MDC	modification detection code
MIB	management information base
MIC	message integrity check
MIME	multipurpose Internet mail extensions
MIT	Massachusetts Institute of Technology
MKMP	Modular Key Management Protocol
MPPE	Microsoft point-to-point encryption
MS-PPTP	Microsoft PPTP
MTA	message transfer agent
NAS	network access server
NASA	National Aeronautics and Space Agency
NAT	network address translation
NBS	National Bureau of Standards
NCP	Network Control Protocol
NCSA	National Center for Supercomputer Application
NCSC	National Computer Security Center
NetSP	network security program
NII	national information infrastructure
NIST	National Institute of Standards and Technology

NLSP	Network Layer Security Protocol
NMS	network management station
NNTP	Network News Transfer Protocol
NRL	U.S. Naval Research Laboratory
NSA	National Security Agency
NSAPI	Netscape server API
NTP	Network Time Protocol
OCSP	Online Certificate Status Protocol
OECD	Organization for Economic Cooperation and Development
OFB	output feedback
OLE	object linking and embedding
ORA	organizational registration agent
ORB	object request broker
OSF	Open Software Foundation
OSI	open systems interconnection
OWHF	one-way hash function
PAC	proxy auto-config
PAP	Password Authentication Protocol
PARC	Palo Alto Research Center
PC	personal computer
PDA	personal digital assistant
PDU	protocol data unit
PEM	privacy enhanced mail
PEP	Protocol Extension Protocol
PER	packet encoding rules
PET	privacy enhancing technology
PFS	perfect forward secrecy

PGP	pretty good privacy
PHP	hypertext proprocessor
PICS	platform for Internet content selection
PIN	personal identification number
PKCS	public key cryptography standard
PKI	public key infrastructure
PKIX	public key infrastructure X.509
POP	Post Office Protocol; point of presence
PPP	Point-to-Point Protocol
PPPEXT	PPP extensions
PPTP	Point-to-Point Tunneling Protocol
PSRG	Privacy and Security Research Group
PSTN	public switched telephone network
P3P	platform for privacy preferences
PUID	Passport Unique Identifier
QoS	quality of service
RA	registration agent; registration authority
RACF	resource access control facility
RADIUS	remote authentication dial-in user service
RFC	Request for Comment
RIP	Routing Information Protocol
ROM	read-only memory
RPC	remote procedure call
RPI	return path information
RSA	Rivest, Shamir, and Adleman
RSAC	Recreational Software Advisory Council
RSACi	RSAC rating service

SA	security association
SAID	secure association identifier
SALS	simple authentication and security layer
SATAN	Security Administrator Tool for Analyzing Networks
SDNS	secure data network system
SDSI	simple distributed security infrastructure
SECSH	Secure shell
SEPP	secure electronic payment protocol
SESAME	secure European system for applications in a multi-vendor environment
SET	secure electronic transaction
SHA-1	secure hash algorithm 1
SHS	secure hash standard
S-HTTP	secure HTTP
SigG	Signaturgesetz (in Germany)
SigV	Signaturverordnung (in Germany)
SILS	standards for interoperable LAN/MAN security
SIP	secure Internet programming
SKIP	simple key-management for Internet protocols
SLIP	serial line IP
S/MIME	Secure MIME
SMS	service management system; short messaging service
SMTP	Simple Mail Transfer Protocol
SNMP	Simple Network Management Protocol
SOAP	Simple Object Access Protocol
SPKAC	signed public key and challenge
SPKI	simple public key infrastructure
SP3	Security Protocol 3

SP4	Security Protocol 4
SPI	security parameters index
SPKI	simple public key infrastructure
SRA	secure RPC authentication
SRI	Stanford Research Institute
SSH	secure shell; site security handbook
SSI	server-side include; single sign-in
SSL	secure sockets layer
SSO	single sign-on
SSR	secure socket relay
STD	Internet standard
STPP	Strategic Technology Protection Program
STS	station-to-station
S/WAN	secure wide-area network
TACACS	terminal access controller access control system
TAN	transaction authentication number
TAZ	temporary autonomous zone
TCB	trusted computing base
TCP	Transport Control Protocol
TCSEC	trusted computer system evaluation criteria
TEK	token enryption key
TESS	the exponential security system
TIS	Trusted Information Systems
TLI	transport layer interface
TLS	transport layer security
TLSP	Transport Layer Security Protocol
TNI	trusted network interpretation

TSA	Time Stamping Authority
TSP	Time-Stamp Protocol
TTP	trusted third party
UC	University of California
UCB	University of California at Berkeley
UDDI	Universal Description Discovery and Integration
UID	user identification
UPP	universal payment preamble
URI	uniform resource identifier
URL	uniform resource locator
URN	uniform resource name
VPN	virtual private network
VTP	Virtual Tunneling Protocol
WAP	Wireless Application Protocol
WG	working group
WIPO	World Intellectual Property Organization
WSDL	Web services markup language
WSIL	Web services inspection language
WTLS	wireless transport layer security
WWW	World Wide Web
W3C	World Wide Web Consortium
XML	extensible markup language
XTACACS	extended TACACS

About the Author

Rolf Oppliger received his M.Sc. and Ph.D. degrees in computer science from the University of Berne, Switzerland, in 1991 and 1993, respectively. After spending one year as a postdoctoral researcher at the International Computer Science Institute (ICSI) in Berkeley, California, he joined the Swiss Federal Strategy Unit for Information Technology (FSUIT) in 1995 and continued his research and teaching activities at several universities and polytechnics in Switzerland and Germany. In 1999, he received the *venia legendi* from the University of Zürich, Switzerland, became the Artech House series editor for computer security, and founded eSECURITY Technologies Rolf Oppliger (http://www.esecurity.ch) to provide scientific and state-of-the-art consulting, education, and engineering services related to information technology security. He has published numerous scientific papers, articles, and books, mainly on security-related topics. He is a member of the Association for Computing Machinery (ACM), the IEEE Computer Society, and the International Federation for Information Processing (IFIP) Technical Committee 11 (TC11) Working Group 4 (WG4) on network security.

Index

A

Abstract syntax notation one, 191
Accept header, 24
Accept-language header, 24
Access control, 14–15, 26–28
Access control list, 361
Acquirer, 253, 260
Active content, 267–72
Active server page, 22, 300, 310, 312–13
ActiveX control, 283–88
Address information restriction, 27–28
Adobe Acrobat Reader, 273
Advanced encryption standard, 96, 136
Aggressive mode exchange, 140
Alert Protocol, 161, 172
American National Standards
    Committee, 242
Andrew file system, 144
Anomaly detection, 381–82
Anonymizing HTTP proxy server, 329–30,
    337–38
Anonymous browsing, 328–36
Anonymous communication, 320–21,
    334–35
Anonymous electronic cash system, 257, 320
Anonymous publishing, 336–41
Anonymous remailer, 321–23
Apache server, 42, 170, 302, 309, 312
Apache server application programming
    interface, 299
AP exchange, 235, 237–38

Application gateway, 52, 64–68, 76, 77
Application-layer security, 143–46
Application-level blocking, 363–65
Application-level gateway, 64–68, 77, 293,
    361, 363
Application programming interface, 22, 142,
    239, 299
Application proxy, 334
Apply action, 131
Arbiter, 253
Asymmetric cryptography. *See* Public key
    cryptography
Attack signature recognition, 381
Attribute authority, 186, 196, 243
Attribute certificate, 186, 242–44
Authenticated Firewall Traversal Working
    Group, 61
Authentication and authorization
    infrastructure, 145, 213–16
    Kerberos-based, 34, 231–41
    PKI-based, 241–44
Authentication and key distribution system,
    144–45, 215–16
Authentication exchange, 15, 140
Authentication header, 128, 131–35
Authentication server, 233–35, 240
Authentication server exchange, 235
Authentication service, 14
Authenticode, 282, 286–87
Author, BETSI, 270–71
Authorization header, 31, 38

B

Babel system, 323
Backbone service provider, 361, 362
Banking software, 169–70
Base-64 encoding, 32–33, 40
Basic authentication, 29–34, 42–45
Basic encoding rules, 191
Bastion host, 64, 69–73
BBBOnLine, 342
Bellcore trusted software integrity system,
    270–71
Best current practice, 75
Binary mail attachment, 271–72
Bind command, 61
Binding framework, 100
Binding information, 8
Black list, 363–65
Bleichenbacher attack, 168–69
Blender server, 331–32
Block cipher, 93, 174
Blowfish algorithm, 95
Browser, 6–7, 76–80, 272–73
Brute force attack, 40, 227
BSD Sockets, 143
Bump-in-the-stack, 141, 142
Bump-in-the-wire, 141–42
Buyer, 250
Bypass action, 131
Bytecode verifier, 280

C

Caching, 26, 34, 39, 170, 182, 197, 324
Card verification code, 261
Card verification value, 261
Cashlike payment system, 254
CAST-128, 95
CCTA risk analysis and management
    methodology, 378
Censorship, 359–60
    content blocking, 360–65
    content rating, 360, 365–71
CERIAS, 53
Certificate, 100, 175–78, 185–86
Certificate authority certificate, 201–3
Certificate-based authentication, 41–42
Certificate message, 164
Certificate owner information field, 189

Certificate practice statement, 194
Certificate repository, 193, 195, 196–97
Certificate request message, 164–65, 194
Certificate revocation, 196–201
Certificate revocation list, 194, 198–99, 288
Certificate revocation system, 200
Certificate revocation tree, 200–1
Certificate verify message, 166
Certification authority, 97, 100, 111, 164,
    175–78, 186, 192, 193, 242
Certification path (certification chain), 192
Challenge handshake authentication
    protocol, 123
Change Cipher Spec Protocol, 161, 163, 166,
    167, 172
Chaum mixing network, 322–23, 324, 330, 334
Checklike payment system, 254
Children's Online Privacy Protection Act, 229
Chosen ciphertext attack, 168–69
Cipher block chaining, 94, 174
Cipher feedback, 94
Cipher suite, 302
Circuit-level gateway, 58–64, 77
Class loader, 280
Client hello message, 162–63, 167
Client key exchange message, 165, 168–69
Client-side security, 267–71
Client software customization, 65
Closed user group, 124
CLUSIF, 378
Code scanning, 292–93
Code signing, 281–83, 286–88
Collision resistant hash function, 91
Collusion attack, 355
Commerce server, 170
Common criteria, 13
Common electronic purse specification, 257
Common gateway interface, 22, 299–309
Common gateway interface directory, 305–6
Common gateway interface script,
    300–1, 304–9
Common Object Request Broker Architecture,
    63, 179
Communication security, 15, 62
Component object model, 283
Compression control protocol, 123
Computational security, 88–90
Computer emergency response team, 3

Computer emergency response team/
    coordination center, 3
Computer oracle and password system, 380
Conditional Access for Europe, 257
Connect command, 61
Connection anonymity, 320–21
Connectionless Network Protocol, 125
Connect method, 180–81
Content blocking, 360–65
Content rating and self-determination,
    360, 365–71
Contents scramble system, 350
Cookie, 139, 223–28, 324–28
Cookie header, 325
Countermeasure, 9
Crowds system, 331–33
Cryptographic algorithm, 88
Cryptographic file system, 144
Cryptographic hash function, 91–92
Cryptographic key protection, 105–6
Cryptographic message syntax, 195
Cryptographic Protocol, 88
Cryptography, 87–90, 111–13
Cryptolope, 350
Cumulative trust model, 190
Customization, 65

D

Data confidentiality, 14, 62, 135, 156
Data encryption standard, 93–95, 108, 135,
    171, 339
Data integrity, 14, 15, 62, 98, 156
Data validation and certification server, 195
Data validation certificate, 195
Decentralized firewall, 53
Delta certificate revocation list, 199
Demilitarized zone, 73, 298, 310
Denial-of-service attack, 3, 4, 276
Deoxyribonucleic acid computer, 90–91
Destination Internet protocol address, 54, 55
Destination port number, 55, 56
DESX protocol, 339
Dial-up client, 120
Differential fault analysis, 9
Differential power analysis, 9
Diffie-Hellman algorithm, 101–2, 137,
    139–40, 165–66, 173, 195, 332–33

Digest access authentication, 34–41,
    45–46, 387
Digital coin, 256
Digital copyright labeling, 349, 351–56
Digital envelope, 103–5
Digital Millennium Copyright Act, 356–57
Digital shrink-wrap, 205–6, 282
Digital signature, 15, 98–99, 100, 101,
    146, 188, 205–6, 281–82
    legislation, 110–11
Digital signature giving message recovery,
    98–99
Digital signature standard, 98, 102,
    140, 173–74
Digital signature with appendix, 99
Digital watermarking, 349, 351–56
Directory information tree, 192
Disable routing/forwarding, 69
Discard action, 131
Distinguished encoding rules, 191
Distinguished name, 187, 191
Distributed computing environment, 145
Domain name system, 23, 27–28, 63, 187, 363
Domain name system security, 144
Domain of interpretation, 138
Donnerhacke's ActiveX control, 286
Dual-homed firewall, 69–71
Dynamic packet filtering, 52, 57–58

E

Electronic cash system, 255–57, 320
Electronic check, 257–59
Electronic codebook, 94
Electronic commerce modeling language, 228
Electronic credit-card payment, 259–61
Electronic payment system, 249–55, 320
Electronic signature legislation, 110–11
Electronic Signatures in Global and National
    Commerce Act, 110
ElGamal algorithm, 102
Elliptic curve cryptography, 102–3
E-mail, 324
E-mail bombing attack, 3, 324
EMV cash card, 257
Encapsulating security payload, 128, 130–36
Encapsulation, 119, 121–23, 126–26, 130–36
Encipherment, 15

Encrypted session manager, 143
Encryption, 105–6
End entity, 193
Environmental variable, 301–2
Ethernet, 118
Europe, 108, 110, 170, 344
Event detection, 15
Excel, 274
Executable content, 267–72
Expired certificate, 197–98
Exploder Control, 287–88
Exponential security system, 145
Express purchase service, 228–29
Extended terminal access controller access
        control system, 68
Extensible markup language, 7, 21–22, 145–46
Extensible markup language digital
        signature, 146
Extensible markup language encryption, 146

F
Fast common gateway interface, 22, 300, 310
Federal information processing standard, 93
Fiber distributed data interface, 118
File permission, 105, 106
File Transfer Protocol, 7, 57–58, 64, 75–76,
        155, 179
Financial services markup language, 259
Financial Services Technology Consortium, 259
Fingerprint, 352
Finished message, 166, 167
FIPS 96, 197
Firewall
    advantages/disadvantages, 53, 81–83
    client-side security, 291–93
    crowds system, 333
    defined, 50–54
    dual-homed, 69–71
    network address translation, 76
    screened host, 71–72
    screened subnet, 72–74
    transparent, 66
Firewall traversal, SSL/TLS, 178–82
Formal risk analysis, 378–79
Fortezza key exchange algorithm, 164, 165,
        166, 171
Fragile digital watermark, 353

Freedom network, 336
Freedom server, 336

G
Gateway, 25
General public license, 293
Generic routing encapsulation, 123
Generic security model, 10–17
Generic security services API, 62, 239
Get message, 5–6, 64, 361
Global information infrastructure, 4
Group-based authorization, 42
Group file, 43, 43–44, 46

H
Hamiltonian path problem, 89–90
Handheld device, 7
Handshake Protocol
    secure sockets layer, 161–67, 179–80
    transport layer security, 171–73, 179–80
Hash function, 90–92
    one-way, 35, 36, 40, 91–92, 106–7, 134,
        170, 174–75, 262
Header
    Hypertext Transfer Protocol, 24–25
    Internet Protocol, 132–33
    packet-filtering rules, 55–56
Helper application, 273–75
Hidden uniform resource locator, 26, 27
Hierarchical trust model, 192
HMAC construction, 134–35, 160–61, 171
Host-based scanner, 380
Host header, 24
Hostname access restriction, 27–28
Host-oriented keying, 130–31
Host security, 13, 50, 52–53
Htpasswd utility, 42, 44–45
HTTPS Protocol, 171, 175, 179, 181, 227, 298
Hybrid cryptography scheme, 103–5
Hypertext markup language, 6
Hypertext markup language tag filtering, 292
Hypertext proprocessor, 307
Hypertext Transfer Protocol, 5–6, 21–26, 166,
        179, 298–99, 303–4, 325, 335, 387
Hypertext Transfer Protocol proxy server, 329–30
Hypertext Transfer Protocol state management,
        325, 327, 328

I

Inbound connection, 51, 55–58
Information Technology Security Evaluation
    Criteria, 13
Initialization vector, 130, 172, 174
Initiator, 334
Inner network segment, 70
Insider attack, 53
Institute of Electrical and Electronic
    Engineers, 118
Integrated Network Layer Security Protocol, 126
Integrated services digital network, 118, 121
Integrity certificate, 271
Intellectual property protection, 347–49
Intermediary, Hypertext Transfer Protocol,
    25–26
Intermediate certificate, 177
Intermediate certificate authority, 192
Intermediate system, 50
International data encryption algorithm, 95
International Electrotechnical Committee,
    187, 198, 242
International Organization for Standardization,
    125, 143, 187, 198, 242
International Standard 15408, 13
International Telecommunication Union
    Telecommunication Standardization,
    187, 198, 242
Internet, 1–5, 117, 169
Internet Architecture Board, 4
Internet Assigned Numbers Authority,
    133, 156, 157
Internet Engineering Steering Group, 175
Internet Engineering Task Force, 61, 76, 122,
    127, 128, 137, 138, 142–44, 146, 171, 175,
    187, 188, 242, 381
    Common Authentication Technology
        Working Group, 239
    Public-Key Infrastructure Working Group,
        185, 187, 193–96, 198, 200
Internet Explorer, 7, 77–78, 154, 176, 181, 201,
    202–5, 207, 273, 275, 286–89, 326, 327,
    343, 368–71
Internet Inter-ORB Protocol, 63, 179
Internet-Keyed Payments Protocol, 261
Internet key exchange, 128–29, 136–41
    security association, 139–40
Internet Key Management Protocol, 127–28

Internet layer security
    architecture, 128–31
    IKE Protocol, 136–41
    implementations, 141–42
    IPsec Protocols, 131–36
    overview, 125–28
Internet message access protocol, 155, 157
Internet Protocol, 119
    address blocking, 361–63
    Secure Tunnel Protocol, 137
    version 4, 63, 74, 127
    version 6, 63, 74, 76, 127
Internet Protocol security, 124
    implementations, 141–42
    protocols, 128, 131–36
    security architecture, 128–31
    security association, 140–41
Internet Protocol security protocol, 127
Internet Protocol Security Working Group,
    127, 128, 137, 142
Internet Security Association and Key
    Management Protocol, 128, 137, 138
Internet server application programming
    interface, 299, 309
Internet service provider, 319, 360, 364
Internet Worm, 3, 272
Internet X.509 public key infrastructure, 196
Internet zone, 288
Interpretation attack, 356
Interpreter application, 274
Interprocess communications facility, 143
Intranet, 50
Intranet firewall, 53
Intrusion detection, 381
Intrusion Detection Exchange Format Working
    Group, 381
Intrusion detection systems, 379, 381–82
Invisible digital watermark, 353
IPX protocol, 119
IRC protocol, 155
Issuer, 253

J

Janus, 336–37
Japan, 108
JAP system, 330
Java, 275–77, 284, 301, 330
Java 2 Platform, Enterprise Edition, 313

Java applet, 278–85
    blocking, 291–92
Java application programming interface, 313
JavaScript, 275–77
Java Server Pages, 22, 300, 310, 313
Java virtual machine, 275, 278, 286
Jondo process, 331–33
JScript, 275, 277, 312–13
Just-in-time compiler, 278

K

Kerberized network, 239
Kerberos, 34, 45, 145, 146, 215–16, 226, 231–40
    version 4, 231–32, 238
    version 5, 231–32
Key distribution, 34, 144–45
Key distribution center, 92–93, 233, 238, 241
Key exchange algorithm, 164, 165, 166, 194
Kids .NET passport service, 229–30

L

Label bureau, 367–70
Layer 2 Forwarding Protocol, 121
Layer 2 Funneling Protocol, 120–21, 124
Layer 2 Tunneling Protocol access concentrator,
    120–23
Layer 2 Tunneling Protocol network server,
    121–23
Layered Security Protocol, 145–46
Leaf certificate, 192
Legal attack, 356
Legal issues, 107–11
Legal security, 17
Lightweight Directory Access Protocol, 195
Link layer encryption, 335
Local-area network, 118
Local intranet zone, 289
Local registration agent, 193
Local registration authority, 193
Locator, 338
Lucifer algorithm, 108

M

Macro virus, 4
Mail order/telephone order, 251
Main mode exchange, 140
Man-in-the-middle attack, 230

MARION, 378
Merchant, 250
Message authentication code, 91, 156, 158,
    160, 172
Message authenticity, 98
Message digest, 91
Message digest, 2, 92, 170
Message digest, 4, 92
Message digest, 5, 35, 92, 134, 170, 270–71
Messaging, Web-based, 7
Metropolitan-area network, 118
MicroMint, 262
Micropayment system, 261–62
Microsoft baseline security analyzer,
    380–81
Microsoft challenge handshake authentication
    protocol, 123
Microsoft .NET Passport, 215–31
Microsoft point-to-point encryption, 123
Microsoft Point-to-Point Tunneling Protocol,
    123–24
Microsoft Word, 274
Millicent Protocol, 262
Modular Key Management Protocol, 137
Mosaic browser, 6, 154
Mozilla browser, 6
Multicast traffic, 127
Multihomed host, 69
Multiprotocol label switching, 124–25
Multipurpose Internet mail extension,
    6, 272, 274, 292
Multitier Web-base application, 298–300
Must-revalidate cache-control directive, 39

N

National Center for Supercomputer
    Application, 154
National Computer Security Center, 13
National information infrastructure, 2, 4
National Institute of Science and
    Technology, 125
National Institute of Standards and
    Technology, 93
National Security Agency, 13, 125
NetBill, 259
NetCash, 257
NetCents, 262
NetCheque, 259

Netscape Navigator, 7, 78–79, 154, 175–76,
    181, 230, 278
Netscape Server application programming
    interface, 22, 299, 309
Network access layer security, 118–25
Network access server, 67, 121
Network address translation, 74–76
Network-based scanner, 380
Network computer, 278
Network computing, 278
Network interface packet-filtering rules, 56
Network layer security, 125–26
Network Layer Security Protocol, 125–26
Network News Transfer Protocol, 181
Network security, 13–16, 52–53
Network security program, 145
Nonce parameter, 37
Non-repudiation service, 14
Non-script-aliased common gateway
    interface, 305
Notarization, 15
Notation, cryptography, 111–13
NSIIOP, 155

O
OAKLEY Key Determination Protocol,
    128, 137–38
Object identifier, 191
Object linking and embedding, 283, 285
Object signing system, 282
Offline payment system, 255
One-way hash function, 35, 36, 40, 91–92,
    106–7, 134, 170, 174–75, 262
Onion, 334
Onion routing, 333–36
Online certificate repository, 193, 195, 196–97
Online Certificate Status Protocol, 195,
    198, 199–200
Online payment system, 254–55
Open Group, 145
Open Pretty Good Privacy, 188
OpenSSL, 170
Open systems interconnection, 14–15, 98, 118
Opera browser, 7, 79–80, 154, 176–78, 181,
    202–3, 318–19, 327
Orange Book, 13
Organizational registration agent, 193
Organizational security, 16–17

Other people's certificate, 177
Outbound connection, 51, 55, 56
Outer network segment, 70
Outer pad value, 134
Output feedback, 94
Ownership labeling, 352

P
Packet encoding rules, 191
Packet filter, 52
    dynamic, 52, 57–58
    static, 52, 54–57
Packet-level blocking, 361–63
Packet logging, 57
Parallel dual-homed firewall, 71
Passive eavesdropping, 33, 168
Passive File Transfer Protocol, 58
Passphrase, 105–6
Passport credentials, 221
Passport unique identifier, 219–20, 224
Passport user profile, 220
Passport wallet, 221
Password cracker, 225
Password file, 42–46
Password security, 216, 227, 232–33
Password sniffing, 3, 4, 8
Patent claims, 108–9
Pay-after payment system, 254
Payee, 250, 255
Payer, 250, 255
Pay-now payment system, 254
PayPal, 253
PayWord, 262
PCMCI card, 106
Perfect forward secrecy, 141
Perl language, 301, 305–6, 333
Personal certificate, 177, 204–5
Personal digital assistant, 7
Personal firewall, 53
Pervasive security mechanism, 15
Photuris Key Management Protocol, 137
Photuris Plus, 137
Physical security, 90
Platform for Internet content selection, 343,
    366–67, 370
Platform for privacy preferences project,
    342–43
Plug-in application, 273–75, 284

Point of Presence 3 Protocol, 155
Point-to-Point Protocol, 118–19, 123
Point-to-Point Protocol extension, 122
Point-to-Point Tunneling Protocol, 122–24
Post method, 223, 303–4
Preferred encryption algorithm, 190
Preimage resistant hash function, 91–92
Prepaid payment system, 254
Presentation attack, 355
Pretty Good Privacy, 270–71
Pretty Good Privacy certificate, 188–90
Principal, 232
Privacy enhancing technology, 317, 343
Privacy protection, 317–24, 341–44
Privacy seal, 341–42
Private communication technology, 154
Private digital watermark, 354
Private key, 97, 105, 106, 202, 258, 322
Privilege attribute certificate, 240
Privilege attribute server, 240
Profile cookie, 223
Protocol data unit, 118, 123
Protocol number, 55
Proxied Application Protocol, 179
Proxy auto-configuration, 78–80, 243
Proxy cache, 39
Proxy-connection header, 24
Proxy server, 25, 39, 59, 68, 77, 179, 181–82,
    291, 293, 324, 330, 361, 363
Pseudorandom bit sequence, 107
Pseudorandom nonce, 140–41
Public cache-control directive, 39
Public database mapping, 340
Public digital watermark, 354
Public key, 96, 322
Public key certificate, 34, 41, 100, 186
    overview, 187–88
    Pretty Good Privacy, 188–90
    X.509, 190–93
Public key cryptography
    overview, 96–100, 103
    provable security, 89
    types, 100–3
Public key cryptography standard 1, 168–69
Public key digital watermarking, 354–55
Public key field, 189
Public key infrastructure, 167, 186–87, 192,
    196, 215, 261

Public key infrastructure authentication and
    authorization infrastructure, 241–44
Public-Key Infrastructure Working Group,
    185, 187, 193–96
Public switched telephone network, 2, 118, 121
Publius, 340–41
Pull model, 244
Push model, 244, 324, 364
Python language, 301

Q

Qualified certificate, 195
Qualitative risk analysis, 379
Quantitative risk analysis, 378–79
Quantum cryptography, 90
Query string, 302–3
Quicken software, 286
Quick mode exchange, 140–41

R

Randomness, 107
RC2/RC4/RC5/RC6, 95–96, 170–71
Realm, 232
Realm parameter, 37, 40–41
Receiver anonymity, 320–21
Recipient labeling, 352
Record Protocol, 159–61, 171–72
Recreational Software Advisory Council rating
    service, 367–70
Registration agent, 193
Registration authority, 193
Regulations, cryptography, 109–10
Remote access server, 118
Remote authentication dial-in user service,
    67–68
Remote system, 120–21
Removable media, 106
Request for comment 822, 366
Request for comment 1851, 135–36
Request for comment 1918, 75
Request for comment 1945, 6
Request for comment 2104, 160
Request for comment 2246, 172, 175
Request for comment 2341, 121
Request for comment 2402, 133
Request for comment 2405, 135
Request for comment 2406, 135

Request for comment 2407, 138
Request for comment 2459, 194
Request for comment 2510, 194
Request for comment 2511, 194
Request for comment 2527, 194
Request for comment 2528, 194
Request for comment 2559, 194
Request for comment 2560, 195, 198, 200
Request for comment 2585, 195
Request for comment 2587, 195
Request for comment 2616, 6, 22, 28
Request for comment 2617, 28
Request for comment 2661, 124
Request for comment 2712, 175
Request for comment 2797, 195
Request for comment 2817, 175
Request for comment 2828, 124, 185, 186,
    196, 242, 319
Request for comment 2875, 195
Request for comment 2965, 325
Request for comment 3029, 195, 198
Request for comment 3039, 195
Request message, 22–24, 30–33, 298
Responder, 334
Response content filtering, 291
Response message, 24–25, 30, 36–38
Response value validity, 38–39
Restricted sites zone, 289
Return path information, 323
Return uniform resource locator, 222, 228
Rewebber, 338–40
RIPEMD, 92
RIPEMD-160, 92
Risk, 376
Risk analysis (risk assessment), 376, 378–82
Risk management, 376–77
Rivest, Shamir, and Adleman, 100–1, 140,
    164, 165, 166, 168, 173
Robust digital watermark, 353
Robustness attack, 355
Root certificate, 192, 202–3
Router, 54–55, 57
Routing control, 15

S
SAFER K-64/K-128, 95
Salt mechanism, 43

Sandbox, 275, 279–80, 282–83
Screened host firewall, 71–72
Screened subnet firewall, 72–74
Screening router, 54–55
Script-aliased common gateway interface, 305
Scripting language, 275–77
Secondary authentication, 68
Second-preimage resistant hash function, 91
Secret key cryptography, 92–96, 103
Secret key digital watermarking, 354
Secret-sharing scheme, 341
Secure channel, 90
Secure channel sign-in, 226–27
Secure data network system, 125, 143
Secured channel, 90
Secure Electronic Payment Protocol, 261
Secure electronic transaction, 259, 261
Secure hash algorithm 1, 92, 134
Secure Hypertext Transfer Protocol,
    153–54, 387
Secure Internet Programming Group, 279
Secure messaging, 145–46
Secure server, 170
Secure shell, 144, 171
Secure sockets layer, 41, 143, 146, 226,
    230, 244, 302, 310, 330, 337, 387
  architecture, 155–59
  certificates, 175–78
  Handshake Protocol, 161–67
  history, 153–55
  implementations, 169–71
  Record Protocol, 158–61
  security analysis, 167–69
  version 1/version 2, 154
  version 3, 154–55, 171, 172
Secure transaction technology, 261
Secure Web tunneling, 182
Security administrator tool for analyzing
    networks, 380
Security association, 124, 129–30, 133,
    138–41
Security association bundle, 130, 138–39
Security association database, 129
Security audit trail, 15
Security engineering, 387
Security-Enhanced Application Protocol, 144
Security gateway. See Firewall
Security Hypertext Transfer Protocol, 144

Security identifier, 241
Security Internet gateway. *See* Firewall
Security label, 15
Security level, 290
Security manager, 280
Security mechanism, 14–15
Security parameters index, 129
Security policy, 10–13, 51, 52, 281, 375
Security policy database, 129, 131, 138
Security Protocol 3, 125
Security Protocol 4, 143
Security Protocol identifier, 129
Security recovery, 15
Security scanner, 379–81
Security service, 14
Security zone, 288–91
Self-labeling, 367, 369–70
Self-signature field, 189
Sender anonymity, 320–21
Sequence number guessing attack, 3, 4
Serial line dial-up, 118
Serial Line Internet Protocol, 118
Server application programming interface, 309
Server configuration, 42–46
Server hello message, 163–64, 167
Server key exchange message, 164
Server-side include, 300, 311–12
Server-side security, 297–300
Server (site) certificate, 203–4
Service ticket, 234–36
SESAME, 145, 240
Session hijacking attack, 156
Session identity field, 162–63
Session key, 105, 107
Session-unique keying, 130–31
Set-cookie header, 325
Simple authentication and security
    layer, 157
Simple distributed security infrastructure, 188
Simple key management for Internet protocols,
    137, 138
Simple Mail Transfer Protocol, 55, 321, 335
Simple Object Access Protocol, 7–8, 146
Simple Object Access Protocol envelope, 8
Simple public key infrastructure, 188
Single sign-in, 217, 222–28
Single sign-on, 217
SKEME, 137

Smart card, 106, 111
SOCKS, 59–65
Socksified client/stack, 60, 61, 65
Software publisher certificate, 205–7
Source Internet Protocol address, 54, 55
Source port number, 55, 56
Specific security mechanism, 14–15
Spoofing attack, 230, 328
SPX Protocol, 145
SSLeay Protocol, 170
SSLref Protocol, 170
Standardization bodies, 187
Standards for interoperable LAN/MAN
    security, 118
Standard sign-in, 226
Stateful inspection, 58
Stateless packet filter, 56–57, 58
Static packet filtering, 52, 54–57
Station-to-Station Protocol, 137
Status code, 25, 30
Strategic technology protection program, 380
Stream cipher, 93, 174
Strong collision resistant hash function, 91
Strong credential sign-in, 227–28
Stunnel software, 170
SubScrip Protocol, 262
Swipe Protocol, 126
Switch debit card, 254
Symmetric key cryptography. *See* Secret key
    cryptography
System administration, 50

T
TAZ network, 340, 364
Telnet, 55, 56, 66–67, 155, 179, 335
Terminal access controller access control
    system, 67–68
Thin client, 278
Threat, 9, 376
Threat analysis, 376–77
Three-key triple data encryption standard, 95
Ticket cookie, 223
Ticket-granting server, 233–37
Ticket-granting ticket, 234–36, 240–41
Time stamping authority, 195
Time-Stamp Protocol, 195
Timing attack, 9
Token bus, 118

Token encryption key, 165
Token Ring, 118
Tool control language, 301
Traffic analysis attack, 156, 319–32
Traffic padding, 15
Transparent application gateway, 76
Transparent firewall, 66
Transport Control Protocol, 5, 54, 57–58, 59,
    62, 64, 300, 308
Transport Control Protocol connection flag, 55
Transport Control Protocol/Internet Protocol,
    60, 71, 117
Transport Control Protocol SYN flooding, 3, 156
Transport layer interface, 143
Transport layer security, 244, 302, 310,
    330, 337, 387
Transport Layer Security Protocol, 41, 143,
    144, 146
    certificates, 175–78
    Handshake Protocol, 171–73
    overview, 171–75
    Record Protocol, 171–72
Transport Layer Security Working Group, 143,
    171, 175
Transport mode, 132
Trapdoor, 287
Triple data encryption standard, 94–95, 136,
    174, 223
TRUSTe, 342
Trusted Computer Security Evaluation Criteria, 13
Trusted functionality, 15
Trusted root certificate, 177
Trusted sites zone, 289
Trusted third party, 98, 100, 186, 195, 215,
    217, 233, 332
Trust management, 214, 214–16
Trustmark, 342
Tunnel, 26
Tunneling Protocol, 119–20, 122–24, 127,
    179–81
Tunnel mode, 132, 133, 136
Two-key triple data encryption standard, 95

U

Unconditional security, 88–89
Uniform resource identifier, 23
Uniform resource locator, 23, 26–27, 222,
    228, 337–40
Uniform resource locator blocking, 361, 363–65
Uniform resource locator rewriting, 337
Uniform resource name, 23
Universal description discovery and integration, 8
Universal serial bus card, 106, 111
UNIX password encryption, 42–43
Unlinkability of sender and receiver, 320–21
Unwanted communication, 52
Usage control, 349–50
User, BETSI, 270–71
User-agent header, 24
User authentication, 14, 28, 52, 62
    basic, 29–34
    digest access, 34–41
    Kerberos, 232–33
    Telnet server, 67–68
User authorization, 28, 42
User Datagram Protocol, 54, 63, 121
User Datagram Protocol associate request, 63
Username, 28
User-oriented keying, 130–31
User password file, 40–41
User procedures customization, 65

V

Validity period field, 190
Value exchange, 140
VBScript, 275, 277, 312–13
Version number field, 189
VirtualPIN, 251–53
Virtual private network, 119, 122, 124–25
Virtual Tunneling Protocol, 119
Virus scanning, 292, 293
Visible digital watermark, 353
Visited sites cookie, 223
Von Neumann architecture, 269
Vulnerability, 8–9, 375

W

Watermarking, 351
Weak collision resistant hash function, 91
Weak one-way hash function, 91
Web bug, 328
Webjacking, 4
Web of trust, 190, 192
Web services, 7–8
Web services inspection language, 8

Web services markup language, 7, 146
Web Transaction Security Working Group, 144
Windows 2000, 240–41
Wireless Application Protocol, 106, 188
Wireless transport layer security, 188
World Intellectual Property
    Organization, 356
World Wide Web, 5–8, 117, 169, 269–71,
    324, 385–87
World Wide Web certificate, 201–7

World Wide Web Consortium, 7, 8, 145–46,
    187, 366, 367
Wrapper, 307–9
WS-Security specification, 146

X
X.500 standard, 187, 190
X.509 certificate, 146, 164, 187, 189, 190–93,
    242–44, 282–83
X.509 certificate revocation list, 198–99

Recent Titles in the Artech House Computing Library

Advanced ANSI SQL Data Modeling and Structure Processing,
Michael M. David

Advanced Database Technology and Design, Mario Piattini
and Oscar Díaz, editors

Action Focused Assessment for Software Process Improvement,
Tim Kasse

Building Reliable Component-Based Software Systems,
Ivica Crnkovic and Magnus Larsson, editors

*Business Process Implementation for IT Professionals and
Managers*, Robert B. Walford

*Configuration Management: The Missing Link in Web
Engineering*, Susan Dart

Data Modeling and Design for Today's Architectures,
Angelo Bobak

Developing Secure Distributed Systems with CORBA, Ulrich Lang
and Rudolf Schreiner

*Future Codes: Essays in Advanced Computer Technology and
the Law*, Curtis E. A. Karnow

Global Distributed Applications with Windows® DNA,
Enrique Madrona

A Guide to Software Configuration Management, Alexis Leon

*Guide to Standards and Specifications for Designing Web
Software*, Stan Magee and Leonard L. Tripp

Implementing Electronic Payment Systems, Cristian Radu

Internet Commerce Development, Craig Standing

Knowledge Management Strategy and Technology,
Richard F. Bellaver and John M. Lusa, editors

Managing Computer Networks: A Case-Based Reasoning Approach, Lundy Lewis

Metadata Management for Information Control and Business Success, Guy Tozer

Multimedia Database Management Systems, Guojun Lu

Practical Guide to Software Quality Management, John W. Horch

Practical Process Simulation Using Object-Oriented Techniques and C++, José Garrido

Risk-Based E-Business Testing, Paul Gerrard and Neil Thompson

Secure Messaging with PGP and S/MIME, Rolf Oppliger

Software Fault Tolerance Techniques and Implementation, Laura L. Pullum

Software Verification and Validation for Practitioners and Managers, Second Edition, Steven R. Rakitin

Strategic Software Production with Domain-Oriented Reuse, Paolo Predonzani, Giancarlo Succi, and Tullio Vernazza

Systems Modeling for Business Process Improvement, David Bustard, Peter Kawalek, and Mark Norris, editors

User-Centered Information Design for Improved Software Usability, Pradeep Henry

Workflow Modeling: Tools for Process Improvement and Application Development, Alec Sharp and Patrick McDermott

For further information on these and other Artech House titles, including previously considered out-of-print books now available through our In-Print-Forever® (IPF®) program, contact:

Artech House
685 Canton Street
Norwood, MA 02062
Phone: 781-769-9750
Fax: 781-769-6334
e-mail: artech@artechhouse.com

Artech House
46 Gillingham Street
London SW1V 1AH UK
Phone: +44 (0)20 7596-8750
Fax: +44 (0)20 7630-0166
e-mail: artech-uk@artechhouse.com

Find us on the World Wide Web at:
www.artechhouse.com